Art Seeking Understanding

Conceptual, Empirical, and Experimental Approaches

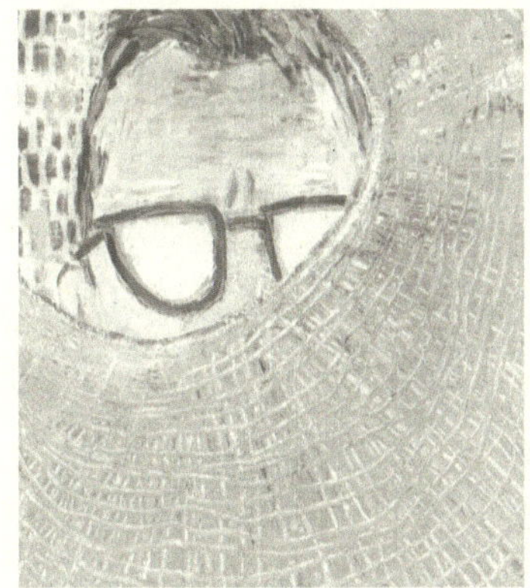

Edited by Christopher R. Brewer

William B. Eerdmans Publishing Company
Grand Rapids, Michigan

Wm. B. Eerdmans Publishing Co.
2006 44th Street SE, Grand Rapids, MI 49508
www.eerdmans.com

Published 2025

ISBN 978-0-8028-8516-6

Library of Congress Cataloging-in-Publication Data

Names: Brewer, Christopher R., editor.
Title: Art seeking understanding : conceptual, empirical, and experimental approaches / edited by Christopher R. Brewer.
Other titles: Art seeking understanding (Wm. B. Eerdmans Publishing Co.)
Description: Grand Rapids, Michigan : Wm. B. Eerdmans Publishing Co., 2025. | Includes index. | Summary: "A collection of essays written by scholars of theological aesthetics, philosophical aesthetics, and empirical aesthetics, examining how art can facilitate spiritual understanding"—Provided by publisher.
Identifiers: LCCN 2024050265 | ISBN 9780802885166 (paperback) | ISBN 9781467469609 (epub)
Subjects: LCSH: Art—Psychology. | Aesthetics—Religious aspects.
Classification: LCC N71 .A74745 2025 | DDC 701/.15—dc23/eng/20250531
LC record available at https://lccn.loc.gov/2024050265

"This book is, in the proper sense, groundbreaking. The astonishing range of the studies on which it reports prepare a terrain from which wholly new ways of thinking may come to fruition. Much remains to be done, but *Art Seeking Understanding* is now the essential starting point for anyone working at the intersection of aesthetics, theology, and empirical psychology."

—GORDON GRAHAM
chair of the Edinburgh Sacred Arts Foundation and
emeritus professor of philosophy and the arts, Princeton Theological Seminary

"*Art Seeking Understanding* is a cornucopia of reports of cutting-edge work. A recent development in philosophical aesthetics is the rise of interest in aesthetic cognitivism: the claim that engagement with works of art often enhances understanding. And a recent development in empirical psychology is innovative inquiries into the psychological dynamics involved in engagement with works of art. *Art Seeking Understanding* honors Sir John Templeton's wish to promote empirical studies into spiritual experience by bringing together these two developments by reports of twenty-three empirical studies, sponsored by the Templeton Foundation, into ways in which engagement with works of art stimulates and enhances understanding of spiritual realities. Groundbreaking contributions to a beckoning new field of inquiry."

—NICHOLAS WOLTERSTORFF
Noah Porter Professor Emeritus of Philosophical Theology, Yale University

"How is engaging art not just an aesthetic or affective experience, but also a cognitive one? With diverse methodologies and disciplinary perspectives, the contributors to *Art Seeking Understanding* offer rich and compelling accounts of how art provokes forms of knowing. In so doing, they chart a vast and fascinating new territory that they invite us to explore. The volume does not resolve the question of art's cognitive significance; it proves why we must keep asking it. For anyone interested in aesthetic cognitivism, this is the place to begin."

—NATALIE CARNES
professor of theology, Baylor University

"By approaching the arts for their capacity to express forms of understanding that are closely connected to our religious sensibilities, Christopher Brewer's team of contributors provide a series of explorations into aesthetic cognitivism. With its empirical and multidisciplinary focus, this volume will provide valuable stimulus for further work on the religious dimension of the arts."

—DAVID FERGUSSON
Regius Professor of Divinity, University of Cambridge

"It has long been acknowledged that we seek meaning in art and interact with art to expand our understanding of the world and ourselves. In this volume, Christopher Brewer has provided leading scholars in various disciplines who are grantees of Templeton Religion Trust's *Art Seeking Understanding* initiative an opportunity to provide updates on their projects, focusing on lessons learned as well as important questions and insights that have emerged in the course of their conceptual and empirical activities. As such, the book provides not only a rich summary of the advances within this grant-making strategy, but also an excellent summary of the state of our knowledge regarding why and how we interact with art."

—Oshin Vartanian
associate professor of psychology, University of Toronto

"Aesthetic cognitivism maintains that art advances understanding. Through a variety of interdisciplinary projects, the Templeton Religious Trust sought to test this hypothesis empirically, particularly but not exclusively with regard to spiritual understanding. *Art Seeking Understanding* is a collection of essays written by grant recipients about their research. The papers detail original hypotheses, methods, pitfalls, preliminary results, and new questions that emerged from the inquiries. These essays afford valuable perspectives not only on the relation of art to understanding, but also on the promise and provisionality of research in progress."

—Catherine Z. Elgin
professor of the philosophy of education, Harvard University

"There is something very heartening about this collection of reflections which diversely brings art back to its familial intimacy with the religious. These two have been long drifting apart, especially since the Enlightenment, but this work is thought-provoking testimony against their divorce. Enabled and gathered under the auspices of the Templeton Foundation, it affirmatively reflects the fertility of the matters at issue. The distinctiveness of art is not lost in the recuperation of this intimacy, nor is the concern of religion with ultimacy diminished. The diverse explorations are wide-ranging, well-informed, and witnesses to impressive scholarship. They are illuminating from both the sides of the aesthetic and the religious, and perhaps most importantly, from the point of view of the challenging intermediation of the two. Impressively brought together under the judicious editing of Christopher Brewer, the work as a whole adds significantly to the Templeton vision."

—William Desmond
David R. Cook Chair of Philosophy, Villanova University

"In this rich and rewarding volume, Christopher Brewer brings together reports on research projects funded by the Templeton Religion Trust on the theme of 'Art Seeking Understanding.' In an echo of Anselm's 'faith seeking understanding,' the participants explore how works of art are themselves able to deepen our understanding of relations between different aspects of our experience. The research projects bring together historians of art, philosophers, theologians, and representatives of the empirical sciences, especially psychology and neuroscience. Not only do the participants explore visual art (including conceptual art, Indian miniature painting, and paratexts in manuscripts), but they also examine architecture, dance, film, music, the novel, and ritual. While much of the volume focuses on issues of morality and character, attention is also given to spiritual values and the way in which aesthetic cognition might open up consideration of transcendent realities. So there is something here for everyone. Careful analysis of aesthetic judgements can indeed provide an alternative access to true knowledge. Brewer's researchers have opened up a plausible path for others to follow."

—David Brown
Emeritus Wardlaw Professor of Theology, Aesthetics, and Culture, University of St Andrews

To my friend and former colleague
W. Christopher Stewart,
with appreciation

Contents

ROUND 2 GRANT PROJECTS

Introduction

Christopher R. Brewer

What is the function of art? Art Seeking Understanding (ASU) is a Templeton Religion Trust (TRT)[1] grant-making strategy that begins with Aesthetic Cognitivism (AC),[2] a theory about the value of the arts that approaches them not simply (or not even) as sources of delight, amusement, pleasure, or emotional catharsis but as sources of understanding. As the philosopher Nelson Goodman (1906–98) puts it, "The arts must be taken no less seriously than the sciences as modes of discovery, creation, and enlargement of knowledge in the broad sense of advancement of the understanding."[3] This advancement of understanding is just the sort of thing that the investor and philanthropist Sir John Templeton (1912–2008) had in mind when he spoke of creative geniuses enlarging our global vision, and "help[ing] god's creation con-

1. Established in 1984, Templeton Religion Trust (TRT) is the first of three charitable entities established by Sir John Templeton. The other entities are the John Templeton Foundation (est. 1987) and the Templeton World Charity Foundation (TWCF, est. 1996). While all three organizations have similar aims, they operate as separate charitable entities. I worked for TRT as Program Officer 2018–21, and now work with TRT as Principal Advisor for the Art Seeking Understanding grant-making strategy.

2. Christoph Baumberger, "Art and Understanding: In Defence of Aesthetic Cognitivism," in *Bilder sehen: Perspektiven der Bildwissenshaft*, ed. Mark Greenlee et al. (Regensburg: Schnell & Steiner, 2013), 41–67. See also Garrick V. Allen, "Aesthetic Cognitivism in the Arts, Theology, Biblical Studies, and Manuscript Cultures: An Annotated Bibliography," online: https://tinyurl.com/2jvxjfuc; Ryan Doran, "Art Seeking Understanding: Annotated Bibliography of Empirical Aesthetics and the Psychology of Art," https://tinyurl.com/zx3en28j.

3. Nelson Goodman, *Ways of Worldmaking* (Indianapolis: Hackett, 1978), 102.

tinue to progress."[4] And who are these creative geniuses? Templeton answers this question with reference to the scholar of religion Huston Smith (1919–2016) who said: "Geniuses in the art of shaping man's imaginings are artists, philosophers, prophets, and seers."[5] Elsewhere, Templeton explains: "In one creative act, a log cabin, an Apollo spacecraft, or a cathedral contains both material and spiritual significance. The idea becomes a material fact; the idea, previously unseen, known only to God or to man, is now visible."[6] What this means is that, for Templeton, the non-material, spiritual dimension is accessible via the creative act, and lest one think that Templeton means only to refer to architecture it is worth noting that a cathedral contains many different art forms. It is a *Gesamtkunstwerk* (total work of art), a point of contact where the unseen ideas of spiritual reality are made visible in architecture, stained glass, painting, sculpture, textile and decorative arts, as well as in (and through) musical instruments of various kinds. And while the Templeton philanthropies are generally prohibited from funding artistic productions or purchases—which some might think suggests total disinterest in the subject—Templeton elsewhere speaks positively of an "expansion of interest in the arts," as well as "a boom in art collecting" before concluding: "The dimensions of this art renaissance are encouraging. . . . This accelerated search for intellectual nourishment, especially for the spiritual side of life, is a primary characteristic of our new era."[7] But is there an empirically demonstrable connection between art and understanding vis-à-vis what Templeton referred to as spiritual reality or spiritual information in particular?[8] And if so, what distinctive cognitive value

4. Sir John Templeton, *Possibilities for over One Hundredfold More Spiritual Information: The Humble Approach in Theology and Science* (Philadelphia: Templeton Foundation Press, 2000), 43.

5. Huston Smith (with Samuel Todes), "Empiricism: Scientific and Religious," in *The Future of Empirical Theology*, ed. Bernard E. Meland, Essays in Divinity, vol. 7 (Chicago: University of Chicago Press, 1969), 143; quoted in Sir John Templeton, *The Humble Approach: Scientists Discover God* (Glasgow: William Collins Sons, 1981; Philadelphia: Templeton Foundation Press, 1998), 58; and also in Templeton, *Possibilities*, 44. It should be noted that in both publications Templeton mistakenly references Smith's chapter (sans Todes) as a book (i.e., with the chapter title in italics and without reference to the Meland volume) rather than a chapter in an edited volume, without a specific page reference, and an incorrect publication date: 1964 instead of 1969.

6. Sir John Templeton, *Humble Approach*, 24. See also Pablo P. L. Tinio, "From Artistic Creation to Aesthetic Reception: The Mirror Model of Art," *Psychology of Aesthetics, Creativity, and the Arts* 7, no. 3 (2013): 265–75.

7. John Marks Templeton, introduction to *Looking Forward: The Next Forty Years*, ed. John Marks Templeton (Philadelphia: Templeton Foundation Press, 1993), 12, 13.

8. For Templeton, spiritual reality includes things like love, purpose, creativity, time, mind, infinity, complexity, understanding, loyalty, friendship, patience, and mercy, to name just a few, and these are just as real as, and perhaps—as in the case of Ultimate reality—even more real than, tangible objects or physical forces like gravity.

does engagement with art (production or consumption) generate? Under what conditions and in what ways does participation in artistic activities encourage or stimulate spiritual understanding, insight, or growth (meaning or sense making)? Relatedly, if art has primarily to do with understanding, then what of beauty? Is it an unrelated aim, or one (in some cases) essential to understanding? And if essential, then what advantages, if any, does beautiful art have over non-beautiful art with reference to understanding?

These are the questions that drive the ASU program strategy as we seek to put AC to the test. Projects in this area bring together artists and art researchers, philosophers and theologians alongside scientists from a variety of subdisciplines within the psychological, cognitive, and social sciences, including developmental psychology, cognitive science of religion, cognitive neuroscience, sociology, social psychology, personality psychology, psychometrics, and clinical psychology to conceive and design empirical and statistical studies of the cognitive significance of art with respect to spiritual realities and the discovery of new spiritual information. More succinctly, ASU is seeking to establish—and indeed has made significant progress toward establishing—a new empirically/experimentally aimed research community at the intersection of philosophical aesthetics,[9] religious/theological aesthetics,[10] and empirical/neuroaesthetics,[11] and all of this in an effort to put AC to the test.[12]

9. See Jerrold Levinson, ed., *The Oxford Handbook of Aesthetics* (New York: Oxford University Press, 2003); and Gordon Graham, *Philosophy of the Arts: An Introduction to Aesthetics*, 3rd ed. (London: Routledge, 2005).

10. See Frank Burch Brown, ed., *The Oxford Handbook of Religion and the Arts* (New York: Oxford University Press, 2014); Gesa Elsbeth Thiessen, ed., *Theological Aesthetics: A Reader* (Grand Rapids: Eerdmans, 2004); and David Brown, *Divine Generosity and Human Creativity: Theology through Symbol, Painting, and Architecture*, ed. Christopher R. Brewer and Robert MacSwain (London: Routledge, 2017).

11. See Marcos Nadal and Oshin Vartanian, eds., *The Oxford Handbook of Empirical Aesthetics* (New York: Oxford University Press, 2022); Pablo P. L. Tinio and Jeffrey K. Smith, eds., *The Cambridge Handbook of the Psychology of Aesthetics and the Arts* (Cambridge: Cambridge University Press, 2014); and Anjan Chatterjee and Eileen R. Cardillo, eds., *Brain, Beauty, and Art: Essays Bringing Neuroaesthetics into Focus* (New York: Oxford University Press, 2022).

12. Cf. David Lyle Jeffrey and Robert C. Roberts, eds., *Art Seeking Understanding* (Waco: Baylor University Press, 2024). It should be noted that it was Templeton Religion Trust (TRT) and not the Templeton Foundation that "published a call for research proposals on the topic 'art seeking understanding,' part of a larger research initiative bearing the same name" (Jeffrey and Roberts, *Art Seeking Understanding*, xiii). The editors also suggest that TRT does not fund conferences, but that is not the case.

The Grant-Making Strategy

Art Seeking Understanding began in earnest with two planning meetings—one in Nassau, the Bahamas (March 2019), and one in Grand Rapids, Michigan (April 2019)—and was originally conceived as a three-phase, $25M grant-making strategy, each phase consisting of two parts: an open Project Grant Request for Proposals (RFP)—eighteen-month projects, $234K maximum request—followed by an invitation only Program Grant RFP—thirty-six-month projects, $1M maximum request. After the second planning meeting, we changed the name of the strategy from AC to ASU. My thinking was that using AC, which is a philosophy of the arts, as the name for the strategy would cause confusion, especially since the strategy was seeking to put AC to the test. Using AC made it seem like we were advocating while foreclosing the possibility that we could be wrong. Clearly based upon Anselm of Canterbury's "faith seeking understanding" (*fides quaerens intellectum*), ASU puts the focus on aesthetic cognition.[13] While some thought the strategy should be called *The Arts* Seeking Understanding, I disagreed.[14] While I understand the reality of pluralism and the pluralization that accompanies that reality, I grow tired of repeated calls to abandon use of the singular in this and other contexts if for no other reason than that the plural—the arts, the sciences, religions, theologies, etc.—is cumbersome. I see no reason why, after acknowledging the fact of the plural, we cannot use the singular (without espousing some form of essentialism), and arguments to the contrary are, from my perspective, pedantic. Must we really say (or imply) everything in order to say anything? Moving on. The Round 1 Project Grant RFP posted in July 2019 and closed in October 2019.[15] Successful applicants were notified in the spring of 2020 and grant projects began in June 2020. The Round 1 Program Grant and Round 2 Project Grant RFPs

13. The only previous usage of this phrase that I was able to find at that time was Jonathan Koestlé-Cate, "The Currency of Belief," *Art and Christianity* 73 (2013): 2. Koestlé-Cate suggests that the British artist John Newling's works can be described as "art seeking understanding."

14. In using the singular—"art"—I am following Nicholas Wolterstorff, *Art Rethought: The Social Practices of Art* (Oxford: Oxford University Press, 2015), xiii: "When I use the term 'the arts' with no qualifying adjective, I will mean the traditional (fine) arts. . . . In the twentieth century a number of additional media have come to be called 'arts,' prominent among them being still-photography, film, and ceramics; I will call these media 'new arts.'" He continues: "When I speak of 'art' rather than 'the arts,' I will mean works of the traditional and new arts along with those artworks that are not works of any of the traditional or new arts."

15. I am grateful to my colleagues at TWCF, Dawid Potgieter (at that time Senior Program Officer) and Syman Stevens (at that time Program Officer), for their advice and assistance with this RFP.

opened simultaneously in June 2021 and closed in October 2021.[16] Successful applicants were notified in the spring of 2022 and grant projects began in July 2022. The Round 2 Program Grant RFP posted in July 2023 and closed in October 2023. Successful applicants were notified in the spring of 2024 and grant projects began in June 2024.

Inspired by the Templeton World Charity Foundation's (TWCF's) Diverse Intelligences Summer Institute,[17] we structured ASU as a community of practice. According to Bev Wenger-Trayner, "A community of practice is a group of people who share a concern or a passion for something they do, and learn how to do it better as they interact regularly."[18] The 2019 planning meetings were the first attempt to build this community of practice, and the June 2022 ASU Workshop at the Caledonian Waldorf Astoria in Edinburgh was a solid second effort with more than fifty grantees in attendance.[19] Robin Jensen and her team at the University of Notre Dame organized a follow-up meeting independently at Notre Dame in May 2023. Five project teams attended that meeting. We then held a second, all-grantee workshop in October 2024 at the University of Notre Dame's Rome Global Gateway.[20] Among other things (and this is no small thing), the community of practice approach has helped us avoid unnecessary duplication while encouraging collaboration and the sharing of results and resources.

From the very beginning, I wanted the strategy to be documented in longitudinal form, and not only for the sake of transparency, but also as a kind of mid- and post-strategy evaluation. Fast forward: two seasons of TRT-funded programming have now been produced by Closer to Truth (CTT),[21] with numerous online inter-

16. For the Round 2 Project Grant RFP, see https://tinyurl.com/54zhdnvz.

17. For more information, see "Diverse Intelligences Summer Institute: Pilot," Templeton World Charity Foundation, https://tinyurl.com/ps6n9dzp.

18. Bev Wenger-Trayner, "What Is a Community of Practice?," https://tinyurl.com/5br3k2an. See also Etienne Wenger, *Communities of Practice: Learning, Meaning, and Identity* (Cambridge: Cambridge University Press, 1998); Etienne Wenger, Richard McDermott, and William M. Snyder, *Cultivating Communities of Practice: A Guide to Managing Knowledge* (Boston: Harvard Business School Press, 2002).

19. "Investigating the Connection between Art and Understanding," YouTube, https://tinyurl.com/yck6mkdv. I am grateful to Justin L. Barrett and Rebecca Dorsey from Blueprint 1543, as well as Sara Merrilees from The Issachar Fund, for their assistance with this workshop.

20. This second workshop was jointly funded by TRT and the Institute for the Scholarship in the Liberal Arts and the College of Arts and Letters at the University of Notre Dame.

21. "Art Seeking Understanding: Season 20," Closer to Truth, https://tinyurl.com/363m9ky7. An additional season is in preparation.

views posted to the CTT website.[22] The plan is to recut this footage for an eventual longitudinal documentary that begins with the 2019 planning meetings and ends with the state of the field. What these episodes and interviews make clear is that building a new research area takes time with progress being made and measured incrementally. In 2019, we didn't even know what the questions were. We now have a list of questions that we have been working on for five years, and we now know individual researchers and research networks that can help us make progress. Again, these things take time, and that is one of perhaps several reasons that Templeton established perpetual philanthropies. Even so, I believe that we have accomplished a good deal over these past five years, moving from conceptual to empirical to experimental approaches. In the next section, I provide additional detail about the contributors to this volume, including the titles of the relevant grant projects, links to online overviews of most every grant (many of which include explainer videos), as well as footnotes listing all publications resulting from these projects in the event that reading through these contributions leads to a desire for even greater detail.

The Book Itself

Rather than merely republishing outputs from their grants, I have invited grantees to submit new essays covering their original research question(s) and method(s), what they have learned thus far, and also any new questions that have emerged. The book is divided into two parts: Round 1 Grant Projects and Round 2 Grant Projects. Of the nine Round 1 projects featured, the first eight moved from project to program stage. Of the fourteen Round 2 projects featured, three moved from project to program stage, including Zorana Ivcevic (chapter 10), Elisabeth Schellekens (chapter 19), and Jonathan Schooler (chapter 21).

- In chapter 1, Judith Wolfe, Marina Iosifyan, and Brendan Wolfe describe three projects: (1) "Text and Image," a Round 1 Project grant led by Brendan Wolfe (2020–22);[23] (2) "Mapping the Imagination," a Round 1 Project grant led by Judith Wolfe (2020–22);[24] and (3) "Art as Revelation," a Round 1 Program grant led by Judith Wolfe (2022–25). A number of publications have resulted from these

22. "Art Seeking Understanding," Closer to Truth, https://tinyurl.com/y2eyk4ds.
23. See Brendan Wolfe, "Reading beyond the Pictures," https://tinyurl.com/bdhb28yy.
24. See Judith Wolfe, "Mapping the Imagination," https://tinyurl.com/42xsxp4j.

grants,[25] including the published version of J. Wolfe's 2022 Hulsean Lectures at the University of Cambridge.[26]

- In chapter 2, Kutter Callaway summarizes work undertaken for (1) "Measuring the (Im)measurable: A Psychological Model of the 'Something More' That Humans Encounter in and through Art," a Round 1 project grant (2020–21);[27] and (2) "Measuring the (Im)measurable in Real Life," a Round 1 program grant (2022–25).[28] Three publications have resulted thus far from these grants.[29]
- In chapter 3, Robin M. Jensen introduces two grant projects: (1) "Understanding the Enduring Impact of Encounters with Sacred Art on Individual Spiritual Reality," a Round 1 project grant (2020–22);[30] and (2) "Assessing the Impact of Sacred Art on Individual Experience, Memory, and Spiritual Understanding," a Round 1 program grant (2022–25).[31] One publication has resulted from these grants with one more in preparation.[32]

25. Judith Wolfe, "The Renewal of Perception in Religious Faith and Biblical Narrative," *European Journal for Philosophy of Religion* 13, no. 4 (2021); Marina Iosifyan, Anton Sidoroff-Dorso, and Judith Wolfe, "Cross-Modal Associations between Paintings and Sounds: Effects of Embodiment," *Perception* 51, no. 12 (2022); Judith Wolfe, "Imagining God," *Modern Theology* 40, no. 1 (2024): 97–109; Marina Iosifyan and Judith Wolfe, "Everyday Life vs. Art: Effects of Framing on the Mode of Object Interpretation," *Empirical Studies of the Arts* 42, no. 1 (2024); Marina Iosifyan and Judith Wolfe, "Buffering Effect of Fiction on Negative Emotions: Engagement with Negatively Valenced Fiction Decreases the Intensity of Negative Emotions," *Cognition and Emotion* 38, no. 5 (2024): 709–26; Marina Iosifyan and Judith Wolfe, "Poetry vs. Everyday Life: Context Increases Perceived Meaningfulness of Sentences," under review; Nicole Ruta and Brendan Wolfe, "Text and Image: Bodily Sensation Maps and Aesthetic Cognition," in preparation.

26. Judith Wolfe, *The Theological Imagination: Perception and Interpretation in Life, Art, and Faith* (Cambridge: Cambridge University Press, 2024).

27. See Kutter Callaway, "Measuring the Spiritual Dimension of Art," https://tinyurl.com/2rrfajbs.

28. See Kutter Callaway, "Measuring Transcendence: IRL," https://tinyurl.com/24sct8ss.

29. Kutter Callaway et al., "Measuring the (Im)measurable: On the Psycho-Socio-Spiritual Effects of Aesthetic Experiences in Art," *Journal of Psychology and Theology* 51, no. 1 (March 2023): 352–74; Rosemary Al-Kire et al., "Original Photographic Art Induces Self-Transcendent Emotions," *Psychology of Aesthetics, Creativity, and the Arts* (December 2023). Advance online publication; Phil Allen Jr. and Justin Ariel Bailey, "A Spacious Place: Blk Halos and the Spirit's Breadth," in *Spirit and the Arts*, ed. W. David O. Taylor and Daniel Train (Downers Grove, IL: IVP Academic, forthcoming).

30. See Robin M. Jensen, "Sacred Art in Context," https://tinyurl.com/ztke396m.

31. See Anjan Chatterjee, "Framing the Experience of Art with Science," https://tinyurl.com/bde8uerc.

32. Sean M. Dageforde et al., "The Effect of Temporal Context on Memory for Art," *Acta Psychologica* 248 (2024): article number 104349, https://doi.org/10.1016/j.actpsy.2024.104349.

- In chapter 4, Eileen Cardillo, Alex Christensen, and Anjan Chatterjee report on two grant projects led by Chatterjee: (1) "Semantic Space of Aesthetic Cognitivism," a Round 1 project grant (2020–21);[33] and (2) "Does Art Promote Understanding? A Behavioural and Neuroscientific Inquiry," a Round 1 program grant (2022–25). In addition to a series of posts on *Psychology Today*,[34] these grant projects have generated four publications.[35]
- In chapter 5, Julio Bermudez and Yoshio Nakamura detail three grant projects: (1) "Cognitive-Aesthetic Effects of Sacred vs. Secular Architecture on Believers: A Neurophenomenological Exploratory Study," a Round 1 project grant (2020–23) led by Bermudez;[36] (2) "How Sacred Architecture Conveys Spiritual Understanding: A Biometric-Based Study," a Round 2 project grant (2022–23) led by Bermudez;[37] and (3) "Spiritual Understanding and Architecture: A Multimethod, Empirical Investigation across Religious and Non-religious Populations," a Round 2 program grant (2024–27) being led by Matthew Niermann.[38]

33. See Anjan Chatterjee, "Coming to Terms with Art," https://tinyurl.com/3zdc36he. This was the second ASU research grant awarded.

34. Natalie Carnes, "Epiphany and Empiricism: A Theological Perspective on Aesthetic Cognitivism," *Psychology Today*, January 18, 2021, https://tinyurl.com/4hucn8m8, accessed August 14, 2024; Noël Carroll, "The Relation of Art and Cognition: A Perspective from the Philosophy of Art," *Psychology Today*, January 11, 2021, https://tinyurl.com/uupv4n62, accessed August 14, 2024; Matthew J. Milliner, "Art and the Apophatic Horizon: An Art History Perspective on Aesthetic Cognitivism," *Psychology Today*, January 25, 2021, https://tinyurl.com/467ew2pn, accessed August 14, 2024; Ellen Winner. "What Does Aesthetic Cognitivism Really Mean, Anyway? Reflections from a Psychologist," *Psychology Today*, January 5, 2021, https://tinyurl.com/msh4jjfp, accessed August 14, 2024.

35. Alexander P. Christensen, Eileen R. Cardillo, and Anjan Chatterjee, "What Kind of Impacts Can Artwork Have on Viewers? Establishing a Taxonomy for Aesthetic Impacts," *British Journal of Psychology* 114, no. 2 (2023): 335–51; A. P. Christensen, E. R. Cardillo, and A. Chatterjee, "Can Art Promote Understanding? A Review of the Psychology and Neuroscience of Aesthetic Cognitivism," *Psychology of Aesthetics, Creativity, and the Arts* 19, no. 1 (2025): 1–14; Vincente Estrada Gonzalez et al., "Art Therapy Masks Reflect Emotional Changes in Military Personnel with PTSS," *Scientific Reports* 14, no. 1 (2024): article number 7192, https://doi.org/10.21203/rs.3.rs-3325596/v1; Kohinoor Darda et al., "A Comparison of Art Engagement in Museums and through Digital Media," *Scientific Reports* 15, no. 1 (2025): article number 8972, https://doi.org/10.1038/s41598-025-93630-0.

36. See Julio Bermudez, "Deconstructing the Effects of Spiritual Architecture," https://tinyurl.com/3cc7rsa3.

37. See Julio Bermudez, "How Sacred Architecture Conveys Spiritual Understanding: A Biometric-Based Study," https://tinyurl.com/bde2h7x7.

38. Bermudez is somewhat of an exception as, after a successful Round 1 project grant, he opted to submit another project grant proposal to Round 2. The Round 2 program grant is now being led by Matthew Niermann (California Baptist University) with Bermudez as co-Project Investigator (co-PI).

These projects have resulted in one publication with additional publication in press.[39]

- In chapter 6, Carl Plantinga provides an overview of two grant projects: (1) "Screen Stories and Moral Understanding," a Round 1 project grant (2020–21);[40] and (2) "Character Engagement and Moral Understanding in Screen Stories," a Round 1 program grant (2022–25).[41] These grants have resulted in a number of publications.[42]
- In chapter 7, Alejandro Bahena-Rivera, Kelsie Rodenbiker, Christoph Scheepers, and Garrick V. Allen present a state of the field report on three field-building projects led by Garrick Allen: (1) "Paratextual Understanding: A Cognitivist Approach to the Aesthetic Features of Manuscripts," a Round 1 project grant (2019–22);[43] (2) "The Paratext Network: Field-Building an Empirical Approach to Literature and Knowledge," a Round 1 bridge grant (2022–23); and (3) "Paratexts Seeking Understanding: Aesthetic Cognitivism, Manuscript Cultures, and Knowledge," a Round 1 program grant / RFP (2023–26).[44] These grants have resulted in several publications, including one monograph.[45]

39. Zakaria Djebbara et al., "Contemplative Neuroaesthetics and Architecture: A Sensorimotor Exploration," *Frontiers of Architectural Research* 13, no. 1 (2024): 97–111.

40. See Carl Plantinga, "Exploring the Moral Impact of Movies," https://tinyurl.com/5n6vunks.

41. See Carl Plantinga, "Developing Moral Understanding at the Movies," https://tinyurl.com/29mkjxj7.

42. Carl Plantinga and Garrett Strpko, "Moral Reflection: On the Reflective Afterlife of Screen Stories," in *What Is Film Good For? On the Ethics of Spectatorship*, ed. Julian Hanich and Martin Roussouw (Berkeley: University of California Press, 2023), 117–27; Carl Plantinga, "Film," in *The Oxford Handbook of Ethics and Art*, ed. James Harold (New York: Oxford University Press, 2023), 391–406; Carl Plantinga, "Bad Fans, Bad Protagonists, and Ethics," in *Cognition, Emotion, and Aesthetics in Contemporary Serial Television*, ed. Ted Nannicelli and Hector J. Pérez (New York: Routledge, 2023), 273–84; Carl Plantinga, ed., *Screen Stories and Moral Understanding: Interdisciplinary Perspectives* (New York: Oxford University Press, 2023); Carl Plantinga and Allison Eden, "Media and Moral Understanding," *Journal of Media Psychology: Theories, Methods, and Applications* 36, no. 4 (2024): 215–9; Carl Plantinga, "The Rhetoric of Empathy in Narrative Film," in *Empathy and the Aesthetic Mind: Perspectives on Fiction and Beyond*, ed. Katerina Bantinaki, Efi Kyprianidou, and Fotini Vassiliou (London: Bloomsbury, 2025).

43. See Garrick V. Allen, "Words Are Not Enough," https://tinyurl.com/bdzbktjr. This was the first ASU research grant awarded.

44. See Garrick Allen, "Mapping the Margins: Understanding Scriptures beyond the Text," https://tinyurl.com/mrxpxrnw.

45. Garrick V. Allen, "The Possibilities of a Gospel Codex: GA 2064 (Dublin, CBL W 139), Digital Editing, and Reading in a Manuscript Culture," *Journal of Biblical Literature* 140, no. 2 (2021): 409–34; Garrick V. Allen, "Paratexts Seeking Understanding: Manuscripts and Aesthetic Cognitivism," *Religions* 1, no. 10 (2020), 523; Anthony Royle and Garrick V. Allen, "GA2604 (CBL W 139) f.176v., f.177r, f.177v and f.178r," *Nakala*. Online: https://nakala.fr/10.34847/nkl.cfac1noc;

- In chapter 8, Jonathan Berger introduces two grant projects: (1) "Sound, Space, and the Aesthetics of the Sublime," a Round 1 project grant (2020–23);[46] and (2) "Sound, Space, and Sensing the Unfathomable," a Round 1 program grant (2022–25). In addition to one publication,[47] these grants have resulted in what I believe is a first for a grant awarded by one of the Templeton philanthropies: two patents.[48]
- In chapter 9, Caleb Froehlich and Alison Jack share about their Round 1 project grant: "Investigating Art and the Sacred at the Edinburgh Festival Fringe: Practice-Based Research with Theological Reflection" (2021–23).[49] This project has resulted in three publications.[50]
- In chapter 10, Pablo P. L. Tinio and Zorana Ivcevic discuss two projects led by Zorana Ivcevic that take Pablo Tinio's "Mirror Model of Art"[51] as their point of departure: (1) "Mirror to the World: The Power of Art to Build Understanding and Creativity" (2022–24), a Round 1 project grant;[52] and (2) "Mirror to the World: The Power of Art to Build Understanding and Creativity" (2024–27), a Round 1 program grant. These projects have resulted in two publications thus far with two more in preparation.[53]
- In chapter 11, Carlos Miguel Gómez-Rincón elaborates the findings from his grant project, "The Hermeneutic Role of Art in Spiritual Experience: Building a

---

Garrick V. Allen, *Words Are Not Enough: Paratexts, Manuscripts, and the Real New Testament* (Grand Rapids: Eerdmans, 2024).

46. See Jonathan Berger, "Seeking the Acoustic Signature of Transcendence," https://tinyurl.com/4dyhnvsa.

47. Jonathan Berger, ed., *Listening in the Past: Sound, Space, and the Aesthetics of the Sublime* (Ann Arbor, MI: Lever, forthcoming).

48. US Patent No. 10812902B1, System and method for augmenting an acoustic space, October 20, 2020; US Patent Application No. 20210037316A1, Networked audio auralization and feedback cancellation system and method, February 4, 2021.

49. See Alison Jack, "Researching Art as More Than Pleasure," https://tinyurl.com/4e82tmk3. The project was to be led by David Fergusson, but, with his appointment as Regius Professor of Divinity in the University of Cambridge, Alison Jack took the lead.

50. Alison Jack, "Poetry, Prayer and Praise" in *The Record* 56 (August 2021): 3–16; Alison Jack, "'The Holy Space Ablaze': New Understandings of Spiritual Reality through Poetry and Music" in *Theology in Scotland* 29, no.1 (2022): 35–47; Gordon Graham, "Art Proper, Perfectionism and the Sacred Arts," in *Imperfectionist Aesthetics in Art and Everyday Life*, ed. Peter Cheyne (London: Routledge, 2022), 54–65.

51. Tinio, "From Artistic Creation to Aesthetic Reception."

52. See https://tinyurl.com/3fts48mt.

53. Zorana Ivcevic and Pablo P. L. Tinio, "Art Builds Understanding," *Psychology Today*, November 3, 2022, https://tinyurl.com/abv5u6xn; Zorana Ivcevic and Pablo P. L. Tinio, "5 Things That Make Art Meaningful," *Psychology Today*, September 12, 2023, https://tinyurl.com/57n5v7vk.

Laboratory for Art and Spirituality" (2022–23),[54] a Round 2 project grant. In addition to a series of short documentaries available on the open-source Convergent Documentary Platform,[55] this project has resulted in two publications.[56]

- In chapter 12, Joshua A. Wilt and Julie J. Exline write about their Round 2 project grant: "Understanding Existence and the Self through Art: Engagement with Art and Life Stories about Ultimate Meaning and Authenticity" (2022–23).[57] This project has resulted in two publications.[58]
- In chapter 13, Lexi Eikelboom and Valerie van Mulukom introduce a Round 2 project grant led by Eikelboom: "Spiritual Understanding in a Secular Age: Engaging Art as Religious Ritual" (2021–23).[59] This project resulted in the publication of an edited volume.[60]
- In chapter 14, Jamal Elias gives background for his Round 2 project grant: "Art and Islam in Society: Aesthetic Cognition Expanding Religious Meaning" (2022–24).[61] This project produced a documentary.
- In chapter 15, Faiz Hashmi, Alejandro Erut, Zachary Taylor, and Cristine H. Legare summarize findings from a Round 2 project grant led by Legare: "The Process of Spiritualization through Artistic Activity and Training" (2022–24).[62]
- In chapter 16, Taylor Worley discusses two grants: (1) "Thinking about Thinking: Conceptual Art and the Contemplative Tradition" (2021–23),[63] a Round 2

54. See Carlos Miguel Gómez, "Exploring Artists' Spiritual Searches," https://tinyurl.com/4dkd9h7j.

55. See https://tinyurl.com/ythc7nep.

56. Carlos Miguel Gómez-Rincón, "Art as a Spiritual Practice: The Interplay between Artistic Creation and Spiritual Search in Seven Colombian Artists," *Journal for the Study of Spirituality* (2023); Carlos Miguel Gómez-Rincón, Natalia Reinoso-Chávez, and Corina Estrada-Barrios, "Unfolding Spiritual Understanding through Artistic Creation: Findings of the Laboratory of Art and Spirituality," *Archive for the Psychology of Religion* (2024): https://doi.org/10.1177/00846724241295783.

57. See Joshua Wilt, "Art as a Way of Becoming," https://tinyurl.com/5t4u9uuj.

58. Joshua A. Wilt et al., "Aesthetic Dispositions, Aesthetic Experiences, and Meaning in Life," *Empirical Studies of the Arts* (2024); Joshua A. Wilt et al., "Engagement with Art and Meaning in Life: The Predictive Roles of Awe, Interest, and Supernatural Attributions," *Journal of Positive Psychology*, forthcoming.

59. Lexi Eikelboom and David Newheiser, "Religious Ritual as a Lens for Understanding Art," https://tinyurl.com/58cxwnx6.

60. Lexi Eikelboom and David Newheiser, eds., *Art-Making as Spiritual Practice: Rituals of Embodied Understanding* (New York: Bloomsbury, 2025).

61. Jamal Elias, "Art and Islam in America Today," https://tinyurl.com/57e98x3d.

62. See Cristine Legare, "The Larger Significance of Miniature Art," https://tinyurl.com/yd27w33h.

63. See Taylor Worley, "Thinking about How We Think about Art," https://tinyurl.com/mrjxvvh2.

project grant; and (2) "Art of Attention: Bridge-Building for Field Experimentation on Conceptual Art," a Round 2 bridge grant (2022–24). These projects resulted in two special journal issues—the first including an introduction plus four articles,[64] and the second consisting of eight articles[65]—and one stand-alone article.[66]

- In chapter 17, Marlene Sophie Altenmüller and Mario Gollwitzer detail findings from a Round 2 project grant led by Gollwitzer: "Art as Bridge to Engagement with the Adversities of Our Time?" (2022–23).[67] This project has resulted in one publication thus far with three more in preparation.[68]
- In chapter 18, Bahador Bahrami and Ophelia Deroy report on a Round 2 project grant led by Bahrami: "Aesthetic Cognitivism for Groups: Collective Ways of Looking and Sense Making" (2022–23).[69] This project has resulted in one publication with two more in preparation.[70]

64. Taylor Worley and Glen G. Scorgie, "Introduction," *Spiritus: A Journal of Christian Spirituality* 23, no. 2 (2023): 187–91; Dennis Kinlaw, "Literary Engagement and the Contemplative Disposition," *Spiritus: A Journal of Christian Spirituality* 23, no. 2 (2023), 192–210; C. M. Howell, "Rhythms of Silence and Space: Contemplation and Architectural Proportion in Dom Hans van der Laan," *Spiritus: A Journal of Christian Spirituality* 23, no. 2 (2023): 211–28; Taylor Worley, "'All Things Visible and Invisible': Conceptual Art and Contemplation," *Spiritus: A Journal of Christian Spirituality* 23, no. 2 (2023): 229–49; Joy Moore, "Before Poetry," *Spiritus: A Journal of Christian Spirituality* 23, no. 2 (2023): 316–30.

65. Alex Sosler, "Going to the Morgue with Andres Serrano: Provocation as Revelation," *Religions* 13, no. 6 (2022): 562; C. M. Howell, "The Edge of Perception: Gordon Matta-Clark's Hermeneutic of Place and the Possibilities of Absence for the Theological Imagination," *Religions* 13, no. 10 (2022): 920; Arthur Aghajanian, "The Readymade as Social Exchange: Everyday Tactics of Resistance in Conceptual Art," *Religions* 13 no. 11 (2022): 1078; Jonathan A. Anderson, "Conceptual Art, Theology, and Re-Presentation," *Religions* 13, no. 10 (2022): 984; Meaghan Burke, "Art Together, Prayer Together: Relational and Revelatory Practices of Jospeh Beuys, Dietrich Bonhoeffer and Leslie Iwai," *Religions* 14, no. 1 (2023): 24; Aixin Zhang, "The Neglected Place of 'Totems' in Contemporary Art," *Religions* 14, no. 6 (2023): 810; Mark Allen, "The Rothko Chapel: Profane or Sacred Space?" *Religions* 14 no. 7 (2023): 853; Stephen M. Garrett, "The Difference of Indifference: Marcel Duchamp and the Possibilities of a Dialogical Personalism," *Religions* 15, no. 4 (2024), 438. See https://tinyurl.com/2j363fxf.

66. Taylor Worley, "Art at the Edge of Mourning," *The Other Journal* 35, "Vice & Virtue" (Spring 2023): 54–66.

67. See Mario Gollwitzer, "Engagement vs. Avoidance: Can Art Be the Difference?," https://tinyurl.com/3xb9dvpn.

68. Marlene S. Altenmüller and Mario Gollwitzer, "Power of Pictures? Questioning the Emotionalization and Behavioral Activation Potential of Aesthetics in War Photography," *Psychology of Aesthetics, Creativity, and the Arts* (2023).

69. See Bahador Bahrami, "Researching Art Experiences as a Group Dynamic," https://tinyurl.com/2sky7856.

70. Ophelia Deroy, Louis Longin, and Bahador Bahrami, "Co-perceiving: Bringing the Social into Perception," *WIREs Cognitive Science* (2024): article number e1681, https://doi.org/10.1002/wcs.1681.

- In chapter 19, Guy Dammann, Elisabeth Schellekens, and John Gibson share findings from a Round 2 project grant led by Schellekens: "Perception, Knowledge, and the Prospects of Criticism" (2022–23).[71] In addition to an online seminar series,[72] this project team is in the process of preparing two papers for publication.[73] The team is now working on a Round 2 program grant: "Aesthetic Cognitivism and the Prospects of Criticism" (2024–27).
- In chapter 20, David Shepherd, Kate Nevin, Elizabeth Mason, and Fiona Newell introduce a Round 2 project grant led by Shepherd: "Through a Glass Brightly: Light Variation and the Perception of Religious Stained Glass" (2022–24).[74]
- In chapter 21, Madeleine E. Gross and Jonathan W. Schooler present findings from a Round 2 project grant led by Schooler: "Expanding Minds: The Cognitive Processes Promoted by Exposure to Art" (2022–24).[75] This project has resulted in two publications thus far with two more under review and four more in preparation.[76] The project team is now working on a Round 2 program grant:

71. See Elisabeth Schellekens, "How Critical Language Lets Us See," https://tinyurl.com/38dxb8ez.

72. Online: https://tinyurl.com/3urd3cta.

73. Guy Dammann, "Criticism in Crisis," *The Times Literary Supplement*, forthcoming; Guy Dammann, John Gibson, and Elisabeth Schellekens, "Critical Cognitivism about Art," in preparation.

74. See David Shepherd, "Art, Light, and Awe: Uncovering the Mysteries of Stained Glass," https://tinyurl.com/mpbzbc4v.

75. See Jonathan Schooler, "Engaging the Brain in Art," https://tinyurl.com/mry52xaw.

76. Madeleine E. Gross and Jonathan W. Schooler, "Standing Out: An Atypical Salience Account of Creativity," *Trends in Cognitive Sciences* 28, no. 7 (July 2024): 597–99; Madeleine E. Gross, James C. Elliott, and Jonathan W. Schooler, "Why Creatives Don't Find the Oddball Odd: Neural and Psychological Evidence for Atypical Salience Processing," *Brain and Cognition* 178 (August 2024): article number 106178, https://doi.org/10.1016/j.bandc.2024.106178; Madeleine E. Gross et al., "When Is a Wandering Mind Unhappy? The Mediating Role of Thought Valence," *Emotion* (2024). Manuscripts under review include Madeleine E. Gross, Claire Zedelius, and Jonathan W. Schooler, "From Curious to Credulous: Information Gaps Inhibit Discernment of Fake News"; and Joshua R. Ortega, Madeleine E. Gross, and Jonathan W. Schooler, "When Life Is But a Dream: Transliminality Predicts Continuity in Bizarreness Across the Sleep-Wake Cycle." Manuscripts in preparation include Madeleine E. Gross and Jonathan W. Schooler, "Aesthetic to Epistemic: Artistic Film Promotes Information Seeking Behavior, Interest-Based and Deprivation-Based Epistemic Curiosity"; Madeleine E. Gross and Jonathan W. Schooler, "Expanding Minds: Artistic Film Promotes Overinclusive Thinking, Verbal Creativity, and State Openness"; Anusha Garg et al., "Mind Wandering Out Loud: Does Think Aloud Change the Phenomenology of Spontaneous Thought?"; Madeleine E. Gross, Todd Kashdan, and Jonathan W. Schooler, "Just Ask: A Novel Method for Inducing and Measuring Interest-Based Epistemic Curiosity." In addition, and as a consequence of Schooler's introduction to Robert Lawrence Kuhn at the 2022 ASU Workshop in Edinburgh, Schooler and Kuhn are working on a collaborative book that will cover the topics under consideration in this project, as well as related topics pertaining to creativity and consciousness.

"Art-Induced Openness: Contexts and Mechanisms Underlying the Cognitive Effects of Art" (2024–27).

- In chapter 22, Stacie Friend outlines progress on her Round 2 project grant: "Art Opening Minds: How Experiences of Cinematic Art Can Transform Perspectives" (2022–23).[77] This project has resulted in three publications with an additional five in preparation or press.[78]
- In chapter 23, Kelly James Clark writes about his Round 2 project grant: "Art, Empathy, and Justice: An Exploration of Cognitive Aesthetics" (2022–23).[79]

It should be noted that not all ASU grantees contributed chapters to this volume, and this for a variety of reasons.[80] Even so, the essays herein provide a collective, representative snapshot of where things stand in this exciting, emerging research area.

I am grateful to my friend and former colleague Chris Stewart for shepherding the development of this strategy through the TRT Steering Committee, and for the support of Justin L. Barrett—who was at that time a Steering Committee member—as well as others along the way. I would also like to thank former and current members of the TRT programs team in Nassau, especially Kara Ingraham (Chief of Staff and Program Officer), Stefen Deleveaux (Program Associate, 2017–20), Sarah Major (Program Associate), and Kimon Sargeant (Vice President of Programs and Evaluation). Thanks also to those who participated in the 2019 planning meetings.[81]

77. See Stacie Friend, "Opening Minds at the Movies," https://tinyurl.com/y9a63jmn.

78. Stacie Friend, "Belief, Imagination, and the Nature of Fiction," in *The Routledge Handbook of Fiction and Belief*, ed. Alison James, Akihiro Kubo, Françoise Lavocat (New York: Routledge, 2023), 15–27; Lena Wimmer et al., "Cognitive Effects and Correlates of Reading Fiction: Two Preregistered Multilevel Meta-Analyses," *Journal of Experimental Psychology: General* 153, no. 6 (2024): 1464–88; Stacie Friend et al., "Moral Understanding and Media: Meeting the Challenges of Interdisciplinary Research," *Journal of Media Psychology: Theories, Methods, and Applications* 36, no. 4 (2024): 220–30.

79. See Kelly James Clark, "Art as a Window into Empathy & Justice," https://tinyurl.com/3382r48s.

80. Significant publications resulting from those grants not featured include Ryan P. Doran, "Thick and Perceptual Moral Beauty," *Australasian Journal of Philosophy* 101, no. 3 (2022): 704–21; Oludamini Ogunnaike, "The Logic of the Birds," *Renavatio*, May 6, 2022; Kevin G. Grove, Christopher C. Rios, and Taylor J. Nutter, eds., *Art, Desire, and God: Phenomenological Perspectives* (London: Bloomsbury Academic, 2023); David Brown, *Gospel as Work of Art* (Grand Rapids: Eerdmans, 2024); and George Corbett and Sarah Moerman, eds., *Music and Spirituality: Theological Approaches, Empirical Methods, and Christian Worship* (Cambridge: Open Book, 2024), https://tinyurl.com/2tvdyjjr.

81. Participants at the March 2019 Nassau planning meeting included Jonathan Anderson (Biola), Justin Barrett (Fuller), Alfonse Borysewicz (Brooklyn-based visual artist), Pascal Boyer (Washington University in St. Louis), David Brown (St Andrews), Gordon Graham (Princeton),

Those discussions shaped the strategy in inestimable ways. On the engagement side, I am indebted to Robert Lawrence Kuhn, Peter Getzels, and the rest of the CTT team. They have repeatedly worked on short notice and in difficult locations—the abandoned South Ocean Golf and Beach Resort in Nassau, for example—to capture the development of this strategy from planning meetings to the present. On the communications side, I am beholden to my friend Scott Heagle from Think Theory with whom I developed the grantee toolkit content generating mechanism that led to all of those grantee stories and videos referenced in the footnotes above, as well as countless others available on the TRT website and YouTube channel. As I have said repeatedly: marketing is programming. Rather than waiting for discoveries to trickle down, storytelling can raise awareness and mainline impact while preparing the intellectually curious general public for deeper engagement. This book would not exist without the help of my wife Rachel Brewer, the persistence of my agents David Bratt and Laura Bardolph from BBH Literary, and the enthusiastic support of Lisa Ann Cockrel from Eerdmans. Thank you. Special thanks to Garrick Allen and Taylor Worley for providing feedback on the arrangement of, and introduction to, this volume. And finally, my heartfelt thanks to all of the ASU grantees, many of whom have become friends over the past five years. I have learned so much from you, and am in awe of your collective and ongoing dedication to our shared task. Sir John Templeton believed that progress is possible when we take the humble approach, admitting we know less than 1 percent of spiritual reality, while at the same time committing ourselves to open-minded research, and the ASU community of practice has been exemplary in this regard.

Antonius Roberts (Nassau-based visual artist), Aaron Rosen (Wesley Theological Seminary), Simone Schnall (Cambridge), Murray Watts (playwright and screenwriter), Judith Wolfe (St Andrews), and Semir Zeki (University College London). Participants at the April 2019 Grand Rapids, MI planning meeting included Joseph Becherer (Notre Dame), Jonathan Berger (Stanford), Anjan Chatterjee (Penn), Nathan Jacobs (writer and director), Jean-Luc Jucker (Independent Researcher), E. Thomas Lawson (Western Michigan University), Matthew Milliner (Wheaton), Carl Plantinga (Calvin), Stephan van Erp (KU Leuven), John Witvliet (Calvin), and Nick Wolterstorff (Yale). Roberta Ahmanson (Fieldstead) and Gabrielle Starr (Pomona) planned to attend, but had to withdraw due to scheduling conflicts.

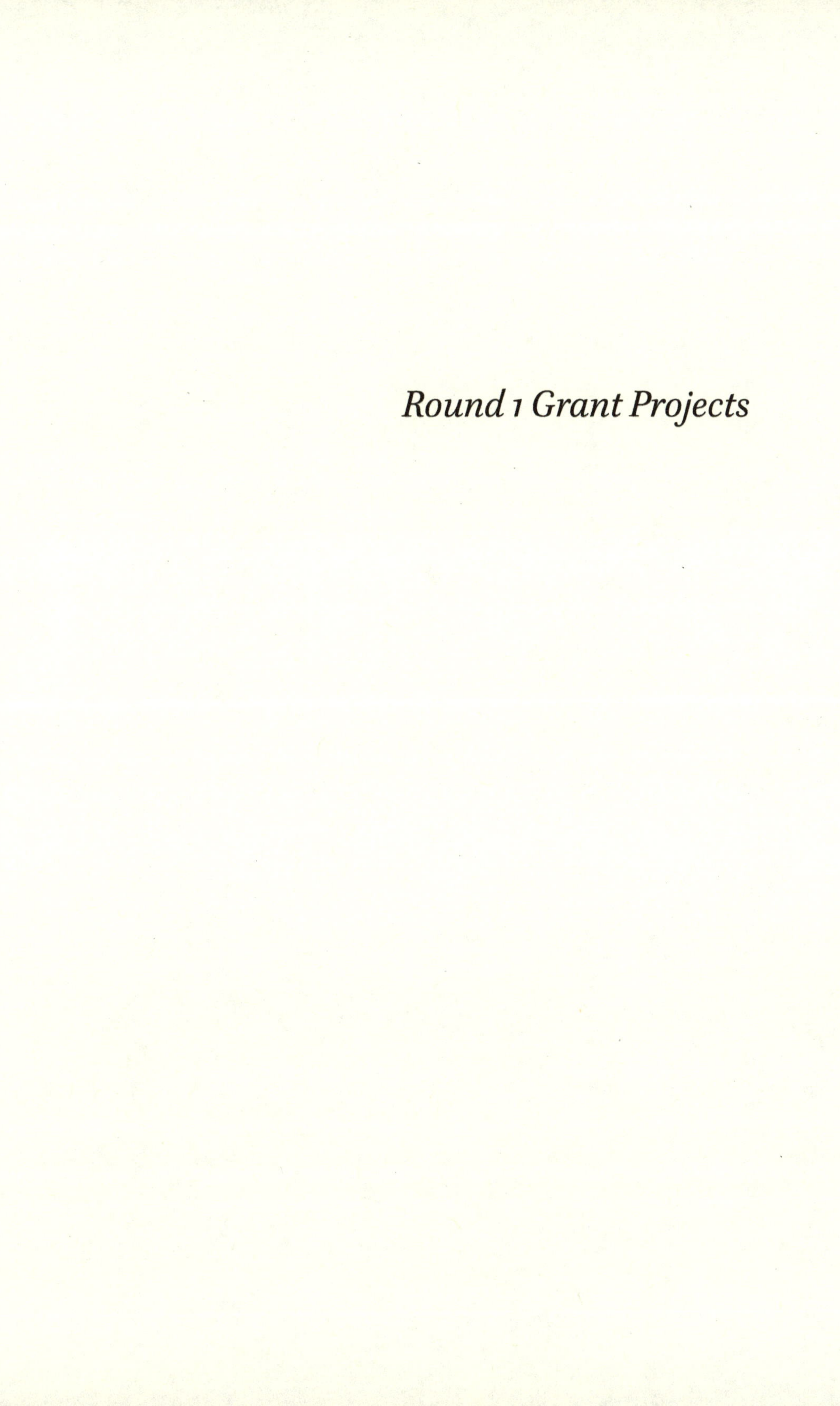

Round 1 Grant Projects

7

Art as Revelation

Judith Wolfe, Marina Iosifyan, and Brendan Wolfe

Our Art Seeking Understanding (ASU) projects arose from a conviction that experiences with art can extend and deepen our understanding of the world, including spiritual realities. To safeguard and increase such understanding, it is important to know more about its four elements: the properties of artworks, the character of aesthetic experience, the form of understanding it engenders, and the spiritual realities which might be understood in this way. And it is important to study these four together, not just separately. However, questions about properties of artworks, types of experience, forms of understanding, and the nature of spiritual realities are not usually studied within the same academic disciplines: they belong to art (and its study), psychology, philosophy, and theology, respectively. To study them meaningfully, therefore, requires bringing practitioners and scholars from within those disciplines together.

The fact that these elements are studied in different academic disciplines is not a merely contingent reality, as easy to overcome as putting four people in the same room. This is partly because although we claim that art engenders a particular kind of understanding, it is in fact more widely the case that different academic disciplines have slightly (and sometimes very) different notions of what it means to understand something, and of what there is to be understood. They think differently about what can become an object of study, by what methods one can investigate it, what kinds of things one can know about it, how one can demonstrate such knowledge, and what conclusions one can draw from it. These different approaches have been refined by long academic traditions, and to learn them is to be formed in a particular tradition of intellectual discipline and virtue. Bringing practitioners of these approaches together has challenges that cannot be neatly separated from a discussion of our subject matter. One such challenge is that epistemology often shapes ontology. In other words, scholars who are committed to a particular academic approach or lens often come to assume that the things they see through this lens are the only things there are to see. This is partly because explanatory schemes often have a sense of (potential or actual) completeness. Someone studying theology will see something very different in a religious experience than someone studying neuroscience; and in each case, the explanation will strive for completeness on its own terms. Sometimes, practitioners will see each other's explanatory schemes as redundant or unserious or reductive; sometimes, they will regard them as incompatible and therefore dangerous. Where different claims challenge each other, where they might be seen to strengthen each other, where they raise questions about what counts as knowledge, and where they simply have nothing to say to one another, are not always immediately obvious. Sometimes there is a common standard by which both can be judged, but often there is not—there are only the discipline-internal standards of what counts as knowledge and understanding. We might appeal to common human sense, but academic disciplines also have different evaluations of how much to trust common sense.

Our projects do not regard these challenges as preliminary to their task—something to be avoided or got out of the way before the real work can begin. Rather, it is precisely this multiplicity of incommensurate or only partly commensurate perspectives that an engagement with art can help us come to grips with. Knowledge *about* these different ways of approaching realities, and ways of negotiating them, are among the cognitive gains that engagement with art can bring. This form of cognitive gain is, in some senses, more essential than a gain in what might be called "propositional knowledge," because it undergirds such knowledge and shapes its limits and possibilities of expansion. Our project teams are composed of theologians, philosophers, and psychologists, and we work closely with artists. The projects are both conceptual and empirical, involving a sequence of experimental studies. Their aim is to make progress on cognitive questions which are difficult to get into view but which engagements with art can help us address.

Project Conception

We have been in charge of a total of three projects: Individually, we led "Text and Image" (2020–22, Brendan Wolfe) and "Mapping the Imagination" (2020–22, Judith Wolfe); together, we have been leading "Art as Revelation" (2022–25).

"Text and Image" deployed and extended a theory of art as communication and intention, focusing on the relationship between viewing effort and the expectation of significance. In normal communication, the "bigger" or more difficult a concept, the more effort is required to convey and understand it. People therefore naturally expect effortful communication to relate to significant messages. The evident effort invested in an artwork by the artist raises an expectation of significance in the viewer, and a consequent willingness to invest reciprocal effort in its discovery. This dynamic raises questions about the viewer that are directly relevant to a research program in aesthetic cognition:

A. In what ways is this investment directed by the artist and/or does it constitute an original contribution by the viewer?
B. What forms does the viewer's reciprocal investment take?
C. Most importantly, what forms of "significance" do viewers seek or expect from art, given that it does not constitute everyday communication with primarily pragmatic or interpersonal aims?

Questions (A) and (B) were the subjects of our planning projects "Text and Image" and "Mapping the Imagination." In relation to (A), "Text and Image" examined the artistic strategy of adding text to images to direct the viewer's attention and imagination. "Mapping the Imagination," by contrast, considered various forms in which the viewer's participation is self-directed. More specifically, in relation to (B), "Mapping the Imagination" argued that one of the chief elements of the reciprocal effort invested in art by viewers is what philosophers term the "imagination," here in the concrete sense of "the power or capacity by which the mind integrates sensory data in the process of perception."[1] The guiding assumption of the project was that works of art deliberately elicit imaginative gestalt-formation; indeed, that such imaginative investment by the viewer is at the heart of what it means to "see" a painting. The project's empirical aim, consequently, was to specify some of the forms this "beholder's share" takes.[2] These separate investigations converge on the larger question (C), which is the governing question of "Art as Revelation." Using but also extending Christoph Baumberger's taxonomy of forms of understanding to which art contributes,[3] "Art as Revelation" uses the planning projects' research into the artist's and beholder's shares in aesthetic cognition to develop and test a theory of art as revelatory.

On the basis of (A) and (B), "Text and Image" and "Mapping the Imagination" developed preliminary hypotheses about question (C). "Text and Image"

1. *Oxford English Dictionary*, s.v. "imagination," https://www.oed.com/view/Entry/91643.

2. E. H. Gombrich, *Art and Illusion* (Princeton: Princeton University Press, 1969).

3. Christoph Baumberger, "Art and Understanding: In Defence of Aesthetic Cognitivism," in *Bilder sehen: Perspektiven der Bildwissenshaft*, ed. Mark Greenlee et al. (Regensburg: Schnell & Steiner, 2013), 41–67.

investigated the hypothesis that religious art, in particular, expands the ordinary model of direct communication between a speaker and a listener (or, in the case of art, an artist and a viewer) to a triangular model of indirect communication that includes not only artist and viewer, but also art's subject matter, God and the divine. "Mapping the Imagination" investigated the hypothesis that viewers bring to art a specific expectation of *figurative* meaning; that is, that they often imaginatively integrate the elements of an artwork into a gestalt that involves not only the literal but also a figurative level. Viewers of Picasso's *Weeping Woman* (1937),[4] for example, resolve the spatial incongruity on the literal plane by appeal to a figurative level, describing the visible female form as broken "because the woman is broken on the inside."

The guiding hypothesis of "Art as Revelation," arising directly from the research pursued in our earlier projects, is that one prominent type of significance that viewers seek in art is "revelatory significance" or, in short, "revelation." In this context, we define "revelation" as the experience of disclosure, by sensory means, of dimensions of reality not directly apprehensible to the senses, promoting a shift in the perception of everyday reality. In adopting this definition and attributing it to art, we are building on the work of phenomenologists such as Maurice Merleau-Ponty and artists such as Paul Klee, who wrote, "Art does not reproduce the visible; it makes visible."[5]

Such a phenomenological description of art complements rather than competes with theological descriptions of art as revelation such as David Brown's.[6] In particular, our definition does not imply any truth claims about the experienced disclosure; rather, it describes a type of cognitive and emotional experience of the viewer. It therefore does not pursue a primarily theological investigation like Brown's, but rather an investigation into the cognitive conditions of the possibility of experiencing "revelation," whether artistic or divine. In doing so, it contributes to Baumberger's taxonomy of forms of epistemic gain afforded by art,[7] and to the study of aesthetic cognition more widely.

As our first projects showed, experiences of "revelation" in our sense are dependent on both artist and viewer: On the part of the artist, they depend on concrete communicative strategies, especially strategies that combine elements which are disparate on a literal level, but congruent on a figurative level, such as images

4. Pablo Picasso, *Weeping Woman*, 1937, oil on canvas, 608 x 500 (23 15/16 x 19 11/16), https://tinyurl.com/yey264sd.

5. Paul Klee, *Schöpferische Konfession* (Berlin: Erich Reiß Verlag, 1920), 1.

6. See especially David Brown, *Tradition and Imagination: Revelation and Change* (Oxford: Oxford University Press, 1999).

7. Baumberger, "Art and Understanding."

incorporating texts that are not immediately descriptive. Thus, "Text and Image" hypothesized and found that integrating pieces of text within the pictorial space which suggest a non-literal dimension to what is seen alters the affective connotations of religious paintings, in terms of physical activation and valence.[8]

On the part of the viewer, such experiences depend on an attenuated kind of gestalt formation, which seeks resolution of visual incongruities not on the literal level of pragmatic connections between objects, but on the figurative level of metaphorical or symbolic connections. Thus, "Mapping the Imagination" hypothesized and found that people have a greater tendency to see connections between incongruous object pairs, often with reference to a non-literal plane, if these pairs are presented in an artistic context than if they are presented in an everyday context.[9]

In "Art as Revelation," we are seeking to refine our theory of revelatory art, and to investigate the processes which underlie this cognitive experience. In doing so, we are drawing on, testing, and extending a recent, integrative model of perception and cognition which has shown great explanatory power in other domains, namely predictive processing.

Predictive processing is the claim that one of the brain's primary functions is to generate predictions about what it will perceive or do.[10] Perception is not a one-way stream of impressions informing the mind, but rather always a two-way interaction: a bottom-up stream of sensory data, and a top-down stream of predictions. The bottom-up stream starts with all the sense impressions we need to process. The top-down stream starts with all our accumulated predictions about the world: our basic concepts and convictions; everything we know from previous experience; our familiarity with a specific context; etc. These priors predict (with lesser or greater force, depending on context) what it is that we are seeing, and perception involves a process of "checking" to what extent the sensory input conforms to those predictions.

Within the predictive processing model, the perception of art has only recently become a subject of interest, but early studies are suggesting results with high

8. See Nicole Ruta and Brendan Wolfe, "Text and Image: Bodily Sensation Maps and Aesthetic Cognition" (in preparation).

9. See Marina Iosifyan and Judith Wolfe, "Everyday Life vs. Art: Effects of Framing on the Mode of Object Interpretation," *Empirical Studies of the Arts* 42, no. 1 (2023): 166–91; and Marina Iosifyan and Judith Wolfe, "Perceived Meaningfulness of Semantically Non-congruent Stimuli Increases in Art Context," *Art and Perception*, preprint, https://doi.org/10.1163/22134913-bja10065.

10. Andy Clark, "Whatever Next? Predictive Brains, Situated Agents, and the Future of Cognitive Science," *Behavioral and Brain Sciences* 36, no. 3 (2013): 181–204.

explanatory power.[11] Building on these studies, we hypothesize that one common function of art is to generate and then resolve prediction errors in unexpected ways, inducing disorientation resolving into reorientation and, consequently, pleasure. More specifically, we hypothesize that some art achieves its revelatory quality by combining sensible elements in ways that do not accord with existing schemata or priors, prompting the brain to revise its schemata or reach for reconciliation on a different (e.g., metaphorical) level. Part of this theory is the claim that the brain is more willing to practice such schematic revision in art conditions than in everyday life conditions. In other words, people display more cognitive flexibility when they take themselves to be viewing art than when they take themselves to be encountering everyday life. We hypothesize that this readiness is determined not only by the qualities of an object of attention (e.g., how good an artwork it is) but also by the context in which it is found: presence in an art gallery or on a cinema screen, for example. It is possible that religious contexts play a further, specific contextual role. The relative importance of quality versus context is a subject of investigation which "Mapping the Imagination" has already begun.

The willingness to revise schemata forms part of what is known in aesthetics, following S. T. Coleridge, as the "willing suspension of disbelief." Key follow-up questions arising from our hypotheses are the upstream and downstream correlations of the cognitive flexibility and innovation that we anticipate being encouraged by art. Upstream, we are going to ask about correlations with associated personality traits (which relate, but are not identical, to spirituality traits). Downstream, we are going to ask whether and how "revelatory" aesthetic experiences interact with the subsequent perception of related objects in everyday life conditions. To what extent does engagement with art heighten a tendency to schema-revision in subsequent engagement with everyday objects? In line with our special interest in religious art and religiosity, we hypothesize that this aftereffect may be moderated by religiosity—specifically, that it is heightened in relation to religious art when encountered by viewers who self-identify as religious.[12] Tanya Luhrmann

11. See, e.g., Stefan Koelsch, Peter Vuust, and Karl Friston, "Predictive Processes and the Peculiar Case of Music," *Trends in Cognitive Sciences* 23, no. 1 (2019): 63–77; Sander Van de Cruys and Johan Wagemans, "Putting Reward in Art: A Tentative Prediction Error Account of Visual Art," *i-Perception* 2, no. 9 (2011): 1035–62; Sander Van de Cruys et al., "Visual Affects: Linking Curiosity, Aha-Erlebnis, and Memory through Information Gain," *Cognition* 212 (2021): 1046–98.

12. We here define religious art as a corpus of artistic production commissioned, inspired, or informed by a specific religion or theological ideas, characterized by the development of defined visual canons or "languages," such as those of the Protestant Reformation. See, e.g., Bridget Heal, *A Magnificent Faith: Art and Identity in Lutheran Germany* (Oxford: Oxford University Press, 2017).

casually assumes such effects and correlations as part of her theory of the nature of religious belief,[13] and operationalizing these assumptions is a significant task.

Empirical Research

Through our previous projects and their various collaborations, we have formed a well-trained and agile team of theologians, philosophers, art historians, and cognitive psychologists, investing significant time and engagement into the cross-training of our research fellows to allow them to move in the interdisciplinary space we are charting. In these projects, we have developed dynamic methods of collaboration in which theological and philosophical questions inform the collaborative formulation of testable hypotheses, followed by the establishment and execution of experimental protocols, whose results reciprocally inform the revision of the theological and philosophical frameworks. This generative method of collaboration also forms the backbone of "Art as Revelation." Beyond the project team, we are drawing on the wider research community of St Andrews's Perception Lab and Institute for Theology, Imagination, and the Arts to help us to map concepts and check external validity.

Our empirical research program, which focuses on visual art, takes a building-blocks approach to our concept of revelation,[14] investigating salient measures that together account for significant aspects of the experience of art as revelatory. We have identified these building blocks on the basis of the research conducted in "Text and Image" and "Mapping the Imagination," although these two projects did not take the further step of contextualizing them within a predictive processing framework. Taking an embodied approach to predictive processing,[15] we hypothesize that the experience of art as "revelatory" includes (among others) the following building blocks:

- more volatile than rigid prediction models in visual processing, involving abstention from pragmatic affordances

13. Tanya Luhrmann, *How God Becomes Real: Kindling the Presence of Invisible Others* (Princeton: Princeton University Press, 2020).

14. Cf. Ann Taves, *Religious Experience Reconsidered: A Building-Block Approach to the Study of Religion and Other Special Things* (Princeton: Princeton University Press, 2009).

15. As developed by Andy Clark, "Busting Out: Predictive Brains, Embodied Minds, and the Puzzle of the Evidentiary Veil," *Nous* 51 (2017): 727–53; Michael David Kirchhoff, "The Body in Action: Predictive Processing and the Embodiment Thesis," in *The Oxford Handbook of 4E Cognition*, ed. Albert Newen, Leon De Bruin, and Shaun Gallagher, eds. (Oxford: Oxford University Press, 2018), 243–60.

- an increased propensity for distal conceptual connections
- rapid perception of unexpected or ambiguous elements
- a tendency toward hypermentalization

We are therefore investigating how and under what conditions people utilize volatile prediction models; are inclined to perceive metaphorical or symbolic meanings in images; rapidly identify unexpected or ambiguous elements; and attribute greater-than-personal agency to makers. We will then pursue important follow-up research about both upstream and downstream correlations, as described above. This building-blocks approach enables us to study individual measures whose significance is not wholly dependent on that of the overall theoretical construct. Should that theoretical construct—i.e., our working definition of art as revelatory—be disconfirmed in external validity checks within our research cluster, the individual measures will retain validity and utility, and be used toward new theoretical developments.

Depending on the variables under consideration, we are using two non-standard types of visual art to allow us to isolate relevant measures and effects:

1. In studies that investigate proactive imaginative investment by viewers, or the framing effects of artistic versus everyday contexts, we are using ready-mades, that is, artworks which involve commonplace objects.[16] Despite the potential limits of their representativeness of art more generally, readymades are useful because they can be perceived differently depending on whether they are presented as everyday objects or artworks, thus permitting an experimental focus on the interpretative work of the viewer.
2. In studies that investigate the perceived intention of the artist, we are using indeterminate art, that is, a seemingly meaningful artistic visual stimulus that denies easy or immediate identification.[17] Despite the potential limits of its representativeness of art more generally, indeterminate art is proven to enable a tight experimental focus on mentalization and hypermentalization.

Our method is dynamic and iterative, and we are still in the early stages of empirical research. In what follows, we describe two areas of study and associated hypotheses relating to the building blocks of our definition of "revelation." These

16. Simon J. Evnine, "Ready-Mades: Ontology and Aesthetics," *British Journal of Aesthetics* 53, no. 4 (2013): 407–23.

17. Robert Pepperell, "Seeing without Objects: Visual Indeterminacy and Art," *Leonardo* 39 (2006): 394–400.

will form the basis for further refinement, extension, and mapping. In particular, as already indicated, one of the remote aims of our project is to expand existing research on religion and predictive processing through a better understanding of aesthetic cognition and its potential upstream and downstream connections to spiritual cognition. Beyond follow-up empirical studies, it will be an important aspect of the later stages of the project to integrate our findings with current predictive processing accounts of religiosity. In doing so, our project aims to complement existing approaches, which focus primarily on "special" experiences (Taves, Schjødt, Andersen, van Elk), meditative practice (Laukkonen), or other ritual or charismatic practices (Schjødt, Andersen). In this context, simply speaking, our project asks, "What if being religious is more like seeing art than like hearing voices?"

Area 1: Embodied Predictive Processing and Art

Our first area advances research into the differences between prediction frameworks operative in encounters with everyday life vs. art. This is a key area for understanding the types of significance looked for in art, and for empirically describing the conditions for experiencing art as revelatory.

Researchers claim that embodiment plays a crucial role in predictive processing.[18] Predictive processing relies not only on exteroception (developing and testing predictions via visual and auditory information), but also on interoception: signals arising from the body. This includes the processing involved in social perception: viz., the fact that when humans perceive actions or emotions of others, they simulate them using their own bodies.[19]

Such a mechanism of embodied simulation is also involved in art perception.[20] Embodied simulation responds both to the imagined process of art making (simulating the actions of the artist who created the artwork) and to the content of an artwork (simulating, e.g., the emotional state of figures in the artwork). Experiments testing embodied simulation have revealed close similarities between the

18. Clark, "Whatever Next?"; Mark Miller and Andy Clark, "Happily Entangled: Prediction, Emotion, and the Embodied Mind," *Synthese* 195 (2018): 2559–75; Ruben T. Azevedo and Manos Tsakiris, "Art Reception as an Interoceptive Embodied Predictive Experience," *Behavioral and Brain Sciences* 40 (2017): article number e350, https://doi.org/10.1017/s0140525x17001856.

19. Vittorio Gallese and Corrado Sinigaglia, "What Is So Special about Embodied Simulation?" *Trends in Cognitive Sciences* 15, no. 11 (2011): 512–19.

20. D. Freedberg and V. Gallese, "Motion, Emotion and Empathy in Aesthetic Experience," *Trends in Cognitive Sciences* 11 (2007): 197–203.

perception of art and perception in everyday life. However, they do not explain the differences between them.

Despite the similarities in embodied simulation, embodied predictive processing may differ in art and everyday life conditions. A prominent hypothesis to explain this difference appeals to the idea of affordances. Affordances are defined as possibilities for action related to ("afforded by") certain objects. (For example, a hammer "affords" grasping and striking.) These affordances shape the generation of predictions. The perception of art generally does not involve classic pragmatic affordances; rather, it may involve what researchers have called aesthetic or "beholding" affordances.[21] The idea behind this concept is that in the context of art, objects can be perceived and processed differently, since they allow perceptual engagement but not action (e.g., the urinal in Marcel Duchamp's *Fountain*[22]). To investigate these differences empirically, we are testing the hypothesis that beholding affordances increase the generation of more volatile prediction models, while classic affordances encourage more rigid prediction models. This study will investigate the generation of prediction models in art versus everyday life conditions, specifically focusing on readymades: artworks which involve commonplace objects.[23] We are choosing readymades because they can be perceived differently depending on whether they are presented as everyday objects or artworks, thus permitting an experimental focus on the interpretative work of the viewer.

Area 2: Religious Art and Predictive Processing

Our second area advances research into the effects that religious art (or art perceived as religious) may have on predictive processing frameworks used in everyday life by religious believers. While area 1 is focused on object interpretation, area 2 is focused on interpretation of artists' intentions and social contexts.

As suggested above, one of the ways in which art may be experienced as revelatory is by encouraging viewers to perceive intentions, purposes, and meanings more richly than in everyday conditions, and in some cases, to see greater, non-mundane agency behind the artist's agency. Seeing a work of art, viewers are aware that it was created intentionally by an artist and thus may attempt to understand the artist's intentions.[24] In psychological terms, engagement with art

21. Maria Brincker, "The Aesthetic Stance—On the Conditions and Consequences of Becoming a Beholder," in Alfonsina Scarinzi, ed., *Aesthetics and the Embodied Mind: Beyond Art Theory and the Cartesian Mind-Body Dichotomy* (Dordrecht: Springer, 2015).

22. Marcel Duchamp, *Fountain*, 1917, porcelain, https://tinyurl.com/yh2v2mh6.

23. Evnine, "Ready-Mades: Ontology and Aesthetics."

24. Michael J. Parsons, *How We Understand Art: A Cognitive Developmental Account of Aes-*

may encourage hyper-mentalizing, and we aim to test this claim. "Mapping the Imagination" experiments have shown that engagement with art has aftereffects on viewers' engagement with scenes and situations encountered immediately afterward, and we intend to design similar experiments to test the effect of religious art on hypermentalization.

Religiosity has independently been shown to relate to attributing intentions to physical objects and nature, since God's intentions may underlie them.[25] It is thus possible that religious art more strongly affects the generation of predictive models which involve attributing secondary meaning to both natural scenes and social situations. Our studies in this area will investigate how religious art affects the generation of prediction models which can also be used in interpretation of everyday life events, involving both natural scenes and social situations.

We expect that the above described experiments will contribute to our understanding of how art generates revelation. Area 1 will contribute to our understanding of object interpretations, such as making distal conceptual connections, rapid perception of unexpected and ambiguous elements, increase in visual exploration and increased salience of symbolic rather than literal meanings of objects. Area 2 will contribute to our understanding of the interpretation of social scenes, such as hyper-mentalizing, or describing events in a projective and symbolic rather than a descriptive and literal way. These studies will be revised and extended in light of the findings of associated pilot projects, as well as through discussion within our research cluster.

Results and Reflections

At this stage, we have completed one major publication: a monograph by Judith Wolfe entitled *The Theological Imagination*.[26] This book lays out the philosophical-theological vision that one project leader is contributing to the interdisciplinary

thetic Experience (Cambridge: Cambridge University Press, 1987); Matthew Pelowski and Fuminori Akiba, "A Model of Art Perception, Evaluation and Emotion in Transformative Aesthetic Experience," *New Ideas in Psychology* 29 (2011): 80–97; Alessandro Pignocchi, *Pourquoi aime-t-on un film? Quand les sciences cognitives discutent des gouts et des couleurs* (Paris: Odile Jacob, 2015).

25. Jesse M. Bering, "The Existential Theory of Mind," *Review of General Psychology* 6 (2002): 3–24; A. Norenzayan, W. M. Gervais, and K. H. Trzesniewski, "Mentalizing Deficits Constrain Belief in a Personal God," *PLoS One* 7, no. 5 (2012): article number e36880, https://doi.org/10.1371/journal.pone.0036880; Michiel van Elk and André Aleman, "Brain Mechanisms in Religion and Spirituality: An Integrative Predictive Processing Framework," *Neuroscience & Biobehavioral Reviews* 73 (2017): 359–78.

26. Judith Wolfe, *The Theological Imagination* (Cambridge: Cambridge University Press, 2024).

work of the team. Although not every aspect of the book is "legible" or operationalizable within an interdisciplinary context, it provides a theological backdrop or horizon to our narrower empirical work. The book argues that to live in the world, we have to imagine it: to make sense of things by seeing coherent wholes in underdetermined data. The book brings together theology, philosophy, psychology, literature, and art to describe and interrogate the human imagination. In five interrelated chapters that draw on the philosophical history of the term "imagination," psychological models and studies (including predictive processing), on the history of art and on literary criticism, the book constructs a phenomenology of imaginative engagement, examining the ways we inhabit our language, our life roles, and our world more widely, often without awareness of the imaginative work that co-constitutes them. Throughout, the book argues that art and poetry loosen the grasp of habituated perception and grant a "double" or "depth" vision of our lives, allowing us to see them from new perspectives or in new ways. The book then discusses Christian liturgy and Scripture as bringing about similar (though more existentially radical) renewals of perception. In its second half, the book investigates the interrelation between these dynamics of imaginative perception and the Christian faith more fully. It argues that faith is both a way of making sense of the world—of seeing it as a whole with depth and significance—and a challenge to our forms of sense making. The book concludes with an account of what it describes as an eschatological imagination.

The empirical portion of the project is well underway, and (as outlined above) is continually raising new questions both about the processes we are investigating, and about their upstream and downstream correlates. All aspects of the research—conceptual, theoretical, and empirical—are confirming that engagement with the arts generates distinctive kinds of understanding, which are more "primary" or basic than propositional knowledge, because they concern the very ways in which we organize the world into concepts. As Albert Einstein wrote: "Imagination is more important than knowledge. For knowledge is limited, whereas imagination embraces the entire world, stimulating progress, giving birth to evolution. It is, strictly speaking, a real factor in scientific research."[27] We look forward to further progress as we continue our work together.

27. Albert Einstein, *On Cosmic Religion* (New York: Covici-Friede, 1931), 49.

2

Measuring the (Im)measurable in Real Life

Kutter Callaway

"My first adult memory . . . is of the Van Gogh museum in Amsterdam. I went there at eighteen, during a break, while I studied my sophomore year in Heidelberg, Germany. I remember thinking that he knew things that I had only felt, and that he was able in canvas after canvas to express the presence of God through the light on canvas. It was the haystack series. I knew he was searching for something, but back then I didn't know it was about light. He deeply influenced both my spiritual life and my filmmaking."

"Jacques Tati's *Playtime* absolutely changed the way I see the world on a very fundamental level—both practically and relationally."

"Walking into the Archbasilica of St. John Lateran in Rome for the first time was a transforming experience. I felt myself transported outside of time and space as I moved among the larger-than-life-sized Rococo statues of the Apostles, each one holding the instrument of their death or a symbol of their contribution to Christianity. I felt myself to be small and insignificant and yet lifted up in spirit."

Transformed understandings of the world, moments of awe and wonder, mystical and even religious encounters—each and every one prompted by art. All of these personal accounts originated from a series of semi-structured interviews with artists and laypersons conducted during the initial stage of a multi-year research project on Art Seeking Understanding (ASU). Taken together, they paint a compelling picture of art's capacity to prompt spiritual and religious forms of cognition. Yet, the primary question this research project aimed to explore was whether these experiences could be assessed scientifically. Are they replicable or even measurable in any meaningful sense? Put differently, when it comes to aesthetic experiences, how can anyone possibly "measure the immeasurable"?

One of our core operating assumptions was that aesthetic experiences of art like those described above are, in fact, vulnerable to empirical investigation. Thus, rather than take the claims of theological and philosophical aesthetics at face value, our project set out to explore their evidentiary basis. If the philosophical and theological accounts of art's capacity to prompt spiritual or religious forms of cognition are reliably accurate (or perhaps even "true"), then what observable evidence might there be to corroborate these accounts, and how might we quantify this evidence in scientifically rigorous ways such that we could reasonably make both predictive and generalizable inferences about the functional value of art? In other words, we asked two big questions: (1) Is it possible to quantify spiritual forms of understanding prompted by art? (2) If so, what difference does it make?

Situated primarily within the disciplines of theology and psychology, but conversant with the more interdisciplinary fields of theological aesthetics and empirical aesthetics, our cross-disciplinary team of psychologists, philosophers, theologians, and even virtual reality designers examined these questions experimentally. The project began with an initial series of studies that were conducted almost entirely online during the COVID-19 pandemic lockdowns. However, upon securing program grant funding, we have continued to build upon these preliminary findings by moving beyond the laboratory, exploring the psycho-socio-spiritual effects of art and art-going "in real life," that is, both in a more ecologically valid setting (in situ) and as a live or living event that unfolds in time (in vivo). In what follows, we not only document our findings from the project grant stage of the research project, but also describe what we have continued to discover during the program grant phase.

A Survey of Scholarship

No empirical study takes place in a vacuum. Thus, in order to provide a rationale for the hypotheses tested over the course of this research project and to offer a robust survey of the extant scholarship, it will be helpful first to identify the key philosophical, theological, aesthetic, and psychological resources that served as the theoretical underpinnings of our approach.

Philosophical Aesthetics

Chief among the intellectual resources informing this project was the work being produced in the field of aesthetic cognitivism, which conceives of the cognitive functions of art in terms of understanding rather than knowledge per se. Art can be said to function cognitively not because it provides a means for acquiring justified true beliefs, but because it is capable of advancing human understanding.[1]

1. Christoph Baumberger, "Art and Understanding: In Defence of Aesthetic Cognitivism," in

Importantly, "understanding" is not about the perceived meaning of the artwork or the semantic knowledge people might abstract from a piece of art, but the ways in which a work of art contributes to an awareness of aspects of the world external to the work itself. Art therefore prompts what might be called "objectual" knowledge of the world.

Far beyond a species of factive belief (i.e., "propositional" knowledge of isolated facts), the kind of understanding artworks deliver (1) provides new categories for classifying real-world objects; (2) presents new perspectives on people, places, and things that enhance people's understanding of them; (3) raises important questions that prompt further inquiry (especially moral inquiry); (4) provides art-goers with opportunities to know what it is like to have certain sensory-motor experiences; (5) serves as thought experiments; (6) enables people to grasp connections between what they already believe; and (7) enhances or refines general cognitive abilities by exercising reasoning, perception, imagination, and memory.[2]

This shift in emphasis from "propositional" to "objectual" knowledge highlights three of the conceptual distinctions that both oriented and animated our approach. First, following Nelson Goodman and others,[3] our driving research questions were not ontological (i.e., What is art?) but functional (i.e., How and why is art?). That is to say, we were far more concerned with how a piece of art functions in the ways that it does and why people in turn do the things they do with art (cognitively, emotionally, behaviorally) than with what art is, what it means, or how it might be valued.

Second, following Berys Gaut,[4] insofar as art does have a cognitive function, the knowledge it provides is non-trivial even if and when it is non-propositional. Although certain artworks may give rise to propositional knowledge, the kind of understanding or "objectual" knowledge that art prompts cannot be reduced to propositional categories alone and, thus, should not be conceptualized as some-

---

Bilder sehen: Perspektiven der Bildwissenschaft, ed. Mark Greenlee et al. (Regensburg: Schnell & Steiner, 2013), 41–67; Gordon Graham, "Aesthetic Cognitivism and the Literary Arts," *Journal of Aesthetic Education* 30, no. 1 (1996): 1–17; Howard Riley, "Aesthetic Cognitivism: Towards a Concise Case for Doctoral Research through Practices in the Visual Arts," *Arts and Humanities in Higher Education* 18, no. 4 (2019): 430–43.

2. Baumberger, "Art and Understanding," 52–59.

3. Nelson Goodman, *Languages of Art* (Indianapolis: Hackett, 1976); Nelson Goodman, *Ways of Worldmaking* (Indianapolis: Hackett, 1978); Ellen Winner, *How Art Works: A Psychological Exploration* (Oxford: Oxford University Press, 2019).

4. Berys Gaut, "Art and Knowledge," in *The Oxford Handbook of Aesthetics*, ed. Jerrold Levinson (Oxford: Oxford University Press, 2003), 436–50; Berys Gaut, "Art and Cognition," in *Contemporary Debates in Aesthetics and the Philosophy of Art*, ed. Matthew Kieran (Oxford: Blackwell, 2006), 115–26.

how deficient or incomplete simply because it cannot be expressed in a logical proof or mathematical theorem. The goal in making this assertion is not to rehash centuries-old arguments regarding epistemology and art. Rather, it is to pave the way for operationalizing the phenomenal or "objectual" knowledge art provides without reducing it.

Third, aesthetic forms of cognition always involve a fully embodied, holistic, sensory-motor perception of the world—a "what-it-is-like" kind of knowledge.[5] A piece of art does not offer a mere depiction or simulation of the world. Rather, it stimulates the sensory-motor capacities of viewers in such a way that they experience what it is like to perceive the world as the artist does, albeit temporarily and imperfectly. Although much of the empirical literature exploring the psychological dimensions of art seems enamored with this notion of "disinterested contemplation,"[6] the cognitive function of a piece of art is rather quite profoundly interested. It is never a purely mental event nor the disinterested contemplation of a universal, transcendental category known as "beauty."[7]

Our primary concern was thus not to defend a particular conception of beauty per se, nor was it to determine whether a given piece of art might be evaluated as "beautiful" or exceptionally well crafted; rather, our aim was to examine the psycho-social-spiritual effects of various kinds of artworks. By conceiving of aesthetics in terms of sensual perception and psychological effects rather than a theory of art or beauty, we approached the functional value of art in a way that aligned well with the most recent developments in empirical aesthetics and neuroaesthetics, which seek to distinguish between the cognitive science of aesthetics and the cognitive science of art.[8] Thus, in our exploration of the kinds of cognition that arise from aesthetic experiences of art, we drew upon the cognitive science of aesthetics, which studies "the aspect of sensory valuation that refers specifically to understanding how and why perceptual representation of a sensory stimulus leads to a given hedonic value,"[9] in order to understand more fully the psychological processes associated with the experience of artistic stimuli, which is the distinct and more narrow focus of the cognitive science of art.

5. Peter Goldie, "Conceptual Art and Knowledge," in *Philosophy and Conceptual Art*, ed. Peter Goldie and Elisabeth Schellekens (Oxford: Oxford University Press, 2007), 157–70.

6. Anjan Chatterjee, *The Aesthetic Brain: How We Evolved to Desire Beauty and Enjoy Art* (Oxford: Oxford University Press, 2014).

7. Alejandro Garcia-Rivera, Mark Graves, and Carl Neumann, "Beauty in the Living World," *Zygon* 44, no. 2 (2009): 243–63.

8. Martin Skov and Marcos Nadal, "A Farewell to Art: Aesthetics as a Topic in Psychology and Neuroscience," *Perspectives on Psychological Science* 15, no. 3 (2020): 630–42.

9. Skov and Nadal, "Farewell to Art," 8.

Theological Aesthetics

By identifying our primary object of inquiry as the cognitive, affective, and behavioral effects of aesthetic experiences with art, we located our exploration within a very particular vein of philosophical aesthetics. But this account had an even more specific focus: art that gives rise to what Sir John Templeton refers to as "spiritual" or "religious" understanding.[10] As a consequence, it was necessary to draw upon theological resources, which provide a kind of domain-specific conceptual scaffolding regarding spiritual understanding that philosophy is unable to supply on its own.

Those contributing to the discourse on theological aesthetics have highlighted the need to consider not merely the function of an artwork, but also the association between the content of an artwork and the content of the cognitive activity it prompts (whether objectual or propositional). A prominent example can be found in the work of Jeremy Begbie, who has asserted that the music of Arvo Pärt, although completely instrumental and without lyrical content, is capable of prompting higher-order reflection on specific theological propositions (e.g., the Christian doctrines of the Trinity and the incarnation).[11] Taking a slightly different angle, James K. A. Smith has suggested that, regardless of the artistic medium in question, the aesthetic content that populates the imaginations of contemporary persons reflects their core desires and shapes their ritual behaviors, both "secular" and devotional.[12] In both cases, however, it is clear that, according to those contributing to theological aesthetics, certain forms of art can give rise to spiritual or religious (even theological) understandings of the world.

That being said, although various forms of understanding might be considered spiritual or theological, they are not always (or even usually) explicitly religious. Indeed, art and aesthetic experiences are increasingly understood by contemporary persons to be primary sites for sustaining their spiritual and religious lives.[13] This is even the case when aesthetic experiences make no reference to anything explicitly religious and take place outside the context of any formal religious tradition or institution. Thus, on one hand, it may be that certain kinds of aesthetic experiences give

10. John Templeton, *The Humble Approach: Scientists Discover God* (West Conshohocken, PA: Templeton Foundation Press, 1981).

11. Jeremy S. Begbie, *Resounding Truth: Christian Wisdom in the World of Music* (Grand Rapids: Baker Academic, 2007).

12. James K. A. Smith, *Desiring the Kingdom: Worship, Worldview, and Cultural Formation* (Grand Rapids: Baker Academic, 2009).

13. Robert K. Johnston, *God's Wider Presence: Reconsidering General Revelation* (Grand Rapids: Baker Academic, 2014).

rise to a constellation of psychological effects that individuals will predictably code as "spiritual" or "religious" even if they do not identify as a religious person themselves. On the other hand, in light of a person's prior metaphysical commitments and religious beliefs, it may also be that certain experiences of profound insight or cognitive reframing, even though not explicitly religious, will be accepted and understood as transcendent, spiritual encounters with the divine. Either way, those operating within the domain of theological aesthetics do not equate or conflate the cognitive function of art with spirituality or religion, but merely recognize that the cognitive, affective, and behavioral effects of art do in fact bear spiritual and religious potential.

The Psychology of Religion and Spirituality

The philosophical and theological literature is instructive, but in order to explore the "spiritual" and "religious" potential of "art" in any meaningful psychological sense, a greater degree of terminological precision is required. Yet, even among those contributing to the psychology of religion and spirituality, there is very little consensus on how best to define religion and spirituality,[14] which are the two objects of inquiry with which we were primarily concerned. Nevertheless, for the sake of clarity with respect to how we intended to deploy these terms and their related constructs, we adopted Peter L. Benson et al.'s stance[15] that religion and spirituality are two distinct but overlapping domains such that (as Sarah A. Schnitker observes): "Most researchers characterize religiousness as engagement with an organized faith tradition that facilitates closeness to the transcendent . . . whereas spirituality is more often typified by private actions and emotions in relation to a transcendent entity."[16] To further clarify what psychological researchers mean by religion and spirituality, a more robust conceptualization of "transcendence" was also needed in order to define the primary object at which religion and spirituality aim. For instance, beliefs about transcendence include at least three discrete but interrelated domains: (1) ontological transcendence, which conceives of reality in terms of supernatural categories of being; (2) phenome-

14. Vassilis Saroglou, "Introduction: Studying Religion in Personality and Social Psychology," in *Religion, Personality, and Social Behavior*, ed. Vassilis Saroglou (London: Psychology Press, 2014), 1–28.

15. Peter L. Benson, Eugene C. Roehlkepartain, and Stacey P. Rude, "Spiritual Development in Childhood and Adolescence: Toward a Field of Inquiry," *Applied Developmental Science* 7 (2003): 205–13.

16. Sarah A. Schnitker et al., "Longitudinal Study of Religious and Spiritual Transformation in Adolescents Attending Young Life Summer Camp: Assessing the Epistemic, Intrapsychic, and Moral Sociability Functions of Conversion," *Psychology of Religion and Spirituality* 6 (2014): 85.

nological transcendence, which focuses on traversing the divide between the self and others or the self and the world; and (3) subjective transcendence, which has in view the ever shifting boundary that constitutes the mundane self, the crossing of which is always yet to come.[17] Although more could be said regarding religion, spirituality, and transcendence, for our purposes it was enough to move forward with these basic definitions in mind.

Evolutionary Psychology and the Art(s)

But what about art? Much like religion and spirituality, art is a construct equally prone to conceptual ambiguity. Indeed, within the field of evolutionary psychology, there is little agreement on how art should be studied or what its adaptive functions (if any) might be.[18] But there is also a lack of consensus regarding something even more fundamental: what art "is" and, thus, how best to define it as an object of scientific inquiry.[19] One of the key problems in this regard is the notion inspired by eighteenth-century European philosophical categories that there is a coherent, overarching category known as "art" that can be distinguished from other human-created artifacts, practices, and experiences.[20] Although certain forms of material culture appear in many if not most contexts,[21] most indigenous languages have no equivalent terms for "art" as it exists in Western societies,[22] which is to say as an all-encompassing concept that includes entities as diverse as painting, carvings, songs, dances, and literature.[23] In other words, given its variety

17. Kutter Callaway, Sarah Schnitker, and Madison Gilbertson, "Not All Transcendence Is Created Equal: Distinguishing Ontological, Phenomenological, and Subjective Beliefs about Transcendence," *Philosophical Psychology* 33, no. 4 (2020), 479.

18. Johan De Smedt and Helen De Cruz, "Toward an Integrative Approach of Cognitive Neuroscientific and Evolutionary Psychological Studies of Art," *Evolutionary Psychology* 8, no. 4 (2010): 695–719.

19. Ellen Dissanayake, "The Arts after Darwin: Does Art Have an Origin and Adaptive Function?" in *World Art Studies: Exploring Concepts and Approaches*, ed. Kitty Zijlmans and Wilfried van Damme (Amsterdam: Valiz, 2008), 241–63; Ellen Dissanayake, "What Art Is and What Art Does: An Overview of Contemporary Evolutionary Hypotheses," in *Evolutionary and Neurocognitive Approaches to Aesthetics, Creativity, and the Arts*, ed. Colin Martindale, Paul Locher, and Vladimir M. Petrov (London: Routledge, 2009), 1–14.

20. Noël Carroll, "Aesthetic Experience, Art, and Artists," in *Aesthetic Experience*, ed. Richard Shusterman and Adele Tomlin (London: Routledge, 2008), 145–65.

21. Donald E. Brown, *Human Universals* (New York: McGraw-Hill, 1991).

22. Denis Dutton, *The Art Instinct: Beauty, Pleasure, and Human Evolution* (London: Bloomsbury, 2009).

23. Dissanayake, "Arts after Darwin."

and complexity, art is likely not a natural kind, which immediately confounds any attempt to define it as such.

That being said, a certain constellation of objects, practices, and experiences does seem to trigger an interrelated set of expectations and mental schemas regarding cultural artifacts that can reasonably be described as "aesthetic."[24] Experimental studies have demonstrated that, cross-culturally, people tend to operate with a folk concept of art that features a strikingly similar set of inferences, expectations, and intentions.[25] For instance, untrained art observers have been shown to prefer pieces of art that align with their evolved cognitive tendencies.[26] Likewise, in most contemporary societies, people think "beauty" is in some way involved in their art making and art appreciation.[27] Experimental philosophers have also investigated these folk concepts, providing compelling evidence that art is very likely a dual-character concept (i.e., it is both descriptive and evaluative), which helps explain at least in part why art-goers' "preferences for" artworks that are "beautiful" (i.e., those embodying certain characteristic values) are closely related to and follow logically from the descriptive features they use as criteria for judging an object to be, ultimately, an actual piece of art.[28]

Marcel Duchamp's *Fountain* offers a well-known example of how these folk expectations operate.[29] A porcelain urinal installed in a restroom is just a plumbing fixture. But when it is located in an art gallery and signed by its creator, that very same material artifact triggers (and upsets) an entirely different set of inferences, mental schemas, and expectations on the part of the viewer. Rather

24. Anton Killin, "The Arts and Human Nature: Evolutionary Aesthetics and the Evolutionary Status of Art Behaviors," *Biology and Philosophy* 28, no. 4 (2013): 703–18.

25. J.-L. Jucker, "Ambiguous Artefacts: Towards a Cognitive Anthropology of Art." DPhil thesis, Linacre College, University of Oxford, 2012; Jean-Luc Jucker and Justin L. Barrett, "Cognitive Constraints on the Visual Arts: An Empirical Study of the Role of Perceived Intentions in Appreciation Judgements," *Journal of Cognition and Culture* 11 (2011): 115–36; Jean-Luc Jucker, Justin L. Barrett, and Rafael Wlodarski, "'I Just Don't Get It': Perceived Artists' Intentions Affect Art Evaluations," *Empirical Studies of the Arts* 32, no. 2 (2014): 149–82; Lauren S. Seifert, "Experimental Aesthetics: Implications for Aesthetic Education of Naive Art Observers," *Journal of Psychology* 126 (1992): 73–78.

26. Colin Martindale, "Bouguereau Is Back," in *Proceedings from the XV Congress of the International Association of Empirical Aesthetics Rome*, September 21–24, 1998 (Rome: La Sapienza, 1998).

27. Winfried Menninghaus, *Aesthetics after Darwin: The Multiple Origins and Functions of Arts*, trans. Alexandra Berlina (Brighton, MA: Academic Studies Press, 2019).

28. Shen-yi Liao, Aaron Meskin, and Joshua Knobe, "Dual Character Art Concepts," *Pacific Philosophical Quarterly* 101, no. 1 (2020): 102–28.

29. Marcel Duchamp, *Fountain*, 1917, porcelain, https://tinyurl.com/yh2v2mh6.

than an a priori classification, these inferences and expectations are not only what constitute the urinal as a piece of art, but also the source of its rejection as a piece of art. Thus, the key question for researchers exploring the psychology of art is not which objects do or do not qualify as art according to a theoretical category, but rather, what are the necessary conditions for activating this folk aesthetic and in what ways do changes to these conditions bring about different psychological effects?

An immediate consequence of targeting folk aesthetics is that it requires a shift away from conceiving of "art" as a monolithic, all-encompassing whole and toward a conceptualization of "the arts" as a wide-ranging group of diverse practices, each of which presents a unique set of circumstances to which psychological researchers must attend. Because different artistic behaviors serve different purposes, and some serve various purposes simultaneously (both now and throughout their evolutionary development), it is unhelpful to approach concrete practices like self-painting and domicile decoration as if they were of the same kind as dancing and music-making.[30] Instead, a diverse and plural conception of the arts is required.[31] For purely pragmatic reasons, it is still helpful to speak of "the arts" as a way of acknowledging the family resemblances that exist between forms as diverse as singing, self-adornment, and narrative fiction, but each of these object categories must be treated individually rather than as a whole in developing testable hypotheses regarding their cognitive, affective, and behavioral effects, for each confers a different set of potential benefits, both to the individual and to the group, and each activates a different set of folk intuitions.

Summary of the Project's Aims

In sum, the approach toward experimentation we adopted emerged from the theoretical discourses of philosophical and theological aesthetics, but it also drew from the psychological sciences in order to pursue the following goals. First, it attempted to provide an account of aesthetic experiences in terms of a broader category of sense perception and, by doing so, conceptualized aesthetic experiences of art as exemplary cases of embodied meaning making.[32] Second, the primary outputs it sought to examine and understand more fully were the

30. Menninghaus, *Aesthetics after Darwin*; Eveline Seghers, "The Artful Mind: A Critical Review of the Evolutionary Psychological Study of Art," *British Journal of Aesthetics* 55, no. 2 (2015): 225–48.

31. Again, see Dutton, *Art Instinct*; Gaut, "Art and Knowledge"; Gaut, "Art and Cognition."

32. Mark Johnson, *The Meaning of the Body: Aesthetics of Human Understanding* (Chicago: University of Chicago Press, 2007).

psycho-social-spiritual effects of material artifacts that activate folk intuitions about art (i.e., a "folk aesthetic"). Third, among the numerous psychological effects we might have explored, the approach we proposed focused on the underlying psychological processes involved in the non-propositional, "what-it-is-like" kinds of objectual knowledge that art prompts and the associated forms of awareness or understanding that lead people to conceptualize their aesthetic experiences in spiritual, religious, or transcendent terms.

Project Phase

Our initial round of studies unfolded in three basic stages. In the first stage, we conducted a comprehensive literature review and published a theory paper that (1) mapped out the current state of research in the two distinct but increasingly interrelated fields of the psychology of art and the psychology of religion and spirituality and (2) identified the most promising avenues of research that psychological scientists in particular might pursue in order to operationalize, quantify, and analyze the psycho-social-spiritual effects of art.[33] Framed by the broader discourses of philosophical and theological aesthetics, this theory paper develops a paradigm for empirical testing organized according to a series of features that are basic to human processing and, thus, familiar to psychological researchers in numerous sub-disciplines.

In the second stage, we developed a set of visual stimuli created specifically for use in experimentation. To do so, we (1) interviewed artists to create basic categories of spiritually evocative art; (2) commissioned original art photographs based upon these categories, which were nature, abstract, human, religious, and unsettling; and then (3) modified those photos by breaking standard aesthetic "rules" of photography (e.g., the rule of thirds). In other words, we made pretty pictures ugly.[34]

In the third stage, we tested whether the original art photos evoked spirituality, connectedness, awe, or other discrete emotions differently from those perceived to be the less aesthetically pleasing photos. The full write-up from these studies has been published in *Psychology of Aesthetics, Creativity, and the Arts*.[35] In sum,

33. Kutter Callaway et al., "Measuring the (Im)measurable: On the Psycho-Socio-Spiritual Effects of Aesthetic Experiences of Art," *Journal of Psychology and Theology* 51, no. 3 (2023): 352–74.

34. See the Online Supplemental Material for Rosemary L. Al-Kire et al., "Original Photographic Art Induces Self-Transcendent Emotions," *Psychology of Aesthetics, Creativity, and the Arts*, advance online publication (2023): https://doi.org/10.1037/aca0000610.

35. Rosemary L. Al-Kire et al., "Original Photographic Art Induces Self-Transcendent Emotions," *Psychology of Aesthetics, Creativity, and the Arts*, advance online publication (2023): https://doi.org/10.1037/aca0000610.

though, our findings were quite promising and support the ideas that, in the first place, photographic artworks can both boost feelings of spirituality, vastness, and awe, and decrease negative states like anxiety and fear. These studies also suggest that the perceived quality of the art and the perception that an image is or is not "art" at all also contribute to shifts in these forms of spiritual cognition.

Moving Out of the Lab

In light of these initial findings, the answer to our first big question (i.e., can spiritual cognition prompted by art be measured?) seems to be a resounding yes. However, as it concerns the question that immediately follows (i.e., what difference does it make?), we still have much to learn. Indeed, based upon the promising data generated during the project phase, we were able to secure program grant funding in order to continue our research. Our current project is thus a direct extension of and an elaboration upon the findings from our initial round of studies. The overarching aim of the studies funded by the program grant is not only to deepen, but also to expand upon our understanding of the underlying psycho-social dynamics of aesthetic experiences of artistic media, specifically as it relates to the different levels of mediation and materiality presented by various artistic media.

In order to expand upon the findings from our first round of experiments, we are currently testing a series of hypotheses regarding the causal associations between the presentational context of artistic media and the psychological insights it generates by conducting a round of experiments using immersive virtual reality (VR) technologies. The primary rationale for incorporating VR interventions into studies examining the positive psychological effects of artistic media is the recent proliferation of empirical research on the benefits of VR technology in both clinical and experimental settings.[36] In terms of experimental design, VR technologies present opportunities for conducting research in a way that allows researchers to maintain a high degree of experimental control over variables without diminishing the ecological validity of the study to the same extent as other

36. Laura Loucks et al., "'You Can Do That?!': Feasibility of Virtual Reality Exposure Therapy in the Treatment of PTSD Due to Military Sexual Trauma," *Journal of Anxiety Disorders* 61 (2019): 55–63; Albert "Skip" Rizzo and Russell Shilling, "Clinical Virtual Reality Tools to Advance the Prevention, Assessment, and Treatment of PTSD," *European Journal of Psychotraumatology* 8, no. 5 (2017), article number 1414560, https://doi.org/10.1080/20008198.2017.1414560; Thomas Talbot and Albert "Skip" Rizzo, "Virtual Human Standardized Patients for Clinical Training," in *Virtual Reality for Psychological and Neurocognitive Interventions, Virtual Reality Technologies for Health and Clinical Applications*, ed. Albert "Skip" Rizzo and Stéphane Bouchard (New York: Springer, 2019).

laboratory studies.[37] What is more, the use of VR technologies has been shown to be an effective way to induce awe and other discrete emotions in controlled experimental settings.[38]

Virtual Reality and Context

Although we are still in the process of collecting and analyzing data, our first VR study is testing the hypothesis that the presentational context of artistic media will prompt significantly different psychological outcomes such as awe, gratitude, elevation, and self-transcendence. In collaboration with a team of VR designers at the University of Notre Dame, we designed an immersive VR experience that allows participants to view the visual stimuli we created during the project phase. Because prior research has demonstrated that distinct situational contexts can prime participants in ways that lead to different psychological outcomes, participants are viewing these visual stimuli in one of three randomly assigned settings (e.g., a museum, a church, a warehouse). Before and after the VR experience, they complete a series of measures that capture state levels of awe, spiritual transcendence, and other "transcendent" or "inspiring" emotions like gratitude and elevation.

Although not yet submitted for publication, early data analyses have produced mixed results. On one hand, the immersive VR experience of art does not seem to shift levels of spiritual transcendence, gratitude, or elevation among participants in any significant way, nor does the context in which the artwork is viewed have any effect on these outcome measures. On the other hand, the VR experience does prompt significant changes in certain subdimensions of state-level awe, namely, a sense of "self-diminishment," "vastness," and the "need for accommodation." Importantly, each of these aspects of awe connects to Baumberger's conceptualization of aesthetic cognitivism, specifically as it relates to the way an experience with art presents new perspectives on people, places, and things that enhance people's understanding of them; raises important questions that prompt further inquiry (especially moral inquiry); and provides art-goers with opportunities to know what it is like to have certain sensory-motor experiences. Again, at this stage, our findings are only preliminary and should not be overinterpreted. However, a recurring theme among all of our studies is that awe and its various subdimensions provide a fertile ground for the empirical examination of aesthetic forms of knowledge.

37. A. "S." Rizzo and S. T. Koenig, "Is Clinical Virtual Reality Ready for Primetime?" *Neuropsychology* 31, no. 8 (2017): 877–99.

38. Alice Chirico et al., "Awe Enhances Creative Thinking: An Experimental Study," *Creativity Research Journal* 30, no. 2 (2018): 123–31.

Virtual Reality and Scale

Shifting from an exploration of context, our second VR study, which launched in early 2024, will test the hypothesis that the scale of artistic media will prompt significantly different psychological outcomes such as awe, gratitude, elevation, and self-transcendence. Because prior research indicates that the scale of artistic media in relation to one's perceived body size is associated with outcome variables like awe,[39] those who consent to participate in the study will be randomly and equally divided into one of two experimental conditions based on the scale of the artworks: small or large.

Although we will be gathering data on a few other outcome variables, the primary hypotheses we will be testing are related to awe and other "positive" emotions like gratitude and elevation. At this stage, we are hypothesizing that there will be differences across the experimental conditions of presentational context (museum, church, warehouse) and scale (small, medium, large) on awe subscales and self-transcendent emotions (e.g., gratitude and elevation). Again, we are still in the process of collecting data, but these VR studies are critical because they are a theoretical and empirical stepping stone to the data we have collected in the "real" world of art galleries.

From the Virtual to the Real

The next hypothesis we are testing is that in-person visual art exhibitions will generate significantly different psycho-socio-spiritual effects among art-goers than replications of exhibitions that are mediated to art-goers entirely by digital technologies. Building upon prior research regarding the psychological effects of live theater and museum attendance,[40] our third study shifts its focus from the "virtually real" world to the "really real" world of in-person aesthetic experiences. In collaboration with Dea Jenkins, a Los Angeles–based visual artist and curator, we created a temporary art exhibition in Pasadena, along with a digital experience of the exhibition that can be accessed on the artist's website (much like the digital 3D tours many museums created during COVID).

39. Michiel van Elk et al., "'Standing in awe': The Effects of Awe on Body Perception and the Relation with Absorption," *Collabra* 2, no. 1 (2016): 1–16.

40. Sara Konrath, "Empathy, Narcissism, and Visual Arts Engagement," in *Designing for Empathy: Perspectives on the Museum Experience*, ed. Elif M. Gokcigdem (Lanham: Rowman & Littlefield: 2019); Steve Rathje, Leor Hackel, and Jamil Zaki, "Attending Live Theatre Improves Empathy, Changes Attitudes, and Leads to Pro-Social Behavior," *Journal of Experimental Social Psychology* 95 (2021): article number 104138, https://doi.org/10.1016/j.jesp.2021.104138.

Our primary objective is to assess the differences between encountering art in a museum and experiencing its digital/virtual analog. There is a growing literature exploring people's psychological and neurological responses to built environments, especially as it concerns spaces designed for a specific purpose, such as a museum or church.[41] Thus, in this study, we are examining the effects of materiality on the degree to which artistic media is experienced as "spiritual" or "transcendent."

In terms of study design, gallery participants attended an in-person exhibition, whereas another set of participants experienced the digital versions of the installation completely online. Before and after they experienced the exhibit (either digitally or in real life), participants completed a series of self-report surveys measuring awe, transcendence, and in-group/out-group biases.

For each of our outcome variables (awe, gratitude, elevation, bias awareness scale, etc.), we conducted a mixed, repeated-measures analysis of variance (ANOVA) with planned contrasts, first comparing within-subject differences across time periods, and then between-subject group differences between the two experimental conditions (digital media or material gallery). Findings from our initial data analyses support our hypothesis that there is a significant between-subjects and within-subjects difference across experimental conditions (digital or in real life) on each of the dependent variables. In other words, just as we anticipated, the in-person museum experience generates greater increases on post-test ratings for positive emotions and self-transcendent emotions such as awe, gratitude, and elevation. This is particularly true of awe, with respect to both "awe self-diminishment" and "awe altered time perception."

Although we are still making our way through all the data, the primary takeaway thus far in our research is that the in-person experience of an artwork is significantly different from the digitally mediated version of the same art, especially as it concerns spiritual cognition. In other words, the question of how and when this art is prompting spiritual cognition has a great deal to do with its materiality. Indeed, what matters most of all is not the content of the artistic media. What matters is, it would seem, matter.

Individual States and Traits

In addition to materiality and mediation, a new question we are asking in light of our research is whether individual factors—both state and trait-like—might also be in play when considering whether media is prompting spiritual forms of

41. Alexander Coburn et al., "Psychological and Neural Responses to Architectural Interiors," *Cortex* 126 (2020): 217–41.

understanding. To explore this notion among those who participated in the art-gallery study, we conducted a series of moderation analyses to test our hypotheses that increases in awe, gratitude, and elevation prompted by exposure to visual art would significantly shift intergroup attitudes, specifically attitudes toward Black, Asian, and Hispanic persons. And as it turns out, these hypotheses were indeed supported by our analysis of the data. Our findings suggest that at least part of the reason certain pieces of art function in spiritual or transcendent ways with respect to intergroup attitudes has to do with the emotional state of the individual as they experience this art. For example, if someone is in a heightened state of awe as a result of viewing art, their positive attitudes toward out-group members increases and their prejudice decreases.

That said, what we are learning is that a state-level emotion like awe is not an uncomplicated good. It can be, and often is, directed by trait-level characteristics. Take social dominance orientation (SDO), for example, which is one of the more powerful predictors of intergroup attitudes and behavior.[42] In the United States, SDO-Dominance is found to be related to old-fashioned racism, zero-sum competition, and aggressive intergroup phenomena. We ran moderation analyses to test our hypothesis that SDO would moderate the association between emotions like awe, gratitude, and elevation and perspectives of White privilege and views toward minoritized racial groups. And just as we anticipated, SDO does indeed moderate this association, such that those who score high on SDO actually see *decreases* in their attitudes toward minoritized racial groups as their experience of awe *increases*. Conversely, those who score low on SDO see increases in their positive attitudes toward minoritized racial groups as their experience of awe increases. Awe, it would seem, is neither a simple nor straightforward emotional state, and it can be co-opted by other trait-level characteristics toward ends that are anything but positive.

Moving Forward

Returning to the "big questions" that have served as the impetus for our research (i.e., Is it possible to quantify spiritual forms of understanding prompted by art, and, if so, what difference does it make?), we are now able to reflect on the ways our research findings are related to the more general concerns of the ASU program. We have attempted to both summarize and describe our project in this

42. A. K. Ho et al., "The Nature of Social Dominance Orientation: Theorizing and Measuring Preferences for Intergroup Inequality Using the New SDO_7 Scale," *Journal of Personality and Social Psychology* 109, no. 6 (2015): 1003–28.

paper without overstating or over-interpreting our data, but we can say with a certain measure of confidence that progress has indeed been made. In the first place, it is clear that there is an empirically demonstrable connection between art and understanding, especially when "understanding" includes not only abstract, propositional reasoning, but also the "what-it-is-like" kind of objectual knowledge that art so often prompts—forms of knowledge most often described in terms of "awe," "self-transcendence," and "spirituality." Second, although our research has focused on a very narrow range of art and art-going, each of our studies has further clarified the ways in which certain underlying psychological mechanisms give rise to aesthetic forms of cognition and, perhaps more importantly, the conditions under which this occurs. Art does not generate a distinctive kind of cognitive value in all places, at all times, and with all people. However, given the right set of circumstances (psychological, contextual, ecological), aesthetic experiences with art can and do give rise to a kind of knowledge of the world (aesthetic, phenomenological, and indeed, spiritual) that simply cannot be reduced to semantic or propositional content alone.

We are of course under no illusion that, by engaging in this kind of experimental research, those who are skeptical about the very idea of "measuring the (im)measurable" will be fully convinced or even partly satisfied. Much more research needs to be done. However, we hope that our efforts provide at least some early evidence regarding the otherwise inaccessible insights that can and do emerge when we allow that which can be measured to inform and enrich our understanding of the spiritual and religious forms of cognition that art prompts.

3

The Impact of Sacred Art on Viewers

Robin M. Jensen

In mid-July 2020, around the time that the pandemic was shutting down schools and sending the world's population into isolation, Templeton Research Trust (TRT) awarded a grant to a team of Notre Dame faculty and graduate students to study the impact of sacred art on viewers. Our proposal focused on how an artwork's context (environment), style, and subject matter might affect both the immediate encounter with the work and the viewers' future recollections of the work and their reaction to it at set intervals over time. In the time between the initial award, which ran for two years (between 2020 and 2022), and the award of a subsequent and much larger three-year grant from TRT (currently in progress), the original research team has developed a series of empirically grounded experiments that can measure the ways encounters with visual art could have enduring influence on an individual's spiritual cognition.

The team consists of three principal investigators, two from the University of Notre Dame Department of Psychology, James Brockmole and Gabriel Radvansky, joined by Robin Jensen from the Departments of Theology and Art History. These three faculty members invited three graduate students to the team, two from the Department of Psychology, Sean Dageford and Dani Parra, and one from the Department of Theology, Lucas Christensen. Supplementing this core group were members of the Art and Art History Department, Michael Schreffler, Maria Tomasula, and the Director of the University's Art Museum, Joseph Becherer, who initially advised the team on the design of the project.

Each of the primary team members brings their particular expertise to the study, which enhances the collaborative and interdisciplinary nature of their research. For example, Brockmole, a cognitive scientist, specializes in vision science. He studies the ways that humans observe, store, and employ representations of art, objects, scenes, and environments.[1] For this project, Brockmole especially

1. James Brockmole, *The Visual World in Memory* (London: Psychology Press, 2009).

focuses on how viewers actually observe works of art. This includes how their eyes move over an image and the length and intensity of their gaze. Radvansky's expertise in human memory and cognition attends to how subjects recall details of their viewing encounters immediately afterward and at increasing intervals in temporal remove. Radvansky also studies the ways viewing experiences are affected by the spatial context of both the viewing subject and the object, as well as the effects of one object's proximity to another.[2] As an art historian and theologian, Jensen is interested in the impact of Christian sacred art on viewers through history and the ways that an art object's surroundings and the viewer's understanding (or interpretation) of the subject matter condition the quality or character of the viewing experience.[3]

An example of the type of initial question that the group posed was whether a viewer engages a statue of the Virgin Mary in a museum context differently than she would in a church. Would the museum experience of the work draw a more formal or historical assessment than a spiritual or devotional response? Is something lost or gained by moving traditionally defined "sacred artworks" from one venue to another?[4] Similarly, in regard to how crucial a viewer's level of background knowledge might be to the quality of the viewing experience, the team wondered whether a viewer unfamiliar with the biblical story could be less affected by an image of Christ's trial and crucifixion than someone who was well-acquainted with the narrative.[5]

As the committee posed these theoretical questions, they also recognized the potential significance of their study for religious leaders, lay committees, architects, liturgists, and interior designers who install and even commission new works of art for different kinds of worship environments. Those who serve in these capacities know that an artwork's style, subject matter, and even medium influence the ways that individuals report their experiences of those works. They also understand that viewers can benefit from even rudimentary instruction about

2. Gabriel A. Radvansky, *Human Memory*, 3rd ed. (London: Taylor and Francis, 2017).

3. Robin M. Jensen, *The Substance of Things Seen: Art, Faith, and the Christian Community* (Grand Rapids: Eerdmans, 2004).

4. A helpful study on this topic is Cynthia A. Hogan, "The Crucifix and the Art Gallery: An Odyssey from Religious Material Culture to Fine Art," *Religions* 12 (2021): https://doi.org/10.3390/rel12070537.

5. Older studies of this question include Guy Bushwell, *How People Look at Pictures: A Study of the Psychology of Perception in Art* (Chicago: University of Chicago Press, 1935); and Michael J. Parsons, *How We Understand Art: A Cognitive Account of Aesthetic Experience* (Cambridge: Cambridge University Press, 1987). More recent relevant bibliography includes Helmut Leder et al., "How Art Is Appreciated," *Psychology of Aesthetics: Creativity and the Arts* 6, no. 1 (2012): 2.

the works, their subject matter, and the artist's process. Yet, because experiences can vary significantly among viewers of different religious, cultural, educational, or other distinctions of background (e.g., gender, age, or political affiliation), discussions about which kinds of artworks are best suited to worship spaces are often subjective and choices are often judged as liturgically unsound, theologically unacceptable, or aesthetically unpleasant. Thus, better understanding of how viewers observe, remember, and report their reactions to sacred artworks can have applied or practical value in such contexts.

Better understanding of how viewers see and are affected by sacred artworks can have application to other settings in which such art is displayed. For example, the Notre Dame University Raclin Murphy Museum of Art has a significant collection of sacred works, spanning times, cultures, and belief systems. This study can help museum curators consider how to design exhibitions and install both sacred and secular works of art in galleries in ways that will enhance visitors' spiritual experience. Others who might benefit from this study include anthropologists, art critics, teachers of art history, and academic theologians.

Thus, this interdisciplinary project starts with the conviction that visual perception is a key element in spiritual experience. Drawing upon the fields of psychology, art history, and theology the team hopes to gain measurable insight into the spiritual impact of contrasting types of artworks (both sacred and secular; abstract and representational) on different types of viewers in varying spatial and temporal contexts. The outcome of this work can inform the scientific community, not only providing information about the ways that viewers are affected by the context, time, and circumstances of their viewing but also assisting those who are charged with choosing and placing works of art in various environments.

Round 1 Project Description and Results

The initial two-year phase of this project focused on how subjects looked at, responded to, and later recalled two cycles of artworks that had closely related subject matter and purpose but were distinctly different in style and context. The first, a series of fourteen traditionally pictorial stations of the cross, are large oil-on-canvas paintings, framed and mounted in two sequences on the north and south nave walls of the University's Basilica of the Sacred Heart. Commissioned for this particular space, they were completed in the late eighteenth century by then artist-in-residence, Luigi Gregori.

The second, a site-specific installation of seventy basalt stone megaliths, is arranged in eight groups to represent episodes from the life of Christ. The series' sculptor, Philip Ricky, completed the work in 2017 for the University's open-air sculpture park and gave it the title "Cycle of Life: Life of Christ." Each of the seven groups is sited along a forty-two-foot-long, meandering pathway that guides viewers through and around them. In addition to being in an outdoor environment, observing these works generally requires more physical interaction with the objects than simply moving from one to another arranged in a proximate series along a straight aisle.

Each cycle was expressly created to serve a devotional purpose, and many of the participants would be familiar with the practice of "praying the stations" at certain times of the Christian liturgical year. Each prompts viewers to encounter the story of Christ's life, passion, death, burial, and resurrection in a visual and even physical mode rather than a purely verbal format (i.e., reading or being read to). While they share this basic purpose, the two cycles were specifically selected for their contrasting styles (representational versus abstract), media (oil paintings versus stone sculptures), and location (indoor/church vs. outdoor/park). Thus, the works present parallel subject matter, albeit in very different ways.

These two installations were the core of the team's two initial experiments, but evolving circumstances and practical issues required certain procedural adaptations. First, because of the COVID-19 pandemic, the team (or assistants) had to maintain social distance from the participants. This limited face-to-face encounters between researchers and participants and their ability to be physically present before artworks in museum or gallery spaces. Second, because both the Gregori and the Ricky works are permanent installations, they were impossible to move into different contexts.

To compensate for these complications, the team first decided to obtain high-quality photographs of the works and manipulate them in a lab setting. Two sets of fourteen photographs (of both Gregori's stations and Ricky's cycle) were superimposed on neutral white fields and then on other backgrounds to suggest environmental changes. These alternatives deliberately included both congruous (expected) and incongruous (dissonant) spaces: a chapel, an office, a casino, a formal garden, and a racetrack.

In this initial trial, over 150 participants, all of them undergraduates at Notre Dame, were asked to view all twenty-two individual images on computer screens. Each person viewed each image for ten seconds while their eye focus, the breadth of their visual exploration, and the physical manner of their actual viewing process were recorded by eye-tracking technology. Participants also received prompts, some of which oriented their viewing to specific details in the works (e.g., What color is the Virgin's dress?) while others inquired about their emotional reactions to and interpretation of the works (e.g., How do you think Christ feels at this moment?). Immediately after each session, the subjects' memory of these details and responses were tested. This process was repeated a day later and then after a week had passed. This procedure aimed at discerning the level of each participant's memory of formal elements (superficial details), and how well they recalled and interpreted the content of the works, as well as how they remembered their own self-reported reactions to it.

This initial round of experiments also considered the possibility that temporal context might affect viewers' encounters with works of art. About half of the 150 students viewed the works during the Christian season of Lent. The team's preliminary hypothesis was that viewing a sacred artwork during certain times of the year could change the level of engagement with or memory of the encounter. Presumably this effect would be more evident in the responses of those who are familiar with (or participate in) certain Christian liturgical seasons. Thus, in temporally congruent contexts, viewers would be more likely to have active knowledge of the event and apply that to their encounter with and subsequent memory of the artworks.

To study these effects of temporal context on both engagement and memory, the team recorded viewers' responses to the two cycles of scenes from the life and passion of Christ both during the Lenten/Easter period and in a non-festal season (i.e., Ordinary Time). Then, participants (and their responses) were grouped according to one of these two time periods. Prior to seeing the selected artworks, they were questioned about their familiarity with the current liturgical season. Each participant also viewed twenty-two other pieces of art, both representational and abstract, and, while viewing, was asked a series of questions about the works. These questions ranged from ones focused on perception of surface details or perceptual memory (e.g., How many halos are in this painting?) to those that attended more to gist memory (e.g., What do these standing stones represent?). Subjects were then asked to self-report their emotional or affective response to the works (e.g., How emotionally engaging is this painting?) and to recall any spontaneous autobiographical memories that arose out of the experience. As before, their memory of the works' subject matter and various details was tested immediately after they had viewed the works, a day later, and then a week later.

Both experiments, the one focused on spatial context and the other on temporal context, yielded noteworthy data. The first revealed that the manipulated backgrounds of the superimposed images made no significant difference in the viewer's visual processing, memory of details, or reported responses. However, the eye-tracking study also showed that participants visually attended to the two types of artworks differently. Overall, the distance between viewer and object was smaller and the time spent in the viewing process itself was greater for the projected images of the non-representational stone sculptures than for the representational paintings of the stations, a difference which correlates to a higher level of mental effort expended in the viewing process. When viewing the paintings, eye movement velocities were slower and blink rates were higher, than when viewing the sculptures. This suggests a lower level of arousal and cognitive engagement, consistent with other scientific eye-tracking studies.[6] These findings suggest that non-representational art elicits a greater level of engagement, perhaps because viewers must try to understand what the works represent or portray.

The memory portion of the study produced a finding similar to the first, insofar as memory of both superficial details and subject matter (interpretive gist) both declined over time, but the rate of decline differed between representational paintings and abstract sculptures. In the case of the paintings, the two types of memory declined at the same rate, but viewers' memory of the subject matter of the non-representational sculptures was more stable than of the details—in fact, subject matter memory even improved over the next twenty-four hours. This suggests that viewers have a greater level of cognitive engagement with abstract artworks, perhaps as they attempt to understand them, which results in a better and more stable memory of the works.[7]

By contrast, when subjects were asked to rate their level of emotional engagement with these works and their responses were then correlated with the results of memory tests, the results were different. A positive result was reported for the representational paintings versus a negative correlation for the abstract sculptures, and this disparity was greatest with respect to superficial details. Perhaps more simply stated, although participants tended to dislike the abstract works, they paid them more attention, while they remembered superficial details of the representational works and reported a higher level of emotional engagement with those (the representational) works.[8]

Finally, the study of the effect of temporal context on viewers' engagement and memory produced some similar results. Again, self-reported engagement with representational art was higher than with abstract artworks, and this was appar-

6. For example, Carolyn Ranti et al., "Blink Rate Patterns Provide a Reliable Measure of Individual Engagement with Scene Content," *Scientific Reports* 10 (2020): 8267; and Sarah Schultz et al., "Inhibition of Eye Blinking Reveals Subject Perceptions of Stimulus Salience," *Proceedings of the National Academy of Sciences of the United States of America* 108 (2011): 21270–75.

7. See the related studies by Astrid Schepman et al., "Shared Liking and Association Valence for Representational Art but Not Abstract Art," *Journal of Vision* 15 (2015): 11; Astrid Schepman and Paul Rodway, "Concreteness of Semantic Interpretations of Abstract and Representational Artworks," *Acta Psychologica* 215 (2021): article 103269, https://doi.org/10.1016/j.actpsy.2021.103269; and David Briebar et al., "Art in Time and Space: Context Modulates the Relation between Art Experience and Viewing Time," *Plos One* 9, no. 6 (2014): doi:10.1371/journal.pone.0099019.

8. A similar conclusion is reported by Eric Kandel, who cites biological evidence that interpreting abstract art requires a greater level of cognitive engagement on the part of the viewer. See *Reductionism in Art and Brain Science* (New York: Columbia University Press, 2016).

ently unaffected by the temporal context. However, although congruent temporal contexts showed a stronger tendency to aid memory of perceptual characteristics of the works (what it looked like), self-reported responses to what it meant or how it was experienced were unaffected by temporal context. This implies that a congruent temporal context provides an activated semantic context that aids the cognitive encoding of what is viewed. Yet, temporal context also influenced the memory for self-reported autobiographical experiences. Specifically, people more accurately remembered their experience with artworks during the temporally congruent time period. By contrast, in a temporally incongruent time period, viewers initially tended to overestimate their engagement because, lacking the semantic cues, they made judgments based on expectations from past experiences rather than reflecting on the actual encounter itself.[9]

An overall conclusion is that the emotional engagement elicited by representational art prompts viewers to focus on what is objectively depicted, while the engagement with abstract art leads to greater thinking about aesthetic qualities of the work along with artistic meaning and intent—overall greater mental effort—when abstracted from the accessible narrative details of the works.

Summarizing, these initial studies indicate that non-representational sacred works (in this instance a cycle of abstract sculptures in an outdoor environment) produce higher levels of arousal, broader scope of attention, and a higher level of cognitive engagement as viewers seek to discern meaning from their perceptual experience. This correlates to a better interpretive memory for these works. Yet, viewers retained a better superficial memory and a stronger emotional response when viewing the representational sacred art.

Meanwhile, on the basis of the experiment as designed, while artistic style appears to affect the viewer's encounter with and understanding of sacred art, environmental context (as manipulated here) does not play a significant role in the experience.[10]

What We Would Like to Have Done Differently

The fact that the team found no evidence that the physical or environmental context played a significant role in the viewer's experience of the works could be explained by the fact that this context variation was not based on actual movement

9. See Sean Dagerforde et al., "The Effect of Temporal Context on Memory for Art," *Acta Psychologica* 248 (2024): article 104349, https://doi.org/10.1016/j.actpsy.2024.104349.

10. For measuring the level of art appreciation, the team drew upon the work of Duane Lundy, "How Important Is Beauty to You? The Development and Desire for Aesthetics Scale," *Empirical Studies of the Arts* 28, no. 1 (2010): 73–92.

to a new place, but simply an artificially constructed change of environment on a computer screen. Spatial context was simply a background issue. Thus, the team wanted to find a means of creating a more realistic and immersive environment that could approximate more realistic encounters with artworks.

At the same time, the team also faced the fact that actually moving precious, fragile, or monumental works of art into diverse spaces is nearly impossible. Moreover, the scientific need to control the variables in the experimental protocols also required that participants needed to have consistent visual experiences in a replicable spatial context. Considering these issues, the team decided that one solution would be to move the participants rather than the objects, allowing them to view a series of prescribed works projected on personal computers in three distinct but easily managed spaces.

The team also pondered the value of using virtual reality (VR) technology to allow viewers to encounter a wider range of both secular and sacred artworks in different types of physical (albeit virtual) spaces. This technology had the potential to create more realistic experiences of art that could also allow control over the viewing conditions and extraneous distractions that might distort the results. This meant that the artworks, still projected but now within virtual rooms, needed to be relatively similar in size and quality, framed much like one another, and placed in carefully managed proximity.

Round 1 Project Description and Preliminary Summary

A second, larger grant from TRT allowed the team to begin this new round of experiments. They were able to build on the conclusions drawn from the completed studies as well as address some of the issues they identified with those studies. They also were able to expand the study to address some of the unanswered questions, and by framing the experiments slightly differently, the team investigated the following: (1) how well the results of the previous studies could be generalized across even more varied kinds of artworks including both secular and sacred subjects, (2) how the experiment might better approximate actual changes in viewers' spatial location or context, and (3) how participants from different educational, cultural, or religious backgrounds vary in their reception and assessment of sacred art.

To study issues one and two, the team worked on creating two more immersive experiences that would allow viewers a more realistic feeling of encountering artworks in different spaces. The first experiment, still ongoing, is relatively simple. Participants are given computer tablets, each with a series of artworks chosen from a group of forty-eight pieces, including both representational and abstract as well as sacred and secular. They are then asked to view them in one of three distinct venues on campus: a chapel, an art gallery, and a faculty office. Before beginning, participants are asked to fill in demographic data (e.g., age, gender identity, ethnicity, education level). They are also to think about their current environment, and how it makes them feel. After viewing the works, lab assistants immediately follow up with a series of questions about the experience. After completion, participants receive a link to respond to questions about a portion of the images they viewed. This process is repeated approximately one day later and, finally, a week later.

The second protocol was far more complicated to design but intended to better approximate a real encounter with art. Using VR technology, participants would have a more immersive and somewhat more realistic encounter with varying types of artworks in three distinct types of settings. Each of these spaces would be populated with projected images of artworks, selected by the team so as to be relatively similar in size and impact while still being distinctly different in style and subject matter.

For this experiment, the team enlisted the assistance of Mike Villano, Assistant Research Professor of Psychology with expertise in virtual reality. Villano, following the direction of the research team, designed the three virtual reality sites: a church-like space, a warehouse-type space, and a museum-like space. Each of these virtual spaces was in some aspects similar in dimension and structure, but each was furnished with selected site-specific objects, set in roughly the same place (e.g., an altar, a supervisor's workstation, and an information desk). Movable walls created individual chapels, rooms, or galleries which supported various secular and sacred artworks in both representational and non-representational or abstract styles. Audio accompaniment (organ music, front-loader activity, or hushed conversations) would further enhance the participants' sense that they were actually inside these spaces.

Each participant, now equipped with a headset, virtually enters and navigates one of these environments. As they move around the rooms, they encounter a series of sixteen artworks that appear to be hanging on the walls. The works are a mixture of overtly religious and more secular subject matter as well as those that are more or less pictorial or abstract in terms of their style. Certain conditions characterize the placement of the works. In some instances, all the artworks are hung in a large open space; elsewhere they are in separate (virtual) rooms or grouped in several rooms based on their conceptual grouping.

Participants are encouraged to spend at least ten seconds viewing each artwork and are informed of the work's title. At the end of each ten-second viewing experience, they are asked a series of questions, including this one: "Did any memories from your life spontaneously come to mind while viewing this painting?" Brief answers are recorded and the process continues through the series.

As in the first protocol, participants respond to questions at several preset time intervals (immediately, a day later, and a week later). They are prompted to recall what they remembered about the works along three different dimensions: the perceptual, the interpretive, and the personal. The perceptual attends to the specific formal aspects of each artwork (e.g., color, content, details). The interpretive refers to how the participant understands what the work is about or communicates. The personal focuses on the work's impact on the viewer, whether it elicited any particular emotions or even involuntary autobiographical memories. Finally, each subsequent report is compared to the previous ones and scored according to the concreteness of the way participants describe their experiences.

In both instances (the experiment with the tablets and the one in the virtual-reality environment) the artworks are still projected but not manipulated, and the viewing contexts are varied. The selected artworks are also varied, and include examples that the team identified as secular (vs. sacred) and abstract (vs. representational). These selections were largely based on the works having familiar subject matter to most participants (e.g., Madonna and Child, Moon Landing, a scene from a well-known fairy tale). Significantly, and especially in the case of the abstract works, titles were supplied to assist identification of the theme or content of the artwork.

Thus, in this set of experiments, instead of prompts directing participants' attention or memory to specific aspects of the works, they are asked to report more freely (and generally) on how they perceived the works in the space, which ones they found most compelling or unappealing, how they interpreted or understood what they saw, and how they judged the work on a personal level (e.g., their emotional reactions to the works or what thoughts or insights the work elicited at a more cognitive level, including unexpected autobiographical memories). The results so far recorded in these cases reveal that in general, the location of the viewing experience did not significantly affect the participants' judgment of the objects' beauty or quality of engagement, while participants' memory for the sacred images was slightly better in the sacred environment. More significantly, their experiences of spontaneous autobiographical memories were significantly more frequent in the office space than in the chapel and stronger and more sensorial when they occurred in the chapel.

Thus, in contrast to the first round of the study, this second round offers a more realistic and immersive experience, includes a wider range of styles (e.g., abstract and representational) and subject matter (e.g., sacred and secular), and pays more attention to the ways participants engage the works across different levels (e.g., perceptual, interpretive, and personal).

The Future

Despite the value and scientific strengths of lab-based experiments, encountering actual artworks in real contexts is a qualitatively different experience for a viewer. Therefore, a final study will be conducted in the University's newly opened Raclin Murphy Museum of Art. Access to the new museum's collection will allow the team to conduct a study "in the wild" in which participants will view a selection of actual artworks in the museum's galleries and allow researchers to ask subjects how they perceive, understand, emotionally respond to, and (subsequently) recall the works. The study will also assess the impact of a first image viewed on the reported engagement with and memory of the next set of images seen in the same visit. This study might also return to the original two cycles of images, used for phase I, the Gregori stations of the cross in the University Basilica of the Sacred Heart and the Philip Ricky installation in the Sculpture Park. Again, in each instance, the team hopes to conduct the studies during at least one of three specific liturgical seasons (Lent/Easter, Ordinary Time, Advent/Christmas) to assess the significance of temporal context on viewers' encounter with these sacred artworks.

Using measures developed in the first phase of the study, participants will be asked to describe any changes in their religious or spiritual perception, practices of prayer, or enhanced sense of the sacred in either or both sites. This information will be key in connecting the data on the knowledge, opinion, and memory with insights into viewers' spiritual growth and cognition.

As before, knowledge and understanding will be assessed at temporally congruent time points (Lent/Easter/Ascension season); related (Advent/Christmas/Epiphany season); and other (Ordinary Time). Returning to the objects used in the first round, participants may view both the Gregori and Ricky works in their entirety, with different people viewing at different times of the year. After a brief ten-minute delay, participants will be assessed using the superficial, interpretive, personal attitude, and religious practices/participation tests for a subset of one-quarter of the elements (e.g., the Stations) of the full works. Sessions 2 and 3 will occur one day and one week later, and participants will be assessed on a different quarter of the initial set.

Each person will see each element in only one of the three temporal contexts, although each art-context combination will be seen the same number of times across participants. Participants will be recruited from the Notre Dame student body; we expect to involve over two hundred of them, none of whom will have been involved in the first two rounds of study.

One of the planned outputs from this final round of experiments is a set of engagement booklets that will translate research findings into suggestions for how viewers might attend to the works in the Museum. The team also plans to hold a conference in the Raclin Murphy Museum at the end of the grant period, inviting attendees from a variety of academic disciplines to discuss the findings and their potential "real-world" applications to different professional endeavors.

Project Questions and Suggestions

Some questions may be fairly posed about these studies in general. For example, because of the need to minimize the effect of prior experiences of specific (or well-known) artworks and to eliminate notable discrepancies in the results that could skew the data, the artworks that were used were, in many cases, generated for the study by artificial intelligence (AI) or chosen from the internet and manipulated to be similar in size and format to one another. Additionally, in the first phases of the study, participants viewed artworks on tablets, computer screens, or in virtual reality settings rather than seeing them "in real life." This led the team's art historians to raise questions about whether the results were not based on encounters with actual artworks in real spaces but rather with artificial, even AI-generated, or poor-quality works projected on screens and viewed in labs. This is an important reason for moving to the third phase of the study, in which viewers would engage actual high-quality artworks in museum, gallery, or church contexts.

A further question arises regarding the demographics of the participants themselves. Most of the participants in the initial studies were undergraduates from a predominantly Roman Catholic student body. As such they were mainly between eighteen and twenty-two-years old, mostly Caucasian, and typically drawn from a population more likely than the general public to be familiar with biblical stories and, in many instances, with some level of art education. The results then favor this group over others and, as such, may not be widely generalizable. Thus, the next phase of this study (as well as the satellite experiments) will draw upon a broader or more diverse group of participants, including more non-Catholics (or non-Christians), older individuals, participants with varying levels of religiosity, and participants from diverse educational backgrounds or academic specialization/college majors. Participants may also differ in their degrees of experience with visual art, formal art training, or familiarity with the stories that are commonly depicted in sacred artworks.[11]

11. For a related study, see Jiwon Song, "Familiarity and Novelty in Aesthetic Preference: The Effects of the Properties of the Artwork and the Beholder," *Frontiers in Psychology* 12 (2021): article 694927, https://doi.org/10.3389/fpsyg.2021.694927.

This last point of divergence raises a related question about how instruction might change the ways that viewers could encounter different types of sacred or secular artworks in a variety of settings (e.g., church, museum, classroom). The team assumes that the educational materials enhance understanding of works of art generally. Thus, a further study might focus on the before and after differences that such knowledge, imparted by gallery labels, museum guidebooks, docents, or art appreciation courses might have on viewers' encounters with art.

Project Relevance

As mentioned in the introduction, we believe that a better understanding of the impact of visual art on spiritual cognition not only allows a better understanding of the process itself, but beyond advancing our knowledge of how art enhances spiritual understanding, these studies may assist religious leaders, liturgy planners, and educators to understand the role of visual perception as a key element in religious formation and development. This may also help artists, museum professionals, and those designing spaces for worship to have a better comprehension of how viewers engage with and are affected by different types of sacred artworks in diverse contexts, during various surrounding events or circumstances, and at different seasons or times of the year.

4

A Scientific Inquiry into the Impact of Art

Eileen Cardillo, Alexander P. Christensen, and Anjan Chatterjee

No one would be surprised to hear that visitors to the Sistine Chapel sometimes feel deeply moved or challenged. One of us (Anjan) was similarly absorbed in Gaudi's La Sagrada Familia, another (Eileen) when first seeing Hilma Af Klint's paintings. We expect big impacts from great art. One of the missions of our research center, the Penn Center for Neuroaesthetics at the University of Pennsylvania is to advance our understanding of the value of engaging with art and exploring its transformative power.

Our foray into exploring transformative encounters includes a large online survey in which we invited participants to describe an engaging experience with the arts. We did not specifically instruct them to share an especially meaningful moment.[1] Nonetheless, people reported memories that remained vivid in their minds for years, even decades. Some described unforgettable encounters in superlative terms, as some of the happiest or most awe-inspiring events of their lives. Reports of otherworldly, magical, dreamlike or self-transcendent states were common. Accompanying physiological responses ranged from feeling breathless, heart palpitations, goosebumps, and tingling to experiencing chills, laughter, butterflies, and tears. Some described mentally challenging encounters ranging from those that "made me look within myself to question the life I am living," to life-altering ones that "shaped me into the person I am today." A few people described their experiences as spiritually enlightening, with hallmark features such as humility ("I felt like my world instantly expanded, as well I felt a bit small in a good way") and a connection to something greater than themselves ("I felt a connectedness with the beauty and intensity of the music, and sensed a togetherness between

1. Yoed N. Kenett, Eileen R. Cardillo, Alexander P. Christensen, and Anjan Chatterjee, "Aesthetic Emotions Are Affected by Context: A Psychometric Network Analysis," *Scientific Reports* 13 (2023): article number 20985, https://doi.org/10.1038/s41598-023-48219-w.

myself and the universe as well"). Participants asked to describe other types of engaging encounters did not produce such language.

How does art enable these experiences of insight, personal growth, and profundity? The wealth of anecdotes attesting to the power of art contrasts with the poverty of scientific evidence or even systematic study. The big question we address is, how does art promote understanding, and can we ground this intuition in scientific evidence?

The humanities have long concerned themselves with the profundity of art engagement. Humans value art for its ability to distill descriptions of the world, its aesthetic appeal, the pleasure it provides, and its ability to express emotions. The way we talk about art also implies a potentially deeper role. For instance, an artwork can be described as "profound" or "insightful," or an encounter as "eye-opening." These descriptions suggest cognitive benefits of art, in addition to its descriptive, formal, pleasurable, or communicative functions.

Aesthetic cognitivism, a philosophical accounting of art, contends just that: the value of art depends on its ability to convey knowledge.[2] Hegel, an early proponent of this view, placed art alongside religion and philosophy in the quest for human knowledge. As Gordon Graham explains (with reference to Hegel), "All three are modes of knowledge and understanding, art no less than philosophy."[3] More recently, philosopher Nelson Goodman took a similar stance, writing, "Art must be taken no less seriously than the sciences as modes of discovery, creation, and enlargement of knowledge in the broad sense of advancement of the understanding."[4] While Goodman argued that the primary purpose of art lies in its cognitive merit,[5] other proponents of aesthetic cognitivism are more flexible. For instance, Graham contends that art's ability to enhance understanding is not the *only* measure of its value—although this capacity makes some art great.[6]

On this view, art's transformative power lies not in factual knowledge that it conveys but instead in its invitation to discover deep and novel ways of understanding our lives. This understanding might take many forms: new concepts or categories, frameworks or perspectives, questions and thought experiments, or

2. Berys Gaut, "Art and Cognition," in *Contemporary Debates in Aesthetics and the Philosophy of Art*, ed. Matthew Kieran (Oxford: Blackwell, 2006), 115–26.

3. Gordon Graham, *Philosophy of the Arts: An Introduction to Aesthetics* (New York: Routledge, 2005), 53.

4. Nelson Goodman, *Ways of Worldmaking* (Indianapolis: Hackett, 1978), 102.

5. Nelson Goodman, *Languages of Art: An Approach to a Theory of Symbols*, 2nd ed. (Indianapolis: Hackett, 1976).

6. Graham, *Philosophy of the Arts*.

possibilities and links between existing beliefs.[7] In sum, art enriches understanding by casting light on the human condition and its many possibilities.

A Challenge for Science

Though much discussed philosophically, and intuitively plausible for those who believe in the power of art, for scientists, aesthetic cognitivism presents a set of hypotheses awaiting verification. Several questions arise. What evidence, beyond anecdotal accounts and personal opinion, exists that art can give rise to impactful understanding? Do all forms of art enrich understanding, and under what conditions? What differentiates an encounter with a great work of art from a pedestrian one? How is a person altered by encountering artistic greatness? Can art evoke epiphany? Do people differ in their susceptibility to the power of art?

With the rapid development of the new field of neuroaesthetics—a subdiscipline of cognitive neuroscience concerned with aesthetic experiences of all varieties—experimental studies are beginning to offer tantalizing hints of the power of art. Pelowski posits that feeling like crying meaningfully indicates an "insightful" experience of art, and provides evidence supporting this claim in museum studies of engagement with abstract art.[8] They infer that feeling like crying is a sign of the transformational capacity of art to invoke epiphany and insight.[9] Others suggest that feelings of wonder[10] and awe[11] or physiological sensations like chills[12] are states that reflect transformative encounters with art. Motivational emotions,

7. Christoph Baumberger, "Art and Understanding: In Defence of Aesthetic Cognitivism," in *Bilder sehen: Perspektiven der Bildwissenschaft*, ed. Mark Greenlee et al. (Regensburg: Schnell & Steiner, 2013), 41–67.

8. Matthew Pelowski, "Tears and Transformation: Feeling Like Crying as an Indicator of Insightful or 'Aesthetic' Experience with Art," *Frontiers in Psychology* 6 (2015): article number 1006, https://psycnet.apa.org/doi/10.3389/fpsyg.2015.01006.

9. Matthew Pelowski and Fuminori Akiba, "A Model of Art Perception, Evaluation, and Emotion in Transformative Aesthetic Experience," *New Ideas in Psychology* 29, no. 2 (2011): 80–97.

10. Joerg Fingerhut and Jesse J. Prinz, "Wonder, Appreciation, and the Value of Art," *Progress in Brain Research* 237 (2018): 107–28.

11. Alice Chirico and David B. Yaden, "Awe: A Self-Transcendent and Sometimes Transformative Emotion," in *The Function of Emotions: When and Why Emotions Help Us*, ed. Heather Lench (Cham, Switzerland: Springer, 2018), 221–33; Dacher Keltner and Jonathan Haidt, "Approaching Awe: A Moral, Spiritual, and Aesthetic Emotion," *Cognition and Emotion* 17, no. 2 (2003): 297–314; Pamela Marie Taylor and Yukiko Uchida, "Awe or Horror: Differentiating Two Emotional Responses to Schema Incongruence," *Cognition and Emotion* 33, no. 8 (2019): 1548–61.

12. Luke Harrison and Psyche Loui, "Thrills, Chills, Frissons, and Skin Orgasms: Toward an Integrative Model of Transcendent Psychophysiological Experiences in Music," *Frontiers in Psychology* 5 (2014): article number 790, https://doi.org/10.3389/fpsyg.2014.00790; Félix Schoe-

like curiosity and interest, may also be important, as they trigger a desire to learn more and understand.[13]

Without directly invoking aesthetic cognitivism, some researchers nonetheless probe outcomes of art engagement that permit cognitive insights,[14] self-transformation,[15] and measures of cognitive challenge or personal meaningfulness.[16] Relatively unexplored is the socio-epistemic value of art: "its communicative nature, its capacity to encourage personal growth, its ability to reveal deep aspects of the human condition, to challenge preconceptions, to help us reconceptualize a question we grapple with, and to provide clarity on ambiguous concepts or ideas."[17]

In reviewing psychological and neural studies relevant to aesthetic cognitivism,[18] we found that such personal gains associated with art engagement largely await experimental testing. That said, people with certain dispositions seem more likely to experience understanding when engaging with art. Greater expertise or training in the arts and openness to novel experiences are associated with enhanced emotional responses to art and reports of greater understanding and appreciation.[19] Given the historical and cross-cultural importance of art in religious traditions, religiosity and spirituality may also be important dimensions to consider.

---

ller, "Knowledge, Curiosity, and Aesthetic Chills," *Frontiers in Psychology* 6 (2015): article number 1546, https://doi.org/10.3389/fpsyg.2015.01546.

13. D. E. Berlyne, "The New Experimental Aesthetics," in *Studies in the New Experimental Aesthetics*, ed. D. E. Berlyne (Washington, DC: Hemisphere, 1960), 1–25; Paul J. Silvia, "Interested Experts, Confused Novices: Art Expertise and the Knowledge Emotions, *Empirical Studies of the Arts* 31, no. 1 (2013): 107–15.

14. Claudia Muth, Vera M. Hesslinger, and Claus-Christian Carbon, "The Appeal of Challenge in the Perception of Art: How Ambiguity, Solvability of Ambiguity, and the Opportunity for Insight Affect Appreciation," *Psychology of Aesthetics, Creativity, and the Arts* 9, no. 3 (2015): 206.

15. Keith Oatley and Maja Djikic, "Psychology of Narrative Art," *Review of General Psychology* 22, no. 2 (2018): 161–68.

16. Gerald C. Cupchik and Robert J. Gebotys, "The Search for Meaning in Art: Interpretive Styles and Judgments of Quality," *Visual Arts Research* (1988): 38–50.

17. Aleksandra Sherman and Clair Morrissey, "What Is Art Good For? The Socio-Epistemic Value of Art," *Frontiers in Human Neuroscience* 11 (2017): 411.

18. Alexander P. Christensen, Eileen R. Cardillo, and Anjan Chatterjee, "Can Art Promote Understanding? A Review of the Psychology and Neuroscience of Aesthetic Cognitivism," *Psychology of Aesthetics, Creativity, and the Arts* 19, no. 1 (2025): 1–14.

19. Kirill Fayn, Carolyn MacCann, Niko Tiliopoulos, and Paul J. Silvia, "Aesthetic Emotions and Aesthetic People: Openness Predicts Sensitivity to Novelty in the Experiences of Interest and Pleasure," *Frontiers in Psychology* 6 (2015): 1877; Helmut Leder, Gernot Gerger, Stefan Dressler, and Alfred Schabmann, "How Art Is Appreciated," *Psychology of Aesthetics, Creativity, and the Arts* 6, no. 1 (2012): 2–10.

Aesthetic experience emerges from interactions of a triad of sensory-motor, emotion-valuation, and meaning-semantic large-scale neural systems.[20] In the context of visual art, the sensory-motor system is attuned to salient visual properties of an artwork such as color, form, brushstroke, texture, and the impression of motion. The emotion-valuation system mediates how an artwork makes us feel. Do we like it? Are we moved by it? Do we desire to stay engaged with it? The meaning-semantic system is engaged when we draw on our pre-existing knowledge of an artwork, or when it takes on new meaning or personal relevance—say, knowing that Wassily Kandinsky's abstract works were informed by his visual-auditory synesthesia or appreciating Frida Kahlo's themes in a new way after learning of her debilitating health issues or political views. Most relevant to the proposition that art serves as a vehicle for understanding is the link between meaning-semantic and emotion-valuation systems. An emotionally impactful engagement may be a necessary precondition for new understanding and insight.

While suggestive, these disparate threads lack common theoretical grounding and conceptual clarity. Constructing a bridge from philosophy and theology to empirical and experimental science requires a clear idea of what constitutes knowledge and understanding in the context of art engagement, the conditions in which they emerge, and for whom.[21] Addressing these questions experimentally requires well-defined and theoretically motivated measures. This gap in appropriate tools motivated our project grant as well as our follow-up program grant.

A Taxonomy for Art and Its Impacts

The primary aim of our pilot grant was to develop a taxonomy of terms that makes explicit concepts both relevant and useful for a scientific study of aesthetic cognitivism. A critical assumption of our approach is that art encounters with strong emotional or cognitive impacts are most likely to elicit new knowledge and understanding. Further, while we acknowledge that profound encounters with art can be challenging to capture in words, we contend that language provides an invaluable glimpse into subjective experience. The words we use to describe art and its effect on us, imperfect as they are, allow us to circle closer to inner states.[22]

Buttressed by these two guiding principles, we recruited five aesthetics experts from different academic disciplines—art history, neuroscience, philosophy, psy-

20. Anjan Chatterjee and Oshin Vartanian, "Neuroaesthetics," *Trends in Cognitive Sciences* 18, no. 7 (2014): 370–75.

21. Again, see Christensen, Cardillo, and Chatterjee, "Can Art Promote Understanding?"

22. Anjan Chatterjee, "Emotion, Language and Aesthetic Expression: On Motherwell and His Art," *Empirical Studies of the Arts* 43, no. 1 (2025): 11–22.

chology, and theology—to help us identify these meaningful impacts.[23] Together, the group proposed a candidate set of words that corresponded to descriptive features of visual art that they believed might be relevant to impactful engagements (124 terms), and their potential cognitive or affective impacts (69 terms). Descriptive terms covered properties like content, form, and evaluations (e.g., geometric, figurative, amateur) and the impact terms captured ways artworks might make a viewer think or feel (e.g., engaged, disgusted, uplifted).

Using these terms as prompts, we asked nearly nine hundred non-experts to generate single-word associations. In this way, we ensured our results would reflect the way the general public understands and uses these terms in the context of viewing art. By applying network-psychometric approaches to these word associations, we were able to map the semantic space of our taxonomy, visually representing the similarity between them at two levels of granularity: a fine-grained network depicted the relationships between all the terms, and a coarse-grained network that summarized these many relationships at a higher order of abstraction.

Our analyses determined that the descriptive terms could be organized into seventeen dimensions, or categories of similar features. For instance, words relating to the engaging nature of an artwork (interesting, striking, absorbing, mesmerizing, arresting) clustered into a single dimension, and words relating to its composition formed another (coherent, balanced, unified, rhythmic, organized, etc.). At a coarser level, these seventeen dimensions could be reduced to five dimensions. These dimensions corresponded to (1) words frequently associated with *artistic greatness* (the fine-grained dimensions of beautiful, innovative, inspirational); (2) words related to an artwork's *form and content* (ambiguous, balanced, concrete, metaphorical, skilled, still life); (3) words related to the *invitingness* (or not) of an artwork (friendly/warm, unimaginative/boring); (4) words related to how *stimulating and positive* the artwork is (colorful, interesting, profound), and (5) words associated with *challenging and negative* qualities (controversial, provocative, sad/melancholic).[24]

Our sixty-nine impact terms organized into eleven dimensions. Noting the three terms most central to each dimension, these were (1) angry/enraged, offended, disgusted/revolted; (2) upset, uncomfortable, unsettled; (3) challenged, paradoxical, curious; (4) interested, engaged, gripped; (5) edified, moralistic, tran-

23. Alexander P. Christensen, Eileen R. Cardillo, and Anjan Chatterjee, "What Kind of Impacts Can Artwork Have on Viewers? Establishing a Taxonomy for Aesthetic Impacts," *British Journal of Psychology* 114, no. 2 (2023): 335–51.

24. For complete descriptions of coarse and fine dimensions and their visual representation see figs. 1–4 of Christensen, Cardillo, and Chatterjee, "What Kind of Impacts," 335–51.

scendent; (6) enlightened, illuminated, revelatory; (7) enraptured, swept away, awe; (8) pleasure, happy/joy, amused; (9) inspired, hopeful, uplifted; (10) compassionate/empathetic, loving, intimate; (11) calm, consoled, grounded. At a greater level of abstraction, our terms cohered into four dimensions: (1) words relating to *enjoyable, positive emotions* (calm, compassionate/empathetic, pleasure); (2) words relating to *negative feelings* provoked by art (angry/enraged, challenged, upset); (3) words relating to *attentional or motivational intensity* (enraptured, interested); and (4) words relating to the *cognitively elevating or epistemic impacts* (edified, enlightened, inspired). This last dimension might be especially relevant to deeper transformative encounters of central relevance to aesthetic cognitivism.

An unanticipated observation from our study is that distinguishing between descriptions of art and their evaluation turns out to be difficult, even for experts. The descriptive terms included positive and negative qualities and words like *mesmerizing* and *inspirational*, which point to effects on the viewer. Classifying art seems to be closely linked to their evaluation.

By integrating the expertise of scholars with the intuitions of laypersons, our taxonomy capitalizes on language to offer a window into a viewer's inner experience when looking at art. We can reasonably assume that any two people gazing at the same canvas on a museum wall are not having identical emotional responses. A common vocabulary can aid the systematic investigation of the variety and nuances of impactful art engagements. By making the taxonomy available to other researchers, our goal is to facilitate future empirical studies of art engagements and to enhance cross-study comparison and conversation.

It is worth noting that our taxonomy is not an exhaustive canvas of the vast and potentially relevant semantic space. Our taxonomy functions much like a geographical map—identifying the major landmarks and communities, and the arteries connecting them or the distances separating them, but omitting minor details that would obscure the general topography. Our descriptive taxonomy focused on words used in the context of visual art. This approach could easily be expanded to incorporate attributes of other domains of art, such as music and architectural design. Our catalog of cognitive and emotional impacts should apply, in principle, to any art form.

Using the Aesthetic Impact Taxonomy

We have come to appreciate that our taxonomy might be useful to enhance people's engagement with art. Standing before a work of art can be overwhelming or intimidating, especially without a solid background in the arts. The cultural elitism often associated with arts institutions does not help. Appreciating these barriers, museums design placards, audio commentary, guided tours, and educational campaigns that aim to facilitate such encounters. Providing information about the artist, the artwork, and the sociocultural context in which it was made and received are common strategies for guiding the experience of visitors. However, tools for enriching the *subjective* experience of viewers are generally overlooked. Just as whiskey tastings provide a vocabulary with which to discern the flavors distinguishing a peaty Scotch from a sweet Kentucky bourbon, we hypothesize that viewing art can be enriched by training in a relevant vocabulary. We are helping design a museum exhibit at the Scottsdale Museum of Contemporary Art organized around the aesthetic triad and our impact taxonomy. The goal is to help viewers engage with contemporary art—typically challenging for many—by giving them a verbal scaffold from which to consider artworks and to identify their own responses to them.

Our taxonomy provides a much needed first step of a careful and programmatic line of research. In several ways, we plan to continue to apply the taxonomy to address foundational questions about the conditions in which art can promote understanding and have transformative effects.

First, we are generating a companion resource to our descriptive and impact taxonomies: a library of images of artworks optimized for empirical studies. Following a method analogous to our approach to developing the taxonomies, we recruited a multidisciplinary panel of experts to propose candidate images. Existing image resources used in empirical aesthetic studies almost exclusively use art from Western Europe and North America, inadvertently perpetuating cultural biases about what constitutes art and which art is worth investigating, and curtailing any claims to generalizability. To address this shortcoming, we included scholars with expertise in the art histories of non-western cultures. Our panel consisted of experts in contemporary European and North American art, Christian art, African art, South Asian art, and Central and South American art. The disciplinary backgrounds of our scholars were similarly diverse, with representatives from art history, art criticism, theology, and African studies, as well as a practicing artist.

Each expert proposed a set of images of artworks they believed might frequently engage each of the eleven impact dimensions we previously identified. Next, we asked lay people to respond to the artworks, generating a cohort of normed images useful for experimental studies. Our aim is to make available to researchers a library of images that covers the range of potential impacts of art and that draws from diverse historical and cultural contexts.

As the deliberations of our expert panel made clear, assigning probable impacts for the artworks was often difficult and uncertain. We anticipate some impacts may be more difficult to elicit or some artworks may evoke more variable response profiles than others. Some impacts—for instance, *edified* and *enlightened*—may be particularly sensitive to differences in pre-existing knowledge and beliefs of individuals than others. Moreover, we anticipate that this library will offer a model for generating a culturally diverse and representative toolbox for empirical studies.

To initiate a programmatic line of research, we ask several questions. How can our taxonomy be used practically to quantitatively assess the impact that art has on viewers? What are the conditions in which understanding is likely to emerge? Are people with certain dispositions or backgrounds more likely to experience art as a vehicle to understanding? What neural systems mediate these behavioral and dispositional influences on art encounters?

Empirical studies of art engagement strongly suggest several important modulators of participants' aesthetic experiences: the context in which they experience an artwork, the length of time they engage with it, and the kind of information they have about it.

The Role of Context

The twenty-first century has seen exponential growth of digitized artworks for online viewing. Led by premier museum collections (e.g., the National Gallery, the Met, the Guggenheim, the Smithsonian, the British Museum, etc.), and capitalized on by cross-collection database platforms like Art UK and Google Arts & Culture, this trend toward digitization took on urgency during the COVID pandemic. Digitization efforts also include world religious and cultural sites, spaces inaccessible to most of the world's population and frequently at risk of being destroyed by political and military conflict.

Digitization of art has clear benefits in democratizing access to the arts and ensuring records for posterity. But these moves may also come with unmeasured costs: Does viewing a work of great art on a screen elide the impact felt when in the physical presence of the art itself? Reproductions of great art shown in the lab are generally smaller, omit tactile features of the originals, and lack the physical remnants of the artist's touch, all features that might diminish the impact of artworks on a viewer.[25] Originals are postulated to evoke more interest, pleasantness, and surprise than reproductions.

25. Matthew Pelowski, Michael Forster, Pablo P. L. Tinio, Maria Scholl, and Helmut Leder, "Beyond the Lab: An Examination of Key Factors Influencing Interaction with 'Real' and Museum-Based Art," *Psychology of Aesthetics, Creativity, and the Arts* 11, no. 3 (2017): 245–64.

We hypothesize that viewing art in person has an impact on viewers in ways that promote understanding, and that this effect is more pronounced for people with limited art experience or low in openness to new experiences. In a current study, we recruited participants from the University of Pennsylvania community and randomly assigned them to one of two art-viewing conditions: in-person or digital. Participants view artworks from one of two internationally renowned art collections in Philadelphia: the Barnes Foundation, which houses one of the largest collections of impressionist and post-impressionist paintings in the world, or the Penn Museum for Archeology and Anthropology, which contains objects of cultural and historical significance from countries all over the world. We chose lesser-known works in the Barnes Foundation and objects from the Native American, African, and Central and South American galleries in the Penn Museum.

To determine the personal impact of viewing the artworks, we used a smartphone survey that queries the relevance of the eleven impact dimensions from our taxonomy, as well as how much participants liked an artwork and found it interesting. Half the participants rated the impact of the actual artworks or objects at the Barnes and Penn Museum, after independently navigating to them, and the other half rated the artworks in the lab, viewing digitized versions of them on a laptop. After completing their ratings, we asked participants in both conditions to return to the single work that most impacted them and spend fifteen minutes further viewing it. Afterward, we asked them (1) to describe the artwork, (2) to describe what the artwork made them feel or think, and (3) to describe any new knowledge or new understanding gained from the object.

From the impact ratings, we will determine the emotional and cognitive impacts these very different collections have on viewers, their intensities, and the difference, if any, between viewing them in-person or on a screen. From their writing samples, we will be able to address the most central question pertinent to aesthetic cognitivism: What kinds of knowledge and understanding do impactful encounters provide? We anticipate we will observe different routes to high-impact encounters. While some participants may be drawn to revisit the works they found most beautiful, others may return to those that they found most challenging. As an exploration, we will determine whether different emotional impacts are associated with different types of understanding.

Looking Time and Contextual Information

Most people spend surprisingly little time looking at paintings in museums. On average, visitors spend just twenty-nine seconds viewing an artwork at which they happen to stop, and that includes time spent reading the placard mounted on the wall beside it.[26] How much can viewers glean from very brief encounters? It is implausible that such short engagements with art could produce deep transformations. Some properties of artworks, such as complexity, ambiguity, and novelty, encourage longer looks.[27] Greater viewing times may assist understanding nonrealistic paintings—for example, surrealist, cubist, and modernist works.[28] However, little is known about the relation between viewing time and the subjective experience of art.

Aesthetic responses to visual images occur in phases. At a minimum, there is a quick reflexive response, followed by a slower reflective phase. We hypothesize that combining the reflective phase of art viewing with additional information about the artwork is most likely to enhance its impact on viewers in ways that promote understanding.

We are initiating a "slow looking" study at the Penn Museum. People will consider artworks for fifteen minutes. We will guide their viewing with respect to the three major dimensions of aesthetic experience: the sensory-motor, emotional-rewarding, and meaning-semantic properties of the object. Our prediction is that such viewing invites greater engagement and affects the impacts of encounters as compared to viewing art in the unguided and more cursory way that people typically experience art in museums. We suspect young people used to swiping quickly through images on their phones will find slow looking a novel and perhaps salutary experience.

How much a person knows about a particular artwork also has an impact on their aesthetic experience. Something as minimal as adding a title can change how an artwork is understood and appreciated.[29] Other studies show that providing

26. Lisa F. Smith, Jeffrey K. Smith, and Pablo P. L. Tinio, "Time Spent Viewing Art and Reading Labels," *Psychology of Aesthetics, Creativity, and the Arts* 11, no. 1 (2017): 77–85.

27. David Brieber, Marcos Nadal, Helmut Leder, and Raphael Rosenberg, "Art in Time and Space: Context Modulates the Relation between Art Experience and Viewing Time," *PLoS One* 9, no. 6 (2014): article number e99019, http://dx.doi.org/10.1371/journal.pone.0099019.

28. Justin Ostrofsky and Elizabeth Shobe, "The Relationship between Need for Cognitive Closure and the Appreciation, Understanding, and Viewing Times of Realistic and Nonrealistic Figurative Paintings," *Empirical Studies of the Arts* 33, no. 1 (2015): 106–13.

29. Manuel Anglada-Tort, Jochen Steffens, and Daniel Müllensiefen, "Names and Titles Matter: The Impact of Linguistic Fluency and the Affect Heuristic on Aesthetic and Value Judgments of Music," *Psychology of Aesthetics, Creativity, and the Arts* 13, no. 3 (2019): 277; Margery B. Franklin, Robert C. Becklen, and Charlotte L. Doyle, "The Influence of Titles on How Paintings Are Seen," *Leonardo* (1993): 103–8; Gernot Gerger and Helmut Leder, "Titles Change the Esthetic Appreciations of Paintings," *Frontiers in Human Neuroscience* 9 (2015): 464; Helmut Leder, Claus-Christian Carbon, and Ai-Leen Ripsas, "Entitling Art: Influence of Title Information on Understanding and Appreciation of Paintings," *Acta Psychologica* 121, no. 2 (2006): 176–98.

information about the maker of an artwork is also influential. People generally like an image more if they believe it to be made by an artist rather than a child or animal,[30] by a human rather than artificial intelligence,[31] or reflects an original versus a forgery.[32] Providing viewers with information about the artwork itself also typically increases how much it is liked.[33] When viewing art from an unfamiliar culture, additional information can also reduce in-group bias, the tendency to show favoritism toward members of one's own culture.[34] The value of added information seems to depend on the type of artwork to which it applies, with abstract and ambiguous images benefiting most. In addition to including standard details like maker and title, our image library will also include brief descriptions of each artwork to enable researchers to explore the relationship between cognitive and emotional impacts and contextual information.

Neural Mechanisms of Impactful Art Engagements

We will use images from our library in an fMRI study to model neural activity based on specific impact variables and determine the neural underpinnings of art impacts and their modulation by individual dispositional differences. This analysis will allow us to infer biological mechanisms in play when people are most likely to be affected deeply by art. The specific design of this experiment will

30. Angelina Hawley-Dolan and Ellen Winner, "Seeing the Mind behind the Art: People Can Distinguish Abstract Expressionist Paintings from Highly Similar Paintings by Children, Chimps, Monkeys, and Elephants," *Psychological Science* 22, no. 4 (2011): 435–41.

31. Rebecca Chamberlain, Caitlin Mullin, Bram Scheerlinck, and Johan Wagemans, "Putting the Art in Artificial: Aesthetic Responses to Computer-Generated Art," *Psychology of Aesthetics, Creativity, and the Arts* 12, no. 2 (2018): 177; Kohinoor M. Darda and Emily S. Cross, "The Computer, a Choreographer? Aesthetic Responses to Randomly Generated Dance Choreography by a Computer," *Heliyon* (2022): article number, e12750, https://doi.org/10.1016/j.heliyon.2022.e12750; Ulrich Kirk, Martin Skov, Oliver Hulme, Mark S. Christensen, and Semir Zeki, "Modulation of Aesthetic Value by Semantic Context: An fMRI Study," *Neuroimage* 44, no. 3 (2009): 1125–32.

32. Yasuki Noguchi and Miharu Murota, "Temporal Dynamics of Neural Activity in an Integration of Visual and Contextual Information in an Esthetic Preference Task," *Neuropsychologia* 51, no. 6 (2013): 1077–84.

33. Kenneth S. Bordens, "Contextual Information, Artistic Style and the Perception of Art," *Empirical Studies of the Arts* 28, no. 1 (2010): 111–30; Gerald C. Cupchik, "The Thinking-I and the Being-I in Psychology of the Arts," *Creativity Research Journal* 12, no. 3 (1999): 165–73; Phil A. Russell, "Effort after Meaning and the Hedonic Value of Paintings," *British Journal of Psychology* 94, no. 1 (2003): 99–110; J. E. V. Temme, "Amount and Kind of Information in Museums: Its Effects on Visitor Satisfaction and Appreciation of Art," *Visual Arts Research* (1992): 28–36.

34. Kohinoor M. Darda and Anjan Chatterjee, "The Impact of Contextual Information on Aesthetic Engagement of Artworks," *Scientific Reports* 13, no. 1 (2023): article number 4273.

be informed by the norms provided in our image library. For example, we might choose a set of images that vary on their negative impacts or those that vary on their cognitively and epistemically elevating impacts. Such a parametric design would help us determine where in the brain neural responses vary parametrically in proportion to the degree of such challenging or complex impacts. Our culturally diverse library will also invite future imaging studies addressing cross-cultural factors in our biological response to art.

Extensions, Lessons Learned, and Challenges Ahead

Urban Neighborhoods

Can public art serve to transform the perception of a neighborhood? The US at present is deeply divided by economic class. Philadelphia has more than four thousand public murals in every neighborhood of this segregated city. We will extend our work at the Barnes Foundation and the Penn Museum into urban neighborhoods and have people engage with select murals in Center City (relatively affluent) and West Philadelphia (relatively low income). Students at our Ivy League university are typically quite privileged. We will query their views of each neighborhood and determine if their impressions of different parts of the city shift when engaging with public art and guided by our taxonomy.

Architecture

Like art, architecture is a human artifact that can have a profound impact on the people inhabiting those spaces. We are now applying our taxonomy to architecture. Some spaces might be more likely to inspire awe and feelings of transcendence and others to encourage curiosity and learning. Presumably religious spaces like churches and mosques structure space for the former and schools and libraries for the latter. In a design parallel to that used to generate our visual art image library, we will examine the emotional and cognitive impacts of different architectural designs, including structures from Africa, Asia, and Latin America in addition to North American and European buildings.

Art Therapy

In a separate study, we are examining the effects of art therapy on PTSD symptoms in veterans. These veterans paint masks as emotional self-portraits at the beginning of an eight-session therapy program and then again at the end. Blinded viewers without knowledge of the stage when the mask was created (onset or end of therapy) read initial masks as conveying more negative emotions (e.g., angry, upset, and challenged) and later masks as conveying more positive emotions (e.g., calm and pleasure). The art-impact taxonomy was used to detect the emotional transition experienced by the participants through therapy as expressed in their art.[35]

Art as Functional Object

The idea of art as an object of distanced contemplation, of disinterested interest, is an eighteenth-century European construction. In all cultures before and in most cultures across the world now, art serves functional purposes, such as mediating rituals that promote social cohesion—a point emphasized by our African art expert when we collected "stimuli" for our art library. For example, the idea of a mask behind a glass case might be regarded as a category mistake—these artifacts are meant to be appreciated in action embedded within a specific cultural practice. As the controversy around objects like the Benin bronzes and repatriation efforts illuminate, the idea of museums as cultural repositories is complex and contentious. How such objects are understood and appreciated is likely to vary widely depending on the knowledge and identity of their viewers. We will try to avoid the narrow cultural lens that many scientists in empirical aesthetics adopt, especially as we proceed with cross-cultural investigations.

The Deepest Challenge

A fundamental challenge for the goals of determining ways in which art seeks understanding is that transformational understanding is qualitative and deeply subjective, while scientific inquiry aspires to be quantitative and broadly objective. How do we bridge this divide? We are beginning to appreciate the force of this fundamental challenge and believe addressing this divide, if possible, is critical to making headway in the goals of this research program. As our own appreciation of this problem evolves through the work we have and are planning to do, we aim to develop methods by which quantitative approaches afforded by our taxonomy and qualitative narratives recounted by viewers of art can converge and narrow the gap between subjective experiences and objective measures.

35. Vincente Estrada Gonzalez et al., "Art Therapy Masks Reflect Emotional Changes in Military Personnel with PTSS," *Scientific Reports* 14, no. 1 (2024): article 7192, https://doi.org/10.1038/s41598-024-57128-5.

Conclusions

Our art-impact taxonomy was designed to be a relevant and useful tool for assessing people's engagement with art. Like discovering that a set of tools developed to construct a table can also be used to make a chair or a cabinet or a bed or a house, our taxonomy is proving to have more uses than we initially anticipated. As planned, we are using it to develop a library of culturally diverse art images normed for their potential impacts, to query differences in impacts of art viewed in person versus digitally, and to begin to probe its neural underpinnings. Along the way, in our scientific pursuit of new knowledge and understanding, we have also discovered novel uses of our taxonomy in architecture, urban design, and mental health.

5

Experimental Theological Aesthetics in Secular and Sacred Architecture

Julio Bermudez and Yoshio Nakamura

Within the Art Seeking Understanding (ASU) program, our two projects would be most closely aligned with theological aesthetics but with an approach that is both empirical and interdisciplinary, having architecture as its focus. Our goal is to make solid progress toward the formation of a new field of study called experimental theological aesthetics, a new interdisciplinary area of scholarly and scientific study focused on the aesthetic and spiritual dimensions of the arts in general and architecture in particular. Our two ASU-funded projects—"Cognitive Aesthetic Effects of Sacred vs. Secular Architecture on Believers: A Neurophenomenological Exploratory Study," and the second, in progress, "How Sacred Architecture Conveys Spiritual Understanding: A Biometric-Based Study"—involved a team of scholars, researchers, and practitioners from different disciplines including architecture, theology, neuroscience, psychology, neurology, and computer science.

Overview

Almost every society since prehistory has entrusted hallowed buildings with recording and teaching their spiritual/religious traditions, thereby advancing access to spiritual information and realities.[1] The fact that this has usually resulted in beautifully designed structures is well documented. Long ago, we learned that

1. Thomas Barrie, *Spiritual Path, Sacred Place: Myth, Ritual, and Meaning in Architecture* (Boston: Shambhala, 1996); Mircea Eliade, *The Sacred and the Profane: The Nature of Religion* (New York: Harcourt, Brace, 1959); A. T. Mann, *Sacred Architecture* (Shaftesbury, Dorset: Element, 1993); Christian Norberg-Schulz, *Meaning in Western Architecture* (New York: Rizzoli, 1974).

we are naturally receptive to and fall in love with what we find beautiful,[2] thus facilitating the pedagogic needs and endurance of faith traditions. The corollary grounding our investigation is clear: there may be no easier or faster way to access spiritual reality than by entering "Domus Dei," the house of God (to cite Christian Scriptures, although this principle applies to all religions).

Following the seminal work of religion scholar Lindsay Jones,[3] we ascertain that sacred architectures encode (1) sacred information (divinity, history, authority, the dead), (2) spiritual orientation (our place in the universe, relation to nature, social order), and (3) holy rituals (practices, contemplation, work). This encoding is accomplished by integrating religious representations into a building's walls, ceilings, windows, and spaces and using its scale and proportions, layout, materials and craftsmanship, acoustics, dark-light ratio, etc. The result is the creation of an all-enveloping, intentionally constructed environment that embodies and communicates spiritual understandings and must be conceived, epistemologically speaking, as a "theotopy" —non-verbal, "place" theology—that is only accessible by inhabiting it.[4] In short, information-rich sacred architectures depend on active human engagement supported by "pre-cognitive" structures before aesthetic and cognitive responses surface in consciousness and behavior.[5]

Once we move beyond such generalizations, we quickly realize that our understanding of why or how all this happens is surprisingly limited. On the one hand, theological aesthetics and related scholarship have advanced reasons for the success of such aesthetic practices,[6] often pointing to architecture.[7] Additionally,

2. Alexander Nehamas, *Only a Promise of Happiness* (Princeton: Princeton University Press, 2007).

3. Lindsay Jones, *The Hermeneutics of Sacred Architecture* (Cambridge, MA: Harvard University Press, 2000).

4. Bert Daelemans, *Spiritus Loci: A Theological Method for Contemporary Church Architecture* (Leiden: Brill, 2015).

5. Leda Cosmides and John Tooby, *Evolutionary Psychology: A Primer* (Center for Evolutionary Psychology, University of California Santa Barbara, 1997), http://cogweb.ucla.edu/ep/EP-primer.html; Grant Hildebrand, *Origins of Architectural Pleasure* (Berkeley: University of California Press, 1999); Stephen R. Kellert, *Nature by Design: The Practice of Biophilic Design* (New Haven: Yale University Press, 2018); Ann Sussman and Justin B. Hollander, *Cognitive Architecture: Designing for How We Respond to the Built Environment*, 2nd ed. (New York: Routledge, 2021); see also Chomskyan linguistics, Jungian psychoanalysis, and Wilberian integral psychology, among other fields.

6. R. Kevin Seasoltz, *A Sense of the Sacred: Theological Foundations of Christian Architecture and Art* (New York: Continuum, 2005); Gesa Elsbeth Thiessen, ed., *Theological Aesthetics: A Reader* (Grand Rapids: Eerdmans, 2004); Richard Viladesau, *Theological Aesthetics: God in Imagination, Beauty, and Art* (New York: Oxford University Press, 1999); Hans Urs von Balthasar, *The Glory of the Lord: A Theological Aesthetics*, 7 vols. (Ignatius Press, 1983–1989).

7. Abbot Suger, *Liber de Rebus in Administratione Sua Gestis* (c. 1140s); Thomas Aquinas,

a growing interest in the relationship among built environment, religion, and spirituality over the past two decades has produced new, valuable insights.[8] However, because these contributions offer no empirical evidence, their arguments cannot survive serious scientific scrutiny nor significantly advance our understanding of how religious buildings facilitate access to spiritual reality. There is also no hard data on the possible causes of such effects. Semiotic studies conducted in architecture and environmental psychology in the 1980s and 1990s only indirectly pointed at possible architectural features that may be involved in communicating and inducing human perceptual and behavioral responses.[9] Similar limitations afflict more recent phenomenological studies of buildings.[10]

Until a generation ago, there was little else to do about empirically gauging how religious buildings could provide access to a spiritual reality. This situation dramatically changed with the advent of human neuroscience—an empirically oriented scientific discipline that studies the relationships between phenomenological states and brain activity. However, most neuroscientific and clinical research on spirituality has focused on internally induced (i.e., self-directed, as

---

Summa Theologiae; Rudolf Otto, *The Idea of the Holy* (New York: Oxford University Press, 1970); John Paul II, *Letter of His Holiness Pope John Paul II to Artists* (1999); Joseph Ratzinger, "Quotes on Architecture by Pope Benedict XVI," *Sacred Architecture Journal* (2019), https://tinyurl.com/yc4z6fvv.

8. Sigurd Bergmann, ed., *Theology in Built Environments: Exploring Religion, Architecture, and Design* (New Brunswick, NJ: Transaction, 2009); Julio Bermudez, *Transcending Architecture: Contemporary Views of Sacred Space* (Washington, DC: Catholic University of America Press, 2015); Renata Hejduk and Jim Williamson, eds., *The Religious Imagination in Modern and Contemporary Architecture: A Reader* (New York: Routledge, 2011); C. Stephen Jaeger, ed., *Magnificence and the Sublime in Medieval Aesthetics: Art, Architecture, Literature, Music* (New York: Palgrave Macmillan, 2010).

9. Geoffrey Broadbent, Richard Bunt, and Charles Jenks, eds., *Sign, Symbols, and Architecture* (New York: Wiley & Sons, 1980); Umberto Eco, "Function and Sign: Semiotics of Architecture," in *The City and the Sign: An Introduction to Urban Semiotics*, ed. Mark Gottdiener and Alexandros Ph. Lagopoulos (New York: Columbia University Press, 1986), 55–86; Bill Hillier and Julienne Hanson, *The Social Logic of Space* (Cambridge: Cambridge University Press, 1984); Donald Preziosi, *The Semiotics of the Built Environment: An Introduction to Architectonic Analysis* (Bloomington: Indiana University Press, 1979); Julia Williams Robinson, *Institution and Home: Architecture as a Cultural Medium* (Amsterdam: Techne, 2006).

10. Tricia Austin, *Narrative Environment and Experience Design: Space as a Medium of Communication* (New York: Routledge, 2020); Julio Bermudez, "Amazing Grace: New Research into 'Extraordinary Architectural Experiences' Reveals the Central Role of Sacred Places," *Faith and Formation* 42, no. 3 (2009): 8–13; Julio Bermudez, "Empirical Aesthetics: The Body and Emotion in Extraordinary Architectural Experiences," in *Proceedings of the 2011 Architectural Research Centers Consortium Conference*, ed. Philip Plowright and Bryce Gamper (2011): 369–80.; Bryan Lawson, *The Language of Space* (Oxford: Architectural, 2001); Sophia Psarra, *Architecture and Narrative: The Formation of Space and Cultural Meaning* (New York: Routledge, 2009).

in prayer or meditation) and not externally induced (i.e., object or environment-driven) spiritual responses.[11] The few studies addressing externally induced aesthetics and spiritual responses have been limited to two-dimensional iconography and music.[12] There have been hardly any neuroscientific studies of architecture dealing with religion or related experiences. Instead, research has been mostly about understanding neural substrates associated with wayfinding, aesthetic judgment, stress, or other non-spiritual responses.[13] Existing scientific work in psychology, neuroaesthetics, and other fields with relevancy to sacred architec-

11. C. Aaen-Stockdale, "Neuroscience for the Soul," *Psychologist* 25, no. 7 (2012): 520–3; Eugene G. d'Aquili and Andrew B. Newberg, "The Neuropsychology of Aesthetic, Spiritual, and Mystical States," *Zygon* 35, no. 1 (2000): 39–51; Di Dio Cinzia and Gallese Vittorio, "Neuroaesthetics: A Review," *Current Opinions in Neurobiology* 19, no. 6 (2009): 682–87; Alexander A. Fingelkurts and Andrew A. Fingelkurts, "Is Our Brain Hardwired to Produce God, or Is Our Brain Hardwired to Perceive God? A Systematic Review on the Role of the Brain in Mediating Religious Experience," *Cognitive Processing* 10, no. 4 (2009): 293–326; Antoine Lutz et al., "Regulation of the Neural Circuitry of Emotion by Compassion Meditation: Effects of Meditative Expertise," *PLoS One* 3, no. 3 (2008): article number e1897, https://doi.org/10.1371/journal.pone.0001897; Andrew Newberg, *Neurotheology: How Science Can Enlighten Us about Spirituality* (New York: Columbia University Press, 2018); Lauren Reinerman-Jones et al., "Neurophenomenology: An Integrated Approach to Exploring Awe and Wonder," *South African Journal of Philosophy* 32, no. 4 (2013): 295–309; Uffe Schjødt, "The Religious Brain: A General Introduction to the Experimental Neuroscience of Religion," *Method and Theory in the Study of Religion* 21 (2009): 310–39.

12. Lorenza S. Colzato, Wery P. M. van den Wildenberg, and Bernhard Hommel, "Losing the Big Picture: How Religion May Control Visual Attention," *PLoS ONE* 3, no. 11 (2008): article number e3679, https://doi.org/10.1371/journal.pone.0003679; Martin Lang et al., "Music as a Sacred Cue? Effects of Religious Music on Moral Behavior," *Frontiers in Psychology* 7, no. 7 (2016): 814; M. J. Lowis and J. Hughes, "A Comparison of the Effects of Sacred and Secular Music on Elderly People," *Journal of Psychology* 131, no. 1 (1997): 45–55.

13. John P. Eberhard, *Brain Landscape: The Coexistence of Neuroscience and Architecture* (New York: Oxford University Press, 2009); Lars Brorson Fich et al., "Can Architectural Design Alter the Physiological Reaction to Psychosocial Stress? A Virtual TSST Experiment," *Physiology and Behavior* 135 (2014): 91–97; Joshua O. S. Goh et al., "Culture Differences in Neural Processing of Faces and Houses in the Ventral Visual Cortex," *SCAN* 5 (2010): 227–35; Ulrich Kirk et al., "Brain Correlates of Aesthetic Expertise: A Parametric fMRI Study," *Brain and Cognition* 69 (2008): 306–15; Qingguo Ma, Linfeng Hu, and Xiaoyi Wang, "Emotion and Novelty Processing in an Implicit Aesthetic Experience of Architectures: Evidence from an Event-Related Potential Study," *Neuroreport* 26, no. 5 (2015): 279–84.

ture also lacks the proper focus due to being too narrow,[14] too general,[15] or at a wrong scale.[16]

Our research program was developed to address these voids by investigating (1) brain and physiological correlates of internal states elicited by two significant buildings—one religious and one secular—in people of faith (project 1), and (2) what architectural features may elicit such responses (project 2). Whereas the first project studies the *effects* of sacred (vs. secular) buildings on people, the second project focuses on the architectural *causes* that produce such effects in the first place. Ambulatory EEG (electroencephalography) for the first project, mobile eye-tracking and AI (Artificial Intelligence)-based visual attention software for the second study, and biometric sensors for both projects are used to analyze the experiential responses of two groups, each one composed of thirty-two individuals of the Catholic faith, to two aesthetic architectural conditions: one religious (the Basilica of the National Shrine of the Immaculate Conception) and one secular (Union Station)—buildings of great significance in Washington, DC.

In this chapter, we mainly focus on project 1, which has been completed. Since project 2 is being finalized at the time of writing this manuscript, we opt to provide some key information about it and point out how the two projects will be integrated to generate new information and knowledge about how sacred architecture can serve as a vehicle for conveying and embodying spiritual information and spiritual reality. By generating scientifically robust data/results, these first-of-its-kind projects will (1) lay the groundwork for a new field of study: experimental theological aesthetics, and (2) contribute to architecture's evidence-based design—a movement that uses science to better understand, teach, plan, construct, and assess the built environment's impact on the human mind, heart, and spirit.

14. Rudolf Arnheim, *The Dynamics of Architectural Form* (Berkeley: University of California Press, 2009); Oshin Vartanian et al., "Architectural Design and the Brain: Effects of Ceiling Height and Perceived Enclosure on Beauty Judgments and Approach-Avoidance Decisions," *Journal of Environmental Psychology* 41 (2015): 10–18.

15. Michael A. Arbib, *When Brains Meet Buildings: A Conversation between Neuroscience and Architecture* (New York: Oxford University Press, 2021); Lynne C. Manzo and Patrick Devine-Wright, eds., *Place Attachment: Advances in Theory, Methods and Applications* (New York: Routledge, 2013); I. Ritchie, ed., "Neuroarchitecture: A Special Issue," *Architectural Design* 90, no. 6 (2020).

16. Harrison Fraker, Peter Siöström, and Atanaska Foteva, *Minding the City: Field Notes on Neuroscience and the Poetics of Sustainable Public Space* (Novato, CA: Oro, 2021); Justin B. Hollander and Eric C. Anderson, "The Impact of Urban Façade Quality on Affective Feelings," *Archnet-IJAR* 14, no. 2 (2020): 219–32.

Theoretical Framework

Our theoretical framework was based on neurophenomenology and aesthetic cognitivism. Neurophenomenology is a scientific approach aimed to create various forms of "bridges" (or correlations) between human experience and neurophysiology—what are usually called the subjective (first-person) and objective (third-person) perspectives of reality—with the aim of developing mutual constraints between the two perspectives.[17] Much of the work on the neuroscience of consciousness that occurred in the past twenty or so years is motivated by neurophenomenology. Aesthetic cognitivism is a philosophical position claiming that the experience of art is inevitably cognitive and, therefore, epistemologically "productive" (i.e., it "produces" knowledge or understanding) and, in principle, empirically measurable.[18] There has been increasing scholarly and scientific attention to aesthetic cognitivism over the past few years, in part due to the success of the Art Seeking Understanding (ASU) program put forward by the Templeton Religion Trust (TRT) and reflected in many chapters in this book.

Based on this theoretical framework and bringing together experts in architecture, psychology, neuroscience, theology, and computer science, our interdisciplinary team (1) employed last-generation technology to measure brain activity, eye-tracking, and bodily states, (2) developed a novel research methodology to investigate architecture's aesthetic capacity to produce spiritual and cognitive outcomes, and (3) collected compelling data to advance our understanding of sacred architecture for further studies.

Project 1 Hypotheses

We aimed to measure differences in brain and physiological activities and cognitive/aesthetic responses to sacred vs. secular buildings. Our objective was similar to the intention of those researchers who have been scientifically documenting the differences between meditative and ordinary mental states. We evaluated the following three organizing hypotheses in project 1:

17. Aviva Berkovich-Ohana et al., "The Hitchhiker's Guide to Neurophenomenology: The Case of Studying Self Boundaries with Meditators," *Frontiers in Psychology* 11 (2020): 1680; Francisco J. Varela, "Neurophenomenology: A Methodological Remedy for the Hard Problem," *Journal of Consciousness Studies* 3 (1996): 330–49.

18. Christoph Baumberger, "Art and Understanding: In Defence of Aesthetic Cognitivism," in *Bilder sehen: Perspektiven der Bildwissenshaft*, ed. Mark Greenlee et al. (Regensburg: Schnell & Steiner, 2013), 41–67; Gordon Graham, *Philosophy and the Arts: An Introduction to Aesthetics*, 3rd ed. (London: Routledge, 2005).

1. Significant differences in EEG-biosensor data, subjective states, and cognitive outcomes triggered by the sacred vs. secular buildings would be observed. For example, relative to secular architecture, we anticipated that sacred architecture would reduce anxiety and mind wandering by absorbing the subjects into its aesthetically rich spiritual environment. We also expected this response to disrupt ordinary mental processes, as reflected in brain activity associated with the operation of the default mode network.
2. Since the sacred space would provide well-defined representational and architectural cues, we expected significantly less self-regulation and executive attention and, therefore, a reduced presence of normal waking EEG patterns than in the less clearly defined conditions of the secular space. Still, we would expect an externally induced (i.e., sense-driven) attention in both architectural conditions, although attention was expected to be higher in the sacred building.
3. Sacred architecture would enable subjects' access to spiritual reality gauged as (1) a heightened sense of connectedness (with self, others, or God), (2) focus on the ongoing moment leading to self-transcendence, (3) contemplative attitude along with feelings of compassion and empathy, and (4) experiences of awe, beauty, and peace.

Since both buildings are aesthetically significant, this study also provided an opportunity to tease out cognitive and aesthetic differences in how the participants would experience the two types of spaces, as reflected in phenomenological responses regarding perception and apprehension of spiritual reality while they visited the two architectural conditions.

Project 2 Hypotheses

We sought to understand how architectural features encode and communicate spiritual understanding by empirically documenting, correlating, and comparing cognitive-aesthetic responses to sacred vs. secular conditions. We define "responses" as data collected from subjects (especially through eye-tracking) that are theoretically and empirically associated with salient objective characteristics shaping the experience. These "responses" are not gauging the subjects' internal states of mind as our project 1. Instead, they are indicators of architectural features that we wish to identify and investigate. We had four organizing hypotheses in project 2:

1. Deep-seated perceptual-behavioral structures will prefigure in observable or self-reported responses to both buildings. Higher communication of spiritual under-

standing is expected when architectural features activate such "pre-cognitive" structures. The same will hold for aesthetic responses in both buildings.

2. Seven unique (unavailable to the other arts) features of architecture play a predominant role in creating unique conditions for aesthetic/functional appreciation, including spiritual understanding and reality: scale, spatial layout and openness, light, formal unity, tectonics, art-integration, and acoustics.
3. Using Baumberger's (seven cognitive contributions of artworks) taxonomy, we hypothesize architecturally induced spiritual understanding as dealing with *perspectives* (e.g., sense making, perspective taking, existential realization), *phenomenal knowledge* (e.g., self-transcendence, timelessness, awe/mystery/sublime, compassion), and *grasping connections* (e.g., new meanings, use/service, liturgy).
4. Spiritual information, orientation, and rituals embedded in the building (e.g., layout, iconography, decorations) will play a direct, conscious, and socially, culturally, and religiously determined role in gaining spiritual understanding. In contrast, architecture's general and environmental properties (e.g., size, space, enclosure, light, acoustics) will provide more intuitive, holistic, and affective types of spiritual understanding. Verbally articulating responses to the first type of aesthetic properties will be easier for subjects than to the second ones. In Baumberger's taxonomy, this translates to gaining perspective and grasping connections vs. phenomenal knowledge. We hypothesize that secular building may elicit phenomenal knowledge of a spiritual kind but little of the former two (i.e., perspectives and grasping connections).

Because cognition is *embodied* (i.e., reality comes through our bodies and senses first, and *pre-attentively*), our empirical work seeks to document and measure the changes in the body as subjects interact with a sacred vs. a secular building. By collecting the physiological data on nervous system arousal, we expect to see how these biomeasurements quickly change, depending on the visual stimuli taken in and recorded with the mobile eye-tracking glasses. By documenting "archetypal" visual responses to architectural scenes predicted by the AI-based visual attention software, we hope to explore the pre-conscious responses of our subjects. We will also monitor the second (and third) layer of cognitive operation, namely the socio-cultural-religious and personal interpretations that we hypothesize are grounded on the former. This multilevel empirical analysis will help us identify the most prominent architectural features that visitors attend to while experiencing the buildings.

Methodology and Study Protocols

We relied on the standard experimental methodology to organize and implement our cause-and-effect study of the two architectural conditions. We conducted two studies, each one approximately eighteen months long, to evaluate (1) the cognitive responses to two magnificent but different architectural conditions—one secular and one religious—of Catholics and (2) the architectural features and conditions that are likely to be associated with such responses. The two buildings were Union Station, the transportation hub that includes a train station, and the Basilica of the National Shrine of the Immaculate Conception (a Catholic Church). Located in Washington, DC, both buildings are architecturally significant, and they have a strong urban presence and serve many thousands of people in the region. While the Basilica is smaller than Union Station, the public areas that most people utilize are comparable (around 110,000 sq. ft. ± 20 percent). Also, because both buildings respond to a traditional premodern orientation and language and seek an aesthetic response, they provided the opportunity to tease out cognitive and aesthetic differences in how the participants will experience the two conditions of spaces/buildings.

Our study participants were recruited from the Catholic University of America community. We used a different group of people for each study. Inclusion criteria for qualifying subjects were English-speaking, between twenty-one and sixty-five years old, healthy enough to walk 1,500 feet and climb stairs, not pregnant, college degree holders, COVID-19 vaccinated, strongly Catholic (measured as getting a score of at least thirty points or higher in the Santa Clara Strength of Belief Questionnaire[19]), and familiar with the two buildings (defined by having had at least two visits in the last two years). Both studies ended up with thirty-two participating subjects (seventeen male and fifteen female). The rationale for selecting believers as our population is similar to that for choosing expert meditators when demonstrating the impacts of meditation. In the case of believers, their sensibility to a sacred space of their own faith would allow them to appreciate, experience, and engage the consecrated building more strongly and more definitively than might be expected of the general population. In other words, this group gave us the best chance to evaluate our hypotheses.

In terms of collecting quantitative data, the first study utilized a mobile EEG system (Cognionics CGX Quick-20r) and biosensors (Empatica E4 wristband) to record the subjects's brain and bodily responses to the two aesthetic structures. In the second study (still ongoing), mobile eye-tracking glasses (Viewpointsystem VPS 19) and biosensors (Empatica E4 wristband) were deployed to gauge the subjects' attentional gaze and bodily reaction to the two buildings in real time. We included a very popular AI-based predictive package (3M VAS—Visual Attention Software) in the analysis of the main architectural scenes in Project 2 with the

19. Thomas G. Plante and Marcus T. Boccaccini, "The Santa Clara Strength of Religious Faith Questionnaire," *Pastoral Psychology* 45, no. 5 (1997): 375–87.

intention of comparing and contrasting real and situated visual attention displayed by human subjects to AI prognostications. In terms of phenomenological or qualitative data, a simple questionnaire (repeated a few times during each visit) and a semi-structured exit questionnaire at the end of each experience were used to collect the subjects' responses to the two architectural conditions. The questionnaires for the two studies shared some of the same questions (to allow us to consider commonalities) but included others that were very different (as each project had different intentions). Both studies were conducted under Institutional Review Board approval at the Catholic University of America.

Half of the subjects were randomly assigned to experience the sacred building first, whereas the other half began with the secular building first. The experimental conditions of the visits were controlled by experiential guidelines (attention, attitude, directionality, social engagement), time of day, and duration. Two visits were scheduled on two different dates (at least three days apart). The protocol guiding the visit to the buildings also followed a strictly predetermined structure, which was the same for both projects. There were five stops resembling an actual visit to the buildings: stop 1: outside and facing the whole structure from about one hundred yards away from the entrance; stop 2: outside in front of the entrance; stop 3: inside after entering the building; stop 4: inside at the center of the main space after five minutes of free movement; and stop 5: outside after exiting the building. Individuals walked from one stop to another. EEG/body measurements (project 1) and eye-tracking recordings/body measurements (project 2) were continuously recorded throughout the path. At each stop, there was a three-minute (project 1) or one-minute (project 2) moment of repose to diminish as much as possible movement-induced artifacts (project 1) and allow subjects to visually explore the view from their location (project 2). The repose was followed by a five-question questionnaire at each stop. In project 1, this quick survey asked subjects to assess their levels of anxiety, aesthetic response, connectedness (to the world, others, or God), internal dialogue, and sense of spiritual reality. In project 2, the short poll requested subjects to share their level of aesthetic response, connectedness (to the world, others, or God), and sense of spiritual reality and report the architectural features attracting most of their (conscious) attention. The total time from stop 1 to stop 5 was around forty-five minutes for project 1 and about twenty minutes for project 2. At the end of each visit, subjects filled out an exit post-study questionnaire with twelve questions about the experience probing subjects' levels of attention; cognitive engagement (e.g., experiential focus, quality, character, and outcome); aesthetic/architectural sensibility; access and retention of spiritual information; degree of transportation to spiritual reality; and disturbance (if any) resulting from following the research protocol. Except for one (that probed the communicative success of the building), the other eleven questions were the same in both studies.

Data Analysis and Results

Since we are still analyzing and interpreting the data gathered in project 2, we will briefly discuss the analytical steps and results from project 1. We will share what we are learning from project 2 at the end of this section.

Due to the ecological conditions (i.e., real-world environment) and the various (and inevitable) noise sources affecting mobile EEG signals, a meticulous and time-consuming pre-processing of the obtained data was required before any analysis. We deliberately chose to use two independent data analytical methods: Machine Learning (AI analysis via a Random Forest Classifier using Python) and EEG Microstate and Frequency Analyses Analysis. For the first analytical method, we only considered EEG data gathered during the five stops. For the second analytical method, we used the whole EEG data recorded during the entire visit. These two analyses delivered distinct but possibly complementary findings, as described below.

The machine-learning analysis indicated that the gamma band operating globally at the intra-subject level (within each subject) and across all EEG sensors played a significant role in classifying any one second of data as belonging to the secular or sacred building. However, the Machine Learning inter-subject analysis was unable to deliver better than chance results. This means that we are unable to make any definitive conclusion about the usefulness of the machine-learning approach at the group level.

On the other hand, the Microstate analysis revealed that the activation of the default mode network (DMN) best explained the variance of the whole EEG data set. We found the average duration of DMN activation to be longer (i.e., a greater time coverage) during the Union Station visit relative to the Basilica visit, although the frequency of DMN activation did not differ across the two buildings. Additionally, a power spectral density analysis in the parietal channels using the sequence of the whole EEG data set uncovered differences between Union Station and the Basilica in all frequency bands (except in the delta band).

Moving now to biometric findings, subjects' blood pressures were significantly lower inside than outside the Basilica (no such result was found in Union Station). Heart rates (HR) were statistically the same across the two buildings, and relative to the baseline, while approaching either structure, but entering the Basilica yielded a measurable increase in HR compared to Union Station. The HR returned faster to baseline while walking through Union Station as compared to the Basilica, keeping a meaningful difference from baseline almost throughout the whole experience. We found increased HRs for both the inside of the Basilica and Union Station compared to the subjects' experience while outside. Given these results and the importance of HR, we analyzed its impact by comparing the overall HR trend (i.e., the slope of a best-fit line) at two important stops: stop 2 (just prior to entrance to each building) and stop 4 (looking around from a stationary position inside each building). We found that there was a significant location effect (Basilica vs. Union Station) and stop effect (stop 2 vs. stop 4) but no interaction between the two factors. In terms of the accelerometer, participants walked at a significantly slower pace inside than outside the Basilica. Finally, temperature-wise, approaching the Basilica significantly decreased subjects' temperatures compared to the baseline. (This was not the case for Union Station.) While exploring the Basilica, the measured temperature consistently remained below the baseline. Comparing being inside with being outside, we found that both the Basilica and Union Station had an apparent cooling effect, but it was stronger for the Basilica.

The phenomenological data showed statistically significant differences between the responses to sacred vs. secular architecture across the five experiential dimensions measured at each stop. The Basilica induced lower levels of anxiety, was considered more beautiful, allowed for a higher level of connectivity, produced less internal dialogue (or mind wandering), and delivered a much higher sense of spiritual reality. Responses to the exit questionnaire have parallels and further define what subjects reported during the five stops. Participants found the Basilica to enhance their connection to a spiritual reality, serve as a spiritual reminder, and enable them to focus on the experience. They also recognized its sacred, peaceful, meaningful, and contemplative nature. In contrast, the experience of Union Station was considered to be of a functional, sociocultural, ordinary, distracted, and self-conscious nature. The overlaps between the participants' assessments of the two experiences are worth mentioning. Both visits occasioned a pleasing (emotionally positive) experience, connections (albeit different), perspective-taking, and a reliance on the building's interior and symbols for semiotic communication. It is evident that both buildings enabled an aesthetic experience but of a different kind.

Taken together, the findings from project 1 provide preliminary evidence for our organizing hypotheses: the study participants showed differential responses to the two buildings, as assessed by (1) EEG measured over the entire duration of the building visits, (2) biometrics, and (3) self-reports of phenomenological experience at the five stops and exit questionnaires.

Discussion

Although the findings are provisional, needing future studies designed to investigate the same or similar set of outstanding issues, we are now able to entertain several generalizations and interpretations of the results from our first project. While brief, this discussion will offer an example of how our empirical approach to sacred architecture may provide meaningful insights and contribute to building what we term an experimental theological aesthetics. Those interested in a longer and more detailed discussion will need to refer to the lectures, conference abstracts, interviews, and journal articles available elsewhere or those to come in the near future.[20]

The statistically significant drops in anxiety and mind-wandering along higher levels of connectivity, aesthetic quality, and a sense of spiritual reality between experiment (sacred) and control (secular) conditions are so consistent with the responses offered in the exit questionnaires (i.e., the visit to the Basilica having an experiential depth—described as sacred and meaningful; character—defined as religious, insightful, and beautiful; outcome—defined as peaceful and contemplative; and levels and directionality of attention) that it is completely justified to define the encounter as aesthetic and spiritual. Such phenomenological characterization aligns well with the measured differential activation of the parietal channels as this area of the brain is in charge of integrating sensory information, something expected in externally induced aesthetic experiences. Most remarkably, the decreased duration of activation of the default mode network during the Basilica visit relative to the Union Station visit indicates the increased presence of a non-ordinary mental state while at the Basilica. The DMN is a signature of ordinary mind wandering or low levels of attention, certainly not with people having aesthetic or religious types of experiences. Furthermore, and while tentative, the gamma band as differentiating secular and sacred conditions (within each subject) resonates with the above-mentioned results because this EEG frequency is associated with higher levels of sense-driven attention. Similarly, lower blood pressure readings inside the Basilica suggest less stress (e.g., anxiety) while increasing heart rate in parallel to decreasing speed in movements inside the holy building (and particularly from stops 2 to 4) insinuates growing excitement or preparation, or both, along with higher demand for attention as the faithful subject prepares to meet their God at the altar.

The results of project 1 suggest that there may be other aesthetic (possibly associated with spiritual) states beyond either judgmental or contemplative.[21] The experience of the Basilica would seem to involve a high level of attention associated more with a semiotic decoding (or "reading") of the religious informa-

20. Refer to the "outcomes" link on our research website for an up-to-date list of such interviews, articles, lectures, etc. Online: https://tinyurl.com/45276pvp.

21. Zaharia Djebbara et al., "Contemplative Neuroaesthetics and Architecture: A Sensorimotor Exploration," *Frontiers of Architectural Research* 13 (2024): 97–111.

tion, spiritual orientation, and holy rituals encoded in the building[22] than with an evaluative pronouncement (it's good or bad, ugly or beautiful) or accessing a contemplative (i.e., non-judgmental, open, non-thinking) state. Rather, the experience that some of the subjects seem to be reporting would be closer to what is called meditation in the Christian tradition, that is, a concentrated (in this case, visually assisted) discursive consideration or thinking about spiritual matters.[23] Enabling this meditative state would require the cognitive processing of the architecturally embedded understandings, which we would expect to be largely unconscious until they surface into awareness at which point the subject's conscious attention and interpretation of the messages presented in and by the building would take place. This obviously raises the question of what architectural features may be actively engaged by people while they experience the sacred or the secular space. Our project 2 precisely investigates this and other related questions by using last-generation eye-tracking devices. We briefly address this effort in the section below.

While not perfect, project 1 demonstrates how neurophenomenology, in coordination with aesthetic cognitivism, can help us build and test specific hypotheses about, arguably, the most qualitative experiences of architecture—something impossible to tackle scientifically until very recently. We believe that the arrival of new and powerful gauging technologies if accompanied by nuanced scientific theories and methods, has the potential to revolutionize our understanding of architecture, religion, spirituality, and beyond.

There are many of us on this path, researchers and scholars in fields as wide apart as theology, musicology, theater, and anthropology who have been demonstrating a greater interest in the relationship between empirical reality and conscious experience.[24] Taken as a whole, this seems to represent a real paradigm shift in studies of art, science, and beyond in contemporary society. It is a movement very much related to experimental philosophy. Starting in the early 2000s, this vision and practice deploy scientific means to respond to old, seemingly intractable philosophical questions.[25] In this context, the ASU-supported projects and programs appear as perfectly timed and likely to have a considerable impact on advancing our understanding of how the arts have managed to communicate and make us experience the immeasurable realm of the transcendent.

22. Jones, *Hermeneutics of Sacred Architecture.*

23. M. Basil Pennington, *Centering Prayer: Renewing an Ancient Christian Prayer Form* (Garden City, NY: Doubleday, 2001).

24. Richard Viladesau, "Art and God," *Artenol* 1 (Spring 2015): 22–30.

25. K. A. Appiah, "The New Philosophy," *New York Times Magazine*, Dec. 9, 2007; Joshua Knobe and Shaun Nichols, eds., *Experimental Philosophy* (New York: Oxford University Press, 2008).

Our Ongoing Project 2

Our first project focused on the *effects* of (sacred vs. secular) architecture on people of faith. But, as mentioned earlier, something crucial remained unattended in that investigation: the *cause*(*s*) producing such effects. In other words, what (and how) do architectural conditions manage to elicit such human reactions? For this reason, our second project has been investigating how architectural properties communicate spiritual understanding by empirically measuring, associating, and comparing cognitive-aesthetic responses to sacred vs. secular conditions. By "responses," we mean data gathered from participants that are theoretically and empirically associated with noticeable objective features present in their experience—not internal mental states as our project 1 investigated. We seek to discover the concrete architectural characteristics (e.g., size, space, symbols, walls, light, decoration, columns, ceiling, bell tower, etc.) that subjects consciously or unconsciously notice or employ to interact with the building. In order to potentially relate the findings of both projects, we are utilizing (1) the same two buildings (Basilica of the National Shrine of Immaculate Conception and Union Station, both in Washington, DC), (2) nearly the same visit protocols, (3) committed Catholics as subjects, and (4) the same biometric device (Empatica E4 wristband) in project 2. The big difference is our use of last-generation mobile eye-tracking (Viewpointsystem VPS 19 glasses) to document our subjects' visual and behavioral responses to the two buildings. Whereas eye-tracking has been used in laboratory settings to study architecture and urbanism in the past, to our knowledge, this is the first time that an ecological experimental paradigm (i.e., one situated in real-life conditions) has been deployed on sacred architecture in particular and one of few in architecture and urbanism in general. Finally, we are also using AI-based scene analysis (3M VAS [Visual Attention Software]) to study architectural "saliency." Of particular interest here is the comparison between AI-based predictions of how people "should" perceive the architectural scenes and the actual, ecologically situated results from actual people visiting the building that we will get using VPS 19 glasses. As of April 2024, we are currently processing data from our second project and are engaged in preliminary analysis of data from the eye-tracking glasses and the Empatica E4 biometric wristband.

Because of the common methodological foundations behind projects 1 and 2, we hope to discern possible relationships between the results of the EEG and the eye-tracking studies. We will not be able to establish solid cause-effect relationships, as this would demand conducting a study with both EEG and eye-tracking in the same experiment. However, the results of both investigations will provide us with solid pointers to support stronger, better, and more empirically testable hypotheses than have been possible or available in the past. Our long-term goal is to contribute to a better empirical grasp of how sacred architecture conveys spiritual understanding and enhances access to spiritual realms, thus laying the groundwork for a new field: experimental theological aesthetics.

Lessons Learned

We believe that we had conceptually sound hypotheses and methodologically appropriate study procedures in our first project. One thing that remained uncertain was the quality of EEG data that we collected with our recording device, Cognionics CGX Quick-20r. The noise artifacts due to movement turned out to be considerable, which forced us to deploy rigorous pre-processing of EEG signals. Because we anticipated this artifact problem to some extent, time-consuming study design included the creation of at least five epochs during which study participants remained still without any movement (i.e., resting in stillness for several minutes). Because our machine-learning data-analytic approach focused on only the EEG data collected from these five epochs, more data would have probably been needed to successfully exploit the use of the machine-learning approach in analyzing EEG data at the group level.

Overall, we believe that many specific implementations of the study were appropriate, and we would not modify specific aspects of the study protocol and implementations for our future studies, if any. However, we would increase the number of subjects in order to have a more robust data set from which the machine-learning algorithm could operate better. Additionally, given the continuous improvements in hardware technology, the 2020 version of our mobile EEG device has already been significantly upgraded, so we would expect that new available hardware and software would allow a better management of the data noise that is inevitably produced by human movement. In other words, we would wait a few more years (three to five) until mobile EEG systems are significantly more advanced to allow us to conduct a similar experimental study.

In contrast, the eye-tracking methodology, protocols, and data processing and analysis behind our project 2 went incredibly smoothly without encountering major hurdles. Because of our experiences with both EEG and eye-tracking technologies, we decided to drop the EEG component in our application for our larger-scale program grant (2024–27).

New Questions

While working on our first project focused on documenting and elucidating effects/impacts resulting from the exposure to the two architectural conditions, we became keenly aware of the need to conduct another study in which the attention would turn to measuring and discerning what and how architectural features were responsible for such effects. For this reason, we came up with the second project grant proposal submitted to the TRT that we were very fortunate to receive.

Based on completing our first TRT project grant and the near completion of our second TRT project grant, we submitted a program grant application to extend the scope of our investigation in several significant ways. Our studies to date focused on Catholic believers who visited both secular and religious buildings. In the new program grant proposal, we will aim to recruit three different groups of participants (Catholics, Protestants, and non-religious) who will visit three different buildings (a church from their own Christian tradition, a church from another Christian tradition, and a secular building) in a counterbalanced manner across the three groups. In other words, our proposed investigation would significantly expand its scope by considering the question of *for whom* the demonstrated findings from project 1 and 2 are applicable, that is, by examining how a person's religious background may play into the experience of architecturally driven spiritual understanding. The sample size for this new study will be large enough to allow us to evaluate the main effects of (1) religious backgrounds and (2) building types, as well as other interaction effects involving these factors. Finally, this new program grant will be conducted in Southern California. This new location makes it possible to select modern buildings in their orientation and style. This is important as there are much and growing interest and discussion in the architectural and theological disciplines regarding the effect of architectural styles on the communicability of Catholic and Christian doctrines. So, building on the success of the first two TRT-funded project grant awards, we hope to evaluate the extent to which observed relationships will be affected by religious affiliations and architectural styles of buildings.

Final Reflections

The findings from projects 1 and 2 are generally consistent with the key promise of aesthetic cognitivism that asserts that the aesthetic engagement of art (in our case architecture) can advance knowledge and enhance appreciation related to said art. On the basis of the subjects' responses to the probing questions during the visits and the exit questionnaires, study participants clearly (statistically significantly so) differentiated their experience of sacred architecture (the Basilica of the National Shrine of the Immaculate Conception) from their experience of secular architecture (Union Station). When we add what we are finding in our project 2 regarding the question of where subjects' visual attention goes vis-à-vis their semiotic interpretation of the architectural scenes, it will be empirically demonstrable that the Catholic church communicates three (out of seven types of) understandings in Baumberger's cognitive taxonomy:[26] *perspectives* (e.g., sense making, perspective taking, existential realization), *phenomenal knowledge* (e.g., self-transcendence, timelessness, awe, compassion), and *grasping connections* (e.g., meanings, use/service, liturgy).

Our studies also shed light on the question of what cognitive value may be activated by an embodied engagement of architecture. Various neurophysiological indicators of brain and somatic activities (i.e., DMN, gamma frequency, various biometrics) are demonstrated to be correlated with specific phenomenological expressions obtained from probing questions during the visits and the exit questionnaires. All things considered, the findings from our project 1 (and what we are discovering in project 2) offer provisional evidence that there is an empirically demonstrable link between art and understanding—in our case, the capacity of architecture to elicit cognitive and aesthetic outcomes resulting from accessing spiritual information and spiritual reality presented by the building itself, at least for devoted Catholic believers. It remains to be seen if this pattern of observations can be generalized to other religious groups of people (such as Protestants) or to a non-religious group of people without any association with organized religion. As we indicated earlier, this is one of the organizing questions and hypotheses of our program grant project at California Baptist University that we hope we will be able to investigate.

26. Baumberger, "Art and Understanding."

6

Screen Stories and Moral Understanding

Carl Plantinga

The projects emerging from this grant examine the relationship between the art of narrative film, or what I call "screen stories," and one sort of understanding—moral understanding. To better understand the aim of the projects, it is useful to first consider a bit of the cultural history of moving image narratives. Whether viewed in the theater, on television monitors, or on computers or other devices, screen stories have become a ubiquitous narrative medium in the contemporary world. Whereas at one time "the movies" were thought to be mere "entertainment" and not an art, perspectives have changed dramatically. In the world's great newspapers and magazines, narrative films are now reviewed alongside venerable forms such as the novel and theater. Elite aesthetics journals such as *The Journal of Aesthetics and Art Criticism* and *The British Journal of Aesthetics* regularly feature studies of narrative film. And the world's most prestigious academic presses regularly publish books on film and television history, theory, and aesthetics. Moving image narratives are today considered to be one of the world's great art forms.

That film is a *popular* art and reaches so many millions of people makes it a particularly important object of study for the Art Seeking Understanding (ASU) initiative of the Templeton Religion Trust (TRT). For decades after its invention in the late nineteenth century, film was considered to be either a mere curiosity or, a few decades later, a vulgar threat to society. Hollywood was considered by many mainstream Americans to be a den of iniquity. To avoid local censorship, the movie industry imposed strict self-censorship on its products in the form of the Production Code of 1934, or what was popularly known as "the Hays Code." The Hays Code governed motion picture content until the US Supreme Court, in the *Miracle Decision* of 1952, ruled that the movies were a legitimate form of expression and thus protected under the First Amendment.

Just as the idea that narrative films are art was slow to catch on, so was the idea that films could make a genuine contribution to our moral and spiritual lives. It was *The Sound of Music* (1965) that convinced many members of the Christian Reformed Church (CRC), a small Protestant denomination, that the movies were a legitimate form of entertainment. It was not until 1966 that the CRC formally ruled that the film arts were a "legitimate cultural medium to be used with discernment by Christians."[1] Few would deny today that many films have morally and spiritually salutary stories to tell, and they do so in the context of an experientially rich and powerful medium. A film can enthrall us and keep our attention for hours on end as few other cultural products or art forms can.

My projects began with a project grant called "Screen Stories and Moral Understanding" (2020–22). The subsequent program grant, entitled "Character Engagement and Moral Understanding in Screen Stories" (2022–25), is a group enterprise for which I am project leader. The focus of our investigation is to discover the ways in which narrative films can contribute to the moral understanding of viewers and audiences. But aside from any specific findings and conceptual clarifications, another important contribution this work will make is to lead to increased interdisciplinary cooperation in examining these issues.

Further below I detail the specific hypotheses we are interested in, but first I will outline some grounding assumptions.

Moral Understanding

Moral understanding begins with the discernment of right and wrong and the moral implications of human action in a wide range of spheres of activity. Moral understanding, however, goes beyond moral reflection and even moral knowledge. As Christoph Baumberger argues, understanding is a complex cognitive achievement that may consist of any or all of the following: categorization, the development of models, the asking of new questions, phenomenal knowledge, and propositional knowledge.[2] Philosopher Allison Hills defines moral understanding in part as "knowing why" in addition to "knowing that."[3]

In the context of both the project and program grants, moral understanding incorporates these broad features in relation to one sort of understanding—*moral* understanding. Films may be able to educate us about human virtues, strengths,

1. "Film Arts," Christian Reformed Church, https://www.crcna.org/welcome/beliefs/position-statements/film-arts.

2. Christoph Baumberger, "Art and Understanding: In Defence of Aesthetic Cognitivism," in *Bilder sehen: Perspektiven der Bildwissenshaft*, ed. Mark Greenlee et al. (Regensburg: Schnell & Steiner, 2013), 41–67.

3. Allison Hills, *The Beloved Self: Morality and the Challenge of Egoism* (Oxford: Oxford University Press, 2010).

and weaknesses in part because *storytelling* is a psychologically gripping means of communication. Stories invariably trace characters as they negotiate serious obstacles and uncertainties and reveal their deepest selves. And as we learn about human virtues, we also see how those virtues (or their lack) play out in specific situations and varied contexts. In *Fargo* (1996), we see the humble Marge Gunderson display tremendous wisdom and judgment in her dealing with dangerous criminals in Fargo, North Dakota. From *The Wizard of Oz* (1939) we may learn from Dorothy's exercise of forgiveness, hope, prudence, and spirituality. Or from Pocahontas in *The New World* (2005), we see honesty, love, kindness, and gratitude in action. Narrative films, like stories in many media, have the capacity to show how various actions play out in specific situations, thus enlarging our understanding not only of the ethical nature of human action, but of what it means to have an ethical outlook on life.

All of this is true. Yet screen stories are a particular sort of narrative in that they are moving *image* narratives that also incorporate *sound*. This contributes to their psychological power, and it also allows such stories to illustrate settings, facial expressions, the complexities of the human voice, and other aspects of our phenomenal existence like no other medium.

That fact that moral learning *may* occur in viewing films does not guarantee that it *will* occur. The purpose of the grant projects is to improve our understanding of when and under what conditions screen stories can impart moral understanding.

Disciplinary Situatedness

Research that bears on these questions has been robust in at least four separate disciplines: film and media studies, psychology, philosophy (aesthetics), and media psychology.[4] Film and media studies and philosophy are conceptual and historical in nature, residing in the humanities, while psychology and media psychology are empirical sciences.

Fellow grantee Murray Smith and I are trained in film and media studies and philosophy. Film and media studies in the late-twentieth century was Brechtian and neo-Marxist in its orientation, and thus interested in the means by which mainstream films inculcate viewers into "dominant ideology."[5] Film and media

4. Media psychologists typically have degrees in communication or media studies, while psychologists, of course, have degrees in psychology. Both of these disciplines share a commitment to empirical research.

5. For a summary and critique of this theory, see Carl Plantinga, "Notes on Spectator Emotion

studies have also been very much interested in postcolonial issues, and in the means by which narrative films play a cultural role in promoting stereotypes for gender, race, nationality, and ethnicity. Neither of these research areas paid much attention to empirical work in psychology and the social sciences, but instead tended to embrace critical or cultural theory. The word "moral" appeared very infrequently; indeed, one cultural theorist, Robert Stam—a graduate of Calvin College, by the way—writes in a review of Murray Smith's book, *Engaging Characters*, that Smith's use of the word "moral" rather than "ideological" is "disastrous" because it locks "complex historical processes into a monadic perceptual prison of the individual psyche."[6]

Such attempts to enforce disciplinary conformity were endemic to the discipline, which manifested a theoretical conformity as imposing as religious dogma. Some film scholars in the 1990s (including myself and Smith) launched a new movement, called cognitive film theory, which focused less on cultural/critical studies and more on the psychological processes of film viewing. Cognitive theorists were much more likely to pay attention to empirical studies of the psychology of viewing moving image narratives. In fact, several psychologists, including fellow grantee Daniel Levin, soon joined the newly formed Society for Cognitive Studies of the Moving Image, began to attend the conferences, and published excellent books on film.[7] Those of us in this group with doctoral degrees in film studies pay close attention to empirical work, while we ourselves are not trained in it.

It is important to note that an interest in psychology is an *addition* to film studies and can contribute to an understanding of the cultural and ethical significance of film. Work on the ethics of engagement in film and in the uses of film in general for the public good has recently become a major topic in film and media studies.[8] What cognitive film and media theory has to offer in particular is an empirically grounded understanding of the nature of the film-viewing experience, especially as it relates to cognition, emotion, and character engagement.[9] Moreover, the

---

and Ideological Film Criticism," in *Film Theory & Criticism*, ed. Leo Braudy and Marshall Cohen, 8th ed. (New York: Oxford University Press, 2016), 374–93.

6. Quoted in Carl Plantinga, *Screen Stories: Emotion and the Ethics of Engagement* (New York: Oxford University Press, 2018), 136.

7. E.g., James Cutting, *Movies on Our Minds: The Evolution of Cinematic Engagement* (New York: Oxford University Press, 2021); Vittorio Gallese and Michele Guerra, *The Empathic Screen: Cinema and Neuroscience* (Oxford: Oxford University Press, 2015); Jeffrey M. Zacks, *Flicker: Your Brain on Movies* (New York: Oxford University Press, 2015).

8. Julian Hanich and Martin Rossouw, *What Is Film Good For?* (Berkeley: University of California Press, 2023); Mette Hjort and Ted Nannicelli, *A Companion to Motion Pictures and Public Value* (Chichester: Wiley-Blackwell, 2022).

9. See Plantinga, *Screen Stories*; Greg M. Smith, *Film Structure and the Emotion System* (Cam-

nature of the film experience has led to ethical considerations of spectatorship.[10] These studies examine the influence of certain sorts of movie experiences on moral understanding.

Now we can turn to another discipline—philosophy. Philosophers, and particularly those working in philosophical aesthetics, have for many decades been interested in aesthetic cognitivism and in the philosophy of film.[11] In particular, philosophers have focused much attention on art in relation to epistemology and morality. What philosophers do well is examine concepts, construct plausible arguments, and consider the work of previous thinkers throughout history. They do not, however, engage in empirical investigation and sometimes pay little attention to empirical work that bears on the topics they discuss.

Now enter the empirical disciplines—psychology and media psychology. Above I mentioned some psychologists interested in the study of film. In relation to film and moral understanding, two areas of psychological research are of particular interest for my grant subject. The first is the study of parasocial relationships that viewers have with film characters. In other words, the thought is that viewers respond to film characters in ways that are similar to actual relationships.[12] Even more important is the study of so-called positive psychology. Responding to the predominance of studies of mental illness in psychology, the positive psychology movement aims to focus on what sort of stimuli lead to mental health and well-being. One branch of positive psychology focuses on the benefits of watching certain movies in relation to their contribution to well-being.[13] The argument is that some narrative films, in the way that they model character strengths and virtues, can lead not only to moral understanding but to positive changes in behavior.

Media psychologists have doctoral degrees in communication rather than psychology, but their work often runs along parallel tracks to psychologists working

---

bridge: Cambridge University Press, 2003); Murray Smith, *Engaging Characters: Fiction, Emotion, and the Cinema*, 2nd ed. (Oxford: Clarendon, 2022).

10. Plantinga, *Screen Stories*, 2018; Wyatt Moss-Wellington, *Cognitive Film and Media Ethics* (New York: Oxford University Press, 2021); Robert Sinnerbrink, *Cinematic Ethics: Exploring Ethical Experience through Film* (New York: Routledge, 2016); Margrethe Bruun Vaage, *The Antihero in American Television* (New York: Routledge, 2015).

11. The literature here is voluminous. For an overview, see these two edited collections: Noël Carroll, Laura Di Summa, and Shawn Loht, *The Palgrave Handbook of the Philosophy of Film and Motion Pictures* (Cham: Palgrave MacMillan, 2019) and Paisley Livingston and Carl Plantinga, *The Routledge Companion to Philosophy and Film* (New York: Routledge, 2009).

12. Karen E. Shackleford, *Real Characters: The Psychology of Parasocial Relationships with Media Characters* (Santa Barbara, CA: Fielding University Press, 2020).

13. Ryan M. Niemiec and Danny Weddings, *Positive Psychology at the Movies 2* (Vienna: Hogrefe, 2014).

on film, and their work is similarly reliant on empirical verification. Prominent among media psychologists is Allison Eden, the co-Project Investigator for our program grant. Media psychologists have long been researching the relationship between media and morality, beginning perhaps with Dolf Zillman and Jennings Bryant's research showing that film viewers are what they call "tireless moral monitors," consistently responding to fictional characters on the basis of moral judgment.[14] Since that time, media psychologists have been developing increasingly sophisticated models of the relationship between the viewing of films and the viewer's moral beliefs and assumptions. Research has been undertaken on what sorts of moral judgments viewers make, how various emotions such as elevation and admiration affect viewers, how moral conflict leads to rumination, and how we enjoy and why viewers seek out morally complex characters.[15]

These disciplines have all featured significant research into the relationship between film and morality, and between film and moral understanding. Each discipline has its own methodologies, and beyond that, diverging understandings of complex terms such as "identification," "empathy," and "immersion" (into the world of the fiction). Each discipline brings characteristic strengths to the investigations. So far there has been far too little interdisciplinary cooperation, however. In addition to advancing our knowledge of how and under what conditions screen stories can lead to moral understanding, that lack of interdisciplinary cooperation is what my project grant, "Screen Stories and Moral Understanding," was designed to address.

Screen Stories and Moral Understanding

The work of "Screen Stories and Moral Understanding" was to examine how and under what conditions narrative films can lead to moral understanding in viewers. The initial work was to bring together scholars from the four disciplines I described above for a seminar entitled "Screen Stories and Moral Understanding." Due to the pandemic, the seminar was held online early in 2021. The seminars were important in beginning to build a community of scholars from the different disciplines and putting together the team for the later program grant. The intent was to engender interdisciplinary cooperation and a common language. The seminar focused on three aspects of the relationship between the viewing of film and moral understanding:

14. Dolf Zillman and Jennings Bryant, "Viewer's Moral Sanction of Retribution in the Appreciation of Dramatic Presentations," *Journal of Experimental Social Psychology* 11 (1975): 572–82.

15. See Ron Tamborini, *Media and the Moral Mind* (New York: Routledge, 2013); Carl Plantinga, ed., *Screen Stories and Moral Understanding* (New York: Oxford University Press, 2023).

1. The transfer of beliefs and responses from the fictional world to the real world, or what we call *transference*.
2. The role of affect in film viewing in such transfer and in moral understanding generally. The fact that watching screen stories is affectively powerful is likely a motivator both for the viewer's intense interest and for possible persuasive effects.
3. How rumination after the viewing, or what we call the "reflective afterlife" of a film, may contribute to moral understanding.

The seminar featured twenty-seven carefully chosen participants from four separate disciplines. The participants included many of the best-known scholars in their respective areas of study. For each of the fourteen presentations, we invited two scholars to respond, then held a general discussion for all participants. In each case, at least one of the respondents represented a different discipline than the speaker. Sample titles included "An Aristotelean Model of Moral Learning in Film," "Moral Beauty and Its Effect on Viewers," and "How Context and Reception Affect Empathy."

The program grant resulted in a book which I edited, published with Oxford University Press, entitled *Screen Stories and Moral Understanding* (2023). The book brings together chapters by many of the participants. The book is notable and will have an influence, in my opinion, not only due to the quality of the individual pieces, but for its demonstration of the benefits of interdisciplinarity. We need collaboration between film and media studies, psychology, media psychology, communication, and philosophy to make the best progress in answering our questions.

In addition to the seminar and published book, the project grant has resulted in other publications, invited lectures, and conference presentations. Publications written by me and completed during the grant period include those listed below, with a brief summary of each.

1. "Moral Reflection: On the Reflective Afterlife of Screen Stories," coauthored with research assistant Garrett Strpko, in *What Is Film Good For? On the Values of Spectatorship*, ed. Julian Hanich and Martin Roussouw (Oakland: University of California Press, 2023). This book chapter examines the ways in which post-viewing reflection leads to moral rumination. It describes many of the institutions and social media sites that encourage such post-film reflection, from Academia to Reddit.
2. "Film," in *The Oxford Handbook of Ethics and Art*, ed. James Harold (Oxford: Oxford University Press, 2023). This chapter is a philosophical overview of the ethical issues surrounding the making and viewing of narrative films.

3. "Bad Fans, Bad Protagonists, and Ethics," in *Contemporary Serial Television: Cognition, Emotion, and Aesthetics*, ed. Hector Lopez and Ted Nannicelli (Abingdon: Routledge, 2022). This chapter examines the ethics of morally complex characters in serial television. Since the phenomenon of the "bad protagonist" or "rough hero" (a term coined by David Hume) is becoming increasingly important in both film and serial television, I plan to devote a chapter to this topic in the monograph I am writing for the program grant (described below).
4. "Phenomenal Experience and Moral Understanding: A Framework for Assessment," in Plantinga, *Screen Stories*. This is my chapter in the edited volume that emerges from the project grant. In this chapter I examine the medium-specific ways in which films can increase moral understanding by providing knowledge of various sorts of experiences that might be unfamiliar to us. Here I focus on the qualities of image and sound that films employ. I use as an example the film *The Sound of Metal* (2020), which examines the experience of a rock drummer who gradually goes deaf.
5. "Screen Stories as 'Imaginative Ecology': A Thought Experiment," in *A Companion to Motion Pictures and Public Value*, ed. Mette Hjort and Ted Nannicelli (Chichester: Wiley-Blackwell, 2022). This chapter performs a utopian thought experiment with clear practical implications related to moral understanding. Suppose that you could design an ideal mix of screen stories to elicit the sort of healthy, productive imaginative lives you might want citizens of your community to share. What would that mix look like?

In addition to this I gave three talks at conferences, including one keynote address:

1. "Phenomenal Understanding and the Peculiar Cognitive Powers of Stories on Screens," Keynote for The Cognitive Impact of Serial Television Virtual Research Seminar, Polytechnic University of Valencia, April 12, 2021. Virtual.
2. "Moral Learning and Phenomenal Knowledge in Narrative Film," Society for Cognitive Studies of the Moving Image Conference, Virtual, June 2021.
3. "The Philosophy of Movie Influence." Society for Cognitive Studies of the Moving Image Conference, June 2022, Valencia, Spain.

Character Engagement and Moral Understanding in Screen Stories

Three of the participants in the virtual seminars—Allison Eden, Daniel Levin, and Murray Smith—and I were later successful in obtaining a program grant from the TRT entitled "Character Engagement and Moral Understanding in Screen Stories." Our program grant narrows the focus of the project grant from screen stories and moral understanding in general to the means by which the spectator's engagement with fictional characters leads to moral understanding. We also want to test the effects of post-film rumination about the characters, or what we call the "reflective afterlife" of a film, on moral understanding. This program grant adds a robust empirical component through which we will test several hypotheses, and it puts the interdisciplinary focus into practice through this collaboration of film and media scholars with psychologists and media psychologists. At the time of this writing, we are one year into the grant work and are now prepared to begin the empirical studies that it funds, in addition to completing the many other outputs of the program grant.

The conception of moral understanding and the interdisciplinary focus, described above, carry on to the program grant. At the heart of the new project will be empirical investigations of: (1) the role of character engagement as a crucial variable mediating the formal structure of stories on screens and moral understanding in viewers and (2) the role of post-viewing reflection in leading to moral understanding in viewers. These studies will assess viewer responses both with questionnaire and online measures of viewer response, including eye movements and EEG (electroencephalography). These experiments will be conducted under Allison Eden, media psychologist at Michigan State University, and Dan Levin, psychologist at Vanderbilt University. Thus, we will leverage exciting recent developments in media technology and neuroscience to connect the cognitive processing that drives media experience with the ultimate impact of these media on moral understanding.

I will write a monograph, to be published with a major university press, that will promote interdisciplinary attention and cooperation. I'll examine the ways that various disciplines have approached film and moral understanding and suggest areas of synthesis and cooperation. This will be the first book of its kind and will, we hope, become influential in academia and beyond.

We will also examine the empirical work from an interdisciplinary perspective and share the results at conferences and in journal articles. This contextualization will be essential to the outcome of fostering interdisciplinary dialogue and cooperation and in encouraging further interdisciplinary research. The interdisciplinary nature of this project will not only increase our knowledge (since the various disciplines shed light on different aspects of the topic) but also lead to long-term relationships that allow constituent groups to make progress on these issues.

We plan to make public an open-source database of coded scenes in films, a measures bank for researchers across disciplines to use to test questions of character engagement and moral understanding, high-impact journal articles, one or more video essays (by co-investigator Murray Smith), and conference panels and presentations.

Our hypothesis, unsurprisingly, is that under certain conditions, viewing narrative films has the capacity to increase viewers' moral understanding of the represented themes. Our work will be to answer several questions that emerge from that hypothesis and our empirical work. What is the role of the viewer's engagement with fictional characters in generating moral understanding? What *kinds* of character engagement generate moral understanding? Admiration? Mixed responses? What is the role of post-viewing reflections in generating moral understanding? How can online assessment of viewer response via eye movements and electrophysiological measures such as EEG reveal cognitions that underlie reflection and understanding? What do the disciplines of media psychology, film and media studies, literary studies, cognitive neuroscience, and philosophical aesthetics have to teach each other about these issues? How can we foster interdisciplinary cooperation in research about the relationship between character engagement, post-viewing reflection, and moral understanding?

Experimental Methods

Within the program grant, we plan to undertake two empirical projects. The first will examine the role of post-viewing reflection in leading to moral understanding. This set of studies will be directed by Project Co-Director Allison Eden of Michigan State University. Eden has an extensive record of empirical research in media and morality, has contributed over thirty journal articles and book chapters on morality and the media, and is the founding organizer of an annual Media and Morality Conference. She is also the head of the Theoretical and Applied Research on Media Affect and Cognition (TARMAC) lab at Michigan State University (https://comartsci.msu.edu/tarmac-lab).

For this project, we have designed an experimental manipulation of film exposure, recall, and post-viewing reflection in which participants engage in a series of guided discussions of moral and aesthetic principles. Based on extensive content analysis of films, as well as expert ratings of content, we will use the films *The Truman Show* and *The Social Network*. The dependent variables will be the degree to which subjects who viewed the film altered their moral understanding via engagement with the characters and moral conflicts presented in the film, as well as the extent to which viewers ruminated about the film in both spontaneous and guided post-film reflections. We will both use existing scales and develop our own scales to measure moral understanding and film viewing parameters that may predict outcomes related to moral understanding, such as empathy and affiliation with characters, parasocial relationships with fictional characters, and the strength of the spectator's engagement with the story-world of the film. We will also use content scales to measure enjoyment, appreciation, and both intellectual and emotional "challenge." Reflection scales for the films have been developed for the specific films used, as well as tailored focus-group discussion guides based on existing work. These studies will provide empirical support for knowledge about the effects of retrospective reflection on moral understanding.

The second empirical project will be directed by co-investigator Daniel Levin. Levin is an expert in human experimental psychology with special expertise in experimental methods involving the study of visual attention, natural events (especially in cinema), and concepts such as agency. Levin leads a lab at Vanderbilt equipped with EEG recording and eye-tracking facilities. The lab has recently completed a National Science Foundation–funded project exploring how eye tracking can reveal learning from instructional videos. In this project, the lab successfully collected and analyzed eye-tracking data from over two hundred participants and developed techniques to efficiently extract interparticipant similarities in eye movements that can be adapted to EEG data. The Levin lab has also been working to incorporate EEG into their research. Levin also has filmmaking experience. His films depicting his research on change blindness have been viewed over three million times on YouTube.

In this second empirical project, we will take advantage of recent developments in neuroscience that allow for the analysis of cognitive responses during film viewing. We have been completing a series of experiments that both prepare for the EEG work for this coming year (2023–24) and explore interesting research questions in their own right. To this end we developed and ran three survey experiments asking participants first to write out the moral lesson from a movie they have seen (from a pre-selected list of popular films well known for their clear moral themes). These experiments tested for the influence of two kinds of predictor variables on the sophistication of the subjects' moral reasoning. First, we tested the degree to which stable individual differences in skills and knowledge relevant to moral understanding may predict moral reasoning about the film. In several of the experiments one of these variables is individual differences in theory of mind (that is, the skills that help people reason about how others' behavior is driven by their beliefs, desires, and goals). Second, we tested whether specific processes mediate the possible link between the enduring individual differences and moral reasoning. These processes included post-viewing reflection on the movies, enjoyment of the movies, and cognitive conflict associated with answering questions about the movies. The specific dependent measures of moral understanding varied across experiments.

Results? First, we observed significant direct and indirect effects linking moral sensitivity with moral understanding. The indirect effect was primarily mediated by post-viewing reflection on the movies. Second, we observed a significant indirect effect linking theory of mind with moral understanding. To our surprise, however, this effect was negative such that increased theory of mind scores were associated with *less* post-viewing reflection! This in turn positively predicted increased moral understanding. Thus, increased theory of mind indirectly predicted less moral understanding. One interesting thing about this surprising finding was that it was foreshadowed in the second experiment's finding that increased theory of mind scores were associated with lower word count in the writing exercise. Thus, there appears to be a range of circumstances in which increased theory of mind leads to less extensive reflection and moral reasoning. We are considering a range of hypotheses that might explain this interesting and paradoxical finding. One possibility is that for these relatively straightforward popular films, individuals with strong theory of mind films "figure them out" relatively quickly and subsequently find little reason to consider them more deeply after viewing them.

In addition to our survey experiments, we have been developing and running a preliminary EEG experiment. In this experiment, participants view nine brief movies (average of 129 seconds): three that are morally charged, three that lack moral content but are emotional, and three that are neutral. While viewing the movies, EEG is recorded across sixty-four scalp electrodes. After viewing each of the films, participants are asked to indicate their emotional state, and to make a range of judgments about the moral themes in the movies, and to describe the "takeaway" message of the movies. Thus far, we have recorded several participants' EEGs to these movies, and we plan to soon complete a small-scale experiment that tests several key hypotheses. Most important, we will test whether measures of interparticipant correlation in alpha power across the timeline of the movies are stronger for moral films than emotional films, and if so, whether this increased correlation is more prevalent across specific brain regions. We can also test for correlational patterns between participants with similar ratings for moral understanding and for theory of mind.

Interdisciplinary and Conceptual Challenges

For the program grant project, we plan not only to learn about the means by which narrative films lead to understanding but also to encourage extensive cross-disciplinary research. Interdisciplinary research, as I described above, faces many obstacles. Consider one example related to fictional characters and moral understanding. If the viewers' engagement with characters can lead to understanding, as we hypothesize in our program grant, we first need to understand the nature of the viewers' interactions with characters. The words used to describe such interactions are legion: sympathy, empathy, identification, perspective-taking, parasocial interaction, immersion, and transportation, for example. Even within each specific discipline, there can be significant disagreements about definitions of these terms and the processes they signify. In aesthetics and film studies, for example, scholars disagree about the word "empathy" and what psychological processes it entails.[16] Some use the word to describe the viewer's care for, or concern about, a character. Others claim that empathy signifies a relationship where the viewer shares all the thoughts and feelings of a character. Still others claim that empathy as shared thoughts and feelings is literally an impossible phenomenon.[17] Others use "empathy" to describe a sharing of congruent emotional states with the character, but also an independent perspective from the viewer's own position.[18]

In the field of moral psychology, the closely related term of "identification" has become somewhat institutionalized. It is held that when viewers identify with a character, they *become* the character in the arena of the imagination.[19] Viewers take on their thoughts and feelings, in fact, their identity. A standard measure of identification has become commonly used in media psychology and has been used in many published studies. Some prominent aestheticians and film and media scholars, however, hold that identification as so defined is psychologically implausible.[20]

Despite such difficulties in moving forward, we hope to encourage future interdisciplinary research and increased collaboration. To that end, co-investigator Murray Smith will publish journal articles and produce a video essay about such interdisciplinarity and both its attractiveness and its difficulties. Smith's original conception of character engagement strongly influences the model we work with for this grant project.[21] Smith is a well-respected film and media scholar with a following in both film and media studies and in philosophical aesthetics, so that these outputs will be well-placed to have some influence. Together with philosopher Stacie Friend, he has written a journal article proposing an interdisciplinary

16. Carl Plantinga, "The Scene of Empathy and the Human Face on Film," in *Passionate Views: Film, Cognition, and Emotion*, ed. Carl Plantinga and Greg M. Smith (Baltimore: Johns Hopkins University Press, 1999), 239–55.

17. Noël Carroll, "On Some Affective Relations between Audiences and the Characters in Popular Fiction," in *Empathy: Philosophical and Psychological Perspectives*, ed. Amy Coplan and Peter Goldie (Oxford: Oxford University Press, 2011), 162–84.

18. Plantinga, "Scene of Empathy."

19. Jonathan Cohen, "Defining Identification: A Theoretical Look at the Identification of Audiences with Media Characters," *Mass Communication & Society* 4, no. 3 (2001): 245–64.

20. Smith, *Engaging Characters*; Carroll, "On Some Affective Relations."

21. Smith, *Engaging Characters*.

methodology for *The Journal of Media Psychology*.[22] This is a special issue on media and morality and is one of the outputs of our Program Grant.

As the Project Leader, I will write a book on film, moral understanding, and interdisciplinarity, with a focus on common areas of focus and what we can learn from the various disciplines. For example, one important focus of research is on how the powerful affective experience of watching films can play a role in moral understanding. Film and media scholars, philosophers, and media psychologists have all written extensively on this topic, but often do not cite or recognize the work in other disciplines, even though such work often runs along parallel tracks. Consider two of the book chapters in *Screen Stories and Moral Understanding* (Plantinga, 2023). Mary Beth Oliver, from the standpoint of media psychology, writes of the emotion of elevation and how that may lead to moral understanding,[23] while philosopher Noël Carroll writes similarly of a different emotion—admiration.[24] We in the various disciplines often have similar concerns and interests, but we need to learn a common language and promote collaboration.

Hypotheses and Findings

While our empirical work is in its early stages, it is still possible to identify the major hypotheses that guide our work. Some of these are supported by extensive empirical research; others await further testing. First, we hypothesize that films offer unique means of imparting moral understanding, given that they employ not only narrative, but narrative in an audio-visual medium.[25] Screen stories are uniquely positioned to provide a sense of what it is like to be someone from a different background, gender, or situation. This is one source of the distinct cognitive value of screen stories. Second, we hypothesize that films must have a strong affective impact to lead to moral understanding.[26] This can come in many ways, in the form of powerful reactions to the film itself, strong attachments to char-

22. Stacie Friend, Angela Nyhout, Murray Smith, and Heather Ferguson, "Moral Understanding and Media: Meeting the Challenges of Interdisciplinary Research," *Journal of Media Psychology* 36, no. 4 (2024): 220–30.

23. Mary Beth Oliver, "Morality and Media: The Role of Elevation/Inspiration," in Plantinga, *Screen Stories*, 146–59.

24. Noël Carroll, "Movies, Examples, and Morality: The Rhetoric of Admiration," in Plantinga, *Screen Stories*, 179–96.

25. Carl Plantinga, "Phenomenal Experience and Moral Understanding: A Framework for Assessment," in Plantinga, *Screen Stories*, 53–68.

26. Robert Sinnerbrink, "Affect and Moral Understanding," in Plantinga, *Screen Stories*, 127–45.

acters as exemplars of virtue,[27] or from morally conflicted attachments to and considerations of characters.[28] Third, we hypothesize that moral understanding through viewing films is much more likely to occur when the viewer reflects on or discusses the film after the viewing.[29] Interestingly, this is much more likely to occur if the film contains moral conflict.[30] But when such reflection is directed or stimulated by an outside source, a morally simple film can also elicit discussion and rumination.

In sum, the ways in which screen stories relate to our lives are diverse and fascinating. We believe that under some conditions, they can contribute to moral understanding, one very significant aspect of human understanding generally. We plan to make significant progress in verifying these hypotheses. May the conversation continue.

27. Carroll, "Movies, Examples, and Morality"; Oliver, "Morality and Media."

28. René Weber and Frederick R. Hopp, "Moral Conflict, Screen Stories, and Narrative Appeal," in Plantinga, *Screen Stories*, 90–104; Allison Eden and Matthew Grizzard, "Media Characters and Moral Understanding: Perspectives from Media Psychology," in Plantinga, *Screen Stories*, 163–78.

29. James Harold, "Audience's Role in Generating Moral Understanding: Screen Stories as Sites for Interpretive Communities," in Plantinga, *Screen Stories*, 197–211; Wyatt Moss-Wellington, "On Reflecting on Reflections: The Moral Afterlife of Screen Stories," in Plantinga, *Screen Stories*, 212–27; Murray Smith, "The Reflective Afterlife and the Ends of Imagining," in Plantinga, *Screen Stories*, 228–45.

30. Weber and Hopp, "Moral Conflict, Screen Stories, and Narrative Appeal," 2023.

7

Paratexts, Manuscripts, Literature, and Understanding

Alejandro Bahena-Rivera, Kelsie G. Rodenbiker, Christoph Scheepers, and Garrick V. Allen

Within the broader philosophical discussion of aesthetic cognitivism, much attention has been paid to the ways that narrative literature can instill knowledge and cultivate understanding. As complex fictional worlds with aesthetic features (e.g., plot, characterization, structure, imagery, symbolism, ambiguity, perspectival play), literature creates the space for readers to improve their conceptual, propositional, and practical knowledge, while also offering opportunities to impart understanding, reconfiguring their existing knowledge into new structures or networks, leading to new perspectives on the world and on themselves.[1] In other words, literature, like other artistic forms, has the potential to produce knowledge. The possibilities for learning and acquiring understanding from literature are multifaceted.

Cognitivist philosophers have pointed out, for example, that literature impinges upon our moral knowledge, acting as a kind of thought experiment or "felicitous falsehood" that can lead to new forms of understanding.[2] Literature

1. See Eileen John, "Fiction and Conceptual Knowledge: Philosophical Thought in Literary Context," *Journal of Aesthetics and Art Criticism* 56 (1998): 331–48; Jukka Mikkonen, "On Studying the Cognitive Value of Literature," *Journal of Aesthetics and Art Criticism* 73 (2015): 273–82; Dennis Kinlaw, "Literary Engagement and the Contemplative Disposition," *Spiritus* 23 (2023): 192–210.

2. Insofar as literature enables us to practice "the application to particulars of abstract moral principles and concepts." Noël Carroll, "Art and the Moral Realm," in *The Blackwell Guide to Aesthetics*, ed. Peter Kivy (Oxford: Blackwell, 2004), 131. See also Oliver Conolly and Bashar Haydar, "Narrative Art and Moral Knowledge," *British Journal of Aesthetics* 41 (2001): 109–24; Gregory Currie, "The Moral Psychology of Fiction," in *Art and Its Messages: Meaning, Morality, and Society*, ed. S. Davies (University Park: Pennsylvania State University Press, 1997), 49–58. On the cognitive value of felicitous falsehood, see Catherine Z. Elgin, *True Enough* (London: MIT Press, 2017), 3; Matthew Kieran, "Art, Imagination, and the Cultivation of Morals," *Journal*

may also yield new propositional knowledge, especially historical novels that rely on factual accuracy for part of their appeal.[3] Regardless of the internal nuances of aesthetic cognitivist discourse on narrative, there is broad agreement that literature, especially narrative fiction, has the potential to lead to knowledge and understanding in those who engage it. Literature can be a learned guide on the road to understanding,[4] an avenue of revelation that may reshape or otherwise disturb our quotidian perceptions of human experience.[5]

If this capacious view of the cognitivist value of literature is valid in some respect, then it ought to be applicable to many literary forms, ancient and modern, presented in various media, whether handwritten, printed, or digital, on papyrus, parchment, paper, or screen. Our project put these cognitivist assertions to the test by exploring the dynamics of ancient religious literature preserved in manuscripts, to control for the specificities of the philosophical conversation that has its own limitations in terms of material and materiality.

There are two major conceptual weaknesses when it comes to analyzing literature within the realm of aesthetic cognitivism. First, the material that forms the basis of analysis in this space tends to be the modern novel or twentieth-century poetry, and it is almost entirely anglophone and tied to modern print culture. The evidentiary basis for these philosophical claims resides in the whole upon modern or contemporary literary artworks. Second, the discourse is preoccupied with the

---

of Aesthetics and Art Criticism 54 (1996): 337–51; Roger Marples, "Art, Knowledge and Moral Understanding," *Ethics and Education* 12 (2017): 243–58; Rafe McGregor, "Narrative Representation and Phenomenological Knowledge," *Australasian Journal of Philosophy* 94 (2016): 327–42; Aleks Zarnitsy, "The Cognitive Value of Fiction in Thought Experiments in Personal Identify," *Journal of Aesthetic Education* 49 (2015): 62–81.

3. Stacie Friend, "Narrating the Truth (More or Less)," in *Knowing Art: Essays in Aesthetics and Epistemology*, ed. Matthew Kieran and Dominic McIver Lopes (Dordrecht: Springer, 2007), 35–49; David Novitz, "Fiction and the Growth of Knowledge," *Grazer philosophische Studien* 19 (1983): 47–68; Peter Swirski, *Of Literature and Knowledge: Explorations in Narrative Thought Experiments, Evolution and Game Theory* (London: Routledge, 2007).

4. See Martha C. Nussbaum, *Poetic Justice: The Literary Imagination and Public Life* (Boston: Beacon, 1995); M. W. Rowe, "Literature, Knowledge, and the Aesthetic Attitude," *Ratio* 22 (2009): 375–97; Peter Goldie, "Charley's World: Narratives of Aesthetic Experience," in Kieran and McIver Lopes, *Knowing Art*, 83–94. Sometimes literature can function as a guide to its own self-understanding. See Peter Jones, *Philosophy and the Novel: Philosophical Aspects of "Middlemarch," "Anna Karenina," "The Brothers Karamazov," "A la recherche du temps perdu," and the Methods of Criticism* (Oxford: Clarendon, 1975).

5. See Gordon Graham, "Aesthetic Cognitivism and the Literary Arts," *Journal of Aesthetic Education* 30 (1996): 1–17. Narrative can also have epiphanic properties according to Colin Lyas, *Aesthetics* (London: UCL Press, 1997), 200–202; and Dorothy Walsh, *Literature and Knowledge* (Middletown, CT: Wesleyan University Press, 1969), 11.

texts of these works, assuming a kind of disembodied ideal form for literary works, something that is unacknowledged but nonetheless ingrained by the replicability of printed books and modern reading cultures. Texts certainly have their own complex aesthetic features (plot, structure, and so on), but readers never engage literary works as pure, unadulterated text free of other influences. Instead, texts are presented in unique material contexts. Printed books, as well as manuscripts and now digital texts, are objects that have their own stories, shaping our reading experiences through their materiality, layout, paratexts, and subsequent evidences of use. There is a substantive discourse in manuscript studies that explores how the transmission of literature in non-typographic cultures impinges on textual interpretation and the aesthetics of the work.[6] The material features of a piece of literature also signify and have their own aesthetic features, features that interact with the texts they transmit in sometimes unexpected ways. We draw on this tradition as a way to test, using both qualitative and empirical methods, the claims made about literature, knowledge, and understanding in cognitivist discourse.

The goal of our project was to begin to put these two discourses together—philosophical attention to the aesthetics of literature and the more material analysis of ancient and medieval manuscript cultures—to begin to better interrogate the role of paratexts on aesthetic evaluations and knowledge transfer. Paratexts are an especially relevant focus since they are both ubiquitous aspects of all literature and highly flexible, existing in various forms in ancient papyri, modern novels, and born-digital works. Paratexts straddle the boundary between text and reader. They represent all the features in a copy beyond the main texts itself—title, page numbers, prefaces, front matter, indices, illuminations, secondary annotations, and so on.[7]

6. See, for example, Garrick V. Allen and Anthony P. Royle, "Paratexts Seeking Understanding: Manuscripts and Aesthetic Cognitivism," *Religions* 11 (2020); Garrick V. Allen, "Text and Tradition: David Brown and New Testament Textual Criticism," in *The Moving Text: Interdisciplinary Studies on David Brown and the Bible*, ed. Garrick V. Allen, Christopher R. Brewer, and Dennis F. Kinlaw III (London: SCM, 2018), 3–16; Garrick V. Allen, *Manuscripts of the Book of Revelation: New Philology, Paratexts, Reception* (Oxford: Oxford University Press, 2020); David Ganz and Barbara Schellewand, eds., *Clothing Sacred Scriptures: Book Art and Book Religion in Christian, Islamic, and Jewish Culture* (Berlin: De Gruyter, 2019); Persis Berlekamp, "Visible Art, Invisible Knowledge," *International Journal of Middle East Studies* 45 (2013): 563–65; Laura Cleaver and Helen Conrad O'Brian, *Latin Psalter Manuscripts in Trinity College Dublin and the Chester Beatty Library* (Dublin: Four Courts, 2015); Stephen G. Nichols, *From Parchment to Cyberspace: Medieval Literature in the Digital Age* (New York: Lang, 2016).

7. On paratexts, see Gérard Genette, *Paratexts: Threshold of Interpretation*, trans. J. E. Lewin and R. Macksey (Cambridge: Cambridge University Press, 1997). On their relevance to manuscript studies, see Allen, *Manuscripts of the Book of Revelation*, 46–52.

To bring these discourses together, we convened multiple interdisciplinary meetings between manuscript scholars, curators, philosophers, artists, and cognitive scientists, using the collection of the Chester Beatty in Dublin as a shared resource for discussion. Holding a world-renowned collection of religious manuscripts, including Christian, Jewish, Islamic, and Buddhist sacred texts, this collection enabled us to have a common critical reservoir for our conversations. We explored ways that we can advance our own disciplines while simultaneously working across boundaries with scholars who hold very different presuppositions, working habits, and critical questions. In addition to these meetings, we crafted an exploratory empirical study based on the collection. The study generated new hypotheses that we can test in the future to address claims made by aesthetic cognitivists, scientists working on reading and perception, and manuscript scholars working to understand how ancient texts were understood by the people that produced and used them.

An Exploratory Empirical Approach to Paratextuality

Although we did not shape our empirical work around a specific hypothesis, we did conduct two exploratory online questionnaire studies. As stimuli, we sampled individual pages from one hundred ancient and medieval manuscripts (and some early printed traditions from Asia) representing various cultures and traditions held in the Chester Beatty collection. Stimuli were drawn from many traditions, including biblical papyri and other early Greek manuscripts, Armenian Gospels, Quranic illustrations, Ethiopian illustrated manuscripts, Japanese wood block prints, Syriac bibles, illuminated Latin books of hours, Turkish illustrations depicting various scenes from Ottoman history, Sumatran bark books, cuneiform tablets, and more. Their materials included papyrus, parchment, clay, paper, and wood, representing text in multiple languages: Arabic, Armenian, Greek, Coptic, Akkadian, Hebrew, Persian, Japanese, Egyptian Hieratic, Turkish, Thai, Latin, and French. The artifacts' times of production cover a nearly four-thousand-year spread, from an Old Babylonian Cuneiform tablet from around 2000 BCE to Thai folding books from the late nineteenth century.

The substantial variety of the stimuli as well as the assortment of their text-to-paratext ratios were intentional: we aimed to ascertain data about participants' engagement with manuscripts containing text as works of art, even (and especially) if they were unable to read the text. One manuscript presents a fish, cleaver, plate, and cup stand with cherry blossoms—a Japanese wood block print also containing a poem; others are highly fragmentary papyri with barely legible Greek or Coptic text (sometimes both); others are from the Latin collection and contain gilded and colorful illuminated folios depicting biblical characters or scenes along with text. The material ranged from the very dull to the highly stimulating, at least as far as manuscripts go.

The manuscript pages were available as high-resolution color images from the digital collection at the Chester Beatty. In each of the two studies, over four hundred participants rated the stimuli on thirteen "features" of the image, which were inspired by previous studies on empirical aesthetics.[8] The features included (in no particular order): likability, lavishness, skillfulness, structuredness, coherence, excitingness, positive feelings, negative feelings, seriousness, distinctiveness, familiarity, value, and purposefulness. Table 1 shows the specific rating instructions given to participants.

Table 1. Features for rating and their corresponding descriptions in the participant instructions. Ratings were provided on a common Likert scale ranging from 1 (very little) to 7 (very much), and their ordering varied randomly across trials.

FEATURE	DESCRIPTION
Likability	How much do you personally like the item?
Lavishness	How elaborate, rich, or intricate do you find the item?
Skillfulness	How much skill do you think went into creating the item?
Structuredness	How clearly organized do you find the item?
Coherence	How well do elements of the item fit together in your view?
Excitingness	How stimulating or exciting do you find the item?
Positive Feelings	How much do you associate the item with positive feelings?
Negative Feelings	How much do you associate the item with negative feelings?
Seriousness	How serious (as opposed to "light-hearted") do you find the item?

8. See A. Dai et al., "Aesthetic Judgment of Architecture for Chinese Observers," *PloS one* 17 (2022); Yi Huang et al., "Cognitive Basis for the Development of Aesthetic Preference: Findings from Symmetry Preference," *PloS one* 15 (2020); A. A. Lavdas and U. Schirpke, "Aesthetic Preference Is Related to Organized Complexity," *PloS one* 15 (2020); I. Reppa and S. McDougall, "Aesthetic Appeal Influences Visual Search Performance," *Attention, Perception & Psychophysics* 84 (2022): 2483–506; D. M. Sidhu et al., "Prediction of Beauty and Liking Ratings for Abstract and Representational Paintings Using Subjective and Objective Measures," *PLoS one* 13 (2018); J. van Paasschen, F. Bacci, and D. P. Melcher, "The Influence of Art Expertise and Training on Emotion and Preference Ratings for Representational and Abstract Artworks," *PLoS one* 10 (2015).

FEATURE	DESCRIPTION
Distinctiveness	How unique or peculiar do you find the item?
Familiarity	How familiar are you with this kind of item?
Value	How valuable or precious do you perceive the item to be?
Purposefulness	How much does the item evoke a sense of purpose or meaning?

We also recorded how long (in milliseconds) participants viewed each image before providing these feature ratings for each stimulus. To avoid demand characteristics (that is, cues that might indicate the study aims to participants), we deliberately concealed this aspect of the design from participants. This contrasts with eye-tracking experiments, where participants are typically aware of the fact that their viewing behavior is being scrutinized. Our instructions only stated that participants could take as much time as they wanted to view each image.

A key difference between study 1 and study 2 was that, before viewing each stimulus for rating, a brief descriptive text vignette (comparable to a museum label) was presented in project 1, whereas no such label was presented in study 2. For example, a label for Study 1 read "Copy of an antiphonary (a songbook for liturgical singing) in Latin and copied sometime between 1330 and 1338. The apostle Paul appears in the large capital 'S.'"

Finally, we also collected demographic data from our participants, including age, gender, country of origin, languages spoken, religious affiliation, and religiosity, without reference to any particular religious tradition. Religiosity was self-assessed using a continuous slider ranging from 0 ("not religious at all") to 6 ("very religious"), preset to the median score of 3 such that participants had to move the slider leftward to indicate lower levels of religiosity, or rightward for higher levels, respectively.

The study was designed to be decidedly data-driven, working without specific hypotheses in mind. Our analyses aimed at answering the following questions: (1) Based on their inter-correlations, how are the thirteen feature ratings related at stimulus level? For this purpose, we conducted Exploratory Factor Analyses (EFA),[9] reducing the thirteen-feature space into a smaller number of *factors* rep-

9. EFA is a technique commonly used in psychometrics, personality research, social sciences, and other fields, to reduce a large number of variables (measured on the same sampling units, in this case, manuscript items) into a smaller number of *factors*. This is achieved on the basis of correlation matrices (variables that are strongly correlated are assumed to be explainable by the same factor), with the goal to explain a large proportion of variance shared between the original variables.

resenting the evaluation of each manuscript in more general, "explanatory" terms. (2) How are viewing times on the stimuli (proxy for attentional engagement) affected by the extracted factors (representing cognitive-aesthetic judgment), and how do person-specific variables, especially self-rated religiosity, interact with the factors in predicting viewing time? These analyses were based on linear mixed effects models with random effects structures that allow for simultaneous generalization of effects across participants and stimuli.[10]

Preliminary Findings

The main findings of our study can be summarized as follows: First, regardless of whether labels were presented (study 1) or not (study 2), ratings for the thirteen features were categorizable into three or four major factors: *impressiveness* (loading positively on ratings of distinctiveness, excitingness, skillfulness, value, lavishness, likability, and positive feelings), *orderliness* (loading positively on ratings of structuredness and coherence), *negative emotion* (explaining ratings of negative feelings specifically), and *gravitas* (loading positively on seriousness and purposefulness).[11] The only notable difference was that *orderliness* and *gravitas* came out as two separate (but positively correlated) factors in study 1, whereas study 2 showed no such separation, meaning that the features structuredness, coherence, seriousness and purposefulness were explained by the same common factor in study 2. Figure 1 shows the factoring structure obtained in study 1, and figure 2 shows the structure for study 2. The four factors identified in study 1 explained approximately 93 percent of the original feature variance at item level, and the three factors in study 2 about 90 percent.

Overall, the outcomes of these related studies show remarkable consistency of the factoring results across different samples of participants and suggest that presence versus absence of labels only played a minor role at best. Participant attention and responses were keyed primarily to the image stimuli in study 1. This conclusion contrasts with previous studies that show that labeling has an influence on aesthetic experience and art appreciation.[12] However, note that the item labels presented in study 1 were chosen to be descriptive and *neutral* in

10. See Dale J. Barr, Roger Levy, Christoph Scheepers, and Harry J. Tily, "Random Effects Structure for Confirmatory Hypothesis Testing: Keep It Maximal," *Journal of Memory and Language* 68 (2013): 255–78.

11. The factor labels suggested themselves after careful inspection of the factor loadings in EFA.

12. See Luise Reitstätter et al., "The Display Makes a Difference: A Mobile Eye Tracking Study on the Perception of Art Before and After a Museum's Rearrangement," *Journal of Eye Movement*

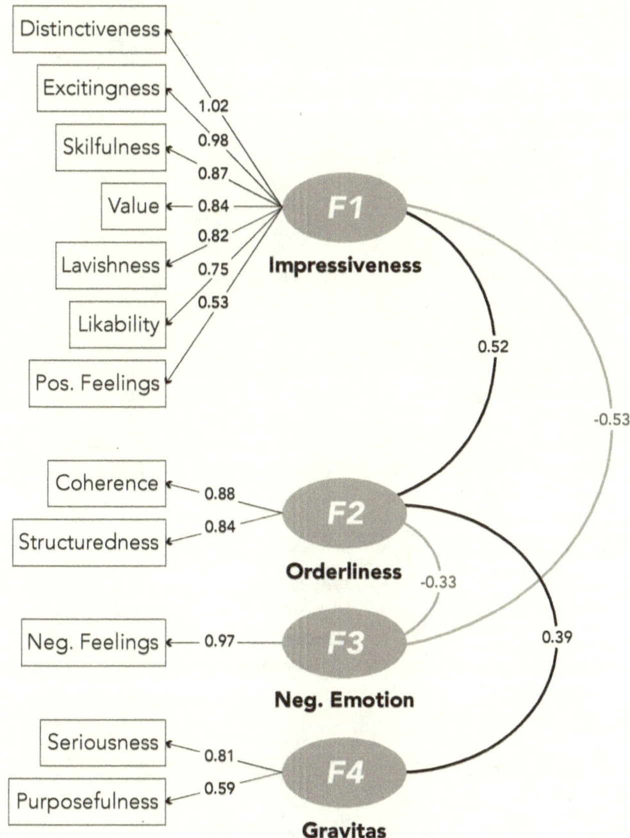

Figure 1. Oblique factor solution for Study 1. Factors are represented as ellipses, the original features (excl. Familiarity) as rectangles. Numbers on the left-pointing arrows indicate strong factor loadings. Numbers on the between-factor arcs highlight substantial factor correlations.

terms of cognitive, aesthetic, and emotional evaluation of the manuscripts. The comparison between study 1 and study 2 appears to confirm this neutrality.

Second, the consistency of the factoring results was further corroborated by strong positive correlations between (by item) factor scores across the two studies (> .8). Since the manuscript stimuli were the same in both studies, such consis-

Research 13 (2020); Claire Bailey-Ross et al., "Aesthetic Appreciation and Spanish Art: Insights from Eye-Tracking," *Digital Scholarship in the Humanities* 34 (2019).

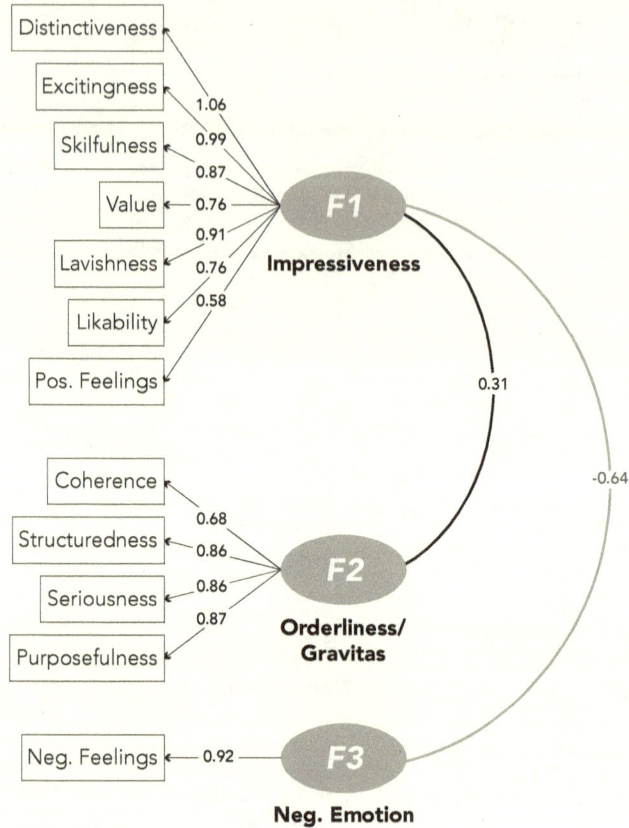

Figure 2. Oblique factor solution for Study 2.

tency—while not unexpected—is very reassuring since it generally validates our approach. The extracted factors characterize the one hundred selected manuscripts well, in a manner that is (1) replicable across different participant samples and (2) reasonably robust against slight variations in presentation context (label present vs. absent).

Third, in terms of viewing times, a similarly consistent picture emerged across the two studies: Items that scored higher on *impressiveness* were viewed for reliably longer periods of time,[13] whereas items that scored higher on *orderliness/gravitas*

13. David Brieber et al., "Art in Time and Space: Context Modulates the Relation between Art Experience and Viewing Time," *PLoS one* 9 (2014) found that people tend to look longer at stimuli

were viewed for shorter periods of time. Interestingly, *negative emotion* was found to be strongly *positively* related to dwell time: items that were judged to evoke more negative feelings were viewed for longer. This finding resonates with the notion of a general *negativity bias* whereby people devote more attentional resources to stimuli they perceive as more negative or unpleasant.[14] While well documented in the psychological literature on general attention, memory, and social judgments, this is the first time (to our knowledge) that such a negativity bias has been registered in the appreciation of cultural artifacts (ancient manuscripts in particular). Indeed, we very recently replicated this finding using more contemporary art as stimuli (paintings from the nineteenth to twenty-first century), suggesting that it reflects a rather general phenomenon which is not specific to ancient manuscripts per se.[15]

Our fourth result was less consistent than the others, but still measurable in study 1: self-rated religiosity significantly modulated the negative effect of *gravitas* on viewing time, such that more religious participants exhibited a reliably less negative effect of this factor on viewing time. However, no such interaction was found in study 2. The reasons for this discrepancy are not entirely clear yet. Apart from the presence versus absence of descriptive labels, the two studies also differed quite markedly in terms of demographic composition of the participant samples (e.g., more male participants in study 1; generally older participants in study 2, among other differences). More critically, a higher percentage of participants in study 2 identified themselves as "atheist" (36 percent, compared to 28 percent in study 1), and this was also reflected in the likelihood of choosing the lowest possible religiosity score in the self-ratings (43 percent in study 2 vs. 25 percent in study 1). The demographic difference could mean that there was not simply enough variability in the religiosity scores in study 2 to detect the interaction between *religiosity* and *gravitas*.

This issue requires further investigation in future research, for example by comparing highly religious people to those who would categorize themselves as

---

for which they have greater aesthetic appreciation (ratings of *liking* and *interest* combined), which (albeit using different stimuli, rating instructions, and experimental contexts) seems to resonate well with this aspect of our findings. Obviously, greater aesthetic valuation (in the broadest possible sense) tends to correspond with prolonged viewing times.

14. See Roy F. Baumeister et al., "Bad Is Stronger than Good," *Review of General Psychology* 5 (2001): 323–70; Maria Lewicka, Janusz Czapinski, and Guido Peeters, "Positive-Negative Asymmetry or 'When the Heart Needs a Reason,'" *European Journal of Social Psychology* 22 (1992): 425–34; Paul Rozin and Edward B. Royzman, "Negativity Bias, Negativity Dominance, and Contagion," *Personality and Social Psychology Review* 5 (2001): 296–320.

15. YuXuan Gao and Christoph Scheepers, "Is There a Negativity Bias in the Appreciation of Art?" (in preparation).

atheists (respectively, rate themselves very low on the religiosity scale). Informed by study 1, we would expect that manuscripts that are judged to be high in *gravitas* (those that exert a strong sense of seriousness and purposefulness) will attract longer viewing times in religious than in non-religious people, even when factors such as familiarity with the manuscript, cultural background, and other issues, are controlled. If confirmed, this would suggest that religiosity is an important mediator in the aesthetic evaluation of religious manuscripts, in the sense that *high gravitas* manuscripts may be perceived as more self-relevant, interesting, and potentially even more enlightening by people who self-identify as more religious.[16]

Despite the demographic diversity and the vast variety of the stimuli, there was a remarkable consistency to both studies' results as far as aesthetic evaluation and these results contrast to earlier studies on the correlation between labeling and aesthetic experience.[17] Would these results be reproducible in studies focused on just one manuscript tradition, or a smaller sampling of correlated features (i.e., language, material, content, religious tradition, etc.)? We are also interested to explore similar questions in contexts where participants read the texts that these works transmit. What is the interplay between text and image in terms of understanding and appreciation?

The relationship between attentiveness and negative emotion may prove an important one for the study of paratextual features. Would the negativity bias toward manuscripts evaluated as invoking negative emotions translate to a similar "difficulty bias" regarding textual content and hard-to-read text? Is there a golden ratio of difficulty that might cause a reader to dwell longer but *not* to evaluate a manuscript as having a lower aesthetic value or affiliation to negative emotion? To put it differently, might paratextual features such as hard-to-read marginal notes or glosses in a language distinct from the main text contribute both to dwell time *and* to perceptions of overall coherence or purposefulness?

Other questions have arisen: How would controlling for participants' levels of expertise, particularly in relation to the languages represented by the various man-

16. On the concept of *self-relevance*, see in particular the landmark paper by Matthew Pelowski et al., "Move Me, Astonish Me . . . Delight My Eyes and Brain: The Vienna Integrated Model of Top-Down and Bottom-Up Processes in Art Perception (VIMAP) and Corresponding Affective, Evaluative, and Neurophysiological Correlates," *Physics of Life Review* 21 (2017): 80–125, who discuss it as an important contributor to the potential *outcomes* of the art perception process, i.e., whether perceivers take a more detached, pragmatic stance on art appreciation, or whether they can gain new insights from the artwork in question.

17. See Serena Castellotti et al., "Psychophysiological and Behavioral Responses to Descriptive Labels in Modern Art Museums," *PloS One* 18, no. 5 (2023); Kohinoor M. Darda and Anjan Chatterjee, "The Impact of Contextual Information on Aesthetic Engagement of Artworks," *Nature: Scientific Reports* 13, no. 1 (2023).

uscript traditions, or their religiosity or cultural background affect future studies' outcomes? Would experts in Greek literature, for example, reliably rate Greek manuscripts as more valuable and more coherent than others? Would people who self-identify as highly religious consistently rate sacred texts from their own tradition as more valuable, or would those who self-identify as atheist consistently rate scriptures from any religious tradition as less valuable? Similarly, how might a participant pool comprised of just one cultural background affect the outcome? For future studies within the life of the *Paratexts Seeking Understanding* project, we will test the limits of these questions from various angles.

Continuing Research on Paratextuality and Knowledge

We have begun to extend these observations further in the form of a larger-scale RFP project entitled *Paratexts Seeking Understanding*. We have made multiple subgrants to scholars working in Jewish, Christian, Islamic, Samaritan, and Buddhist manuscript cultures.[18] These teams are charged to carry out research on the cognitive potential of the paratexts of their traditions, while also working with a scientific team at the University of Glasgow (Christoph Scheepers, Alejandro Bahena-Rivera, Xuanyi Ma, and Mirza Iqbal) to craft empirical studies on the effects of these features on reading, cognition, and knowledge transfer, using primarily psychometric, physiological, and eye-tracking as measurement tools. Additionally, the subgrant teams will work with the Chester Beatty and Scientific Team to craft an exhibition at the Chester Beatty that doubles as an experimental space. This event will showcase the project's empirical and qualitative aspects while simultaneously functioning as an experimental space where further data can be gathered to address questions related to the project's objectives.

Paratexts and Art Seeking Understanding

Given that participants viewed each stimulus in our studies for only a few seconds before providing the feature ratings for it, combined with the fact that the manuscripts were in various ancient languages and mostly handwritten, we do not believe that our findings have strong implications for "deeper" levels of understanding which would require actual reading of the texts. However, we believe that the

18. Subgrantees include Jull Unkel (Chester Beatty), Elvira Martín-Contreras (Institute of Languages and Cultures of the Mediterranean and the Near East, Madrid), Francis Watson (Durham University), Stefan Schorch (Hebrew University), Dorji Wangchuck (University of Hamburg), Asma Helali (University of Lille), Matthew Keegan (Barnard College), as well as Stephen Carlson and Jonathan Zecher (Australian Catholic University).

study results are very informative in terms of *initial impression formation* on the basis of general layout, font, illuminations, color profiles, ornaments, and other paratextual elements in the presented manuscripts, each of which constitute aesthetic features. Regardless of their cultural background or level of expertise, perceivers use this information to consistently evaluate the stimuli along three to four psychological dimensions, including aesthetic pleasure (factor *impressiveness*), structure/coherence (factor *orderliness*), emotional valence (factor *negative emotion*) and seriousness/purposefulness (factor *gravitas*). The average viewing times from both studies suggest that these evaluations must be formed within less than eight seconds of self-paced exposure to the images. Moreover, these evaluations have consequences for attentional engagement with (or interest in) the manuscripts such that more aesthetic pleasure predicts longer viewing times, for instance. We believe that first impressions matter as much for the engagement with art as they do for engaging in social relations, albeit the parameters for evaluation are potentially very different between aesthetics and social judgments.

Clearly, our research at this stage touches only lightly upon questions concerning the consequences of these first impressions for actual *understanding* of the manuscripts—what participants actually take home from them at deeper levels of cognitive-emotional engagement. For instance, how do perceived *impressiveness*, *structuredness*, *negative emotion*, and *gravitas* combine to predict peoples' feelings of enlightenment, transcendence, or some other higher-order quality in relation to the individual manuscripts? We are currently preparing another study to address such questions in a scientifically rigorous manner. We will use the same set of one hundred manuscript images as stimuli, without presenting labels (same as in study 2). The factor norms from the previous two studies combined (based on data from more than eight hundred participants) will now be used to predict new ratings of *ambiguity*, *cognitive(-emotional) involvement*, *spiritual well-being*[19] and *self-transcendence*.[20] We will also ask participants to intuitively classify each presented manuscript into categories such as *religious text, poetry, musical lyrics, scholarly text,* or *literature* to investigate whether and how the first impressions identified

19. This is a validated questionnaire developed from a theoretical perspective that considers spiritual well-being as expressed through the quality of relationships that a person has across different domains. For example, the relationship with a transcendent other, the environment, the connection with the own self, and the relationship with others. See John W. Fisher, "Validation and Utilisation of the Spiritual Well-Being Questionnaire: SHALOM," *Journal of Religion and Health* 60 (2021): 3694–715.

20. Self-transcendence has been defined as the virtue of expanding personal boundaries in different ways. See Gørill Haugan et al., "The Self-Transcendence Scale: An Investigation of the Factor Structure among Nursing Home Patients," *Journal of Holistic Nursing* 30 (2012): 147–59.

in our previous studies can enable naive participants (those who cannot read the actual text, or simply do not read it very carefully) to make informed guesses of what the manuscripts may actually be about. Future work will also incorporate *qualitative* studies in which we ask participants to freely associate what comes to their mind when exposed to the manuscript examples, combined with eye-tracking to identify hotspots of attention during visual information processing.

Using a *qualitative* approach, we will incorporate participants' own experiences associated with the artworks. This could include individual interviews or focus groups with participants familiar with the manuscripts, for example, students and lecturers in theology and art, to contrast with naive ones. Also, we could use a more participatory approach,[21] inviting participants from different backgrounds to co-create based on their experiences with manuscripts, new materials, and activities to explore the development of understanding and art appreciation in a more proactive way. This can also give us the opportunity to tease out the relationship between aesthetic experiences and people's well-being.[22] We are in the early stages of exploring the relationship between manuscript cultures and aesthetic cognitivism, but our early data suggest that our approach will make a meaningful contribution to this discourse in multiple directions.

21. See Flora Cornish et al., "Participatory Action Research," *Nature Reviews Methods Primers* 3 (2023).

22. See E. Bradfield, "Subjective Experiences of Participatory Arts Engagement of Healthy Older People and Explorations of Creative Ageing," *Public Health* 198 (2021): 53–58; Nicola J. Holt, "Using the Experience-Sampling Method to Examine the Psychological Mechanisms by Which Participatory Art Improves Wellbeing," *Perspectives in Public Health* 138 (2018): 55–65.

8

Sound, Space, and the Aesthetics of the Sublime

Jonathan Berger

Why can music cause people to feel transported? Descriptors of affective response to music—to be "moved," "uplifted," "transported"—underscore the dynamic nature of music listening. For this reason, the intrinsic temporality of music[1] provides a useful framework to study dynamic perceptual and predictive processes[2] and gain empirical insights on aesthetic responses. Over the past few decades, a wealth of studies investigated how musical processes arouse affective response resulting from violated expectations.[3] Most experiments of these types evaluate anomalous events in rhythmic, melodic, or harmonic sequences.[4] Typically, to minimize experiment confounds, stimuli necessarily comprise synthetic sounds heard over headphones with invariant timbre, loudness, and source location. Recordings of listener brain activity when these stimuli are played implicate regions in the brain responsive to violated expectations.[5] Behavioral researchers rate preferences and describe aesthetic responses of pleasure and excitement. These empirical studies identify musical correlates

1. Jonathan D. Kramer, "Studies of Time and Music: A Bibliography," *Music Theory Spectrum* 7 (1985): 72–106.

2. Devarajan Sridharan et al., "Neural Dynamics of Event Segmentation in Music: Converging Evidence for Dissociable Ventral and Dorsal Networks," *Neuron* 55, no. 3 (2007): 521–32.

3. Patrik N. Juslin, *Musical Emotions Explained: Unlocking the Secrets of Musical Affect* (Oxford: Oxford University Press, 2019), https://doi.org/10.1093/oso/9780198753421.001.0001.

4. Patrik N. Juslin et al., "From Sound to Significance: Exploring the Mechanisms Underlying Emotional Reactions to Music," *American Journal of Psychology* 128, no. 3 (2015): 281–304.

5. Almudena González and M. Santapau, "EEG Analysis during Music Perception," in *Electroencephalography: From Basic Research to Clinical Applications*, ed. H. Nakano (London: IntechOpen, 2021).

of the experience of beauty[6] in response to music listening.[7] They consider select acoustical parameters, privileging pitch and rhythm over other dimensions. While the resulting research is often enlightening, the lack of ecologically valid stimuli and conditions pose limits to the insights that can be drawn. Overcoming this constraint by exploring alternative research methods that approach real-world situations has been central to my research.[8]

Further limiting music perception research is the pervasive reliance on the notated score. Indeed, the lion's share of research in western musicology and theory considers the notated score as the primary source of study. Aside from the fact that most of the world's music is not amenable to being recorded in western notation posing a Eurocentric bias, scores provide an impoverished and partial representation of at best approximating the actual sound with quantized units of time and discretized pitches.[9] Traditional western music notation has only occasional tempo directives. Phrasing, articulation, and timbre are typically vaguely suggested or ignored. Indeed, a great deal of the qualities of musical performance are left to conjecture. It is precisely those attributes—particularly timbre and agogics—that are absent or necessarily vaguely represented that are key factors in the evocation of aesthetic responses.[10] These limitations have inspired me to consider the acoustic characteristics of musical sound as a gateway to a deeper understanding of how music can move us. Timbre, or the "color" or "quality" of a sound, has defied an accepted metric.[11] An often-disregarded contributor to timbre is the amount of reverberation in the signal. Here we introduce the role of architectural acoustics.

6. Luke Harrison and Psyche Loui, "Thrills, Chills, Frissons, and Skin Orgasms: Toward an Integrative Model of Transcendent Psychophysiological Experiences in Music," *Frontiers in Psychology* 5 (2014): 790.

7. Diana Omigie et al., "Experiencing Musical Beauty: Emotional Subtypes and Their Physiological and Musico-Acoustic Correlates," *Psychology of Aesthetics, Creativity, and the Arts* 15, no. 2 (2019).

8. Blair Kaneshiro et al., "Natural Music Evokes Correlated EEG Responses Reflecting Temporal Structure and Beat," *Neuroimage* 214 (2020): article number 116559, https://doi.org/10.1016/j.neuroimage.2020.116559.

9. Norman Cazden, "Staff Notation as a Non-Musical Communications Code," *Journal of Music Theory* 5:1 (Spring 1961): 113–28.

10. Oliver Grewe et al., "Listening to Music as a Re-Creative Process: Physiological, Psychological, and Psychoacoustical Correlates of Chills and Strong Emotions," *Music Perception: An Interdisciplinary Journal* 24, no. 3 (2007): 297–314.

11. Hiroko Terasawa and Jonathan Berger, "The Thirteen Colors of Timbre," *Proceedings of the 2005 IEEE Workshop on Applications of Signal Processing to Audio and Acoustics* (2016): 323–26.

Largely absent from research on music cognition is consideration of the effect of room or ambient acoustics on the musical signal. Architectural acoustics comprises the missing musical "voice" that implicitly controls the temporal and timbral dimensions of music. The acoustic effects of sound filtered by the geometries, proportions, and materials of an architectural structure play a fundamental role in the way the sound is perceived and processed. The way in which sound is reflected essentially renders an architectural space a "large instrument . . . collecting sound, amplifying it and transmitting it elsewhere."[12]

A wide range of acoustic variation and a great deal of sonic subtlety define how a given room "treats" a sound within its space. However, a gross binary distinction can be made between the acoustic clarity of a sound and the degree to which the signal is heard as blurred. In architecture maximizing acoustic clarity is key in designing spaces in which speech is intelligible.[13] In music, the degree to which the sound is obscured by reflection and resonance accounts for a great deal of how that sound is perceived. The polarities of acoustical clarity and sonic obfuscation have been determinants in the development of ritual and cultural practices and styles. Consideration of the architectural and environmental conditions that contain the experience of sound is a critical and underexplored aspect of how humans engage with both musical and ritual sound. Empirical studies of aesthetic and affective responses to sound, whether eliciting calm or awe, transcendence or chills, must consider the key role of architecture in generating deep affective response to music. This is the central premise of our research.

We approach this research with particular focus on sacred spaces and the sacred music of these spaces that is often described as *awesome*. Our core research questions are:

- What role does architecture play in evoking deeply affective aesthetic responses to sound?
- What are the underlying principles in which musical and ritual sounds modulated by the physical spaces in which they are created, transmitted, and perceived elicit powerful aesthetic or spiritual responses in listeners or congregants?

12. Peter Zumthor, *Atmospheres: Architectural Environments, Surrounding Objects* (Basel: Birkhauser Architecture, 2006).

13. Vern O. Knudsen, "Architectural Acoustics," *Scientific American* 209, no. 5 (1963): 78–95; Robert S. Shankland, "The Development of Architectural Acoustics: The Application of the Science of Acoustics to Architectural Designs Has Produced Greatly Improved Halls for Both Speech and Music," *American Scientist* 60, no. 2 (1972): 201–9.

- Can we earmark those sonic attributes, and their associated physical and architectural features that, through the diffusion and dispersal of both musical and ritualistic sounds in space, create a sense of wonder and awe?

An additional question involves not only the role of the coloration imposed by the architectural acoustics, but also the role of the architecture itself on how sound is perceived and processed—that is, what is the effect of the visual environment on the affective nature of sound?

Like music, architecture affects people. Sacred architecture can trigger deep aesthetic responses. A wide range of emotions are used to describe responses to sacred architecture, including admiration, beauty, delight, goose bumps, aesthetic chills, fear, dizziness, romance, or hope.[14] Some monumental structures evoke a sense of awe (generally the response to stimuli with a characterization of "vastness," or a thing larger than oneself compared to a particular frame of reference).[15] Awe promotes a sense of the spiritual,[16] of "oneness" with the world,[17] and alters one's sense of time.[18] Among the factors that trigger a sense of awe are height and a perceived contradiction to the law of gravity. Schopenhauer described the interior of Gothic churches with "the groined vaulting borne by slender, crystalline, aspiring pillars, raised high aloft, and, all burden having disappeared, promising eternal security, impresses the mind."[19]

Music and architecture share roles in evoking spirituality. Music is transitory, ephemeral, and intangible; it affects our aesthetic feeling. Architecture is voluminous, stationary, and material. At times, it alters our sense of relative size. Somehow, in their interplay, a sense of the spiritual sometimes emerges. Thus, we add the following questions to our research agenda:

14. Yannick Joye and Jan Verpooten, "An Exploration of the Functions of Religious Monumental Architecture from a Darwinian Perspective," *Review of General Psychology* 17, no. 1 (2013): 53–68.

15. Dacher Keltner and Jonathan Haidt, "Approaching Awe, a Moral, Spiritual, and Aesthetic Emotion," *Cognition and Emotion* 17 (2003): 297–314.

16. Vassilis Saroglou, Coralie Buxant, and Jonathan Tilquin, "Positive Emotions as Leading to Religion and Spirituality," *Journal of Positive Psychology* 3 (2008): 165–73.

17. Michelle N. Shiota, Dacher Keltner, and Amanda Mossman, "The Nature of Awe: Elicitors, Appraisals, and Effects on Self-Concept," *Cognition & Emotion* 21, no. 5 (2007): 944–63.

18. Melanie Rudd, Kathleen D. Vohs, and Jennifer Aaker, "Awe Expands People's Perception of Time, Alters Decision Making, and Enhances Well-Being," *Psychological Science* 23 (2012): 1130–36.

19. Arthur Schopenhauer, *The World as Will and Idea*, trans. R. B. Haldane and J. Kemp (London: 1883; reprint, Routledge and Kegan Paul, 1964), 3:191.

- Why do some of us, when certain music is played, and when we are in certain architectural structures, feel like we are in the presence of majesty, of something overpowering, awe-inspiring, reverential?
- How does music interact with visual perception of architectural space to engender a feeling of the transcendent? What aspect of the acoustics of sacred spaces induces spiritual feelings? Is it measurable? Is it replicable?

We approach these questions from a perceptual and cognitive orientation in which acoustical models generated from analyses of site recordings provide methods and materials for experiments in perception and cognition. We propose the following underlying assumptions:

1. Each architectural space has an acoustic signature that can be captured and analyzed.
2. A computational analysis of sonic reflections and resonance will reveal particular acoustic features of sacred structures. For example, in spaces of great tranquility, we predict a lower spectral centroid which reduces the perceived brightness of sound. In spaces appreciated for grandeur we predict complex patterns of sound reflection and extensive decay times, which exaggerate a building's scale.
3. Computational modeling of sacred acoustic signatures can be used in experiments to study why certain acoustic-architecture interactions cause some listeners to experience the numinous.
4. Some acoustic signatures regularly produce aesthetic characteristics unconsciously exploited by performers or composers of sacred ritual music.

During the data collection phase of our research, we have been capturing the acoustic signatures of selected sacred spaces and acquiring appropriate musical excerpts to use as experiment stimuli. With the acoustic measurements we build computational models and mathematically analyze them to characterize distinct attributes and determine commonalities. Convolving the recording of a strategically placed sound source (typically a speaker playing a sine sweep, or a loud impulse such as a balloon pop) with a measured characterization of how the human ear receives a sound from a location (known as a head related transfer function, or HRTF), the acoustic features and characteristics of a measured space can be applied to any sound. Such re-creations of how a sound in a measured space (called an auralization) have provided new theories about musical performance practices,[20] and are

20. Braxton Boren, "Computational Acoustic Musicology," *Digital Scholarship in the Humanities* 34 no. 4 (2019): 707–15.

currently being created as a preservation method in re-creating the acoustics of lost or significantly altered sites such as the sounds of Byzantium,[21] or those of the cathedral of Notre Dame prior to the recent catastrophic fire.[22] With sufficient knowledge of the size and geometries that comprise a structure, along with absorption and scattering coefficients of the materials of surfaces within the structure, an acoustical model can be approximated by computing an impulse response (IR). This allows for the creation of virtual acoustic auralizations of lost and inaccessible sites.

Using the auralizations, we design experiments to determine the nature of the interaction between acoustics, architectural space, and human judgment and feeling. Our experiments test auditory response to musical excerpts subjected to digital filtering created with our computational models. We then add high-resolution imagery of the sacred sites we use based upon photogrammetric and LIDAR (Light Detection and Ranging) scans of the structures we measured. We developed and implemented a novel method of presenting virtual acoustic environments in free space (that is, not constrained by headphones).[23] This system (called Chamber for Augmented Virtual and Interactive Audio Realities or CAVIAR) allows us to process our experimental stimuli, as well as to virtually place the subject within the acoustics of any of the sites we measured and modeled.[24]

In addition to our goal of characterizing deeply affective responses in listeners, we observe and test how musicians are affected by the acoustics of the sacred spaces for which they compose and in which they perform, specifically, how they adapt in subtle ways to the resonance, reverberation, and reflectance that make them unique.

Across millennia and cultures, structures have been constructed to house ritual and sonic practices including oration, chanting and music. The sounds that were designed and created for these spaces adapted to, and perhaps influenced,

21. Spyridon Antonopoulos et al., "Soundscapes of Byzantium," *Speculum* 92, no. 1 (2017).

22. Julien De Muynke et al., "Ears of the Past, an Inquiry into the Sonic Memory of the Acoustics of Notre-Dame before the Fire of 2019," *Journal of Cultural Heritage* 56 (2022): 130–37. For an interactive article with spatial sound, see Madeleine Schwartz et al., "A Cathedral of Sound," *New York Times* (March 3, 2023), https://www.nytimes.com/interactive/2023/03/03/magazine/notre-dame-cathedral-acoustics-sound.html.

23. J. S. Abel, E. F. Callery, and E. K. Canfield-Dafilou, "A Feedback Canceling Reverberator," in *Proceedings of the Digital Audio Effects Conference*, Aveiro, Portugal, 2018; E. K. Canfield-Dafilou et al., "A Method for Studying Interactions between Music Performance and Rooms with Real-Time Virtual Acoustics," in *Proceedings of the 146th Audio Engineering Society Convention*, Dublin, 2019; E. F. Callery, J. S. Abel, and K. S. Spratt, "Synthesizing Reverberation Impulse Responses from Audio Signals: Auto-Reverberation and Interactive Environments," in *Proceedings of the 151th Audio Engineering Society Convention*, Las Vegas, 2021.

24. J. S. Abel and Eoin Callery, Networked audio auralization and feedback cancellation system and method, US Patent 11589150B2, filed November 18, 2020, and issued February 2, 2023.

the acoustical characteristics of these structures. While some structures are purposed for speech or music, others, such as churches, include both speaking as well as singing. Lecturing and sermonizing demand acoustic clarity to render the speech intelligible. Much music, in particular vocal music, is sonically enriched by reverberation. The delicate and shifting balances between acoustical clarity and intentional sonic blur reflect divergent tastes, varying religious priorities, and evolving aesthetic ideals of particular cultures and subcultures. Performance practices affecting the transmission and reception of music change in tandem with architectural modifications.

Beyond this, we seek to understand the perceptual and cognitive effects of architectural acoustics in general, and in the interactions of sound and space in sensing the unfathomable. Resonance, reflection, and decay filter a sound, rendering it into an object that could be beautiful or irritating, transcendent or disconcerting.[25]

Despite a wide-ranging variety of architectural styles and plans, many sacred structures share acoustical features whose complex geometric structures and use of reflective materials compromise intelligibility and reduce the clarity of auditory signals. Cathedrals create imposing volumes whose play with light and height project a sense of awe. The sense of mystery is amplified by the highly reverberant acoustics which evoke a sense of timelessness.

The empirical goal of our initial research thrust was to measure behavioral responses to auditory stimuli (specifically excerpts of sacred music) recorded under near-anechoic conditions (that is, with no audible reverberation) when heard in various acoustical modifications that accurately simulate the acoustics of specific places that we measured and modeled.

We next added a visual component to our experiment; specifically, using virtual reality, we placed the subject within various architectural spaces. While in pilot studies our expectation that the combined effect of visual and auditory stimuli would amplify the affective response was confirmed, we observed a striking effect resulting from *sensory integration confusion* (that is, when audition and vision each justify different judgments of distance or volume).

We hypothesize that cross-modal confusion has the capacity to elicit temporal and spatial ambiguities that may be factors in the sense of timelessness and transcendence associated with moments of awe. Specifically, we propose a sensory mismatch between auditory estimates of size and shape and visual estimates based on observing the architectural space from whence the sound and music are heard.

25. Regula Qureshi, "How Does Music Mean? Embodied Memories and the Politics of Affect in the Indian 'Sarangi,'" *American Ethnologist* 27, no. 4 (2000): 805–38.

Much of my research has aimed to gain empirical aesthetic insights using real-world stimuli and listening situations. Along the way, I became increasingly cognizant of the crucial role of room acoustics on the way music is created and received. Templeton Religion Trust provided an opportunity to develop methods to study this phenomenon.

Great cathedrals are places of splendor and awe. Soaring spires, majestic naves, and imposing domes evoke awe. Plays of light and darkness evoke mystery, and the reverberation in the space can create a sense of timelessness.[26] The residue of decaying sound can confuse contradicting percepts of size and spatial orientation.

Studies of musically evoked frisson[27] provided insights into deeply affective musical experiences,[28] and recent studies on the neuroaesthetics of architecture[29] argue for further research into affective responses to buildings. However, to my knowledge, no research considers the spiritually transformative role of the integration of music and architecture. We hope our experiments will contribute to determining the nature of the interaction between acoustics, architectural space, and human judgment and feeling.

Our most recent publication[30] describes three projects that demonstrate the breadth and scope of our work, particularly methods of integrating virtual reality with virtual acoustics. We describe how we acquire, analyze, and re-create sounds with examples of our studies of Chauvet, a necropolis in Saqqara, and the Ospedaletto in Venice.

Our initial goal was to study deep affective response to music by identifying and measuring behavioral response to ecologically valid auditory stimuli (specifically excerpts of sacred music from fifteenth- to eighteenth-century Italy) heard under

26. Scott R. Reidel, *Acoustics in the Worship Space* (St. Louis, MO: Concordia, 1986); Jürgen Meyer, *Kirchenakustik* (Frankfurt: Verlag Erwin Bochinsky, 2003).

27. Harrison and Loui, "Thrills, Chills, Frissons, and Skin Orgasms."

28. Stange and Taylor (2008) characterize the commonality between mystical and aesthetic experience in terms of "1) a feeling of highly abnormal intensity to the experience; 2) a deep sense of the profundity of the experience; 3) an inability to adequately express the experience in words; 4) a feeling of unity with all; 5) a feeling that all is as it should be; and 6) an altered perception of time." Ken Stange and Shelley Taylor, "Relationship of Personal Cognitive Schemas to the Labeling of a Profound Emotional Experience as Religious-Mystical or Aesthetic," *Empirical Studies of the Arts: Journal of the International Association of Empirical Aesthetics* 26, no. 1 (2008): 40.

29. Alex Coburn, Oshin Vartanian, and Anjan Chatterjee, "Buildings, Beauty, and the Brain: A Neuroscience of Architectural Experience," *Journal of Cognitive Neuroscience* 29 (2017): 1–11.

30. Luna E. Valentin, F. Farzanah Murakami, and Jonathan Berger, "Exploring the Past with Virtual Acoustics and Virtual Reality," *Proceedings of the 2023 International Immersive Audio Conference (I3DA 2023)*, Bologna, Italy.

varying acoustic manipulations. The stimuli were recorded in near-anechoic conditions (that is, with no perceptible reverberation). In the experiment subjects heard the stimuli both in their original "dry" state (i.e., with no reverberation) and acoustically modified by adding reverberation based upon acoustical models of specific architectural spaces to the music using a process called convolution. By adding computationally modeled reverberation of sites studied in our site visits (including Byzantine, Gothic, and Renaissance churches, a paleolithic cave, and a mosque) we could observe how architectural design features affect the music, and how these adaptations influence listener responses. Our underlying objective was to identify, qualify, and attempt to quantify the sense of awe (that is, the emotion that arises when one encounters something so strikingly vast that it provokes a need to update one's mental schemas[31]) reported by congregants and audience members while hearing music.

To identify perceptual thresholds marked by altering acoustic conditions we asked instrumental musicians and singers to perform musical excerpts using the acoustic conditions but varying them progressively. We observed precisely when the changes caused them to deviate from the tempo indicating when they became conscious of the altered acoustical condition. In addition to being a useful indicator, this method raised an important musicological issue relating to historically informed performance practices, an area of music research that, through archival study of primary sources, documents historically accurate performance practices such as types of embellishment, number and type of instrument, methods of execution, etc.

Among the least studied aspects of historically informed performance practice is the selection of tempo in performance. Recognizing the effect of reverberation time on tempo choice, the question of how architectural space influences tempo decisions arose. Among the examples we are currently investigating is the sacred music of Florentine composer Marco Da Gagliano (1582–1643). Gagliano composed works for two principal churches in Florence, the Cathedral of Santa Maria del Fiori (the Duomo) and the Basilica of San Lorenzo. These two churches have remarkably distinct acoustic signatures. The reverberation decay times between the Gothic style Duomo and the Renaissance style San Lorenzo differ significantly. The same work would sound radically different in each of the two churches, and the degree of tonal blur sets a boundary of coherence based upon these decay times. Thus, the general question, what was the role of architecture on musical tempo, raises two significant corresponding questions. First, Is musical style, particularly in terms of rhythm and tempo, influenced by architecture? And second, more specifically, Might the distinct sonic differences imposed upon the music by the two churches indicate the intended church for a specific work?

31. Devin M. Gill et al., "The Perceived Duration of Vast Spaces Is Mediated by Awe," *Attention, Perception, and Psychophysics* 84 (2022): 2562–81.

Analyzing the music from the church archives, we classify the music according to rhythmic complexity, vocal range and density, to conjecture about which architectural structure best fits the work. Models created from in-situ studies assume accessibility and historical integrity of the architectural structure under study. However, the vast majority of historically and culturally significant sites are inaccessible or no longer extant. To address this, we adapted methods of creating virtual acoustic models from archival documents and architectural plans. These models generate approximations of how a sound would have been altered and processed by the imagined space.

This approach piqued the interest of several archaeologists, who typically reimagine architectural structures that are in ruins based upon limited evidence. Working with a prominent Egyptologist, we created an acoustic model of two funerary sites in third dynasty Saqqara. Modeling the inside of the tomb, the entry path, and the outer platform allowed us to re-create the approximate sounds created both inside and out, as heard within and outside of the tomb. Although (aside from wall paintings of musical instruments) nothing is known about the ritual music of the time, archaeologists created hypotheses of how sound may have played a role in ancient burial rituals.[32]

Although both invisible and ephemeral, sound is at the core of human social interaction including communications, ritual, and music. It is inconceivable to imagine cultures or to reimagine ancient human social structures without considering the role of sound.[33]

Throughout time humans have endowed special significance to places with specific acoustical properties.[34] These signature characteristics were, as suggested by artistic and textual evidence, integral to ritual. More generally, the ephemerality of sound challenges any definitive statement regarding aural communications. No sooner than a sound is created and, in the absence of recording, disappears without a trace. Measuring, modeling, and reproducing the acoustic signature of a site allow us to conjecture as to the nature of sonic environments in past epochs.

32. Luna E. Valentin et al., "Exploring the Past with Virtual Acoustics and Virtual Reality," *Proceedings of the 2023 International Immersive Audio Conference (I3DA 2023)*, Bologna, Italy.

33. Rupert Till, "Sound Archaeology: A Study of the Acoustics of Three World Heritage Sites, Spanish Prehistoric Painted Caves, Stonehenge, and Paphos Theatre," *Acoustics* 1, no. 3 (2019): 661–92.

34. Jose Valenzuela, Margarita Díaz-Andreu, and Carles Escera, "Psychology Meets Archaeology: Psychoarchaeoacoustics for Understanding Ancient Minds and Their Relationship to the Sacred," *Frontiers in Psychology* 11 (2020).

9

Practice-Based Investigations of Art and the Sacred at the Edinburgh Festival Fringe

Caleb Froehlich and Alison Jack

Our project at the University of Edinburgh, "Investigating Art and the Sacred at the Edinburgh Festival Fringe," was one of several interdisciplinary studies in the theological aesthetics stream of Templeton Religion Trust's Art Seeking Understanding (TRT; ASU) program. This project was empirical, involving quantitative and qualitative research into peoples' experience of art at the Festival of Sacred Arts (FSA) during the Edinburgh Festival Fringe in 2021 and 2022. It was also conceptual, as it involved theological and philosophical reflection that drew on this empirical data.

Within the broader field of theological aesthetics, several theologians[1] and some religion scholars[2] consciously or unconsciously reflect the claims of *aesthetic cognitivism*,[3] asserting that more than simply offering emotional and aes-

1. See, for example, Douglas Hedley, "Revelation Imagined: Fiction, Truth, and Transformation" in *Theology, Aesthetics, and Culture: Responses to the Work of David Brown*, ed. Robert MacSwain and Taylor Worley (Oxford: Oxford University Press, 2012), 79–88; Ben Quash, *Found Theology: History, Imagination and the Holy Spirit* (London: Bloomsbury, 2013); David Brown, *Divine Generosity and Human Creativity: Theology through Symbol, Painting and Architecture*, ed. Christopher R. Brewer and Robert MacSwain (London: Routledge, 2017); Paul Fiddes, "The Trinity, Modern Art, and Participation in God" in *Christian Theology and the Transformation of Natural Religion: From Incarnation to Sacramentality—Essays in Honour of David Brown*, ed. Christopher R. Brewer (Leuven: Peeters, 2018), 81–100.

2. See, for example, Frank Burch Brown, "Musical Ways of Being Religious" in *The Oxford Handbook of Religion and the Arts*, ed. Frank Burch Brown (Oxford: Oxford University Press, 2014), 109–29; Allen Speight, "Religion, Art, and the Emergence of Absolute Spirit in Phenomenology" in *The Oxford Handbook of Hegel*, ed. Dean Moyar (Oxford: Oxford University Press, 2017), 148–65.

3. See, for example, Catherine Elgin, "Art in the Advancement of Understanding," *Philosophical Journal* 39, no. 1 (2002): 1–12; Berys Gaut, "Art and Knowledge" in *The Oxford Handbook of Aesthetics*, ed. Jerrold Levinson (Oxford: Oxford University Press, 2003), 436–50; Gordon Gra-

thetic pleasure, art is valuable because it can promote new spiritual knowledge and deepen understanding of spiritual realities.[4] According to these scholars, artworks can "help break down barriers between the invisible world of the divine and our own,"[5] becoming sources of revelation and transcendence[6] by representing and transmitting theological knowledge[7] and leading, in some instances, to greater insight into the spiritual realities of this world.[8] This seems intuitive, especially if the artwork makes explicit reference to a religious context and subject matter. However, while many scholars in theological aesthetics largely agree that religious art contains "a strong didactic component"[9] and may encourage "new thinking about God, providing deeper understanding,"[10] there remains a critical need to verify these claims empirically through an analysis of everyday people's lived experiences of artworks.

Our project,[11] led by Alison Jack, directly addressed this need by examining the experiences of artists, performers, participants and audiences in the context of

---

ham, *Philosophy of the Arts: An Introduction to Aesthetics*, 3rd edition (New York: Routledge, 2005); Christoph Baumberger, "Art and Understanding: In Defence of Aesthetic Cognitivism" in *Bilder sehen: Perspektiven der Bildwissenschaft*, ed. Mark Greenlee et al. (Regensburg: Schnell & Steiner, 2013), 41–67. Aesthetic cognitivism makes an epistemic claim and an aesthetic claim: (epistemic) art can be a source of knowledge and understanding and (aesthetic) this function partly determines the artwork's aesthetic value. See Baumberger, "Art and Understanding," 1.

4. For example, Hedley, "Revelation Imagined," 84–85.

5. David Brown, *God and Grace of Body: Sacrament in the Ordinary* (Oxford: Oxford University Press, 2007), 237.

6. For example, David Brown, "In the Beginning There Was Image," "The Annunciation as True Fiction," and "Artists on the Trinity," in Brewer and MacSwain, *Divine Generosity and Human Creativity*, 7–22, 105–12, 130–49; Trevor Hart, *Between Image and Word: Theological Engagements with Imagination, Language and Literature* (London: Routledge, 2013); Frank Burch Brown, "Musical Ways of Being Religious," 109–29; Christopher R. Brewer, "'Surely the Lord Is in This Place': Jacob's Ladder in Painting, Contemporary Sculpture and Installation Art," in *The Moving Text: Interdisciplinary Perspectives on David Brown and the Bible*, ed. Garrick V. Allen, Christopher R. Brewer, and Dennis F. Kinlaw III (London: SCM, 2018), 107–21; Gordon Graham, *The Re-enchantment of the World: Art vs. Religion* (Oxford: Oxford University Press, 2007).

7. See, for example, Quash, *Found Theology*, xvii, 93–94; Gesa Thiessen, "Artistic Imagination and Religious Faith" in Brown, *Oxford Handbook of Religion and the Arts*, 77–90; Speight, "Religion, Art, and the Emergence of Absolute Spirit," 148–65; Fiddes, "Trinity, Modern Art, and Participation in God," 81–98; Natasha O'Hear, "Understanding John's Visions: Unlocking the Insights of Revelation's Visual History," in Allen, Brewer, and Kinlaw, *Moving Text*, 122–42.

8. Graham, *Re-enchantment of the World*, 59.

9. Hedley, "Revelation Imagined," 85.

10. Brown, *Divine Generosity and Human Creativity*, 38.

11. For a video and information about the project, see Alison Jack, "Researching Art as More Than Pleasure," https://tinyurl.com/4y4vj56p.

a Sacred Arts Festival, asking whether these experiences extended and enriched their understanding of spiritual reality. To do so, we used a twofold methodology: (1) we conducted in-depth interviews with twenty-four participants who varied in age, background, gender, and faith-commitment who attended festival events in music, visual art, iconography, dance, theater, poetry, and architecture about their experiences of these artworks. We supplemented this data with around seventy responses from online and in-person surveys with festival audiences. (2) We also engaged in theological and philosophical reflection with a symposium of eleven academics and practitioners from a range of disciplines and artistic media drawing on the data gathered at the FSA and analyzed by Caleb Froehlich, the project's postdoctoral research associate.

In this article, we will summarize the project and its findings. First, we will describe our key findings and, in retrospect, reflect on what we would have done differently with the project as a whole. We will then outline key questions which emerged from this research and plans to pursue some of these questions in another funded project examining peace-building arts and how they might enhance understanding of spiritual reality through the experience of and building of peace. Finally, we will relate our research to the more general concerns/goals of the ASU program, describing how it contributes to the progress of this strategy more generally.

Project Findings

Did the experiences of artists, performers, participants, and audiences with art in the context of the FSA extend their knowledge and understanding of spiritual reality? For our study participants, the answer to this question was generally yes. In fact, many of these experiences of sacred art corresponded closely to several of the ways Christoph Baumberger describes artworks as contributing to knowledge and understanding more generally.[12] These included: creating new spiritual categories which reorganize knowledge domains; altering perspectives of the spiritual by drawing attention to previously unnoticed features or concepts; raising new questions about the spiritual for further exploration; and offering a phenomenal knowledge by broadening spiritual experience and encompassing emotions participants had previously never undergone or felt. In many instances, these different ways artworks extended or enhanced spiritual understanding overlapped or were interwoven in participants' experiences of art at the festival.

In listening to these participant accounts, however, we were surprised to find that the spiritual significance or non-significance of an artwork had as much or

12. Baumberger, "Art and Understanding," 41–67.

even more to do with elements external to the artwork than with the artwork itself. This was especially clear in the FSA in August 2021, which took place within the context of the wider COVID pandemic. These participants had just come out of lockdown and, for some of them, their physical proximity to other people in these live festival settings distracted them from any kind of spiritually meaningful engagement. One visitor, for example, stated that she was "a little stressed because I wasn't sure how people would be masked up" and did not "feel that connected to what was going on" in a performance of Haydn's *Seven Last Words from the Cross* because "there was a man next to me who wasn't wearing a mask, so I was stressed and I kept looking at him and he was coughing."[13] Similarly, another participant remarked that a vestments exhibition talk she attended "wasn't really that spiritual to be honest . . . because of the pandemic, I didn't want to squeeze in with all the people, so I just sort of stood back."[14]

For other participants, however, the live setting of the FSA encouraged spiritual engagement with the artworks. For instance, one of the participants who had emerged from the 2021 lockdown remarked that the music performances "brought people together" out of isolation and created a space with a "spiritual ambience, an enriching spiritual ambience for me to go in." Another 2021 participant similarly stated that the "shared experience of the music or the artwork of the embroideries" connected the audience: "We're all tied together from that shared experience. So that shared experience is extremely spiritual."[15] Post-lockdown participants in the FSA in August 2022 also found the live setting of the artworks spiritually significant. One even shared that, for him, the spiritual impact of the FSA was "not so much the art itself," but "the community of it." The "spiritual community" of the festival was "alien" for him and engaging with art in the sacral context of the festival prompted him to consider "spiritual matters. Things I just haven't considered for years and years."[16]

The non-artwork elements participants drew on were not merely the wider social context, but the immediate material contexts in conjunction with their own backgrounds with religion, both positive and negative. From a negative background, for example, one visitor shared that she "didn't feel a sacred connection"

13. Meera, *Art and the Sacred* [Interview transcript] (August 31, 2021; September 8, 2022): https://doi.org/10.7488/8e0e7b8d-c7a3-4935-b42a-f043669153b3.

14. Tracey, *Art and the Sacred* [Interview transcript] (September 14, 2021; August 31, 2022): https://doi.org/10.7488/8e0e7b8d-c7a3-4935-b42a-f043669153b3.

15. Tyler, *Art and the Sacred* [Interview transcript] (September 2, 2021): https://doi.org/10.7488/8e0e7b8d-c7a3-4935-b42a-f043669153b3.

16. Dale, *Art and the Sacred* [Interview transcript] (September 2, 2022): https://doi.org/10.7488/8e0e7b8d-c7a3-4935-b42a-f043669153b3.

with the *Seven Last Words* performance because the sacral setting of the chapel in which it was performed together with the poetry readings interspersed between the sonatas reminded her of "Christmas mass," which she was forced to attend as a child in a Catholic School despite her Hindu upbringing.[17] Similarly, from someone with a more positive background, one visitor who identified as a Christian minister stated that "the setting [of Saint Michael and All Saints Church] didn't quite work" for a dance performance he attended. The minister explained the juxtaposition of the setting and performance in this way: "The lady who did the dancing, the belly dancing, was sort of dancing right in front of an altar in a Roman Catholic Church. And for me, that setting just didn't match, um . . . I just got really distracted. For me there was just a discrepancy between seeing what effectively was belly dancer in front of, you know, the altar where . . . the Eucharist is served."[18] While it may seem counterintuitive, what became clear from these and other participant experiences was that positive backgrounds with religion seemed just as influential as negative backgrounds in steering participants away from any theological/spiritual engagement with certain artworks.

However, these varied backgrounds with religion also primed visitors for more meaningful spiritual engagements with FSA artworks. For instance, one visitor said that while he was used to "hearing stories [about Jesus] growing up," the fact that *Hope Rises*, a passion play he attended, was a "promenade performance" made the stories "more real" and "come alive" for him.[19] Similarly, a doctoral theology student remarked that he found the performance of a "Marian hymn" spiritually meaningful because of his theological education: "I was able to, I guess, read my theological education back into that hymn and to the whole experience throughout . . . I was pulling a lot of my own experience, what I understood of God, of Scripture, into the text. Which I'm not sure whether someone without my theological education would have appreciated."[20] These accounts suggested to us that participants' spiritual understanding as a result of these artworks was manifestly determined by what art historian Ernst Gombrich calls the "beholder's share," or the inner and outer resources audiences bring to their engagements with an artwork, and by which they actively "complete" their experience of the work.[21]

17. Meera, *Art and the Sacred.*

18. Hendrik, *Art and the Sacred* [Interview transcript] (September 14, 2022): https://doi.org/10.7488/8e0e7b8d-c7a3-4935-b42a-f043669153b3.

19. Isaac, *Art and the Sacred* [Interview transcript] (September 1, 2022): https://doi.org/10.7488/8e0e7b8d-c7a3-4935-b42a-f043669153b3.

20. Kevin, *Art and the Sacred* [Interview transcript] (August 31, 2022): https://doi.org/10.7488/8e0e7b8d-c7a3-4935-b42a-f043669153b3.

21. E. H. Gombrich, *Art and Illusion: A Study in the Psychology of Pictorial Representation*, 5th ed. (New York: Phaidon, 1993), 155.

In this way, festival visitors became active participants in the artwork's spiritual functioning.[22]

One of the clearest examples of this active participation was one participant's engagement with a performance of Haydn's *Seven Last Words of Christ.* He arrived at the performance after having just come from mass at St. Mary's Cathedral where they were celebrating the Feast of the Assumption and, as a result, "was associating everything with Mary that day." This led him to reflect on "the life of Christ with Mary during peaceful times leading up to his ministry and crucifixion" during the "Passiontide piece," rather than on the crucifixion itself. He explained his interaction in this way:

> In my view, I saw this wonderful photo, or this banner or something, a picture of this very solemn looking Madonna and Child and then in the stained glass to the right of me on the right side of the church, if you enter into it, there were some Latin quotes in the stained glass that I think were very much related to how I received all of the music. . . . One of the quotes read *super astra spero*, I hope beyond the stars, I think. And that one is very much related to encountering Christ in the *Seven Last Words*. It gave primacy to the divine.[23]

These various elements—the mass leading into the performance, the stained glass images and quotations in the setting of St. Vincent's Chapel—became resources he brought to his interpretation of the music, shaping the performance into what he described as a "spiritual experience in its full sense."[24] Other visitors also drew on a wide range of external and internal resources in the constitution of spiritual insight, ranging from their own histories and experiences leading into the events to social/material elements in the church settings, such as audiences, windows, texts, altars, and the artists and art tools they were using at events. One participant even shared that the spiritual significance of the FSA for her was not so much the images and music of festival events, but the musician's "interaction with the strings . . . directing notes . . . the eminence of the sound afterwards . . . and the interplay between liminal space just before the sound then released and let loose." These interactions became the participant's resources for thinking dif-

22. John Shearman, *Only Connect . . . Art and the Spectator in the Italian Renaissance* (Princeton: Princeton University Press, 1992), 57.

23. Gerard, *Art and the Sacred* [Interview transcript] (September 22, 2021): https://doi.org/10.7488/8e0e7b8d-c7a3-4935-b42a-f043669153b3.

24. Gerard, *Art and the Sacred.*

ferently about the "tensions of the world and the divine" in Christ's incarnation and connecting her own artistic practice to her spirituality.[25]

What became increasingly apparent when interviewing participants about their experiences of artworks at the FSA was that, in bringing these different external elements into their interpretive engagements with the works, the contributions to their spiritual understanding involved what we described as a "reciprocal interpretive interplay" between participants and the artworks within their broader and more immediate social/material contexts. We found that these different enhancements and extensions to participants' understanding emerged through a process of reflexive construction—namely, the knowledge and experience participants brought to their engagements with the artworks (i.e., the beholder's share) was both shaping and simultaneously being shaped by the artworks within their particular church settings in the constitution of new spiritual insight.

We might recall, for instance, the aforementioned participant who came to the performance of the *Seven Last Words* from a celebration of the Feast of the Assumption. This initial reflection on Mary seems to draw his attention to the Madonna and Child image and Latin script next to his seat, and these together colored his interpretation of the Passiontide piece as "the life of Christ with Mary during peaceful times leading up to his ministry and crucifixion." Likewise, the music of the *Seven Last Words* performance seemed to simultaneously color the particular way he viewed these other elements as lending themselves to that interpretation. He stated that he was surprised by how "uncharacteristically not sad" the music was and "may have been more surprised hearing that on . . . Good Friday than hearing this on the Assumption." It is telling that he wrote down a description of his emotional response to the music during the performance as "loving."[26]

Another clear example of this reflexive construction was a minister viewing the acclaimed Phoebe Traquair murals in the former Catholic Apostolic Church, now transformed into a night club. He shared that before encountering the murals, he had been thinking about "Christian universalism," but had not given much serious consideration to "universal salvation" because it was "more on the fringes of . . . Orthodox Christianity." However, upon looking at the murals, he was surprised to discover that hell was missing from scenes of the last judgment. He was also drawn to an image of Jesus's parable of the "five foolish virgins lying asleep" and an image directly below this one depicting the account of Jesus knocking at the door from the book of Revelation, which he connected as "Jesus was standing and

25. Nancy, *Art and the Sacred* [Interview transcript] (September 6, 2021): https://doi.org/10.7488/8e0e7b8d-c7a3-4935-b42a-f043669153b3.

26. Gerard, *Art and the Sacred.*

knocking at the door . . . to wake them up." The minister described the impact of these images in this way:

> I just walked in a church, not expecting any of this. And then just sort of seeing, like, this lady, this extraordinary lady who had painted all these murals. And it almost felt like she was, you know, like we were in conversation through those paintings. . . . I thought it was just to help me to see, hey, [universalism] is not something that is necessarily on the fringes. And it's also not something that you necessarily have to . . . it's a genuine belief in how things will end according to the Christian story that can be a very powerful and joyful expression of your faith. And that became very visual to me there.[27]

This visual "conversation" with the artist did not simply provide him with a new perspective, it also seemed to heighten the way he engaged with the idea of universal salvation on a cognitive level. This corresponds with Baumberger's description of cognitive contributions that reach beyond knowledge, improving cognitive capacities and enabling participants to grasp connections between things they already knew or believed. Within this particular encounter, however, the visual conversation refined his previous, dismissive understanding of universal salvation, making him a "hopeful universalist," not in the sense of "I hope it's the case, but I'm not sure it may be," but "more towards hopeful in the sense that I actually think that's probably how the story will end." Through this process, it seemed this reciprocal process with the murals, what he described as a "conversation," contributed to his spiritual understanding in a way that reached beyond mere spiritual knowledge; it transformed his spiritual outlook, changing the way he engaged cognitively with his own spiritual and religious beliefs, which could perhaps extend into other areas and realities in his life, spiritual or otherwise.

Project Publications

As a result of the symposium meetings and reflections on the data gathered at the FSA, a range of publications have been produced by the academics and artists involved and more are in process. Alison Jack's keynote address on "Poetry, Prayer and Praise" given to the Church Service Society in Edinburgh in May 2021 was subsequently published in their journal *The Record*.[28] Her article "'The Holy Space Ablaze': New Understandings of Spiritual Reality through Poetry and Music" has

27. Hendrik, *Art and the Sacred.*

28. Alison Jack, "Poetry, Prayer and Praise," *The Record* 56 (2021): 3–16.

been published in *Theology in Scotland*.[29] Both contributions explored some of the literary aspects of the Festival of Sacred Arts.

In addition to setting up the transcript database for the project,[30] the project website[31] and the "Art and the Sacred" podcast series,[32] Froehlich has written an article on "Assessing Sacred Art and Spiritual Understanding at the Edinburgh Fringe Festival," and is currently in the process of securing an academic publisher. He has also contributed a chapter in the collected volume *Art as Revelation* (forthcoming with Open Book Publishers) entitled "Art as Revelatory Means: Continuing the Creative Process," drawing on the project's findings at the Festival Fringe.

Also from an academic perspective, Gordon Graham has contributed a chapter, "Art Proper, Perfectionism, and the Sacred Arts," to an edited volume, *Imperfectionist Aesthetics in Art and Everyday Life*.[33] His contribution to the Catholic University of America's Symposium on Neurophenomenology and Sacred Architecture: Toward an Experimental Theological Aesthetics in March 2023, which was entitled "Spiritual Reality and Its Investigation," was published online.[34]

Several of the artists taking part in the project have produced publications of various kinds. Visual artist Peter Gardner has published a zine including photographs documenting people's interactions with their Peacemaker's Loom art installation, a theological reflection on the installation within a church written by Rev. Dr. Doug Gay, and reflections on the relationship between the art and understanding of spirituality by Gardner and Gardner.[35] Another of our visual artists, Carol Marples, has published an article for *Transpositions*, an award-winning online journal hosted by the Institute for Theology, Imagination, and the Arts at the University of St Andrews, based on her "7 Days: Art and the Sacred."[36]

Other artists have prepared material for publication and are in the process of securing a publisher. The poet Christine de Luca engaged with a visual artist, a film-maker and a theologian. This resulted in a film contextualizing the collaborative work between Christine and the artist Brigid Collins in the context of Dr. Neil's Garden, Duddingston, and a series of her ekphrastic poems written in

29. Alison Jack, "'The Holy Space Ablaze': New Understandings of Spiritual Reality through Poetry and Music," *Theology in Scotland* 29, no.1 (2022): 35–47.

30. "Investigating Art and the Sacred at the Edinburgh Festival Fringe—Interview Transcripts," https://doi.org/10.7488/8e0e7b8d-c7a3-4935-b42a-f043669153b3.

31. Online: https://tinyurl.com/mrxj47m4.

32. Online: https://tinyurl.com/yezbeu72.

33. Gordon Graham, "Art Proper, Perfectionism and the Sacred Arts," in *Imperfectionist Aesthetics in Art and Everyday Life*, ed. Peter Cheyne (London: Routledge, 2022), 54–65.

34. Online: https://tinyurl.com/57s9arfy.

35. Gardner and Gardner, Ciara Menzies and Doug Gay, *Peacemakers* (Self-published, 2023).

36. Carol Marples, "7 Days: Art and the Sacred," September 12, 2022, https://tinyurl.com/3k6z8k58.

response to Brigid's drawings and paintings of the plants and plant communities. Three theological reflections on these outputs and the relationship between the art and spiritual reality were written by the university chaplain, Kitty Whitear. Finally, Christine produced a reflective report on the experience of writing the poems and engaging with the chaplain's theological reflections. Christine is working with a publisher and hopes a book will result from the wealth of material produced.

The composer on the project, Harry Whalley, ran a workshop with musicians at St. Vincent's Chapel, "Understanding the Spiritual Intentions of the *Quartet for the End of Time* through Practice." He produced a transcript of these discussions as well as a recorded compositional response to the quartet, "Le Ton Beau De Marot." He plans to submit a paper based on his reflections on the process for the *Scottish Journal of Performance*.

Finally, four of the project's academics collaborated to run an "Art as Means (Not End)" workshop in the Hunter Lecture Theatre at the Edinburgh College of Art in August 2022, engaging with the findings of the project in a variety of contexts. Juliette MacDonald presented "Curating the Ineffable: Henri Matisse's Chapelle du Rosaire de Venice"; Caleb Froehlich presented "The Rothko Chapel as Process"; Carol Richardson presented "Getting It Together: The Ignatian Spiritual Exercises and the Purposes of Art in Sixteenth-Century Rome"; and Lisa McCormick presented "The Festival as Means (Not End)." The organizers are seeking a publisher for a volume based on these and the other contributions to the workshop.

Project Reconsiderations

While the project was a success overall, there were a few things we would have done differently to take full advantage of the research findings. The symposium, for instance, was generative of ideas and supportive to the research team; but the timescale for the project (two years, 2021 and 2022) was too short to really make in-depth use of the data produced at the FSA in symposium reflections. This was exacerbated by the first year of the research being conducted in 2021 while pandemic restrictions were still in place, limiting the possibilities for data collection—for example, we conducted audience surveys online rather than in-person that year. Moreover, the Fringe Festival takes place in August, which was very close to the end of our "project year." This meant that there was little time for analysis, synthesis, and interpretation of data from both years before the end of the project timeframe, even though we were granted a short extension by the Trust. The project would have benefited from another year, which would have contributed to data availability and more in-depth symposium engagement.

Emergent Questions

One of the most surprising discoveries from our investigation of artist, performer, and audience experiences of sacred art at the Edinburgh Festival Fringe was the prominence of the FSA's sacral settings in determining whether or not an artwork was spiritually significant to participants and contributed to their understanding of spiritual reality. Also prominent was the visitor's own expectations when entering these sacral spaces. This led us to recognize that there was a need for further empirical research on whether and how spiritual understanding is or is not extended or enriched in settings which ostensibly do not have sacred arts as their focus or make explicit reference to a religious context or subject matter. For instance, how might non-religious settings impact the way religious artworks are perceived and engaged with? Can non-religious works be spiritually significant and contribute to spiritual understanding, insight, and growth, whether performed in a sacred setting or not? If so, how is this best characterized? Does sacred art have a uniquely religious significance or are there ways in which all artistic work must be understood as directed toward the spiritual?

Jolyon Mitchell and Froehlich are currently working on another grant application which aims to explore these questions in relation to the use of the arts in and around international peace museums. There are well over one hundred peace museums around the world and different arts (e.g., paintings, drawings, wall art, murals, sculptures, photographs, banners, interactive displays, films, music, literature, drama, memorabilia, historical artifacts, and garden displays) are commonly used to educate, to inform, and to entertain. These museums employ the arts to explore themes such as the effects of war and conflict, peace movements, the lives of peacemakers and peace builders, pacifism, nuclear disarmament, the arms trade, the search for just peace, human rights, peace and ecology, and the relation between religion and peace. Religious or spiritual themes and symbols are commonplace in these artworks and peace settings, coming in many different forms, sometimes explicit and sometimes very implicit. We hope to investigate whether different kinds of art within these peace-making settings, through challenging and altering perceptions on conflict and violence, would also contribute new spiritual insight and growth for those who encounter them.

Project Findings and ASU Goals

Art Seeking Understanding aims to empirically test the central claims of aesthetic cognitivism—that is, that the special value of art is that it can be a source of knowledge and understanding, especially as this relates to spiritual realities and the discovery of new spiritual information. The focus of this kind of exploration lends itself to approaches which consider the cognitive value of artworks themselves, as we did at the start of our project, asking questions like, What spiritual qualities or meanings does an artwork "contain"? Is the work superficial or profound? Engaging or a turn-off? Beautiful or not? If the artwork itself displays a spiritual dimension or intent, does that mean that it communicates this quality to all who engage with it? Our study of participant experiences of sacred art at a Sacred Arts Festival in the Edinburgh Festival Fringe led us to recognize that this line of questioning is not sufficient in itself. We discovered that an artwork's contribution to a person's spiritual understanding is not necessarily something intrinsic to the artwork but is manifestly dependent on a variety of other factors outside the artwork itself, including, but not limited to, an individual's personal background in terms of spirituality and religion and, indeed, the broader and more immediate socio-material contexts in which they perceive and interpret the artwork. Moreover, we discovered that artworks function not as ends for understanding, but more often as means, extending interpretive possibilities and inviting further responses which continue to inform and reform participants' understandings of spiritual reality. This prompted us to consider different questions, like how might non-religious settings impact the spiritual significance of an artwork? And, given the prominence of people's background with spirituality and religion, can non-religious artworks in ostensibly secular settings (or, indeed, in sacred settings) have similar cognitive effects as sacred arts with explicit reference to religious context and subject matter? These are questions which require further empirical study.

Round 2 Grant Projects

10

The Power of Art to Build Understanding and Creativity

Pablo P. L. Tinio and Zorana Ivcevic

The scholarship on art experiences is vast. Empirical aesthetics—the interdisciplinary study of the nature of aesthetic experiences and behavior—is the second oldest field in psychology (after psychophysics).[1] However, researchers have yet to adequately describe and understand the thoughts and insights we have after engaging with art, such as when walking out of a museum, and have yet to document and explain changes in thinking after meaningful encounters with art. These experiences can be inspiring, spiritually enlightening, and contribute to well-being.

"Mirror to the World: The Power of Art to Build Understanding and Creativity" is a project situated within empirical aesthetics. Gustav Theodor Fechner conducted the first empirical aesthetics study when he systematically compared people's reactions to two paintings of the Madonna during an exhibition in Dresden in 1871, one of which was rumored to be by Holbein the Younger. Fechner hypothesized that greater preference for one version over the other would serve as evidence for the painting's authenticity. Fechner asked visitors which of the two paintings they found more appealing but, sadly, only 113 of 11,842 visitors completed his survey and many of the participants did not follow the instructions correctly.[2] As far as distinguishing the authenticity of the Madonnas based on visitor reactions, the findings were inconclusive. However, Fechner's study marked

1. William P. Seeley, "Philosophy of Art and Empirical Aesthetics: Resistance and Rapprochement," in *The Cambridge Handbook of the Psychology of Aesthetics and the Arts*, ed. Pablo P. L. Tinio and Jeffrey K. Smith (Cambridge: Cambridge University Press, 2014), 35–59.

2. Gustav Theodor Fechner, *Bericht über das auf der Dresdner Holbein-Ausstellung ausgelegte Album* (1872); Philip H. Marshall, James H. Shrader, James Worthen, Del Kahlstorf, Linda Brant, and Charles Pickeral, "Fechner Redux: A Comparison of the Holbein Madonnas," *Empirical Studies of the Arts* 13, no. 1 (1995): 17–24; and Marcos Nadal and Oshin Vartanian, "Empirical

the beginning of empirical aesthetics, and although his research method lacked experimental control and was largely ineffective in answering the question, it foretold the approach that empirical aesthetics researchers would employ in many decades to come.

Through the years, empirical aesthetics has experienced various phases, ups and downs of popularity in the scientific community, major debates, and identity crises, which is not unusual for a scientific field that crosses disciplinary lines. However, the last two decades have been marked by tremendous growth in the number of researchers entering the field, noteworthy findings, and formal organizational structures such as conferences, journals, and volumes dedicated to "the study of our experiences of the visual arts, music, literature, film, performances, architecture and design; our experiences of beauty and ugliness; our preferences and dislikes; and our everyday perceptions of things in our world."[3] Our project focused on visual arts—paintings, sculptures, conceptual works, and other artifacts that might be displayed as art in a home, museum, or public space.

Research in empirical aesthetics has led to many notable findings related to each of the three main components of the aesthetic experience: the artwork, the viewer, and the context in which the artwork is viewed. We briefly review prior work on each of these components in order to set our project within the larger context of scientific findings and methods. Based on these discussions, we identify limitations associated with the field's emphasis on measuring largely basic outcomes of art engagement, such as art viewers' liking and preferences for certain types of artworks. The "Mirror to the World" project addresses these shortcomings by capturing cognitive and emotional outcomes of art engagement including personally meaningful associations, existential or spiritual understandings and insights, intense emotional reactions, intellectual humility, and deep reflection about the human condition.

The Artwork

A major area of research in empirical aesthetics is centered on the effects that visual features have on judgments about preference, liking, and appeal toward a variety of stimuli, such as basic shapes, faces, and objects. Stimuli are varied in

---

Aesthetics: An Overview," in *The Oxford Handbook of Empirical Aesthetics*, ed. Marcos Nadal and Oshin Vartanian (Oxford: Oxford University Press, 2022), 3–38.

3. Pablo P. L. Tinio and Jeffrey K. Smith, introduction by the editors, Tinio and Smith, eds., *Cambridge Handbook of the Psychology of Aesthetics*, 3.

terms of symmetry,[4] complexity,[5] contrast,[6] contour,[7] and other low-level visual characteristics. Changes in these characteristics are easily made by the researcher. For example, the symmetry and complexity of an image composed of rectangles, triangles, and circles could be varied for the purpose of making experimentally controlled comparisons.[8] Unlike these basic stimuli, artworks are complex visual objects with features that have been developed by their creators through preliminary studies, experimentation, and ongoing refinements. As a result, artworks have largely been used in studies in an unmodified state, with a few exceptions where studies had elements in artworks moved or altered. However, these modifications often lead to significant changes in how the works are perceived and evaluated, with participants seemingly knowing that something is "off" with the modified versions.[9] Because of the difficulty in modifying artworks for use as stimuli in controlled experimental studies, studies using basic stimuli have dominated the field.

A popular type of research using real artworks has focused on examining preferences for two broad categories of art: representational works (e.g., landscape paintings such as those by Albert Bierstadt and Susie M. Barstow or portraits by Johannes Vermeer and James Whistler) and abstract works (e.g., paintings similar to works by Kazimir Malevich and Joan Mitchell). Importantly, preference for one of these broad categories over another is related to viewers' art knowledge. Those with little knowledge about art tend to prefer representational works over abstract works, whereas those with more knowledge do not show a clear preference.[10] Viewers with more art knowledge seem to draw on what they *know* about

4. Thomas Jacobsen and Lea Höfel, "Descriptive and Evaluative Judgment Processes: Behavioral and Electrophysiological Indices of Processing Symmetry and Aesthetics," *Cognitive, Affective, & Behavioral Neuroscience* 3, no. 4 (2003): 289–99.

5. Thomas Jacobsen and Lea Höfel, "Aesthetic Judgments of Novel Graphic Patterns: Analyses of Individual Judgments," *Perceptual and Motor Skills* 95, no. 3 (2002): 755–66.

6. Pablo P. L. Tinio, Helmut Leder, and Marlies Strasser, "Image Quality and the Aesthetic Judgment of Photographs: Contrast, Sharpness, and Grain Teased Apart and Put Together," *Psychology of Aesthetics, Creativity, and the Arts* 5, no. 2 (2011): 165–76.

7. Helmut Leder, Pablo P. L. Tinio, and Moshe Bär, "Emotional Valence Modulates the Preference for Curved Objects," *Perception* 40, no. 6 (2011): 649–55.

8. Marcos Nadal, Enric Munar, Gisèle Marty, and Camilo Jo Cela-Conde, "Visual Complexity and Beauty Appreciation: Explaining the Divergence of Results," *Empirical Studies of the Arts* 28, no. 2 (2010): 173–91.

9. Viren Swami and Adrian Furnham, "The Effects of Symmetry and Personality on Aesthetic Preferences," *Imagination, Cognition and Personality* 32, no. 1 (2012): 41–57.

10. Elina Pihko, Anne Virtanen, Veli-Matti Saarinen, Sebastian Pannasch, Lotta Hirvenkari, Timo Tossavainen, Arto Haapala, and Riitta Hari, "Experiencing Art: The Influence of Expertise

art to make sense of abstract works in terms of their stylistic characteristics.[11] The impact of art knowledge on viewers' reactions to representational and abstract works has also been shown at the neural level, with artists having the highest neural activity (measured using event-related potentials) in response to abstract art as compared to representational and semi-abstract art. In contrast, non-artists had the lowest neural activity in response to abstract art.[12]

While searching for meaning in an artwork, art novices identify and interpret recognizable elements, such as people, places, and things. These elements can be more difficult to identify or be nonexistent in abstract works. In contrast, art experts, in addition to identifying depicted people, places, and things, are able to interpret the structural, compositional, and stylistic elements of a work—elements that are present in both representational and abstract art. Without clearly depicted objects to think about, art novices base their search for meaning and aesthetic judgments not on what they see, but on how they feel about a work.[13]

In addition to differences between representational and abstract art, researchers have also focused on the compositional structure of artworks. Even without much prior knowledge about the artworks that they are viewing, people are sensitive to any researcher-produced changes to the original compositional structure of artworks. For example, Paul Locher presented participants with unaltered reproductions of artworks (e.g., Félix Vallotton's *Still Life, Red Peppers on White Table* and Hans Hoffman's *The Golden Wall*) and their corresponding altered versions in which shapes and objects were moved.[14] He found that participants were able to identify originals from the altered versions. This sensitivity is also reflected in

---

and Painting Abstraction Level," *Frontiers in Human Neuroscience* 5 (2011): article number 94, https://doi.org/10.3389/fnhum.2011.00094; Liisa Uusitalo, Jaana Simola, and Jarmo Kuisma, "Consumer Perception of Abstract and Representational Visual Art," *International Journal of Arts Management* 15, no. 1 (2012): 30–41.

11. Camily J. Cela-Conde, Gisèle Marty, Enric Munar, Marcos Nadal, and Lucrecia Burges, "The 'Style Scheme' Grounds Perception of Paintings," *Perceptual and Motor Skills* 95, no. 1 (2002): 91–100.

12. Jane E. Else, Jason Ellis, and Elizabeth Orme, "Art Expertise Modulates the Emotional Response to Modern Art, Especially Abstract: An ERP Investigation," *Frontiers in Human Neuroscience* 9 (2015): 525.

13. Pablo P. L. Tinio, Jeffrey K. Smith, and Lisa F. Smith, "The Walls Do Speak: Psychological Aesthetics and the Museum Experience," in Tinio and Smith, *Cambridge Handbook of the Psychology of Aesthetics*, 195–218; Pablo P. L. Tinio and Eva Specker, "For Emotion's Sake . . . The Centrality of Emotions in the Art Experience," in *The Cambridge Handbook of Creativity and Emotions*, ed. Zorana Ivcevic, Jessica D. Hoffman, and James C. Kaufman (Cambridge: Cambridge University Press, 2023), 358–75.

14. Paul J. Locher, "An Empirical Investigation of the Visual Rightness Theory of Picture Perception," *Acta Psychologica* 114, no. 2 (2003): 147–64.

how quickly—in mere milliseconds—people are able to form stable judgments regarding aspects of composition, like the extent to which elements of artworks are orderly or harmonious.[15]

Studies on how specific characteristics of artworks, such as those discussed above, impact how the artworks are perceived and evaluated have dominated empirical aesthetics. In contrast, our project focuses on viewers' experiences of artworks in their genuine and unaltered states. Instead of examining specific features of artworks, we focus on them as wholes. This decision is based on the goal to study and connect the processes of art creation and art appreciation and to capture meaningful and profound outcomes of art engagement. Along the continuum of analyses from more molecular to more molar aspects of experience, the "Mirror to the World" project falls firmly in the molar end of the spectrum. Because much research has historically focused on specific molecular features of artworks, we purposefully take a complementary approach and start our research by inductively examining experiences of viewer-selected art.

The Viewer

Viewer characteristics comprise the second main component of the aesthetic experience of art. Although we have already discussed art expertise in relation to preference for representational and abstract art, expertise has other significant effects, such as on people's emotional reactions to art. Leder et al. used facial electromyography (fEMG) on art experts and novices while the participants looked at positively (e.g., joyful) and negatively (e.g., disturbing) valenced art.[16] The fEMG method distinguishes between a primarily positive or primarily negative emotional response indicated by greater activation of the zygomaticus major (smiling muscle) or corrugator supercilii (frowning muscle). Compared to art novices, art experts showed stronger zygomaticus muscle activations to positively valenced artworks and weaker supercilii muscle activations to negatively valenced ones. Expertise seems to help temper extreme negative reactions to art.

Another important viewer characteristic that impacts engagement with art is personality. Much research employed the Big Five model of personality traits, which summarized personality differences into five broad dimensions: extraver-

15. Kana Schwabe, Claudia Menzel, Caitlin Mullin, Johan Wagemans, and Christoph Redies, "Gist Perception of Image Composition in Abstract Artworks," *i-Perception* 9, no. 3 (2018): 1–25.

16. Helmut Leder, Gernot Gerger, David Brieber, and Norbert Schwarz, "What Makes an Art Expert? Emotion and Evaluation in Art Appreciation," *Cognition & Emotion* 28, no. 6 (2014): 1137–47.

sion, agreeableness, conscientiousness, neuroticism, and openness to experience.[17] Of the five trait dimensions, openness to experience—how intellectually curious, imaginative, and creative one is, and how open to ideas, actions, and values they are—has been most reliably and strongly associated with art, with those highly open to experiences showing greater interest in and liking for art,[18] as well as greater engagement in art appreciation activities (e.g., visiting art museums).[19]

Those who are open to experiences tend to prefer artworks that are unusual, unappealing to most, and more difficult to understand, such as surreal, abstract, and less popular and avant-garde art. In contrast, those who are low in openness to experience tend to prefer more traditional portraits or paintings of landscapes.[20]

Another personality trait that has shown similar associations with art preference as openness to experience is sensation seeking. Those who are high in sensation seeking—who crave diverse, novel, and intense experiences and are willing to pursue such experiences even at significant cost—are more likely to prefer complex and more difficult to understand art.[21]

17. Lewis R. Goldberg, "An Alternative 'Description of Personality': The Big-Five Factor Structure," *Journal of Personality and Social Psychology* 59, no. 6 (1990): 1216–29; Oliver P. John, Lauren P. Naumann, and Christopher J. Soto, "Paradigm Shift to the Integrative Big Five Trait Taxonomy," *Handbook of Personality: Theory and Research* 3, no. 2 (2008): 114–58.

18. E.g., Adrian Furnham and Margaret Avison, "Personality and Preference for Surreal Paintings," *Personality and Individual Differences* 23, no. 6 (1997): 923–35; Adrian Furnham and John Walker, "Personality and Judgements of Abstract, Pop Art, and Representational Paintings," *European Journal of Personality* 15, no. 1 (2001): 57–72; Ian C. McManus and Adrian Furnham, "Aesthetic Activities and Aesthetic Attitudes: Influences of Education, Background and Personality on Interest and Involvement in the Arts," *British Journal of Psychology* 97, no. 4 (2006): 555–87; and Paul J. Silvia, Emily C. Nusbaum, Christopher Berg, Christopher Martin, and Alejandra O'Connor, "Openness to Experience, Plasticity, and Creativity: Exploring Lower-Order, High-Order, and Interactive Effects," *Journal of Research in Personality* 43, no. 6 (2009): 1087–90.

19. Zorana Ivcevic and John Mayer, "Mapping Dimensions of Creativity in the Life-Space," *Creativity Research Journal* 21, no. 2–3 (2009): 152–65.

20. Tomas Chamorro-Premuzic, Charlotte Burke, Anne Hsu, and Viren Swami, "Personality Predictors of Artistic Preferences as a Function of the Emotional Valence and Perceived Complexity of Paintings," *Psychology of Aesthetics, Creativity, and the Arts* 4, no. 4 (2010): 196–204; Tomas Chamorro-Premuzic, Stian Reimers, Anne Hsu, Gorkan Ahmetoglu, "Who Art Thou? Personality Predictors of Artistic Preferences in a Large UK Sample: The Importance of Openness," *British Journal of Psychology* 100, no. 3 (2009): 501–16; Gregory J. Feist and Tara R. Brady, "Openness to Experience, Non-Conformity, and the Preference for Abstract Art," *Empirical Studies of the Arts* 22, no. 1 (2004): 77–89; and Adrian Furnham and John Walker, "Personality and Judgements of Abstract, Pop Art, and Representational Paintings," *European Journal of Personality* 15, no. 1 (2001): 57–72.

21. Adrian Furnham and Melinda Bunyan, "Personality and Art Preferences," *European Jour-*

The Context

In addition to features of artworks and characteristics of the viewer, the nature of the context in which art engagement takes place has a significant impact on the aesthetic experience. Consider the typical empirical aesthetics study in which researchers bring participants into the lab to look at and evaluate images of artworks presented on a computer screen. These participants are often college students who receive course credit or a small incentive for their participation. Studies usually last less than an hour, and after a debrief with the researcher, the participants are thanked and sent on their way. Lab studies such as these have led to important insights regarding the experience of art, as shown in the many studies described above. However, one of the issues that arises is related to ecological validity—the extent to which the findings reflect the experience of art beyond the lab. We argue that examining the experience of art in everyday life environments is one of the ultimate goals of empirical aesthetics research and that engagement with art in contexts designed to display it, especially museums and galleries, contributes to the effects of that engagement.[22]

It may seem superfluous to state that lab participants and museum visitors are not the same, but there are key differences between them that should be explicitly acknowledged when the ecological validity of empirical aesthetics research is being discussed. Unlike participating in a lab study for course credit, going to a museum is usually a planned and intrinsically motivated event. Some have even likened the experience to going to church.[23] People research the museum, make travel plans, dress up for the occasion, and sometimes pay a not insignificant sum of money to enter the museum. In essence, the museum visitor has committed to and invested in the museum visit long before setting foot in the museum, and upon entering, the visitor is at once immersed in an environment designed to optimize engagement with art.

From small and simple galleries to the major art museums—the Louvre, British Museum, Museo Nacional del Prado, Metropolitan Museum of Art, Whitney

---

nal of Personality 2, no. 1 (1988): 67–74; and Marvin Zuckerman, *Sensation Seeking: Beyond the Optimal Level of Arousal* (Hillsdale, NJ: Erlbaum, 1979).

22. Aniko Illes and Pablo P. L. Tinio, "Experiencing Art in Museums," in *The Routledge International Handbook of Neuroaesthetics*, ed. Martin Skov and Marcos Nadal (New York: Routledge, 2022), 423–37; Matthew Pelowski, Helmut Leder, and Pablo P. L. Tinio, "Creativity in the Visual Arts," in *The Cambridge Handbook of Creativity across Different Domains*, ed. James C. Kaufman, Vlad P. Glaveanu, and John Baer (Cambridge: Cambridge University Press, 2017), 80–109.

23. Jeffrey K. Smith and Lisa F. Smith, "Spending Time on Art," *Empirical Studies of the Arts* 19, no. 2 (2001): 229–36.

Museum, and the like—art exhibitions are curated spaces with specific elements that have been meticulously researched and designed with the visitor in mind. Individual galleries and special exhibitions are thematically organized. Artworks displayed might be from the same artist, art style or school, or historical era, or introduce contemporary art into historical galleries to deliberately present different perspectives and pose questions aimed at inspiring new understandings. They might also represent works from a group of artists known to have worked, socialized, or even lived together in the same neighborhood, such as the 1950s Abstract Expressionists from New York. The visitor is made aware of the organizing theme through labels accompanying each artwork, wall texts and brochures presented at the entrance to the gallery, and audio or docent-led tours.[24]

Art exhibitions in museums are therefore designed to maximize art engagement, both physically and intellectually, which is an experience wholly different from the typical lab study. Specker et al. showed the significance of experiencing a genuine artwork in an actual museum space when they compared people's experiences of a painting displayed in a museum and its reproduction in the lab.[25] Participants reported more intense aesthetic experiences and learning more about the genuine artwork in the museum. However, it is important to note that studies that directly compare responses to genuine artworks in a museum with their reproductions in the lab confound the stimulus with the context. Studies are needed to tease apart the effects of these two factors.[26]

Another feature that defines the majority of modern empirical aesthetics research conducted in the lab is the use of digital reproductions of artworks that participants rate on a number of dimensions such as liking and beauty. The sizes of these stimuli are limited by the sizes of the screens on which they are presented, and their image quality depends on the width and height of the screens as measured in pixels. Also dependent on the characteristics of screens is the color fidelity or accuracy of the reproductions. Given these image factors, it is entirely possible to have a reproduction of an artwork that is much bigger or smaller, more or less visually clear, and of a different color profile than an original, authentic

24. Pablo P. L. Tinio, Jeffrey K. Smith, and Kathryn Potts, "'The Object and the Mirror': The Nature and Dynamics of Museum Tours," *International Journal of Creativity and Problem Solving* 20 (2010): 37–52.

25. Eva Specker, Pablo P. L. Tinio, and Michiel van Elk, "Do You See What I See? An Investigation of the Aesthetic Experience in the Laboratory and Museum," *Psychology of Aesthetics, Creativity, and the Arts* 11, no. 3 (2017): 265–75.

26. Eva Specker, Anna Fekete, MacKenzie D. Trupp, and Helmut Leder, "Is a 'Real' Artwork Better than a Reproduction? A Meta-Analysis of the Genuineness Effect," *Psychology of Aesthetics, Creativity, and the Arts* 17, no. 3 (2023): 294–306.

artwork, which the artist has continually refined during the process of creation. Genuine works are valued more than their corresponding reproductions because people assume that more effort and skills were needed to produce them and because people attach importance to the artist's *touch* that is presumably intrinsic to the genuine artwork.[27]

Fundamental Gaps in Research and Our Approach

Empirical aesthetics research has elucidated much about how the characteristics of the artwork, the viewer, and the context impact the aesthetic experience. However, as the brief survey of the literature above shows, the majority of these studies have taken place in the lab, with research participants not prepared or intrinsically motivated to engage with art, and with reproductions of artworks serving as stimuli. Researchers themselves have usually done the job of selecting the artworks that were presented to the viewers. Moreover, the participants' engagement with art is short, usually limited to under an hour, with the amount of time spent on each stimulus being dictated by the research design. As a result, the pace of viewing is mostly predetermined. After viewing each artwork, usually on a screen, participants indicate their liking or preference for, interest in, or beauty judgments of each work using rating scales. Even the fairly limited number of studies conducted in museums and galleries have used versions of these methods.

One of the consequences of the traditional approach to aesthetics research is that we have not been able to capture the most profound and personally meaningful outcomes of engaging with art, especially those that are cognitive in nature. Put simply, judgments of preference or liking or beauty do not adequately represent the full range of outcomes of engaging with art. Some of these other reactions evoke memories from the viewer's life or prompt reflection on their relationships with others. The reactions could be spiritually and existentially profound, deeply emotional, intellectually humbling, awe-inspiring, and potentially transformative. These are the very experiences that we wanted to capture empirically in our project.

To allow the possibility of identifying the full range of experiences during engagement with art, especially cognitive experiences that we know little about, we included in our research design the following key features. First, the studies were conducted at the Whitney Museum of American Art (New York, NY, USA), a space possessing attributes that could facilitate the deep engagement with genuine artworks presented within a thoughtfully crafted curatorial context. Second,

27. George E. Newman and Paul Bloom, "Art and Authenticity: The Importance of Originals in Judgments of Value," *Journal of Experimental Psychology: General* 141, no. 3 (2012): 558–69.

the study participants were museum visitors who were primed to engage with art (unlike the typical lab participants). Third, instead of viewing researcher-selected stimuli, we asked each participant to select an artwork that would be the subject of the study, a piece that most resonated with them or that they found most meaningful. They were therefore more invested in their chosen piece than if one was just presented to them. Fourth, to capture the full range of visitors' experiences of art, we took an open-ended and emergent approach that gave the visitors the opportunity to verbalize, for as long as they thought necessary, what they were seeing, feeling, and thinking as they stood in front of the artworks. Collectively, these methodological design features allowed us to identify the potential cognitive effects of art that would not be detectable in the laboratory context, with reproductions of art, and with participants who might not be motivated to engage with art.

We combined these research design features with two theoretical frameworks that describe outcomes of engagement with art: *aesthetic cognitivism* from philosophy,[28] and the *mirror model of art* from psychology.[29] The theory of aesthetic cognitivism posits that the value of art stems from its ability to enhance human understanding of reality, including understanding of ourselves and our relation to the world, human nature, individual and social conditions, as well as moral and spiritual concepts. Aesthetic cognitivism describes the relationship between the artwork and the perceiver in which artworks are vehicles that move perceivers from one way of seeing and thinking to another. Furthermore, the theory proposes that it is possible to learn from art and that engagement with art affects our cognition and mental faculties. Our project builds on these propositions and examines what are the understandings that people gain from encounters with art and how they affect our creative thinking abilities.

Whereas aesthetic cognitivism proposes a big idea, the mirror model of art describes how art can create new understandings and prime creative thinking. According to this model, the process of aesthetic reception is a mirror reverse of artistic creation. Artists, through their work, convey meanings, ideas, and messages to their audience. Wassily Kandinsky in his book *Concerning the Spiritual in Art* (2002) explicitly described the role of the artist and art as conveying meaning: "The artist must have something to say, for mastery over form is not his goal,

28. Christoph Baumberger, "Art and Understanding: In Defence of Aesthetic Cognitivism," in *Bilder sehen: Perspektiven de Bildwissenschaft*, ed. Mark Greenlee et al. (Regensburg: Schnell & Steiner, 2013), 41–67; and Gordon Graham, *Philosophy of the Arts: An Introduction to Aesthetics*, 3rd ed. (New York: Routledge, 2005).

29. Pablo P. L. Tinio, "From Artistic Creation to Aesthetic Reception: The Mirror Model of Art," *Psychology of Aesthetics, Creativity, and the Arts* 7, no. 3 (2013): 265–75.

but rather the adapting of form to its inner meaning."[30] He specifically noted the spiritual purpose in art: "The work of art is born of the artist in a mysterious and secret way. From him, it gains life and being. Nor is its existence casual and inconsequential, but it has a definite and purposeful strength, alike in its material and spiritual life."[31]

Whether something that the artist has to say includes expressing their perspectives on the human condition, beliefs about social and spiritual realities, or critiques of the art world and artistic practice, artists begin the art-making process with exploratory studies and sketches that outline what they are trying to accomplish in a work. Taking painting as an example, the first marks on canvas are often comprised of the underdrawing, which serves as a visual and conceptual guide for the artist as they develop the work. Over time, additional layers of materials are added, lines, contours, and shapes are outlined, and the structural composition is solidified. For representational works, people, places, and things become more defined. For example, Edgar Degas's *Woman Combing Her Hair* started with a contoured shape that was built with pastel strokes in multiple layers. Shades of green and blue, pink and orange, brown and red, are juxtaposed to create optical color mixing. Finally, as the work nears completion, finishing touches are added to the surface of the work.

According to the mirror model, a viewer's initial interaction with the work begins where the artist left off—right at the surface. This early stage of the aesthetic experience transpires quickly and often beyond the viewer's conscious awareness. However, if the viewer continues to engage with the work, their memory processes are activated, they begin to try to make sense of what they are seeing, and identify anything depicted that is familiar. Even in completely abstract works, there is the tendency to try to recognize objects or make associations. If the viewer continues to engage with the work, they might begin to think and wonder about its more substantive aspects: When was it created and what was happening in the world during that time? Who was the artist, where are they from, and what artistic style or school are they associated with? Eventually, the viewer might reach the point at which the artist began by contemplating why the artist created the work, and finally, what the artist intended to communicate to the audience. At each stage of processing, viewers can reach new understandings. Personal memories and associations can create understandings of oneself and our relationships with others or our place in the world. Viewers can also gain understandings of the artistic

30. Wassily Kandinsky, *Concerning the Spiritual in Art* (1911; reis. 2002), 37. Online: http://www.public-library.uk/ebooks/22/92.pdf.

31. Kandinsky, *Concerning the Spiritual in Art*, 36.

process. Finally, it may become possible for the viewers to intuit the meanings, ideas, and perspectives that motivated the artist.

Although the model accounts for both emotional and cognitive correspondences,[32] we focused on the latter in our project. We hypothesized that the mirroring process underlies the cognitive outcomes of engagement with art. Furthermore, we hypothesized these outcomes to manifest particularly in situations in which the viewer is absorbed in an artwork and immersed in the ideas associated with its creation. Such sustained engagement is more likely to occur when encountering personally meaningful works within a context in which visitors themselves are dictating their engagement with art. These are the very conditions that form the basis for our project.

In addition to capturing the understandings gained from art, we also aimed to examine another major cognitive impact of engagement with art: the enhancement of creativity. Support for this hypothesized outcome of art comes from applied research that tested educational programs developed to build creative thinking abilities. For example, participants in a course that included eight sixty-minute sessions of art engagement activities in a museum described gaining both self-knowledge and developing thinking abilities. After the course, they recounted being better at "extrapolating art to personal life," described realizing that "the association of real problems with possible solutions shows the utility [art] has," and appreciated being able "to improve personal abilities you generally don't work on."[33] Compared to a matched control group, those who completed the course showed significantly higher creative thinking abilities (both idea generation and problem construction) and these gains were sustained in a two-month follow-up.[34] The "Mirror to the World" project asks whether creative thinking is primed

32. Eva Specker, Pablo P. L. Tinio, and Michiel Van Elk, "Do You See What I See? An Investigation of the Aesthetic Experience in the Laboratory and Museum," *Psychology of Aesthetics, Creativity, and the Arts* 11, no. 3 (2017): 265–75; and Pablo P. L. Tinio and Andreas Gartus, "Characterizing the Emotional Response to Art beyond Pleasure: Correspondence between the Emotional Characteristics of Artworks and Viewers' Emotional Responses," *Progress in Brain Research* 237 (2018): 319–42.

33. Marina Ebert, Jessica D. Hoffmann, Zorana Ivcevic, Christine Phan, and Marc A. Brackett, "Creativity, Emotion and Art: Development and Initial Evaluation of a Workshop for Professional Adults," *International Journal of Creativity and Problem Solving* 25, no. 2 (2015): 47–59; Jessica D. Hoffmann and Zorana Ivcevic, "Creativity, Emotions, and the Arts Courses: An Art Center at the Center," in *Creativity, Emotion, and the Arts: Research, Application, and Impact*, ed. Zorana Ivcevic (Santander: Fundación Botín, 2022), 45–55.

34. Jessica D. Hoffmann, Zorana Ivcevic, and Nadine T. Maliakkal, "Creative Thinking Strategies for Life: A Course for Professional Adults Using Art," *Journal of Creative Behavior* 54, no. 2 (2020): 93–310.

after meaningful engagement with art in an art museum, even when not paired with structured educational activities, and if so, what the necessary conditions of such effects of art are.

Study 1: What Makes Art Meaningful?

The goal of our first study was to inductively examine what makes art meaningful to museum visitors. What kinds of understandings and insights do they gain from pieces that are most evocative to them and that they find the most remarkable? We approached seventy visitors to the Whitney Museum of American Art, asked them to view art in the galleries as they normally would, and to return to the researcher after approximately fifteen minutes. They were then asked to identify an artwork that they found most meaningful. As they stood in front of it, the think-aloud protocol was used to capture what they were seeing, feeling, thinking, and otherwise experiencing. Given our focus on capturing as wide of a range of experiences as possible, it was important for visitors to know that their individual voice mattered. During the think-aloud process, the researchers gave the visitors the time and space to verbalize their thoughts and provided additional prompts as needed.

All think-aloud recordings were transcribed and subjected to a formal and systematic thematic content analysis that included verification of all transcriptions by two research assistants; primary and secondary read-throughs of all think-aloud transcripts prior to the start of the coding process; line-by-line coding; identification of initial categories; category refinement and extraction of textual units; and final category refinement and development of overarching themes. The ultimate goal of the analysis was to "assign symbolic meaning to the descriptive or inferential information compiled during a study."[35] Although we could have taken the approach of deductive or a priori data analysis in which there is a search for predetermined patterns and themes in the data, we did not believe that prior research would have enabled us to formulate categories of understandings gained from art that are comprehensive.

Study 1 resulted in the identification of five overarching themes: (1) self and life history; (2) others and the world; (3) artist and the creative process; (4) search for meaning and creation of an aesthetic narrative; and (5) art techniques and materials. Furthermore, each broad theme included several narrower sub-themes. For example, a sense of spirituality is included in the theme others and the world.

35. Matthew B. Miles, A. Michael Huberman, and Johnny Saldana, *Qualitative Data Analysis: A Methods Sourcebook*, 4th ed. (New York: SAGE, 2019).

The themes are briefly described below and illustrated with textual extracts from the think-alouds.

The *self and life history* theme refers to the experience of something personally meaningful resulting from engagement with an artwork and an artwork's connection to the visitor's life history. It also refers to acquiring new learning and ways of seeing oneself, as well as experiencing inspiration, transformation, and intellectual humility. This theme is prominently associated with the expression of emotions or stimulation of emotions in the visitor.

Referring to Georgia O'Keeffe's *Flower Abstraction* (1924), one of O'Keeffe's early flower paintings, a visitor stated: "I was drawn to this painting because it looked like it was giving you an embrace, like it was embracing you. It was like a hug and it's ready to blanket you and hold. I just felt like I could fit into the painting and then you zoom out, then it looks like a flower. I think it's a flower and it's just so peaceful and so comforting. The pink is so caring and I guess that's what I need now." For this visitor, O'Keeffe's painting elicited emotions of comfort and serenity and thoughts about the work fulfilling a psychological need at that particular moment. The theme of *self and life history* is inward-looking, which contrasts with the next theme.

The theme of *others and the world* involves thoughts and understandings of a visitor's relationships with and connection to others, thoughts about society, politics, and history, and a sense of spirituality, religion, and existence. In essence, this theme includes experiences evoked by art that are beyond the individual.

Describing the experience of Edward Hopper's *Two Comedians* (1965), a somber painting of two figures on a stage, a visitor said: "I feel like this genre, what it does for a lot of people, is just sort of like turns up their sympathy. So maybe you'll leave here and give a dollar to the guy on the subway. That is beyond the museum, I feel like. . . . So maybe it makes you more sympathetic." This sentiment speaks to one of the main tenets of aesthetic cognitivism: art's ability to increase sensitivity to and understanding of others. The artwork "turned up" feelings of sympathy that the visitor anticipated to still be present after they leave the museum.

The theme of the *artist and the creative process* includes visitors' reflections about the artist's life, ideas, intentions, and motivations. This theme lies at the heart of the mirror model as the visitor, after sustained engagement and thorough absorption in the work, begins to engage with the ideas, concepts, and meanings that are most closely associated with the creation of the work.

Reflecting on Edward Hopper's *A Woman in the Sun* (1961), a work depicting a female nude, a visitor stated: "He made some sketches. Probably he made sketches of the face; you could see that there is a good work on the body also, so this is not a piece of art that he made up some simple strokes. He spent a lot of time thinking about this." Here, the visitor has engaged with the Hopper painting and was reflecting on the process associated with its creation.

The *search for meaning and creation of an aesthetic narrative* theme represents a visitor's search for meaning and their attempts to interpret and understand the work, as well as any resulting aesthetic judgments. This theme also involves visitors creating narratives that describe what they are seeing in an artwork and showing empathy toward depicted subjects.

Speaking about George Tooker's painting *The Subway* (1950), which depicts subway commuters staring at an anxious-looking person at the center of the composition, a visitor wondered: "I would say that it seems really pertinent to our day and age right now. Seems like there's a certain amount of you know, obviously, depression era aesthetic to it. And there's a lot of staring going on of the woman that's in the photo, or that's in the painting. And she seems kind of isolated in this world where it's pretty much entirely men. And she seems scared, just generally, maybe not necessarily of the other men, but it's possible." This visitor seems to have immersed themselves in the scene and has created a story that helps them to understand what is depicted in the painting. The visitor is also empathizing with the central figure in the painting.

The theme of *art techniques and materials* refers to visitors' thoughts about the creative techniques and materials that comprise an artwork. Regarding Malcolm Bailey's *Untitled* (1969), a painting depicting a cotton plant and numerous human bodies that are reminiscent of slaves from Africa being transported on crowded ships: "I think it was pretty meticulous and intentional in its technical approach in that these android figures are repetitive and I've looked at them closely they're sort of beautifully simple in their construction. But the picture of the botanical picture of the cotton plant, which for being such like the turn of a page of a textbook, says so much more than a typical text would say to you, especially juxtaposed with the, with the slave ship shapes of the bodies." This visitor speaks about the techniques that the artist used to create a piece that is at once methodological (textbook-like) and historical (commentary on the slave trade).

Study 2: Does Art Engagement Prime Creativity?

The goal of our second study was to start the line of research examining the extent to which engagement with art in a museum primes or stimulates creativity, as well as under which conditions and for whom this happens. We hypothesized that deep and self-referential engagement with meaningful art would result in higher creativity than art engagement that does not include such explicit reflection. One-hundred twenty visitors to the Whitney Museum were recruited to participate in one of three conditions. In the experimental condition, participants viewed art in the galleries, identified an artwork that they found meaningful, and as they stood in front of the work, they reflected on what made that specific piece meaningful to them. In another condition, participants also viewed art, but instead of reflecting on a personally meaningful piece, they were asked about the percentage of all art shown that they spent time on and about the physical sizes of the art that they saw. If explicit reflection about what makes art personally meaningful is not essential for priming creative thinking, participants in this condition would perform similarly to those in the first condition on tasks assessing creativity. Finally, in the third condition, visitors were recruited as they entered the museum and did not yet look at art. These participants had the intention and motivation to engage with art and had put in the effort to visit the museum (as those in the other conditions), but only anticipated an art experience.

All three groups were administered two creativity tasks: art creation and metaphor generation. The first was a collage-making task in which participants were provided a standard set of digital images on a large handheld device and asked to create a design using the images as materials. These materials were reproductions of twenty abstract (e.g., Jean Hélion's *Composition*, 1935) and semi-abstract (e.g., August Macke's *Zoological Garden I*, 1912) artworks that visitors could manipulate by using them whole or cutting out pieces to make new images from different pieces. If the effect of art appreciation in a single museum visit is akin to a priming effect on creativity, it could be most relevant to art-related tasks. Because of this, we decided to administer the art creation task first. The second task measured whether art engagement has an effect on creative thinking that does not involve images or art creation. Thus, we opted for a verbal task asking participants to think of a metaphor about what it is like to experience great art. Participants were introduced to different kinds of metaphors and asked to generate a creative metaphor of any type. Data analysis for Study 2 is in progress.

Project Outputs

The "Mirror to the World" project has two sets of outputs: scholarly publications and presentations and broader public communications. The full set of results of our empirical studies will be reported in articles in journals in empirical aesthetics and psychology of art. To share our research, we organized a symposium at the Annual Convention of the American Psychological Association in Washington, DC. We presented results about what makes art meaningful, along with papers by Rebekah Rodriguez-Boerwinkle and colleagues who examined behavioral indicators of engagement with art, Jeffrey Smith who discussed the deep sense of sadness in the art of Chaim Soutine, and Anjan Chatterjee and colleagues who developed a taxonomy of impacts of art on viewers. Furthermore, our project sparked interest in the greater research community, leading to a collaboration on an article reporting on a neuroscientific test of the mirror model of art, as well as invitations to present our research in a colloquium series at the University of Pennsylvania and at a symposium on psychology of creativity and art at the University of Tokyo.

We have introduced ideas of aesthetic cognitivism and the mirror model of art in four articles published in *Psychology Today*.[36] In "Art Builds Understanding," we described the basis of our project and the search for cognitive outcomes of art. "Unlocking the Emotional Code of Abstract Art" described new research showing that viewers agree on what colors and lines communicate different emotions.[37] Whereas brown, green, and ocher communicate the moral emotion of disgust, yellow, orange, cyan, and pink evoke joy and wonder. "Your Brain on Art" presents the neuroscientific evidence for the correspondence between art creation and art appreciation hypothesized by the mirror model.[38] Finally, in "What Makes Art Meaningful?," we present the findings on the kinds of understandings people derive from art, from drawing on personal memories to insights about social and spiritual realities.[39]

In addition to writing for the broader public, at the Designing for Empathy Summit we reached out to the community of museum professionals—those who work with art and create programs to enhance the effects of art. We conducted a workshop about the cognitive benefits of art at the Phillips Collection and presented about understandings of art at the Fashion Institute of Technology.

The final output of our project was the "Mirror to the World: Exploring the Power of Art" symposium at the Glencairn Museum (Bryn Athyn, PA, USA), an institution devoted to religious and spiritual art and history. Uniting the themes of basic research that builds new knowledge and dissemination of the insights it provides about the benefits of art in the museum and broader communities, the event included presentations by the authors; Katherine Cotter, Associate Director of Research at University of Pennsylvania's Positive Psychology Center; and Elif Gokcigdem, art historian and founder of ONE (Organization of Networks for Empathy). The event also featured workshops demonstrating the mirror model of

36. Zorana Ivcevic and Pablo P. L. Tinio, "Art Builds Understanding," *Psychology Today*, November 3, 2022, https://tinyurl.com/535u5bmx.

37. Dirk B. Walther, Claudia Damiano, and Zorana Ivcevic, "Unlocking the Emotional Code of Abstract Art," *Psychology Today*, May 16, 2023, https://tinyurl.com/ycyf6j4x.

38. Oshin Vartanian and Zorana Ivcevic, "Your Brain on Art," *Psychology Today*, March 7, 2023, https://tinyurl.com/2reuu85y.

39. Zorana Ivcevic and Pablo P. L. Tinio, "5 Things That Make Art Meaningful," *Psychology Today*, September 12, 2023, https://tinyurl.com/yeau48mj.

art and the ability of art to build empathy as well as a panel discussion about understanding through art that included the authors; Elif Gokcigdem; Aisha Imam, Founder and Director of the Reed Society for the Sacred Arts; Brian Henderson, Director of the Glencairn Museum; and Amelia Winger-Bearskin, artist and Associate Professor and Banks Preeminence Chair of AI and the Arts, University of Florida.

Reflections

The primary goal of our project was to go beyond the traditional focus of empirical aesthetics research on basic outcomes, such as judgments of pleasantness, interest, or liking, and to capture the more profound cognitive outcomes of art engagement. Reaching this goal required a research design that centered around the art viewer's perspective, as well as a data collection method that involved an authentic experience with genuine artworks in a real museum setting.

Museum visitors sought and gained meaning and understanding from the artworks they were viewing. As predicted by the theory of aesthetic cognitivism, engagement with art clearly has cognitive value. The results showed that museum visitors were able to articulate what art they found meaningful and why. They related what they were seeing to aspects of themselves, their life histories, and their relationships with others. Museum visitors also spoke about things beyond themselves such as society, political realities, and the human condition, as well as spiritual understandings and insights that go beyond ourselves and the material world. They also related to themes depicted in the works—they created stories and narratives and empathized with protagonists in pieces of art to which they were drawn. Especially pertinent to the mirror model of art, the visitors engaged with the creators of the works and with the process of creation.

As we reflect on a new line of research, we realize the importance of exploratory work. We are scientists who have developed theories of the creative process and theoretically connected processes of artistic creation and appreciation; we value and know the importance of theory. But this project reminded us that equally important is the inductive approach that listens and learns from the lived experiences of those it aims to understand. This method opened up new questions and hypotheses that await to be examined. For example, what understandings tend to co-occur? Do different kinds of insights and thoughts reflect levels of processing proposed in the mirror model of art? Is emotional processing related to cognitive understanding? And, to fully put the mirror model of art to the test, to what extent does the creative process in artists correspond to the process of art appreciation in their audience? Previous research has provided evidence that such correspondence exists for emotional content of art,[40] and our continued research will take the next step and examine cognitive correspondences. Our future work will include a collaboration with artists as we study how they create, with emphasis on their cognitions, ideas, insights, and emotions as they make art and test how these are identified and experienced by viewers when engaging the studied works. Based on the interest and feedback that we have received from scholars in the field of empirical aesthetics, we expect that the results of this research will make an impact on the field and inspire others to put aesthetic cognitivism to the test, especially in the context of museums, where the experience of art is at its most powerful.

As science is a process of asking new questions and addressing new problems, we want to conclude this chapter by looking ahead. Scientific research is built on measurement. Well-constructed measures draw attention to an area of inquiry and lower the barrier to entry into a research domain by providing the means to address research questions from different perspectives and take an area of inquiry into new directions. The use of think-aloud protocols was an effective method for capturing visitors' experiences in a museum in the exploratory stage. However, it will be crucial for the field to have a measure of cognitive responses to art that could be used in quantitative and hypothesis-driven studies. Such measures exist for so-called aesthetic emotions, but none exist for cognitions in response to art. We are planning to create such a measure. As we take a long view to the emerging field of empirical aesthetics that tests propositions of aesthetic cognitivism, we look forward to developing the key measurement infrastructure and to putting it to use to understand the cognitive effects of art.

40. Pablo P. L. Tinio and Andreas Gartus, "Characterizing the Emotional Response," 319–42.

11

The Hermeneutic Role of Artistic Creation in Spiritual Experience

Carlos Miguel Gómez-Rincón

With the aim of contributing to the Art Seeking Understanding (ASU) program strategy's goal of exploring whether there is an empirically demonstrable connection between art and understanding, we designed a novel, interdisciplinary methodology that we are calling "Laboratory of Art and Spirituality" (LAS). We assembled a group of seven Colombian artists from different disciplines (music, visual arts, dance, and poetry) working together with a philosopher, a social psychologist, and a film director. The methodology included three main components: (1) spaces of spiritual practice in seven residential workshops for the artists, designed around different aspects and dimensions of spiritual experience (spiritual experience in diversity, in daily life, in nature, in love, in crisis, before death and in joy); (2) artistic exploration of the themes and contents of the project, using the artistic mediums and languages of each participating artist; and (3) tools for artists' self-description and reflection on the relationship between their creative process and spiritual experience. These tools included journals, autoethnographies, interviews, and philosophical dialogues, all of which were coded and analyzed using a hermeneutic phenomenological approach. The whole process was recorded to produce eight short documentary films that are presented, together with samples of the artist's works and journals, the methodological design, and the research results, in the open-source Convergent Documentary Platform.[1]

Some Problems with the Concept of Artistic Understanding

The idea that the arts offer unique forms of understanding and knowledge that cannot be reduced to or replaced by other types of understanding, such as scien-

1. Online: https://www.spiritualartlab.com/en.

tific theories and explanations, discursive thinking, or common-sense language, has a long tradition in Western history. It reaches back to antiquity, when poets were considered interpreters of nature, which would itself act as a poet by creating meaningful relationships among its parts and components.[2] Notions such as likeness, correspondence, consonance, emulation, analogy, and sympathy were epistemic principles used to read the semantic interconnection of reality until the end of the sixteenth century.[3] German Romanticism continued exploring and deepening art and poetry as forms of knowledge that would overcome the limitations of a purely intellectual and mechanistic understanding of nature and the human heart. This enterprise deeply influenced Spanish and Latin American poets. Antonio Machado (1993), María Zambrano (2016), and the Mexican Nobel Laureate Octavio Paz (2014) are prominent examples of the search for what they called "poetic thinking," which through images and rhythm would allow for a more integral apprehension of reality, able to reconcile opposite and apparently contradictory terms and to access dimensions of reality inaccessible to scientific and discursive thinking.

However, defining how art and poetry generate understanding, and what that understanding is, is not a simple task. Researchers have tended to focus on reception. Martha Nussbaum, for example, has explored how reading novels enhances moral understanding and contributes to political and democratic education.[4] David Perkins moved toward a definition of the understanding achieved through contemplation of art by identifying some of its characteristics. According to Perkins, understanding would entail the generation of relationships between elements, showing how things hang together in a web that must be coherent according to different contextual standards of coherence, so that a person can act based on what she understands without ever exhausting what can be understood.[5]

Likewise, Christoph Baumberger offered a characterization of artistic understanding in terms of cognitive success. He differentiated understanding from knowledge, pointing out that the cognitive achievements proper to the former do not require belief formation and are not evaluated in terms of their truth or falsehood, but rather using aesthetic criteria such as simplicity, applicability, and in general the abil-

2. Pierre Hadot, *The Veil of Isis: An Essay on the History of the Idea of Nature* (Cambridge, MA: Belknap, 2006), 201.

3. Michel Foucault, *The Order of Things: An Archaeology of the Human Sciences* (London: Routledge, 2002), 19.

4. Martha Nussbaum, *Poetic Justice: The Literary Imagination and Public Life* (Boston: Beacon, 1995).

5. D. Perkins, "Art as Understanding," *Journal of Aesthetic Education* 22, no. 1, Special Issue: Art, Mind, and Education (1988): 111–31.

ity to use information in particular scenarios.[6] Developing new categories to order elements and aspects of things, creating models to account for complex processes and objects, suggesting thought experiments, and raising new questions are examples of the sort of cognitive achievements possible in artistic understanding.

In all these efforts the notion of cognition remains linked to a mental process that, even if not completely identical to conceptual or discursive thinking, does not significantly differ either. Understanding appears as the result of certain intellectual, linguistic, or artistic processes or operations performed, in these cases, by the receptor of an artwork. It would be something that needs to be produced and could be described in terms of the processing of information, as if we started from an absolute lack of understanding and then managed to incorporate and learn how to use data.

On the contrary, as hermeneutic phenomenology has shown, understanding is primordially related to our embodied, enacted, lived experience of meaning.[7] Before any propositional, thematic, or explicit formulation of meaning, we already move and act in a meaningful world, and it is in our dealing with reality and in our relationships with others that we express what the world and others signify to us. Our pre-theoretical, non-thematic, tacit forms of living and coping with reality constitute the fundamental form of understanding.[8] Starting from this horizon of "fore-understanding" we move by means of diverse interpretative acts toward the elucidation, elaboration, and gradual enlargement of meaning, discovering new aspects and nuances of significance.

Based on this basic phenomenological image of understanding, our project focused on the artists' side, striving to explore the ways in which artistic creation contributed to the unfolding of meaning in relation to experiences they considered "spiritual." This is a necessary starting point, we believe, to explore whether there is "an empirically demonstrable connection between art and understanding *vis-à-vis* spiritual information" and "what the distinctive cognitive value engagement with the arts generate," which are two of the fundamental aims of the ASU program strategy. Our project reformulated them in the following three questions:

6. Christoph Baumberger, "Art and Understanding: In Defence of Aesthetic Cognitivism," in *Bilder sehen: Perspektiven de Bildwissenschaft*, ed. Mark Greenlee et al. (Regensburg: Schnell & Steiner, 2013), 41–67.

7. Martin Heidegger, *Being and Time*, trans. John Macquarrie and Edward Robinson (Oxford: Blackwell, 2001); Hans-Georg Gadamer, *Truth and Method* (New York: Continuum, 2004).

8. Hubert L. Dreyfus, *Being-in-the-World: A Commentary on Heidegger's Being and Time, Division 1* (Cambridge, MA: MIT Press, 1995), 18; Maurice Merleau-Ponty, *Phenomenology of Perception* (London: Routledge, 1981), ix.

1. What are the characteristics of artistic understanding and how can we differentiate it from other forms of understanding (e.g., conceptual comprehension, discursive thinking, everyday knowledge, and scientific explanation)?
2. How does artistic creation make meaning of experiences that seem to occur beyond words and concepts?
3. What are the cognitive, emotional, and existential processes implied in this form of interpretation?

The Interdisciplinary, Practice-Based, Phenomenologically Oriented Methodology of the LAS

The notion of understanding in aesthetic cognitivism needs to be enlarged and further developed to include the embodied and lived experience of meaning in artists' spiritual and aesthetic experiences, which is then elaborated through their creative processes. How can we study the ways in which artistic creation generates and elaborates spiritual meaning? This requires an empirical investigation that allows for the observation and description of artists' inner processes. We must integrate their first-person perspectives. As a lived, embodied experience, meaning making cannot be reduced to a physical process or behavior only observed from a third-person perspective. It needs to be studied in its own terms.[9] This makes it necessary to treat artists as co-researchers of their own experiences and inner life, instead of as passive, disengaged research subjects.[10]

Using a call for applications we recruited a group of artists committed to a spiritual search, who were willing to engage in a process of self-observation, self-description, and reflection of their inner processes. The final configuration of the LAS included three musicians, one dancer, one photographer, one painter, one poet/philosopher, one social psychologist, one philosopher and cultural studies scholar, and one philosopher and film director. Five were female, and five were male, aged between their late twenties and early fifties. All the artists were professionally trained in their disciplines and had a significant artistic trajectory. As

9. Edmund Husserl, *The Crisis of European Sciences and Transcendental Phenomenology* (Evanston, IL: Northwestern University Press, 1970), 7; Wilhelm Dilthey, *Hermeneutics and the Study of History: Selected Works, Vol. 4*, ed. Rudolf Makkreel and Frithjof Rodi (Princeton: Princeton University Press, 1996), 229.

10. Gadamer, *Truth and Method*, 292; Jonathan A. Smith, "Towards Reflexive Practice: Engaging Participants and Co-researchers and Co-analysts in Psychological Inquiry," *Journal of Community and Applied Social Psychology* 4, no. 4 (1994): 253–60; Jonathan A. Smith, "Participants and Researchers Searching for Meaning: Conceptual Developments for Interpretative Phenomenological Analysis," *Qualitative Research in Psychology* 16, no. 2 (2019): 166–81.

co-investigators, they participated in a ten-month research-creation process that integrated three components.

Spiritual Practice

We adopted spiritual experience as a theme for experiential and artistic exploration. Even if there is no single characterization of spiritual experience, in the call for application we offered the following working definition: "For this project spiritual experience is characterized as an individual's sense of existing in relation to the divine or some transcendent dimension of reality, which includes the feeling of gaining deep understanding and insight about the meaning of life and existence, and as a result of which observable positive transformations are produced in people's lives." We then designed and conducted seven three-day residential workshops, each around one aspect or dimension of spiritual experience: spiritual experience in diversity, in daily life and the extraordinary, in love, in nature, in uncertainty and crisis, in finitude and death, and in joy. These retreat-like encounters occurred every five weeks and included different practices of contemplation, meditation, breathing, psycho-physical exploration, artistic creation, reflection, and discussion. These exercises were conceived with a pluralistic orientation, responding to the diverse religious and spiritual backgrounds of the artists. Their basic aim was to allow for the experiential emergence of meaning around the topics explored, which could then trigger creative processes as forms of further artistic interpretation.

In keeping with our phenomenological image of understanding and the extensive literature on religious experience, we postulate that spiritual experience is itself a source and form of insight that cannot be reached or replaced by other means. A deep meaning of reality and our place in it, linked to the lived presence of the divine, is often reported as a key element of spiritual experience, together with the sense that this meaning cannot be easily expressed in words and concepts.[11] We carefully explored how this experiential discovery of significance and value relates to artistic creation, sometimes motivating it and other times merging with it.[12] The following journal entry from one of the musicians summarizes the complex nature of lived spiritual and artistic understanding:

11. William James, *The Varieties of Religious Experience* (Mineola, NY: Dover, 2002), 380; John Hick, *An Interpretation of Religion: Human Responses to the Transcendent* (New Haven: Yale University Press, 2004), 161; Carlos Miguel Gómez-Rincón, *Racionalidad y trascendencia. Investigaciones en epistemología de la religión* (Bogotá: Sal Terrae, Universidad del Rosario, 2020), 119; Carlos Miguel Gómez-Rincón, "Diversity and Interpretation: Toward a Pluralist Realist Description of Religious Experience," *Religions* 12 (2021): 848.

12. Carlos Miguel Gómez-Rincón, "Art as a Spiritual Practice: The Interplay between Artistic

> I have realized that understanding itself is something related to the spiritual order. It is more a matter of feeling than of thinking. And that feeling is mainly a feeling of the essence of love. To feel that force that nourishes, that connects us with the divine and with others. To understand that a life full of love is a life full of fulfillment. Through music, I can understand and feel deeply the power of love. And nurture and share it. I can feel its transforming and healing power. I understand that through music I can tune into the frequency of divine love, resonate with it, and at the same time transmit and imprint this in the music I make. I understand that when I make music from a state of love and serenity, creativity emerges more easily, and more fluidly. I understand that music reinforces my spiritual purposes. I understand that my art is in itself a method, a way to connect with something that goes far beyond my ego. I understand that music made in this way has a profound transformative and healing power. I understand that music allows me to empty myself in order to fill myself with joy and wholeness. I understand that music allows me to enter into a flow, into a state of harmony.[13]

Artistic Exploration

Between the workshops, the artists committed to the development of art pieces and the description in their journals of the ways in which the experience of grasping and elaborating meaning manifested. Given that their artworks were themselves the main vehicle to grasp and express these meanings, which were felt to be impossible to translate into other mediums without a loss of significance, we opted for acknowledging this untranslatability. The study of artistic and spiritual understanding requires accepting that there is a plurality of forms of meaning-making that need to be first presented in their own terms and then interrelated to show their connections. For this, we envisioned the main product of the project as a Convergent Documentary Platform (CDP), a website including documentary production, samples of artworks, autoethnographic explorations, and academic products.

None of these different forms of language and investigation are given epistemological priority. Rather the CDP aims to be a sort of ecosystem presenting the

---

Creation and Spiritual Search in Seven Colombian Artists," *Journal for the Study of Spirituality* (2023).

13. Rodrigo Restrepo, artist's journal, workshop 4. Even though the artists' journals have not been published, a further elaboration of them resulted in a collection of autoethnographies that can be found online: https://tinyurl.com/45nv8rr9.

richness, complexity, and diversity of spiritual understanding reached through artistic creation. Two of its sections present the interconnection between the artists' self-descriptions of their creative processes and the resulting art pieces.[14] They show the complementarity between artistic languages—which explore aspects of significance that are non-discursive, symbolic, material, intuitive, and emotional—and the verbal description of these processes and contents. This required a long training in self-observation and self-description abilities, as well as the development of certain techniques and strategies.

Tools for Self-Observation and Self-Description

One of the main methodological challenges of a phenomenologically oriented approach is to design appropriate instruments to access lived experience. As co-researchers of the processes related to meaning making through artistic creation, the lab artists undertook four strategies:

- The *river of life visual method* was an initial exercise to elucidate the spiritual background and previous history of integration between art and spirituality in each artist's life. It consisted of the presentation of key moments and experiences by means of drawings and symbols, which were then developed using in-depth interviews.[15]
- Artists were given a *journal* designed as a semi-structured tool for registering their experiences, reflections, and ideas. It was divided into seven sections, corresponding to the workshop themes, using relevant images and inspirational quotes. It also included a *toolbox for self-exploration* consisting of thirty-nine questions to help artists direct their attention toward different moments, aspects, and characteristics of meaning making through artistic creation. These questions were organized into ten groups: (1) spiritual experience as a form of understanding, (2) from experience to creation, (3) the integration of life in the work of art, (4) glimpses of grace, (5) looking for the form, (6) the revelation of meaning, (7) the others meet my work, (8) the transformative power of art, (9) art as a form of self-knowledge, and (10) from art to life.
- To generate collective reflection and intersubjective points of view, we carried out regular *philosophical dialogues* that often began from the self-descriptions of the artists. They helped to deepen and expand certain narratives, as well as

14. Online: https://tinyurl.com/szedp4h9 and https://tinyurl.com/2rbk65sr.

15. Kathleen Pithouse, "Picturing the Self: Drawing as a Method for Self-Study," in *Picturing Research: Drawing as Visual Methodology*, ed. Linda Theron et al. (Rotterdam: Sense, 2011).

to enlarge the interpretations made by artists while listening to the questions, ideas, and remarks of others.

- At the end of the laboratory, artists went back to their journals and the toolbox for self-exploration and wrote a final autoethnography.[16] In these texts they explored in detail one aspect of spiritual understanding developed through artistic creation, focusing on what they considered their central discoveries and experiences during the lab.

With these tools, we constructed a corpus of forty-nine journal entries (one per artist per workshop topic), fourteen transcripts of dialogues, seven in-depth interviews, and seven final autoethnographic texts, which were analyzed using a hermeneutic phenomenological approach. Initially, a group of three researchers (the philosopher, the social psychologist, and the cultural studies scholar) individually coded these materials with the help of software for qualitative analysis. Gradually, a detailed book of codes emerged, using as categories both the main themes and concepts implicit in the toolbox and the emergent themes discovered during the analysis. These codes present the common patterns, processes, and motives related to spiritual search and experience, their relationship to artistic practice, and the generation of spiritual meaning through artistic creation. In research meetings, these interpretations were triangulated, while we strived to bring to light the researchers' presuppositions, which guided their readings of the materials. Thus, it was possible to review and enlarge the researchers' interpretations vis-à-vis artists' self-descriptions and reflections.

The final moment of the hermeneutic phenomenological analysis consisted of the construction of nineteen cases in which it was possible to clearly appreciate how understanding emerged in the creative process of specific artworks. As a result, we developed a model of artistic understanding that identifies five moments or "places" through which spiritual meanings are elaborated in a process of artistic exploration, as well as five meaning-making mechanisms characteristic of this interpretative unfolding.

Findings

The analysis of the materials produced by the artists led to the identification of the ways in which spiritual search and artistic practice interrelate in pluralistic milieus typical of contemporary societies, and to development of a comprehensive model of artistic understanding.

16. Carolyn Ellis, Tony E. Adams, and Arthur P. Bochner, "Autoethnography: An Overview," *Forum Qualitative Social Research* 12, no. 1 (2011).

Art as a Spiritual Practice

In a preliminary paper, we explored the ways in which the artists' spiritual searches and backgrounds interrelate with their artistic careers.[17] This contributed to the study of the shapes and transformations spirituality is taking in pluralistic, secular societies, insofar as the lab artists' views and practices resonate with categories recently elaborated in the sociology of religion to describe "progressive,"[18] "subjective-life oriented" spiritualities.[19] In this regard we found some common traits among the artists' understandings and practices of spirituality, such as the emphasis on a non-denominational and extra-institutional search for the direct experience of the divine, which is concomitant with the search for meaning and well-being that engenders long histories of spiritual wandering; the tendency to integrate spirituality with bodily and earthly concerns; and the constant need to elaborate personal syntheses among diverse elements, practices, and sources, coming from different religious traditions. We saw how artistic techniques offer models for elaborating these fusions. This is one of the reasons why, as Robert Wuthnow claims, people "are now turning to artists for spiritual guidance."[20]

In this context, artistic practices are regarded by the lab artists as a fundamental part of their spiritual adventures. This is so for three reasons: artistic explorations induce forms of spiritual experience; the works of the LAS artists attempt to express or transmit what they discover in these experiences; and their arts have spiritual properties. Frequently, they described inner states linked to artistic creation as forms of meditation and spiritual connection similar to "mystical" experiences. This is clearly shown in the following passage from the photographer's journals:

> How could I describe this experience of "vanishing when I observe"? When I am totally perceiving the phenomena of the world I feel the autonomy, infinitude, harmony, perfection, and independence of the world . . . I stop existing. It is as if I discovered certain perfection of the world without me, a break from

17. Carlos Miguel Gómez-Rincón, "Art as a Spiritual Practice: The Interplay between Artistic Creation and Spiritual Search in Seven Colombian Artists," *Journal for the Study of Spirituality* 13, no. 2 (2023): 132–46.

18. Gordon Lynch, *The New Spirituality: An Introduction to Progressive Belief in the Twenty-First Century* (London: I. B. Tauris, 2007).

19. Paul Heelas and Linda Woodhead, *The Spiritual Revolution: Why Religion Is Giving Way to Spirituality* (Oxford: Blackwell, 2005).

20. Robert Wuthnow, *Creative Spirituality: The Way of the Artist* (Berkeley: University of California Press, 2001), 10, 275.

> the need for my presence. This is something so subtle that these words cannot express it. The feeling is of peace and joy as if that sort of perception of the mechanism of the world moving on its own gave me tranquility . . . the certainty that everything, absolutely everything is fine.[21]

This preliminary exploration allowed us to situate our investigation of the processes linked to the generation of meaning regarding spiritual experience through artistic creation, better appreciating the artists' previous experiences and interpretations regarding the interconnection between their art and their spiritual lives.

The Unfolding of Spiritual Understanding through Artistic Creation

We found that the understanding reached through artistic creation is not a single cognitive event, but rather consists of a gradual elaboration of lived, embodied meaning that goes through different interpretative moments and integrates diverse meaning-making mechanisms. We call these interpretative moments "loci of understanding," since they refer both to temporal stages in the process of discovering meaning and to "places" in which meaning appears. They are:

Locus 1 (L1): The *artist's spiritual experience*, in which meaning manifests not as the result of an inferential process but as the realization of a deep sense of the world and the self. This includes both moments of spiritual practice, such as prayer and meditation, and spontaneous moments in which the presence of the divine is felt. Here we also find crucial moments in life in which important realizations are gained.

Locus 2 (L2): The *creative process* by means of which what was first grasped in experience is elaborated. Very often artists seek to express, investigate, and expand what they discovered in experience by means of their artistic explorations. Thus, new and deeper aspects of signification are disclosed. We found that in the case of the lab participants artistic practices frequently merge with their spiritual searches. Spiritual experience does not only motivate artistic creation, but at crucial moments aesthetic experience is lived as a form of spiritual experience. In these moments artists reported experiencing something described with terms such as "artistic revelation," "being a channel for something bigger than the ego," and "connecting to the Source."

Locus 3 (L3): An *artwork* is the result of the previous loci. In the artwork, meaning acquires a level of independence in relation to its creator, insofar as the work

21. Guillermo Santos, artist's journal, workshop 1.

can be differently interpreted by diverse spectators.[22] Even though we did not explore the reception process, we allowed for spaces of reflection in which artists were the first spectators of their own works. Previously elaborated meanings received then a further moment of elaboration. New points of view and insights emerged from the contemplation and presentation of drafts and works.

Locus 4 (L4): The embodied, enactive, pragmatic character of understanding can be clearly appreciated in its *effects on artists' lives*. These effects include transformations in their ways of seeing themselves and previous experiences, changes in previous beliefs, and calls to adopt new habits, practices, and forms of life.

Locus 5 (L5): Given that artists participated as co-researchers, the use of the tools for self-observation and self-description constituted a further moment for the unfolding of understanding. While describing and reflecting on their inner processes they gained new perspectives and insights, which, unlike the previous loci, commonly implied the use of more discursive forms of language. We denominated this moment *autoethnographic reflexivity*.

We identified and described five meaning-making mechanisms that work differently at each of these loci: perception, emotional understanding, knowing-how, seeing-as, and perceiving mystery. Each one makes it possible to grasp specific contents and kinds of meaning, which could not be accessed through a different mechanism. They represent the forms of understanding proper to artistic creation and commonly reinforce each other.

Let us briefly see how these meaning-making mechanisms work in the case of the production of one of the artworks resulting from the LAS experiment. It is chapter 5 (*capítulo* 5) of the seven chapters of the filmic poem created by Guillermo Santos. The chapter is entitled "The Texture Needed to Be an Angel" (*La textura necesaria para ser un ángel*).[23]

Understanding started with a diffuse, intuitive grasp of significance through the visual *perception* of the statues of three angels during one of the retreats:

> I wanted to take a walk around the place, with the only intention of getting to know it and enjoying it. I entered the mountain and suddenly found a sort of altar. There were, in their niches, the statues of three angels: Gabriel, Rafael,

22. Paul Ricoeur, *From Text to Action: Essays in Hermeneutics*, vol. 2, trans. Kathleen Blamey and John B. Thompson (Evanston, IL: Northwestern University Press, 1991), 105.

23. Guillermo Santos, "Diario de una pregunta Poema fílmico en siete capítulos." Online: https://www.spiritualartlab.com/en/visuales.

> and Michael. . . . I was fascinated, shocked, by the texture of their faces and the imperfections of their skins. It was both disturbing and moving, and I said to myself: "Wahhh, wahhhh, I must take a picture of this!!!!" The shape came to me through my senses and impacted me in an aesthetic manner, without asking about its meaning, except for certain feelings of compassion.[24]

At the level of experience, perception is always a form of interpretation of the world.[25] Instead of receiving and processing in a disengaged way bits of information, to which we afterward attach certain "meaning," we grasp meaningful totalities in which we know how to act and live. In John Hick's words, "Meaning is the most general characteristic of conscious experience as such. For being conscious is, normally, to be discriminatingly aware of various features of our surroundings in such a way that we can act appropriately in relation to them."[26] In this case, together with this regular interpretative character of visual perception, there is a sort of suggestion of spiritual significance or an awareness of a kind of "message" present in ordinary things, which invites further elaboration through artistic creation at L2.

Here perception already works in solidarity with another meaning-making mechanism: *emotional understanding*. There are certain meaningful contents that can be only grasped through emotional feelings. This implies that emotions, far from opposing rationality and knowledge, have intentional content and cognitive value.[27] Through them, we become aware of certain properties of reality, and thus they play a fundamental role regarding moral and spiritual understanding. Thus, in the case of the angels, the feeling of compassion gradually evolved:

> It was the attraction to those worn textures that later seemed to me like my imperfections, shortcomings, defects, and barbarities. . . . It was seeing those textures with their aesthetic potentials that allowed me to understand the tender feeling of loving the imperfections of those surfaces, to feel the pertinence of those figures' defects. To let oneself be moved by them.[28]

These perceptual and emotional meaningful contents were further elaborated by another meaning-making mechanism, which has been identified as a funda-

24. Guillermo Santos, artist's journal, workshop 6.

25. Heidegger, *Being and Time*, 187.

26. John Hick, *An Interpretation of Religion: Human Responses to the Transcendent* (New Haven: Yale University Press, 2004), 130.

27. Mark Wynn, *Emotional Experience and Religious Understanding: Integrating Perception, Conception and Feeling* (Cambridge: Cambridge University Press, 2005).

28. Guillermo Santos, artist's journal, workshop 6.

mental aspect of understanding: *knowing-how*.[29] In this sense, to understand something is to be able to do something, since understanding goes implicit in our forms of acting and dealing with the world.[30] Additionally, the LAS exploration showed how mastery in an artistic practice, which implies knowing how to use certain instruments and materials, leads to the discovery of new aspects of signification in the very use of those instruments and materials: "That is why I decided to film them in a detailed plane and then manipulate the photographic form. The drastic changes in image definition gradually brought me an understanding of how the pain of crises opens the path toward beauty."[31] Form and content cannot be separated in an artwork, and there is a direct relationship between the development and production of elaborated aesthetic resources and a deeper understanding.

Even if meaning has a lived, embodied character, and understanding cannot be accounted for only in terms of an intellectual process, concepts, ideas, and beliefs nonetheless play an important part. To account for this role of concepts and ideas we formulated an additional meaning-making mechanism denominated *seeing-as*, after Ludwig Wittgenstein's idea that we perceive things as we *see* them, deploying concepts.[32] In the artists' materials, we found two different ways in which concepts and ideas work in artistic understanding: they provide an interpretative clue to read certain experiences and situations or to direct a creative exploration (guiding seeing-as), or they are produced as the result of the creative process (generative seeing-as). The latter may imply the use of notions proper to an artistic discipline that are now applied to a different situation to make sense of a new experience. This typically implies establishing analogical relationships between the two domains. Generative seeing-as also includes the formulation of new questions that allow reinterpreting past experiences and provide self-knowledge, as well as the formulation of definitions, which tend to occur particularly at L5. The following quotations of the photographer show these aspects of generative seeing-as:

> How to face texture, understood as I intuited it when filming the angels? That is to say, as a manifestation of one's defects, one's own shortcomings? How to love texture? How to love one's own faults and defects without falling into a kind of "self-pity" . . . how to recognize that sensation, those textures without judgment, but without surrendering to them . . . to witness them without judgment and at the same time working on oneself. . . . That has been the search . . . that is the question.

29. Dreyfus, *Being-in-the-World*, 18.
30. Heidegger, *Being and Time*, 182.
31. Guillermo Santos, artist's journal, workshop 6.
32. Ludwig Wittgenstein, *Philosophical Investigations*, 2nd ed. (Oxford: Blackwell: 1999), 193.

> How unpleasant is my texture! The vanity and pride that is in it . . . the desire sometimes to put oneself above others . . . for example. . . . How does one face that? . . . And how do I make art looking at myself in that process? I have no idea.
>
> To be an angel, one must finally get dirty going through crises, to find the light within oneself.[33]

Seeing-as thus leads both to transformations in the artist's self-understanding and form of life (L4) and to the development of more theoretical formulations (L5), which frequently referred to the very nature of artistic understanding, since artists were committed to the project's goals. Reflecting on the process leading to the creation of the angels piece, the photographer claimed:

> Understanding came after the encounter with the form, and that is why I say that the form can be magical, because it comes before rational understanding; and it can even come before in time than knowing its meaning; or before knowing that it is going to be a work. That is why I believe that this movement of the form toward me does not respond to a linear logic of time and, therefore, I believe that this movement is mysterious, intuitive (I doubt that it comes from chance), and not rational.
>
> Understanding is also that clarity that occurs in me when that sensation penetrates my intellect. That is to say, when these ideas are clear within me not only discursively, but when that discussion is pierced by that sensation.[34]

A final meaning-making mechanism we identified has to do with a central trait of spiritual experience, which was denominated by William James its noetic quality. It refers to "states of insight into depths of truth unplumbed by the discursive intellect."[35] Artists reported moments of "illumination," "direct intuition of the divine," and "disclosure of deep significance," which resist expression in ordinary language and cannot be conceptually grasped. They were frequently referred to as ineffable, and artistic creation was considered one of the only means to try to express or point toward them. In the words of the photographer:

33. Guillermo Santos, artist's journal, workshop 6.
34. Guillermo Santos, artist's journal, workshop 6.
35. James, *Varieties of Religious Experience*, 380.

> What is it to feel another dimension of what we are? Evidently, the answer is ineffable but... I recognize with enough clarity... that the limits of my rational cognition, the restrictions of my intellect, do not allow me to approach that answer, and that instead perhaps I can approach it by honoring the capacity of knowledge that feeling offers. During the Laboratory, at a certain moment, it appeared to me, following this way of thinking (or feeling?) that what happens to me when I happen to feel or touch that other deep part of who we are is similar to what I feel when I touch or get close to the seed of what might later become an artistic piece. In both situations, I find a degree of subtlety, an intensity, and a power of feeling that makes them difficult to grasp with words. Both situations then seem to evolve in a sort of decantation that little by little permeates the grounds of reason until they "land" in a concrete way in my life.[36]

We called this kind of intuitive realization of spiritual meaning *perceiving mystery*. Artists frequently affirmed that their artistic practices not only are attempts to express this kind of insight, but that they also can generate it.

This model contributes to the characterization and study of the forms in which artistic creation generates spiritual understanding, based on empirically gathered data. It is presented in detail in the main paper resulting from the project[37] and in the interactive infographics of the CDP.[38]

Questions for Further Research

The model of understanding we have developed allows for the incorporation of third-person approaches for a richer and more comprehensive study of meaning making through the arts. The loci and meaning-making mechanisms may be used as basic descriptions of processes and states whose neurophysiological correlates could be identified, advancing toward a neurophenomenological study.[39] Thus, new questions to continue with our research emerge:

36. Guillermo Santos, autoethnography, 92–104. Online: https://tinyurl.com/45nv8rr9.

37. Carlos Miguel Gómez-Rincón, Natalia Reinoso-Chávez, and Corina Estrada-Barrios, "Unfolding Spiritual Understanding through Artistic Creation: Findings of the Laboratory of Art and Spirituality," *Archive for the Psychology of Religion* (2024), https://doi.org/10.1177/00846724241295783.

38. "Results: Elaborating Meaning through Artistic Creation Interactive Infographics," https://www.spiritualartlab.com/en/resultados.

39. F. J. Varela, "Neurophenomenology: A Methodological Remedy for the Hard Problem," *Journal of Consciousness Studies* 3, no. 4 (1996): 330–49.

1. What neurophysiological correlates of the processes of artistic understanding can be identified at each locus of understanding?
2. How do different forms of language (e.g., narrative, symbolic, analogical, and discursive) relate to the different loci of understanding and meaning-making mechanisms?
3. What experiential contents (e.g., emotional feelings, thoughts, ideas, tendencies) are linked to the five meaning-making mechanisms at each locus?
4. How can first- and third-person approaches fruitfully combine to create a non-reductionist theory of spiritual experience and artistic understanding?

The attempt to find correlates, instead of one-directional causal relationships, between neurophysiological processes and phenomenological experiences implies that neither of them is considered more basic or essential. Thus, a full non-reductionistic model could be developed by integrating first- and third-person approaches. This implies establishing relationships between the subjective content of artists' experiences, registered through meaning-capturing techniques such as the ones we developed, and neurophysiological records, which allows us to contrast changes at the somatic level with the characteristics of the reported experiences.[40]

This would allow us to test and expand our descriptive approach, supplementing it with the investigation of the brain processes associated with artistic and spiritual understanding, while simultaneously avoiding losing sight of the irreducible character of the experience of meaning, which needs to be presented in its own terms.

40. Christopher Timmermann et al., "A Neurophenomenological Approach to Non-ordinary States of Consciousness: Hypnosis, Meditation, and Psychedelics," *Trends in Cognitive Sciences* 27, no. 2 (2023): 139–59.

12

Understanding Existence and the Self through Art

Joshua A. Wilt and Julie J. Exline

Might involvement with art lead to deeper understandings of the world and the human condition?[1] The philosophical position of aesthetic cognitivism helps to capture this idea. If indeed art and understanding share an intricate bond, this would mean that art transcends its role as a source of pleasure, beauty, and aesthetics, extending into the realm of cognition. The idea of a link between art and cognition might seem intuitive; art is both culturally and personally meaningful, often serving as a profound source of significance for societies and individuals alike. However, empirical exploration of the potential connection between art and understanding remains a largely uncharted territory.

As part of our project grant, we examined the relationship between engagement with art and spiritual understandings. We specifically focused on *authenticity* (understandings about one's true self and one's place in the world) and *ultimate meaning* (understandings about the deeper meaning of life and existence). We asked whether and how art might reveal insights into these existential issues that have provoked deep and profound interest throughout human history. We approached engagement with art both from the perspective of the artist and the audience: Might creating art and interacting with the artworks of others relate to a sense of deeper existential understanding?

Another goal of our project grant was to look at connections between engagement with art and meaning in life. If art can yield existential meaning, then engagement with art may help people to experience their lives as more comprehensible, purposeful, and significant.

1. Christoph Baumberger, "Art and Understanding: In Defence of Aesthetic Cognitivism," in *Bilder sehen: Perspektiven der Bildwissenshaft*, ed. Mark Greenlee et al. (Regensburg: Schnell & Steiner, 2013), 41–67; Gordon Graham, *Philosophy of the Arts: An Introduction to Aesthetics* (London: Routledge, 2005).

Psychological-Sciences Approach to Aesthetics

Within the Art Seeking Understanding (ASU) community of practice, our project is situated within the sciences. Specifically, we take a psychological-sciences approach to our research questions, relying on empirical studies to test hypotheses and generate conclusions. Psychological science involves the systematic study of human and nonhuman animal behavior, cognition, emotion, and other psychological concepts.[2] An important point here is that psychological science is agnostic about the accuracy of existential theories or ideas. For instance, psychological science does not try to discover the meaning of life or to reveal a person's true life purpose. Rather, psychological scientists would focus on people's thoughts, feelings, and experiences about existential issues. Indeed, there is an entire subfield of psychology, existential psychology, that delves into how people confront existential issues, such as personal identity, freedom and responsibility, isolation and connectedness, the search for meaning, spirituality, and the inevitability of death.[3] Because we studied existential psychological experiences around art, our project bridges psychology and aesthetics. Thus, our project fits in the interdisciplinary field of empirical aesthetics.

In the upcoming sections, we summarize our work related to the two main goals of our project: seeing how engagement with art relates to spiritual understandings around (1) authenticity and ultimate meaning and (2) overall meaning in life. For each research topic, we start with a literature review and conceptual background, followed by a brief overview of our methods, analyses, and results. We close the chapter by reflecting on lessons learned during the research and emerging questions.

Understandings about Authenticity and Ultimate Meaning

Art could connect with understanding in many ways, especially since the broad concept of understanding can take on various forms and dimensions. Empirical researchers often try to distill general claims or theories into more specific and manageable hypotheses that can be rigorously tested. Along these lines, the ASU grant-making team focused its lens on a distinct subset of understanding: spiritual understanding. Within the boundaries of spiritual understanding, we first zoomed in on two areas: authenticity and ultimate meaning.

2. Elizabeth A. Phelps, Elliot T. Berkman, and Michael Gazzaniga, *Psychological Science*, 7th ed. (New York: Norton, 2022).

3. Jeff Greenberg, Sander L. Koole, and Tom A. Pyszczynski, *Handbook of Experimental Existential Psychology* (New York: Guilford, 2004).

Philosophy, psychology, and religious/spiritual teachings often talk about the quest for authenticity—the attempt to find one's true essence.[4] Current psychological theories focus on several aspects of authentic functioning: self-awareness, knowing positive and negative aspects of oneself, enacting personal values, and being open and honest in relationships.[5] Ultimate meaning refers to a deeper, "ultimate" level of significance to one's own life or life in general.[6] Psychological studies of ultimate meaning focus on how people grapple with the nature of existence, identity, the significance of suffering, and spirituality.[7]

Could involvement with art be a meaningful part of this process? We expected that it would. Artists often try to convey deep meaning through art, and audiences might extract meaning from art as well.[8] Engagement with art, on the part of the artist or audience, may lead to meaning making by encouraging reflection.[9] For instance, powerful personal responses to art, such as feeling chills or a sense of awe, could lead people to contemplate themselves and the world.[10] There are also

4. M. Craig, "To Be or Not to Be: Understanding Authenticity from an Existential Perspective," *Existential Analysis* 20, no. 2 (2009): 292–98; Alexis T. Franzese, "To Thine Own Self Be True? An Exploration of Authenticity," abstract (PhD diss., Duke University, 2007), https://hdl.handle.net/10161/431; Brian M. Goldman and Michael H. Kernis, "A Multicomponent Conceptualization of Authenticity: Theory and Research," *Advances in Experimental Social Psychology* 38 (2006): 283–357.

5. Michael H. Kernis and Brian M. Goldman, "A Multicomponent Conceptualization of Authenticity: Theory and Research," in *Advances in Experimental Social Psychology*, vol. 38, ed. M. P. Zanna (Cambridge, MA: Elsevier Academic, 2006), 283–357; Alex Matthew Wood et al., "The Authentic Personality: A Theoretical and Empirical Conceptualization and the Development of the Authenticity Scale," *Journal of Counseling Psychology* 55, no. 3 (2008): 385–99.

6. Viktor E. Frankl, *Man's Search for Meaning: An Introduction to Logotherapy* (Boston: Beacon, 1992); Viktor E. Frankl, *Man's Search for Ultimate Meaning* (Cambridge, MA: Perseus, 2000).

7. Kenneth I. Pargament and Julie J. Exline, *Working with Spiritual Struggles in Psychotherapy: From Research to Practice* (New York: Guilford, 2022); Joshua A. Wilt et al., "Authenticity, Presence of Meaning, and Struggle with Ultimate Meaning: Nuanced between-and within-Person Associations," *Journal of Research in Personality* 93 (2021); Paul T. P. Wong, "Meaning-Seeking, Self-Transcendence, and Well-Being," in *Logotherapy and Existential Analysis: Proceedings of the Viktor Frankl Institute Vienna*, vol. 1, ed. Alexander Batthyány (Switzerland: Springer, 2016), 311–21.

8. Melissa J. Dolese and Aaron Kozbelt, "Communication and Meaning-Making Are Central to Understanding Aesthetic Response in Any Context," *Frontiers in Psychology* (2020): 11; Pablo P. L. Tinio, "From Artistic Creation to Aesthetic Reception: The Mirror Model," *Psychology of Aesthetics, Creativity, and the Arts* 7, no. 3 (2013): 265–75.

9. A. P. Christensen, E. R. Cardillo, and A. Chatterjee, "Can Art Promote Understanding? A Review of the Psychology and Neuroscience of Aesthetic Cognitivism," *Psychology of Aesthetics, Creativity, and the Arts*, advance online publication, 2023.

10. Aleksandra Sherman and Clair Morrissey, "What Is Art Good For? The Socio-Epistemic Value of Art," *Frontiers in Human Neuroscience* 11 (2017): 411.

some important similarities between aesthetic and religious/spiritual processes, which suggest that engagement with art may relate to existential understandings. Both artistic and religious/spiritual practices could stimulate imagination and poignant emotions related to existential issues.[11] For example, explorations of art and religion/spirituality may both relate to *subjective transcendence*, in which a person perceives the self as part of a greater whole.[12]

Life Stories about Engagement with Art

If engagement with art does result in greater understandings about authenticity and ultimate meaning, where might those understandings reside psychologically? We approached this question with a simple idea: Behind every artwork is a story, authored by the artist. Bringing art into being involves connected stages and events, such as conceptualization, initiation of the work, refinement, and finishing touches.[13] Just as stories typically have a beginning, middle, and end, the artist may recount these stages in narrative form. Similarly, people who have profound experiences with an artwork created by others may find material for new stories. Interactions with art may move from a gradual awareness of sensations (e.g., visual, auditory, emotional) to the features of the artwork itself, the concepts at play, and perhaps even the motivations behind the artwork.[14] Based on these ideas, we proposed that people could find understandings in life stories about creating art and interacting with art produced by others.

Even though life stories are subjective, personal, and idiosyncratic, it is still possible to do empirical research on them. In psychology, a *narrative identity* framework can guide these types of studies.[15] Rooted in the idea that humans are natural storytellers, narrative-identity approaches focus on how the stories we create about our lives can help to shape and express our sense of self.[16] The most engaging or important stories may be emotionally powerful ones in which people

11. Benjamin Beit-Hallahmi, "Understanding Religion through the Psychology of Art," *Leonardo* 16, no. 3 (1983): 237–40.

12. Kutter Callaway et al., "Not All Transcendence Is Created Equal: Distinguishing Ontological, Phenomenological, and Subjective Beliefs about Transcendence," *Philosophical Psychology* 33, no. 4 (2020): 479–510.

13. Tinio, "From Artistic Creation to Aesthetic Reception."

14. Tinio, "From Artistic Creation to Aesthetic Reception."

15. D. P. McAdams, *The Stories We Live By: Personal Myths and the Making of the Self* (New York: William Morrow, 1993).

16. D. P. McAdams, "Narrative Identity," in *Handbook of Identity Theory and Research*, ed. Seth J. Schwartz, Koen Luyckx, and Vivian L. Vignoles (New York: Springer, 2011), 99–115.

can clearly connect the story content with key parts of themselves.[17] For people who have a strong passion for art, stories about artistic creation and engagement may be very valuable, both emotionally and in terms of personal identity.

Understanding and Meaning-Making around Authenticity and Ultimate Meaning

Next, we will summarize our research to date, which focuses on how stories about art experiences can convey understandings. We offer only a brief discussion of our research questions, methods, and results here; we describe the studies in more detail elsewhere.[18]

Aim 1: Understandings about Authenticity and Ultimate Meaning

First, we wanted to focus on understandings about authenticity and ultimate meaning as reflected in these art stories. What did people learn about their true nature and about existence, the world, and the nature of reality? Because previous research has not addressed these questions, we did not have specific hypotheses about what kinds of understandings would emerge. Instead, we chose an exploratory approach, one in which we looked closely at the data to see what types of understanding emerged.

Because we wanted to capture a wide array of understandings around authenticity and ultimate meaning, we sought out people who would represent a diverse spectrum of art expertise and training. Our participants ranged from hobbyists and art students to faculty and professional artists. We also aimed for diversity in art forms (e.g., visual art, performance art, music, sculpture, architecture).

We recruited three samples of participants: one undergraduate sample of art enthusiasts, an online adult sample of art hobbyists, and a sample of art students,

17. Jefferson A. Singer and Pavel Blagov, "The Integrative Function of Narrative Processing: Autobiographical Memory, Self-Defining Memories, and the Life Story of Identity," in *The Self and Memory*, ed. Denise R. Beike, James M. Lampinen, and Douglas A. Behrend (New York: Psychology, 2004), 117–38; Jefferson A. Singer et al., "Self-Defining Memories, Scripts, and the Life Story: Narrative Identity in Personality and Psychotherapy," *Journal of Personality* 81, no. 6 (2013): 569–82.

18. Joshua A. Wilt et al., "Art as a Portal to Narrative Understanding of the True Self and Existence: A Mixed-Methods Study," Association for Research in Personality Conference, Evanston, IL, July 2023; Joshua A. Wilt et al., "Engagement with Art and Meaning in Life: The Predictive Roles of Awe, Interest, and Supernatural Attributions," *Journal of Positive Psychology*, forthcoming; Joshua A. Wilt et al., "Understanding Existence and the Self through Art: Phenomenological Analysis of Life Stories about Art Creation and Interaction," *Existential Psychology Preconference* (online conference), February 2023.

faculty, and staff from university visual and performing arts departments and art schools, as well as members of arts organizations. We collected interviews from 119 participants (62 percent of them female). Of those, 61 percent had formal training in the arts (e.g., faculty at a university or art school, professional artist, current or former art student) and 39 percent reported no formal training but a "lot of experience in the arts." Many reported expertise in music (35 percent) or painting (17 percent), and between 5 and 10 percent reported expertise in dance, drawing, literature, performance art, theater, or photography. Most participants identified as White/Caucasian/European American (56 percent), with more than 10 percent of participants identifying as African American/Black or Asian/Pacific Islander. In terms of religion and spirituality, most identified as Christian (32 percent) or as nonreligious (35 percent).

To gather stories about creating art (creation stories) and interacting with artworks created by others (interaction stories), we used structured interviews, asking all participants a predetermined set of questions. Interviews took place either through videoconferencing (Zoom) or via an online survey. In each interview format, we informed participants that they could select an artwork across a wide range of art forms: "painting, drawing (such as graphic design, illustration), sculpture, stained glass, installation, music, songs, dance, performance art, film, literature (such as poetry, drama), theater, fashion, crafts, mixed media, furniture design, architecture, interior design, plastic arts, or another art that we have not mentioned." To get a sense of these personal stories involving art, we asked participants a variety of questions. For example, we asked about how the story began and unfolded over time, along with high points, low points, and turning points in the experience. To tap into potential existential understandings, we posed targeted questions about authenticity and ultimate meaning.

We used a technique called Interpretative Phenomenological Analysis (IPA)[19] to identify spiritual understandings. Interpretive Phenomenological Analysis is a qualitative method that aims to deeply explore human experiences, seeking to understand the personal significance of lived experiences and the ways that people make sense of them.[20] Research assistants (called "coders") carefully read

19. Jonathan A. Smith, "Beyond the Divide between Cognition and Discourse: Using Interpretative Phenomenological Analysis in Health Psychology," *Psychology and Health* 11, no. 2 (1996): 261–71; Jonathan A. Smith and P. Shinebourne, "Interpretative Phenomenological Analysis," in *APA Handbook of Research Methods in Psychology*, vol. 2, *Research Designs: Quantitative, Qualitative, Neuropsychological, and Biological*, ed. H. Cooper et al. (American Psychological Association, 2012).

20. Pnina Shinebourne, "The Theoretical Underpinnings of Interpretative Phenomenological Analysis (IPA)," *Existential Analysis: Journal of the Society for Existential Analysis* 22, no. 1 (2011).

the responses of study participants, with the aim of trying to immerse themselves in the perspectives of the participants. Table 1 shows some key findings from this analysis. Participants reported understandings about the self, identity, emotions, others, the world, and spirituality. These themes align well with fundamental existential issues.[21]

Table 1. Themes Identified through IPA

AUTHENTICITY THEMES	ULTIMATE MEANING THEMES
Authentic abilities or skills	Connection to nature
Authentic passion for art	Creating art creates meaning
Authentic purpose in life	God controls higher meaning
Authenticity embodied in the artwork	Infinite nature of existence
Authenticity is found in being present	Intuition is connected to ultimate meaning
Clarifying core values	Life is about increasing understanding
Decreased negative evaluation of self	Life is constantly changing
Deep connection to emotions	Life is imperfect
Growth/learning through creating art	Life repeats experiences
Importance of safety for developing authenticity	Love is a fundamental essence
Importance of spirituality	Love is the highest value
Increased trust in core self	Oneness of existence
Increased understanding of beliefs	Other people are here to teach lessons
Inherent generativity and creativity	People are connected
Inherent positivity	Personal truths can be shared through art
Insight into inauthentic aspects of self	Reality is both positive and negative

21. Paul T. P. Wong, "Existential and Humanistic Theories," in *Comprehensive Handbook of Personality and Psychopathology*, ed. Jay C. Thomas and Daniel L. Segal (Wiley & Sons, 2005), 192–211; Paul T. P. Wong, "What Is Existential Positive Psychology?" *International Journal of Existential Psychology and Psychotherapy* 3, no. 1 (2010).

AUTHENTICITY THEMES	ULTIMATE MEANING THEMES
Insight into true interests	Reality is contained in the present moment
Intuition reflects authentic self	Reality is positive
Rediscovery of inner child, youthfulness	Suffering is a part of life
Relational authenticity: connection to others	True nature of reality is spiritual
Revealing personality traits	Uniqueness of each person
Spiritual nature of true self	
Vision of future growth toward authentic self	
Vulnerability	

Aim 2: Predicting Meaning Making around Authenticity and Ultimate Meaning

We expected that some interview responses would reflect more existential insight and meaning making than others. Our second aim, then, was to consider how certain psychological experiences might relate to higher levels of meaning making around art. For these analyses, we went back to the same group of participants described above, but this time we interpreted the data in a different way: Instead of identifying key themes in the responses (as with the IPA technique described above), here we assigned different types of numeric responses (codes) to each response, so that we could analyze the data with statistical techniques.

Coders rated responses to the authenticity and ultimate meaning prompts using the following scale: 0 (no meaning), 1 (specific lesson), 2 (vague meaning), and 3 (insight). For instance, we applied a code of 0 (no meaning) to this response excerpt: "I don't think that this piece necessarily told me something about myself that I didn't already know." We scored the following response excerpt as a 1 (lesson) because there was some meaning focused on a specific piece of information: "One thing I learned about myself with this piece was that I have an eye for color." Here is an excerpt of a response scored as 2 (vague meaning): "something of that idea of unity in the cosmos and in reality." Here, the person had a potentially important realization, but it was not elaborated very thoroughly. And here is an example of a response excerpt coded as a 3 (insight): "I was exploring that part of myself and then coming to the conclusion that okay, I needed art in my life, art was important to me, and I really wanted to help other people." This response showed clear links between the experience and understandings about greater areas of the person's life. We added the scores for authenticity and ultimate meaning responses to create a variable focused on existential meaning making, which we used in later statistical analyses.

We focused on three psychological experiences with art as potential predictors of existential meaning making: interest in art, awe around art, and supernatural attributions around art experiences. Interest in art is an enduring, long-term engagement with art shown through creative practice, learning, or thinking about art.[22] We reasoned that people with strong interest in art might be motivated to search for meaning in art. Awe is a complex emotional experience that involves reverence, wonder, and uncertainty, as well as altered perceptions of time and self-awareness.[23] Awe-inspiring experiences might draw attention to knowledge gaps and prompt searches for meaning and understanding to fill those gaps.[24] Some people might also make supernatural attributions for art experiences;[25] in other words, they might believe that God (or gods), human spirits, or cosmic forces like fate/destiny or karma are playing a role in their art experiences. These types of supernatural explanations might help people to feel connected with something greater that transcends the material world. We used survey measures to assess interest in art,[26] awe around art,[27] and supernatural attributions for art experiences.[28]

22. Christensen, Cardillo, and Chatterjee, "Can Art Promote Understanding?"

23. Dacher Keltner and Jonathan Haidt, "Approaching Awe, a Moral, Spiritual, and Aesthetic Emotion," *Cognition and Emotion* 17, no. 2 (2003): 297–314; David B. Yaden et al., "The Development of the Awe Experience Scale (AWE-S): A Multifactorial Measure for a Complex Emotion," *Journal of Positive Psychology* 14, no. 4 (2019): 474–88.

24. Jonathon McPhetres, "Oh, the Things You Don't Know: Awe Promotes Awareness of Knowledge Gaps and Science Interest," *Cognition and Emotion* 33, no. 8 (2019): 1599–615; Grace N. Rivera et al., "Awe and Meaning: Elucidating Complex Effects of Awe Experiences on Meaning in Life," *European Journal of Social Psychology* 50, no. 2 (2020): 392–405.

25. Julie J. Exline and Joshua A. Wilt, "Supernatural Attributions: Seeing God, the Devil, Spirits, Fate/Destiny, and Karma as Causes of Events," *Annual Review of Clinical Psychology* 19 (2023): 461–87.

26. James Rounds et al., *O* NET Interest Profiler Short Form Psychometric Characteristics: Summary* (National Center for O* NET Development, 2010).

27. Michelle N. Shiota, Dacher Keltner, and Oliver P. John, "Positive Emotion Dispositions Differentially Associated with Big Five Personality and Attachment Style," *Journal of Positive Psychology* 1, no. 2 (2006): 61–71.

28. Joshua A. Wilt et al., "Who Engages with Supernatural Entities? An Investigation of Personality and Cognitive Style Predictors," *Imagination, Cognition, and Personality* 41, no. 4 (2022): 373–414.

Using the statistical technique of correlation, which looks at relationships between variables, we examined how each of these psychological variables related to the existential meaning-making variable that we created from our numerical coding process. We found that interest in art and awe around art were clearly associated with meaning making, but supernatural attributions were not.

Aesthetic Dispositions, Aesthetic Experiences, and Meaning in Life

The research questions above focused on specific existential understandings about authenticity and ultimate meaning. But how might engagement with art relate to an overall experience of life as meaningful? Experiences with art—creating art and interacting with the art of others—have been highly meaningful to humans throughout history and across cultures.[29] Thus, it seems natural that involvement with art would relate to a greater sense of meaning in life—an idea that has been supported in some research studies.[30]

Research Questions. We wanted to build on this prior work in two ways. First, we wanted to focus on how people differ in some specific psychological experiences with art (which we called *aesthetic experiences* here) that may relate to meaning in life. We focused on the same three psychological factors described above as our aesthetic experience variables for this study: interest in art, awe around art, and supernatural attributions around art experiences. We also included *aesthetic fluency*, which refers to knowledge about art.[31]

In this study, we were interested not only in these aesthetic experiences, which any person could have in response to art; we were also curious about whether these aesthetic experiences around art might serve as pathways, helping to explain why certain types of people might report more meaning in life. Here, we were interested in people who had higher vs. lower levels of *aesthetic dispositions*, which are a person's typical, fairly stable levels of engagement with art in daily

29. Henrik Hagtvedt and Kathleen D. Vohs, "Viewing Challenging Art Lends Meaning to Life by Stimulating Integrative Complexity," *Journal of Positive Psychology* 17, no. 6 (2022): 876–87.

30. Hagvedt and Vohs, "Viewing Challenging Art"; Peter Totterdell and Giulia Poerio, "An Investigation of the Impact of Encounters with Artistic Imagination on Well-Being," *Emotion* 21, no. 6 (2021): 1340–55.

31. Paul J. Silvia, "Knowledge-Based Assessment of Expertise in the Arts: Exploring Aesthetic Fluency," *Psychology of Aesthetics, Creativity, and the Arts* 1, no. 4 (2007): 247; Lisa F. Smith and Jeffrey K. Smith, "The Nature and Growth of Aesthetic Fluency," in *New Directions in Aesthetics, Creativity, and the Arts*, ed. Paul Locher, Colin Martindale, and Leonid Dorfman (London: Routledge, 2006), 47–58.

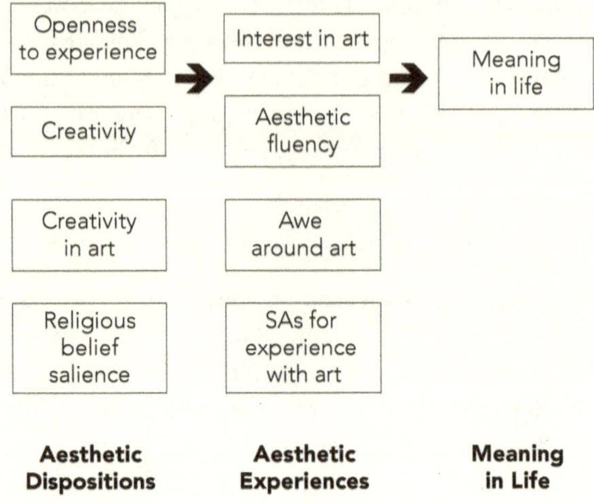

Figure 1. Conceptual Model Relating Aesthetic Dispositions Aesthetic Experiences, and Meaning in Life

life. Might these aesthetic experience variables help to explain why people higher in aesthetic dispositions report more meaning in life?

We drew the expected relationships as part of a model (figure 1). We wanted to see how well our data would fit this model. And, as stated above, we were especially interested in how the aesthetic experiences (middle column of boxes) might serve as routes by which the aesthetic dispositions (left column of boxes) might relate to meaning in life.

Figure 1 lays out the specific variables that we examined. The left section includes three aesthetic dispositions that we included in our study: openness to experience, creativity, and religious belief salience. Openness to experience is a personality trait encompassing tendencies for open-mindedness, curiosity, and intellect.[32] People with greater openness experience more awe around art and typically have higher levels of aesthetic interests and knowledge.[33] Creativity in-

32. C. G. DeYoung, L. C. Quilty, and J. B. Peterson, "Between Facets and Domains: Ten Aspects of the Big Five," *Journal of Personality and Social Psychology* 93, no. 5 (2007): 880–96; Robert R. McCrae and Angelina R. Sutin, "Openness to Experience," in *Handbook of Individual Differences in Social Behavior*, ed. Mark R. Leary and Rick H. Hoyle (New York: Guilford Press, 2009), 257–73.

33. Susan K. Chen and Miriam Mongrain, "Awe and the Interconnected Self," *Journal of Positive Psychology* 16, no. 6 (2021): 770–78; Christensen, Cardillo, and Chatterjee, "Can Art Promote Understanding?"

volves generating novel and useful ideas.[34] Because creativity is central to art,[35] it is important to explore its unique effects, in general and in art specifically, apart from openness. Religious belief salience indicates how central religious beliefs are in a person's life.[36] Because religion often includes supernatural beliefs,[37] we reasoned that people with greater religious belief salience would make more supernatural attributions around art.

Predicting Meaning in Life

We next briefly describe our research looking at predictors of meaning in life. See the referenced sources for more details.[38]

Aim 1: Predicting Meaning in Life from Aesthetic Experiences

We recruited participants from the same groups described above: (a) undergraduates with experience in art, (b) an online sample reporting art as a hobby, and (c) people affiliated with university arts departments, art schools, or community arts organizations. We collected data from one hundred participants from each group, for a total of three hundred participants (64 percent female). This sample was divided quite evenly between those with formal arts training (53 percent) and those without formal training, who pursued art as a hobby (47 percent). Again, music (22 percent), painting (23 percent), and drawing (17 percent) were highly represented. Most participants identified as White/Caucasian/European (65 percent), with more than 10 percent of participants identifying as African American/Black, Asian/Pacific Islander, or Latino/Hispanic. And again, most participants identified either as Christian (43 percent) or as nonreligious (e.g., agnostic, atheist, none) affiliations (33 percent). We used an online survey to measure interest

34. James C. Kaufman and John Baer, "Sure, I'm Creative—but Not in Mathematics! Self-Reported Creativity in Diverse Domains," *Empirical Studies of the Arts* 22, no. 2 (2004): 143–55.

35. Gerald C. Cupchik, "The Thinking-I and the Being-I in Psychology of the Arts," *Creativity Research Journal* 12, no. 3 (1999): 165–73; Tinio, "From Artistic Creation to Aesthetic Reception."

36. Bruce Blaine and Jennifer Crocker, "Religiousness, Race, and Psychological Well-Being: Exploring Social Psychological Mediators," *Personality and Social Psychology Bulletin* 21, no. 10 (1995): 1031–41.

37. Exline and Wilt, "Supernatural Attributions."

38. Joshua A. Wilt et al., "Aesthetic Dispositions, Aesthetic Experiences, and Meaning in Life," *Empirical Studies of the Arts* (2024); Joshua A. Wilt et al., "Experiences with Art and Meaning in Life: The Predictive Roles of Interest, Awe, and Supernatural Attributions," Association for Psychological Science Convention, Washington, DC, May 2023; Wilt et al., "Engagement with Art and Meaning in Life."

in art,[39] aesthetic fluency,[40] awe around art,[41] supernatural attributions for art experiences[42] and meaning in life.[43]

We computed correlations between each aesthetic experience variable and meaning in life, and we looked at these across all participants and within each individual sample. We found positive links among all the aesthetic experience variables and meaning in life in the full sample and in the online sample of art hobbyists. We did not find associations between predictors and meaning in life in the undergraduate sample. And, in the sample of individuals affiliated with art schools and organizations, we found that only awe related positively to meaning in life.

These results yielded rather mixed support for our hypotheses; only the online sample of hobbyists showed results consistent with our predictions. We speculate that the differences in these results may be due to differences in the relative importance of art between the groups. Among undergraduates with relatively little formal training, art experiences may not be central to one's life and therefore not strongly related to meaning in life. For people affiliated with art schools/organizations and high levels of formal training, art may be uniformly important. Therefore, interest in art and aesthetic fluency might not differentiate these individuals. Instead, only extraordinary, awe-inspiring experiences were highly relevant to meaning in life. People in the online sample of hobbyists may have fit into a sort of "middle ground"; they probably placed varying levels of importance on art, and this variation may be what allowed us to detect more relationships between the factors.

Aim 2: Testing a Model Relating Aesthetic Dispositions, Aesthetic Experiences, and Meaning in Life

Our final aim was to try to replicate and build on the findings predicting meaning in life from the previous study. Because findings from the online hobbyist sample fit best with our predictions, we now turned to a larger sample of hobbyists with moderate levels of formal art training. We also tested the figure 1 model again. As a reminder, the overall logic behind the figure 1 model is that aesthetic dispositions would relate to aesthetic experiences, which in turn would relate to meaning in

39. Rounds et al., *O*NET Interest Profiler.*

40. Smith and Smith, "Nature and Growth of Aesthetic Fluency."

41. Shiota et al., "Positive Emotion Dispositions."

42. Joshua A Wilt et al., "Who Engages with Supernatural Entities? An Investigation of Personality and Cognitive Style Predictors," *Imagination, Cognition, and Personality* 41, no. 4 (2022): 373–414.

43. Login S. George and Crystal L. Park, "The Multidimensional Existential Meaning Scale: A Tripartite Approach to Measuring Meaning in Life," *Journal of Positive Psychology* 12, no. 6 (2017): 613–27.

life. Therefore, aesthetic dispositions may relate to meaning in life in part because of their associations with aesthetic experiences (which we tested through statistical mediation). We made the following specific predictions. First, we predicted that openness would relate to meaning in life through each aesthetic experience. Second, we predicted that creativity variables would relate to meaning in life through interest in art, aesthetic fluency, and awe around art. Third, we predicted that religious belief salience would relate to meaning in life through supernatural attributions (SAs) for art experiences.

We surveyed 691 art hobbyists. A little more than half of the hobbyists were informally involved in art, and nearly half of the sample had experience as an art student or professional. Many were engaged with drawing, painting, music, digital art, or photography. This sample was demographically similar to the others; most participants were White/Caucasian/European American (75%) and identified as Christian (40%) or nonreligious (41%). Participants completed the online survey measures of aesthetic experiences and meaning in life reported previously, as well as measures of aesthetic dispositions: openness,[44] creativity in general and in art specifically,[45] and religious belief salience.[46]

Correlational analyses replicated key results from the previous study: Once again, interest in art, aesthetic fluency, awe around art, and SAs for art experiences were positively related to meaning in life.

In the path analysis and our tests of statistical mediation,[47] we found that aesthetic dispositions related positively to aesthetic experiences. However, only a few effects of dispositions on meaning in life were explained, or statistically mediated, by experiences: All dispositions related to meaning in life through interest in art, and creativity in art related to meaning in life via awe (and not through the other variables shown in the middle column of figure 1). We speculate that this narrower aspect of creativity, because it is specifically about aesthetics, may be more tightly tied to awe-inspiring and meaningful experiences with art.

Research Challenges and Solutions

Some of the major lessons we learned concerned recruitment of participants—an area where we ran into some challenges. We originally planned to recruit partic-

44. M. B. Donnellan et al., "The Mini-IPIP Scales: Tiny-Yet-Effective Measures of the Big Five Factors of Personality," *Psychological Assessment* 18, no. 2 (2006): 192.

45. Kaufman and Baer, "Sure, I'm Creative."

46. Blaine and Crocker, "Religiousness, Race, and Psychological Well-Being."

47. David P. MacKinnon et al., "A Comparison of Methods to Test Mediation and Other Intervening Variable Effects," *Psychological Methods* 7, no. 1 (2002): 83–104.

ipants for interview studies through an online research firm only. Though the research firm collected survey data efficiently, we observed a low opt-in rate to the interview, and so we sought other means to recruit participants. We reached out to administrators at universities, art schools, and art organizations, and many were receptive to advertising our study via emails, listservs, and websites. We achieved much higher opt-in rates to interviews through these additional means of data collection. We were also able to reduce costs due to being able to pay participants directly rather than using the research firm as an intermediary. We originally planned for data analysis to focus heavily on interview data rather than survey data. However, conducting, transcribing and qualitative coding of more than one hundred thirty-minute interviews proved to be more time-intensive than anticipated, even with ten research assistants each working three to six hours per week. Therefore, while continuing to work on qualitative coding, we pivoted to quantitative analysis of survey data. These latter analyses proved fruitful, and the results formed the basis of our second major aim.

Progress Made and Emerging Questions

ASU projects endeavor to reveal whether and how art relates to greater spiritual understandings. Our project grant has yielded intriguing empirical findings about the spiritual understandings that people convey in life stories about emotionally salient experiences with art. For example, for authenticity, participants have elaborated on how they have come to understand their true feelings, thought processes, interests, and personalities. For ultimate meaning, participants have narrated understandings about life and death, the significance of suffering, the universality of loss and change, the nature of love, and the underlying fabric of reality. Further, we discovered that psychological experiences with art (e.g., awe, interest, supernatural attributions) predict variation in meaning making around authenticity and ultimate meaning. These findings suggest that art may possess cognitive value by sparking critical thinking and prompting people to engage in self-reflection about their identity, their place in the world, and the fundamental essence of reality.

Beyond examining how engagement with art relates to specific spiritual understandings, we are also making progress toward comprehending the interplay between art engagement and meaning in life. The psychological experiences of awe, interest, and supernatural attributions are relevant here as well. Further, they may work in conjunction with dispositional variables such as openness, creativity, and religious belief salience to potentially influence meaning in life. Again, these findings may suggest associations between art and understanding, as art may encourage individuals to contemplate and grasp the profound connections between their artistic experiences and the core purpose and significance of their existence.

Our findings lead naturally to additional questions, four of which we are particularly interested in exploring further. First, how are understandings from stories about emotionally salient experiences with art incorporated into broader life stories? For example, do such understandings permeate one's stories in art, religious/spiritual life stories, and life stories in general? Second, how do storied, spiritual understandings achieved through engaging with art develop over the course of weeks to months? Do they emerge gradually, or are there "aha" insights or epiphanies that guide the understanding process? Third, do spiritual understandings conveyed in stories about specific art forms (e.g., visual art, literature, dance, and music) differ from each other? Though any art form may lead to understandings, the different arts may emphasize different skills and thought processes which may lend themselves to different understandings. And finally, what are the roles of aesthetic dispositions and experiences in predicting understandings in broader life stories, how do understandings develop, and are understandings associated with specific art forms? In exploring these questions, we aim to delve deeper into the transformative potential of art in shaping life stories and spiritual understanding.

13

Spiritual Understanding in a Secular Age and Art as Religious Ritual

Lexi Eikelboom and Valerie van Mulukom

The Art Seeking Understanding (ASU) program naturally invites interdisciplinary work, but what such interdisciplinarity entails can vary dramatically. Perhaps one of the greatest contributions of the project "Spiritual Understanding in a Secular Age: Engaging Art as Religious Ritual" is that it pushed the boundaries of what interdisciplinary work can look like. Because our project approached art practice as a form of knowledge in its own right, the relationship between art and more traditional academic disciplines offered an opportunity for interdisciplinary innovation. Moreover, because we sought to understand the spiritual significance of this way of knowing the world through a comparison with religious ritual, which has been studied by many disciplines, our approach naturally invited perspectives from across the humanities and the social sciences. What we hope to show here is that pushing the boundaries of interdisciplinarity in these ways, while challenging, has been essential to developing methodological innovations for unearthing the distinctive cognitive value of the arts.

The field of ritual studies is characterized by many disciplines and methods. We are perhaps disposed to think first of the classic texts by anthropologists like Victor Turner, Mary Douglas, and Catherine Bell. However, alongside the persistence of anthropological approaches, there exist also literary and psychological approaches, as well as treatments from philosophy and theology. Where sociologists and anthropologists unearth the social functions of religious rituals, psychologists attempt to identify how rituals affect individuals, whether physically or psychically.[1] Philosophers and scholars of religion seek to make claims about

1. Valerie van Mulukom, "Remembering Religious Rituals: Autobiographical Memories of High-Arousal Religious Rituals Considered from a Narrative Processing Perspective," *Religion, Brain & Behavior* 7, no. 3 (2017): 191–205; Sarah. J. Charles et al., "Blocking Mu-Opioid Receptors

the role of ritual in religion or what ritual reveals about some aspect of being human,[2] while theologians focus on the significance of particular rituals, such as the Christian liturgy, in the context of the doctrines and beliefs that render them meaningful to those who undertake them.[3] Some of these approaches are combined harmoniously.[4] At other times, however, serious methodological differences create disagreements over how the object of study—ritual—ought to be defined or whether the term ought to be used at all, a question commonly raised about the term "religion" as well.[5]

The challenge of studying a diversity of human expressions from multiple perspectives, all with reference to a common heading such as "ritual," reflects the complexity of the phenomena to which the term "ritual" refers, and it is this tension between a theoretical category, on the one hand, and complex human behavior, on the other, that makes ritual studies a helpful lens for approaching art practice as well. Among other things, religious rituals are complex embodied activities that engage both social norms and metaphysical beliefs. They thus involve multiple aspects of human existence—embodiment, belief, sociality, questions about human essence and significance, etc.—and different disciplines and methods necessarily prioritize one or more of these aspects or envision their inter-relationship in different ways. If art practice is, like ritual practice, a complex

Inhibits Social Bonding in Rituals," *Biology Letters* 16, no. 10 (2020): article number 20200485, http://dx.doi.org/10.1098/rsbl.2020.0485; Ronald Fischer and Janpaphat Kruekaew, "Synchrony vs. Pain in Males and Females: An Examination of Differential Effects on Social Bonding in a Naturally Occurring Ritual," *Religion, Brain & Behavior* 10, no. 4 (2020): 407–27; Nicholas M. Hobson et al., "The Psychology of Rituals: An Integrative Review and Process-Based Framework," *Personality and Social Psychology Review* 22, no. 3 (2018): 260–84.

2. Talal Asad, "Toward a Genealogy of the Concept of Ritual," *Genealogies of Religion: Discipline and Reasons of Power in Christianity and Islam* (Baltimore: Johns Hopkins University Press, 1993); Amy Hollywood, "Performativity, Citationality, Ritualization," *History of Religions* 42, no. 2 (2002): 93–115; Kevin Schilbrack, *Thinking through Rituals: Philosophical Perspectives* (New York: Routledge, 2004).

3. Terence Cuneo, *Ritualized Faith: Essays on the Philosophy of Liturgy* (Oxford: Oxford University Press, 2016); Theodore W. Jennings, "On Ritual Knowledge," *Journal of Religion* 62, no. 2 (1982): 111–27.

4. Catherine Bell's classic text *Ritual Theory, Ritual Practice* (Oxford: Oxford University Press, [1990], 2010) engages literary theorists alongside anthropologists and philosophers.

5. Two of our project contributors wrote essays on this subject for the project's edited volume: Marko Geslani, "The Temporality of a Medieval Brahmanical Procession: Ritual Time and the Time of 'Ritual,'" and Elayne Oliphant, "Subtraction in Ritual" in *Art-Making as Spiritual Practice: Rituals of Embodied Understanding*, ed. Lexi Eikelboom and David Newheiser (New York: Bloomsbury, 2025). See also Catherine Bell, "Modernism and Postmodernism in the Study of Religion," *Religious Studies Review* 22, no. 3 (1996): 179–89.

embodied activity undertaken by humans and couched in both social norms and metaphysical beliefs, then the conversations and disagreements involved in attempts to talk about religious rituals may likewise be important for approaching art practice responsibly as an object of study. It is this complexity and the challenges revealed by the study of ritual that demand the kinds of interdisciplinary innovation this project exemplifies.

Research Questions

Beyond this methodological usefulness, ritual theorists also sometimes suggest that particular functions of ritual—the construction of identity and subjectivity, the production of culture, the activation of a symbolic universe, for example—are likewise associated with art.[6] Victor Turner, for example, suggests that rituals and artists both rearrange elements of culture into new patterns. Both instantiate an escape from social structure so that those structures can be reinstituted in new forms.[7] Such functions would, moreover, qualify as developments in insight or understanding as defined by aesthetic cognitivists,[8] suggesting the possibility of a connection between ritual and art in terms of epistemic function.

Continuity between ritual and art practice has haunted art theory and criticism as well. Deborah Lewer claims that the ritual function of art "has been a strikingly recurrent concern for historians of (primarily) Western art."[9] Beyond the obvious ritual origins of art, it has been argued that contemporary artists and curators both carry ritualizing agency in secular society.[10] Walter Benjamin suggests that, while art has become progressively distanced from its ritual functions, it has retained its aura as something almost magical, to be experienced with

6. Victor Turner, *Dramas, Fields, and Metaphors: Symbolic Action in Human Society* (Ithaca, NY: Cornell University Press, 1974); Robert E. Innis, "The Tacit Logic of Ritual Embodiments: Rappaport and Polanyi between Thick and Thin," in *Ritual in Its Own Right*, ed. Don Handelman and Galina Lindquist (New York: Bergham Books, 2005), 197–212; Margo Kitts, "Discursive, Iconic, and Somatic Perspectives on Ritual," *Journal of Ritual Studies* 31, no. 1 (2017): 11–26.

7. Turner, *Dramas, Fields, and Metaphors*, 255–56.

8. Gordon Graham, *Philosophy of the Arts: An Introduction to Aesthetics* (London: Routledge, [1997] 2005); Christoph Baumberger, "Art and Understanding: In Defence of Aesthetic Cognitivism," in *Bilder sehen: Perspektiven der Bildwissenschaft*, ed. Mark Greenlee et al. (Regensburg: Schnell & Steiner, 2011).

9. Deborah Lewer, "Theorising Ritual and Art After Modernity," in Eikelboom and Newheiser, *Art-Making as Spiritual Practice*.

10. Hans Belting, "Image, Medium, Body: A New Approach to Iconology," *Critical Inquiry* 31, no. 2 (2005): 302–19, 309; Carol Duncan, *Civilising Rituals: Inside Public Art Museums* (London: Routledge 1995).

reverence, on display particularly in the autonomy of art movement. As this way of thinking about art as autonomous becomes increasingly discredited, Lewer nevertheless suggests that "if solipsistic and expressionist forms of auratic art have been discredited, and the ethical imperatives of participatory art circumscribed, the potential ritual has for endowing meaning, structuring experience, challenging injustice, seeking better ways of being in the world and demarcating the distinctiveness of the sacred, may yet signal a renewal of its relationship with art, however technologically mediated."[11] In other words, ritual has been a reference point for articulating the significance of art in both art history and ritual studies and, moreover, continues to offer new resources in the face of our changing ideas about the significance of art.

In response to these associations, we were interested in whether a kind of spiritual insight could result from engaging with art through practices like preparing materials, attentive observation, and repetitive motion, which share features with ritual practices. By focusing on the cognitive effects of art practices, we asked whether art may be a source of spiritual understanding regardless of the thematic content of the art or the beliefs of the artist or audience. More specifically, we framed our research questions in terms of a comparison between art practice and religious ritual:

- In what ways, if any, are art making and art reception analogous to participation in religious rituals?
- Does art contribute to spiritual understanding in ways that can be likened to a religious ritual's contribution to spiritual understanding?
- What tools, methods, and frameworks does the field of ritual studies offer to help researchers better understand art's contribution to spiritual understanding?

Recent studies in experimental psychology have shown that ritual practices share underlying cognitive processes regardless of whether they are performed in a religious or a non-religious setting.[12] Since these processes do not depend on the belief-content of ritual but pertain to its form, including its temporal features, its violation of intuitive causal relations, and its transformation of an object beyond

11. Deborah Lewer, "Theorising Ritual and Art After Modernity," in Eikelboom and Newheiser, *Art-Making as Spiritual Practice*.

12. Pascal Boyer and Pierre Liénard, "Why Ritualized Behavior? Precaution Systems and Action Parsing in Developmental, Pathological and Cultural Rituals," *Behavioral and Brain Sciences* 29 (2006): 1–56; Robert N. McCauley and E. Thomas Lawson, *Bringing Ritual to Mind: Psychological Foundations of Cultural Forms* (Cambridge: Cambridge University Press, 2002).

the observable effects of the action[13] (features which may be part of art practice as well), engagement with art may likewise have similar effects. We hypothesized that practices of art making and art reception make use of similar affective, social, and cognitive processes as those that underwrite religious rituals.

The project involved two strands: one conceptual and the other experimental. The experimental strand tested for effects of engagement with a choreographed dance performance, that is, an artwork without religious thematic content but with ritualized, synchronous movements. The conceptual strand worked with practicing artists to identify possible epistemic aspects of art making and compared them to the working of those aspects in ritual.

The hypothesis guiding the experimental study was that, for both religious and non-religious participants, perceiving a choreographed performance is associated with feelings of self-transcendence and positive affect, and leads to a significant subsequent increase in social bonding—effects that are similar to those generated by religious rituals.[14] Psychologists Valerie van Mulukom and Miguel Farias, together with choreographer Robert Clark, proposed, specifically, that "the main effect of interest that may be shared between religious rituals and artistic experience is *self-transcendence*. Self-transcendence is what happens when (1) self-boundaries are reduced, or a focus on the self becomes less salient, and when (2) one becomes connected to (even merged with) something bigger than oneself (whether one's surroundings, group, or even the universe), potentially via the expansion of self-boundaries (Yaden et al., 2017)."[15]

The experimenters examined whether an arts performance, like a religious ritual, could induce these effects by testing for the following three hypotheses, which were based on their previous research on religious rituals:[16] (1) experiencing an art performance together increases social bonding with coattendees as

13. Boyer and Liénard, "Why Ritualized Behavior?"; Justin L. Barrett and E. Thomas Lawson, "Ritual Intuitions: Cognitive Contributions to Judgments of Ritual Efficacy," *Journal of Cognition and Culture* 1, no. 2 (2001): 183–201; Justin L. Barrett and Brian Malley, "A Cognitive Typology of Religious Actions," *Journal of Cognition and Culture* 7, no. 3–4 (2007): 201–11.

14. Boyer and Liénard, "Why Ritualized Behavior?"; Sarah J. Charles et al., "United on Sunday: The Effects of Secular Rituals on Social Bonding and Affect," *PLoS One* 16, no. 1 (2021): article number e0242546, https://doi.org/10.1371/journal.pone.0242546.

15. Valerie van Mulukom et al., "Blurring of Self-Other Boundaries Is Associated with Awe and Social Bonding in an Art Ritual Performance," *PsyArXiv* (2025): https://doi.org/10.31234/osf.io/6atkp_v1, 2.

16. Sarah Charles et al., "Religious Rituals Increase Social Bonding and Pain Threshold," *PsyArXiv* (2020); Sarah J. Charles et al., "Blocking Mu-Opioid Receptors,"; Sarah J. Charles et al., "United on Sunday"; Sarah Charles et al., "Bending and Bonding: A Randomized Controlled Trial on the Socio-Psychobiological Effects of Spiritual versus Secular Yoga Practice on Social Bonding," *Current Psychology* (2022): 1–17.

does a religious ritual; (2) the increase in social bonding is predicted by positive affect and feelings of self-transcendence as well as awe during the experience; (3) perceiving blurred boundaries between self and other predicts (a) increased feelings of self-transcendence and (b) associated increased social bonding.[17]

Thus, the experiment tested our main hypothesis that practices of art reception make use of similar processes as those that underwrite the experience of religious rituals by testing, specifically, for experiences of self-transcendence, positive affect, and social bonding, which have been shown to be operative in rituals, both religious and non-religious.

The conceptual strand of the study, in contrast, focused on art making and sought to test the hypothesis by beginning, not from processes that have already been shown to be operative in religious rituals, but from the making practices of artists themselves in order to identify additional promising processes that contribute to art making as a way of knowing, and that may have spiritual significance. Only then did we ask scholars of ritual to write about these features in relation to a particular ritual in order to identify whether or not any overlaps were suggested that might offer promising avenues for future research. The conceptual strand of the study thus tested our main hypothesis that practices of art making make use of similar processes as those that underwrite religious rituals by identifying such processes in specific art-making practices and then observing how scholars studying ritual practices spoke about similar processes in religious rituals.

Methods and Outcomes

Experimental

Van Mulukom and Farias's experimental intervention was a ten-minute adaptation of the performance "MASS" choreographed by Robert Clark. In the adaptation, two participants sat opposite one another while a dancer moved behind each of them in synchrony, the two dancers mirroring one another. Participants could see the mirroring through their peripheral vision and eventually experienced synchronous touch as well, intended to cause a sense of blurred boundaries between the participants' bodies, which van Mulukom, Farias, and Clark called "mirror fusion." In the control condition, the dancers moved in near synchrony but with a five- to ten-second delay. Using surveys administered both before and after the experience, the experimenters tested participants for the same sorts of effects of self-transcendence and social bonding for which they test in religious rituals.

17. Van Mulukom et al., "Blurring of Self-Other Boundaries," 3.

If the results showed an experience of self-transcendence and a subsequent significant increase in bonding from before to after the performance, the experimenters would interpret this as supporting our hypothesis that engagement in artistic performance relies on similar affective, social, and cognitive processes as is the case for religious rituals, which may, in turn, indicate an increase in a certain kind of embodied spiritual understanding. Moreover, through comparing the results of the main condition (i.e., the dancers moving in synchrony with each other) with the control condition (i.e., the dancers moving in canon, with a five- to ten-second delay between them), the researchers would be further able to distinguish the effects of synchronous movement—a highly important component of many religious rituals around the world,[18] which would itself be an instance of artistic contribution to academic knowledge concerning spiritual matters since the experiment relied on a choreographer's artwork in its design. The experimental method and outcomes are all detailed in the forthcoming article "Blurring of Self-Other Boundaries Is Associated with Awe and Social Bonding in an Art Ritual Performance."[19]

The experimenters found that, in both conditions, social bonding significantly increased from before to after the performance. Moreover, social bonding overall was greater in the main (synchrony) condition than in the control (canon) condition, but this did not interact with the comparison from pre- to post-performance, meaning that the *increase* in social bonding was not greater in the main condition than in the control condition. This seems to suggest that synchronous movement was not a driving factor of the social bonding in the artistic performance, as it likely is in religious rituals. This was somewhat surprising, given that the researchers did find that the experience of "mirror fusion" was greater in the main condition than in the control condition, as was participants' experience of feelings of connectedness to the world around them.

However, the researchers suggest that in order to really understand what is happening in this experiment, we should look at individual differences. That is, we should ask: "What needs to be in place for someone to experience social bonding

18. Léon Turner, "Synchronous Rituals and Social Bonding: Revitalizing Conceptions of Individual Personhood in the Evolution of Religion," *Zygon* 56, no. 4 (2021): 898–921; Michele J. Gelfand et al., "The Cultural Evolutionary Trade-off of Ritualistic Synchrony," *Philosophical Transactions of the Royal Society B* 375, no. 1805 (2020): article number 20190432, https://doi.org/10.1098/rstb.2019.0432; Martin Lang et al., "Sync to Link: Endorphin-Mediated Synchrony Effects on Cooperation," *Biological Psychology* 127 (2017): 191–97.

19. Valerie van Mulukom et al. offer more of the theoretical framework that makes sense of this research in their essay "Art Performances and Religious Rituals: How Transformative Experiences Can Foster Knowledge," in Eikelboom and Newheiser, *Art-Making as Spiritual Practice*.

(in whichever condition)?", thereby focusing attention on the underlying processes rather than the experimental context. Through analyzing such individual differences, the experimenters found that when an individual experienced an increase in social bonding, this was preceded by an experience of "mirror fusion" during the performance. In other words, these participants experienced a strong feeling of dissolution of the self-other boundary. This was a very strong effect, and the strongest effect of all the measurements, suggesting that the experience of mirror fusion may have been a requirement for social bonding to take place. The experience of awe was similarly (though less strongly) predictive of increases in social bonding. Together, these findings suggest that when an artistic performance reduces a person's sense of his or her boundaries, it may also allow for an experience of merging with others, much like the effect of self-transcendence in religious rituals.

From this experiment we learned that a feeling of self-transcendence may be bound up with experiences of social bonding, suggesting that social, affective, and perspective-shifting events occur together and can perhaps even predict one another. In the context of aesthetic cognitivist theories, which argue that works of art contribute to knowledge or understanding, it is significant that increases in social bonding could also indicate perspectival shifts. Moreover, as a prominent feature of religious rituals, it may suggest a perspectival shift of a particularly spiritual kind, which can be induced by encounters with art.

Conceptual

The outcome of the experiment, in which the art performance functioned in ways that are both similar to and different from religious ritual, is consistent with the starting point for the conceptual work undertaken as part of the project in that we did not begin from a presumption of any particular direct parallels between art making and ritual. While some ritual theorists, as outlined above, have drawn direct parallels between the functions of ritual and the functions of art, we chose not to impose such expectations onto artists. In this, we took our cue from research that problematizes the term "ritual" as universalizing and as servicing the needs of theory rather than the practices it seeks to name,[20] and instead attempted to go back to the practices themselves, so to speak.[21]

20. E.g., Bell, *Ritual Theory, Ritual Practice*, 19–49.

21. The theoretical foundation for this approach was presented in the conference paper by Lexi Eikelboom, "How Do We Approach Art Practice through Ritual Theory?" The European Academy of Religion, August 2021.

Sarah Tomasetti, David Newheiser, and Lexi Eikelboom collected a group of scholars in Melbourne, Australia, and together watched footage of seven artists working, visited their studios, and had several conversations with them about their art-making practices. The task given to this group was simply to understand as best as possible if and how these artists' practices functioned as a kind of knowing. The scholars came from a range of disciplines—theology, religious studies, sociology, literary studies—each bringing their own disciplinary perspectives, methods, and interests to their analyses. The artists worked in a variety of visual media—drawing, painting, photography, video, movement—and had a wide variety of spiritual commitments. Our final conversation took place during a workshop in which each scholar presented his or her interpretation of one of the artist's practices as a way of knowing through the lens of his or her discipline and in conversation with a particular feature of art making (movement, medium, attention, subtraction, invention, time, and listening), which we identified over the course of our observations. The artist then had an opportunity to respond to the presentation and correct any misunderstandings.

Much of what was learned about the distinctiveness of art practice during this project came about through discussions with the artists, which made clear that while we can learn something about how an artist's practice works by watching the movements involved, hearing descriptions, and asking questions, we nevertheless cannot understand the practice *in the same way* that the artist does because the practice is a distinct way of knowing that cannot be translated into another (discursive, academic) practice of thinking. Moreover, it is impossible to isolate the embodied dimensions and processes of an art practice from the larger social and linguistic frameworks within which those processes take place. While we started by attempting to focus on the bodily mechanisms of particular practices, we found that this was impossible to separate from the language that the artist used to communicate the significance of these processes, and that this language manifested and imported commitments and contexts that were always already in play.

Only after these practices were fully explored did we gather a separate group of scholars who study ritual from a variety of disciplinary perspectives—anthropology, psychology, theology, religious studies, literary studies—to each present on one of the same features (movement, medium, attention, subtraction, invention, time, and listening). Each scholar writing on an art practice then incorporated any relevant elements from the corresponding ritual essay into his or her analysis. The resulting seven pairs of essays—one on the noetic elements of a ritual practice and one on the noetic elements of an art practice—both responding to the same theme, appear in an edited volume *Art-Making as Spiritual Practice: Rituals of*

Embodied Understanding. Rather than making any direct claims for art making as a spiritual practice or any claims about the parallels between art making and ritual as such, the volume simply puts practices next to one another under the same feature or process (movement, medium, time, attention, subtraction, invention, listening). The result is a series of what Bruce Lincoln calls "weak comparisons,"[22] in which a small number of examples are compared in the complexities of their respective contexts in ways that highlight similarities and differences in the service of making modest claims. We assume that the practices we pair are different in many ways and that each is contextualized in its own set of conflicts, but that their differences might be instructive "when set against their shared nature as practices that are adaptations of social, spatial, and temporal realities in response to particular issues in their contexts."[23]

We learned that while religious rituals and art making are very different sorts of practices, they both rely on and employ these same aspects of embodied processes (movement, medium, attention, time etc.) for different but related purposes. Multiple contributors suggested, for example, that rituals and art making involve inviting an experience of vulnerability, as opposed to mastery and management. The idea of subtraction and similar concepts (e.g., erasure) also frequently emerged. Whether a necessary and inherent feature of what makes both kinds of practices work (i.e., that in subtracting some things other things are permitted to emerge) or a discursive construction that preserves a duplicitous purity for domains like "art" and "ritual," subtraction nevertheless seems to be an event that makes the practices work in certain ways, whether for good or for ill. Many of the practices are likewise presented in terms of the kinds of attention they enable or where or to what they direct attention. The noetic significance of these functions is also clear. Shifts in attention are directly related to insight, while subtraction is likewise a tool by which some things are cleared away so that others become more prominent to perception and thus in one's mental landscape. Vulnerability too, as an antidote to mastery, is a prerequisite for new insight.

The pervasiveness of these themes across such divergent practices suggests that they are candidates for further study—even, perhaps, empirical study—concerning connections between religious ritual and art practice as sources of spiritual understanding. This reorients the intellectual space by showing how the embodied practices and processes of art practice that appear opaque are an

22. Bruce Lincoln, *Apples and Oranges: Explorations in, on, and with Comparison* (Chicago: University of Chicago Press, 2018), 11.

23. Lexi Eikelboom, "Challenges in Approaching Art-Making across Practice and Discourse," in Eikelboom and Newheiser, *Art-Making as Spiritual Practice*.

externalized and embodied form of seeking understanding such that its spiritual significance may likewise lie, in part, in this embodied quality.[24]

Moreover, insofar as considering these practices raises questions for the researcher and the reader about how we attend to the world, which sorts of attention should be privileged, how and where we allow, expand, and meet vulnerability, and what we subtract in various contexts, whether consciously or unconsciously, and insofar as these are also questions of spiritual concern, art making has contributed to the spiritual understanding of scholars themselves through their scholarly engagements and the resulting essays.[25] In other words, if engagement with art making can change the ways that scholars think about the spiritual significance of invention, time, movement, vulnerability, subtraction, and attention, then it likewise makes a second-order contribution to spiritual understanding in addition to being its own kind of spiritual understanding. Art making has, if nothing else, made a contribution to spiritual understanding through this project by forcing us, the researchers and the readers, to consider our answers to questions about the nature of vulnerability, subtraction, invention, and attention (among others) in relation to the practices through which we engage the world, one another, and the divine.

Future Inquiry

At the outset of this essay, I suggested that one of the primary contributions of this project to the larger ASU program is that it shows how pushing the boundaries of interdisciplinarity is both challenging as well as essential for developing the kind of methodological innovations that will make it possible to unearth the distinctive cognitive value of the arts. In this project, we did not merely bring together two or three disciplines as is often the case in interdisciplinary research. We made the unusual choice to include a large number of disciplines. This enabled us to cast a wide net. It enabled us to produce a kind of tasting menu of available options for thinking about art practice commensurate with the wide range that exists for

24. See Benjamin R. DeSpain, "Invention in Dominic Redfern's Video Practice: The Art of Discovery," in Eikelboom and Newheiser, *Art-Making as Spiritual Practice*.

25. In addition to these themes, which emerge through the edited collection, I also gave a conference paper, "Place-Making as Paradox: Making and Given-ness in Practices of Art and Liturgy," at the conference "Catholicism, Literature, and the Arts III: Poetics of Liturgy and Place," July 2022, London, UK. The paper became an article "Presence and Grace: What Can Artmaking Teach Us about Liturgy?" for *Religion and Ethics, Australian Broadcasting Corporation*, April 18, 2023. Online: https://tinyurl.com/595pe67b. In addition to these publications, Lexi Eikelboom and artist Sarah Tomasetti gave an interview, "Art after Religion? Artmaking as a Spiritual Practice," on *Soul Search*, ABC Radio National (March 20, 2022), https://tinyurl.com/msbm7u2d.

thinking about ritual practice. Putting this diversity on display as we have done here will help future researchers to choose the right methodological tools and disciplinary perspectives for the aspects of art practice that they would like to better understand. The disciplinary diversity also allowed methodological questions to come to the surface through the juxtaposition of perspectives. For example, we grappled with questions like: what sort of intellectual work does the category "art" do for us, and what is the value of this category given the diversity of practices and artefacts that it encompasses? Which disciplinary commitments determine which aspects of art practice we pay attention to? If art making is spiritual, who is best qualified to understand and describe that spirituality?

Because we have understood this project to be initiating a new field of research on art practice analogous to ritual studies, this disciplinary diversity has been essential for marking out parameters and identifying central questions for this field. As described above, because art making is a complex human activity, it cannot be reduced to any one or two particular disciplinary perspectives. It always exceeds any one frame. It was through this approach that our innovative process of shared attention on practices despite disciplinary difference, the identification of themes through such shared attention, and the process of "weak comparison" of practices emerged, providing a coherent approach to the spiritual and noetic significance of such practices that could encompass multiple disciplines while respecting the individuality of both the disciplines and the practices. If we could do things differently, we would put more structures in place to scaffold some of this complexity effectively from the outset, but these were also true methodological innovations, hard-won through the struggle involved in the process of inquiry.

Likewise, by including artists as producers of knowledge and not merely subjects to be studied, we introduced yet another vocabulary into the conversation, pushing the boundaries of interdisciplinarity by attempting to include a knowledge practice that is different from other academic practices. Because scholars in the humanities and practicing artists are working in relation to different institutional structures and expectations, the conversations in which they are interested are often quite different. Vocabulary is similar, but the questions that each group seeks to answer differ. This illustrates the importance of considering art making a way of knowing in its own right, as distinct from academic reflection, but it also makes conversation challenging.

This too was a key methodological innovation but, of everything, it is also the one that could have been scaffolded more effectively. Our focus was the particular practices themselves, not the structures of the art world in which artists practice, but we now understand that those structures are indispensable for understanding the practices. It would have been worth devoting more time upfront to learning those structures, the vocabulary, questions, and concerns that operate in the background as artists work and that could have helped us make better sense of how they talk about their work. We wanted to invite artists to contribute to the process of knowledge creation but we did not always have the tools to receive what they had to offer. In the end, the limitations of our capacities meant that we prioritized the creation of an interdisciplinary academic field rather than the artist-scholar collaboration.

Nevertheless, this points the way to future research questions. Now that some of the markers for such a field are in place, it is easier to see more sustained artist-scholar collaborations in relation to questions of spiritual significance with different kinds of scholars. We can more clearly see the noetic contributions that art making may be able to make, what conversation and engagement look like, and what collaboration with different kinds of scholars might be able to offer. Now that this is in place, there is the question of what insights might be possible when only two or three dedicated researchers work more closely with artists to identify and analyze practices using resources from ritual studies. This may offer a more precise, albeit circumscribed, theory of the ways in which the study of ritual might make sense of art practice as a spiritual knowledge practice.

There are also research questions emerging from the themes uncovered through the scientific and the conceptual work. Our experiment raises questions about what might happen in other kinds of art encounters. Would similar or different patterns of experience of self-transcendence and bonding occur in different kinds of art engagement? And what would happen if one ran an experiment in which an isomorphic art and ritual experience were compared? Likewise, the themes identified through our conceptual work raise questions about whether it would be possible to test for experiences like vulnerability or shifts in attention and the effects of these experiences in art and ritual practices. Moreover, is it possible to assess the effects of subtraction by, for example, removing different sorts of things in different iterations of an art experience or a ritual?

Finally, the observations I have here made about procedure and method raise questions about the kind of contribution that art can make to more discursive forms of knowing. Art making may be a form of knowing in its own right, but this project showed that engaging with artists and art making can also change the conceptual thinking of scholars such that it can make a contribution to discursive knowledge through such interdisciplinary, or perhaps, inter-practical, engagement. The contributions of art to understanding may come from studying the ways in which scholars themselves are changed by their engagements with art and art practices. This may be a fruitful locus of empirically demonstrable connection because it presents a clear and articulated shift (because of the nature of scholarship) that might in other ways and circumstances be difficult for participants to articulate.

In particular, there is still much to be learned about the epistemic value of the practices of art making for the practice of theology, a discipline that is expressly devoted to spiritual understanding. The idea that art making constitutes a form of knowledge has been well supported from within the art world,[26] but we do not yet have a clear sense of how this way of knowing affects the study of theology, specifically. The outcomes of this project suggest that art making may be a distinct, context-dependent practice in relation to which new theological insights are possible. But how does this particular form of knowledge illuminate spiritual realities of the kind investigated by theology specifically? What might taking art making seriously as a practice of knowing make possible for theology in terms of new ways of thinking and new approaches to doctrines that theorize and interpret spiritual realities?

Conclusion and Questions

An empirical connection between art and understanding is incredibly difficult to demonstrate. How exactly one tests for the myriad and subtle processes and changes involved in understanding is a difficult question.[27] This project, however, has uncovered another reason for the difficulty, namely, that "art" can mean many things and with each meaning come multiple possibilities for its contribution. This project has suggested that we consider testing, not just for the effects of artworks, but art practice.

We here hypothesized that we might be able to get at the distinctive cognitive value of engagement with the arts through a comparison with religious rituals, that art's distinctive cognitive value in relation to spiritual understanding might share something with religious ritual. In a number of ways, we were right about this. Thinking about art practice through the lens of religious ritual led us to think of its cognitive value as an embodied reality. Thus, the cognitive value of art engagement for spiritual understanding, according to our experiment, may, for some individuals, be related to perspective shifts involved in experiences of self-transcendence and social bonding induced by artworks that engage and draw

26. Elizabeth Fischer and Rebecca Fortnum, eds., *On Not Knowing: How Artists Think* (London: Black Dog, 2013); Mara Ambrozic and Angela Vettese, eds., *Art as a Thinking Process: Visual Forms of Knowledge Production* (Berlin: Sternberg, 2013).

27. A. P. Christensen, E. R. Cardillo, and A. Chatterjee, "Can Art Promote Understanding? A Review of the Psychology and Neuroscience of Aesthetic Cognitivism," *Psychology of Aesthetics, Creativity, and the Arts*, advance online publication, 2023.

attention to the boundaries of the body. And, according to our interviews with artists, the cognitive value of art making, specifically, may be the ways it enables vulnerability, leverages subtraction, or enables particular kinds of attention, all of which may make contributions to or set the cognitive stage for spiritual insight. Finally, because our researchers, both scientific and conceptual, worked with artists as agents of knowledge who, by virtue of their art-making practices, have a particular kind of understanding, we have shown that the cognitive value of engagement with the arts may also lie in the ways that scholars engage artists as contributors to academic thinking about spiritual realities.

14

Islam, Arts, and Artists

Jamal J. Elias

There is excellent scholarship on the history and production of Islamic art and architecture across time. It covers the rich and broad range of Muslim-majority societies across multiple continents, and it focuses on minor arts in addition to well-known visual art forms such as calligraphy, miniature painting, and architectural ornamentation. By comparison, the role of the arts in religious and social understandings among Muslims is woefully understudied both in the past and the present. In contrast to exploring aesthetic concerns centered around beauty, or technical aspects of art production, it is considerably more challenging to study human responses to art, and even more so to analyze religious, affective, cognitive and other forms of understanding. This essay is an attempt to place Islamic arts in a social context in order to understand the place of art in society. The focus is on visual and material arts, but it bears noting that there are rich traditions of non-visual arts such as music and dance in all Muslim-majority societies.

Outside of art-historical circles, much of the scholarship on the arts in Islamic society continues to focus on issues of religious legitimacy. A preoccupation with questions of whether or not Islam allows visual representation, or on the nature of what does and does not qualify as being religious, misses the crucial fact that Muslims have historically possessed rich artistic traditions and that the arts contribute centrally and directly to understanding for contemporary Muslims.

Didactic Purposes of Art

Medieval writings on artistic visual and material objects stress their didactic importance, especially for eliciting wonderment in the viewer. The influential Muslim theologian and philosopher, al-Ghazali (d. 1111) addressed questions of aesthetics and beauty in several of his works, shedding light on the value of art in Islamic contexts. According to al-Ghazali, beauty is important because it reflects an inner perfection. Physical appearances on their own can be deceptive, because our physical senses can only perceive the apparent level of things, and appearances can be deceiving. In contrast, he argues that the heart (understood as the location of the inner senses) is able to discern the real nature of things. For this reason, simply contemplating beautiful visual objects runs the risk of leading the observer to think that the visible world is an accurate representation of all reality. Al-Ghazali outlines a number of categories of beauty which he arranges hierarchically, and also describes the ways in which one can see the inner beauty and goodness behind externally beautiful objects. So, for example, seeing a beautiful person helps one understand divine goodness because God is the creator of human beings.[1]

Al-Ghazali encourages one to love all forms of beauty because they lead to a love for divine beauty. Love, in this sense, is different from desire and is selfless and internal, but it can be cultivated by contemplating the beauty of external, visual things. According to him, physical beauty is a gift from God and, since in his view beauty and virtue are inseparable, appreciating physical and visual beauty is evidence of the inner virtue of the viewer.[2]

Such traditions of thought bear directly on premodern schools of artistic representation in the Islamic world, and also on the cognitive role of amazement and wonderment in relation to visual art and material objects.

Amazement, Wonderment, and Visual Art

Concepts of visual and physical beauty as windows into the contemplation and understanding of supernatural beauty and goodness are intimately connected to ways of artistic representation. Al-Ghazali was not interested in art for its own sake but for its relationship to aesthetics, morality, emotions, and imaginative understanding. He discusses the beauty of art in terms of the moral qualities and spiritual insights of the artist, not in terms of the aesthetic qualities of the work. But he combines this with the opinion that the contemplation of visual art enables human beings to contemplate the physical universe. And just as admiring visual art makes us admire the artist's qualities, admiring the physical universal makes us admire and gain some understanding of the divine artist behind it.

Related to al-Ghazali's encouragement to contemplate beautiful objects as a way of understanding, Islamic scholarship contains an explicit exhortation to

1. Abu Hamid Al-Ghazali, *Kīmiyā-i sa'ādat*, 2 vols., ed. Husayn Khadivjam (Tehran: Shirkat-i intishārāt-i 'ilmī wa farhangī, 1975; rpt. 2001), 1:586.

2. Abu Hamid Al-Ghazali, *Iḥyā' 'ulūm al-dīn*, 4 vols., introduction by Badawi Tabana (Cairo: Dār iḥyā' al-kutub al-'arabiyya, 1975; rpt. Istanbul, Çağrī Yayınları, 1985), 2:291.

cultivate wonderment, which is understood to be a doorway to knowledge. The cultivation of this sort of wonderment also involves recognizing portents in one's contemplation of objects, in the sense that seeing awe-inspiring objects serves as a reminder of the transitory nature of human life. Such objects can be natural, but they are very often made by humans. The pyramids in the Nile Valley are evoked commonly by premodern writers as precisely such an object to contemplate: their magnificence reflects the artistry of their makers who have now all turned to dust, reminding the viewer of the transitory nature of their own lives.[3]

Emotional Response to the Arts

This very brief overview of the history of the place of visual and material objects in Islamic societies is necessary to make a number of points, most significant among them that Islamic aesthetic, philosophical, and moral thinkers recognized that visual perception results in emotional responses that are identifiable. There is little debate on whether or not images judged to be beautiful elicit emotional or pleasurable responses. The issue is whether or not these responses are appropriate. It is this concern, that of the propriety of images and our reactions to them, that informs important aspects of responses to the arts in contemporary Islamic societies.

The Visual Arts and Islam

There is a widespread understanding (both among Muslims and others) that Muslims do not have visual representations of human beings, particularly of religious figures such as prophets. This idea extends beyond questions of the acceptability of figural religious images to say that Muslims are opposed to all visual images. The truth is somewhat more complicated.

Viewed globally and historically, there is undoubtedly an antipathy in many Muslim social contexts to the visual depiction of God or human religious figures. The rejection of such images is the norm, rather than the exception. There are complex reasons for this, but it bears remembering that a broad taboo on religious figural representations does not mean that such opposition extends to all figural representations of humans, animals, and supernatural beings. Furthermore, this rejection of specific categories of figural representations exists within a broader

3. For more on the cultivation of wonderment, see Jamal J. Elias, *Aisha's Cushion: Religious Art, Perception, and Practice in Islam* (Cambridge, MA: Harvard University Press, 2012), esp. chapter 5.

religious culture that embraces images and material objects in a variety of ways. There is also a long history in a number of different Muslim-majority societies of visually representing religious figures, including the prophet Muhammad.[4]

It is for such reasons of the moral and spiritual function of visual religious art that certain forms of non-figural representation have been popular in some societies, and that calligraphy, in particular, has enjoyed pride of place among the visual religious arts in the Islamic world.

Even though the extensive Islamic traditions of visual representation are frequently non-figural, it is difficult to argue that they are non-representational. There are widespread practices of using the Ka'ba in Mecca and the Prophet's Mosque in Medina to represent God and His prophet. Similarly, holy relics such as stylized images of Muhammad's footprint clearly stand in for the religious personage who cannot be depicted figuratively. Non-figural representation can be taken a step further to be iconic, in the sense that a visual image represents something else.

Another tradition of representing Muhammad aniconically is to make lavishly illuminated panels featuring a textual description of his physical appearance and personal qualities. Typical of such works is one created by the noted Ottoman calligrapher, Hafiz Osman (d. 1698). The textual description of the Prophet is drawn from a ninth-century text by an important scholar named al-Tirmidhi, and is attributed to Muhammad's cousin and spiritual successor, 'Ali, who was also the first male convert to Islam:

> He was neither too tall nor too short, rather he was of medium height. . . . His hair was neither short and curly, nor was it long and straight, it hung in waves. His face was neither fleshy nor plump, but it had a roundness, rosy white, with very dark eyes and long eyelashes. He was large-boned as well as broad-shouldered, hairless except for a thin line that stretched down his chest to his navel. His hands and feet were coarse. When he walked, he would lean forward as if descending a hill. When he turned [toward someone], he turned with all his body. Between his two shoulders was the Seal of Prophethood.[5]

The word commonly used for these pieces of religious art is "*hilya*" (or "*hilye*"), an Arabic term referring to a person's appearance. The use of the term in this

4. For a history of the visual representation of the prophet Muhammad, see Christiane Gruber, *The Praiseworthy One: The Prophet Muhammad in Islamic Texts and Images* (Bloomington: Indiana University Press, 2019).

5. Abu 'Isa al-Tirmidhi, *Shamā'il al-nabī*, ed. Mahir Yasin Fahl and Bishar 'Awad Ma'ruf (Beirut: Dār al-gharb al-islāmī, 2000), 36–37.

context also derives from a saying attributed to 'Ali and recorded by al-Tirmidhi: "The Prophet of God . . . said: 'Whosoever sees my *hilya* after me, it is as if he had seen me; and whosoever sees it, longing for me, God prohibits Hell-fire from him and he will be protected from the trials of the grave, and he will not be resurrected naked on the Day of Judgment.'"[6]

These textual works of art are intended as visual representations, a point made clear by the fact that the various elements that are brought together to create a *hilye* panel are bodily: a place for the head (*başmakam*), torso (*göbek* or *gövde*), belt (*kuşak*) and skirt (*etek*). Very frequently, *hilye* panels also have four medallions containing the names of the first four Caliphs, their placement suggesting four limbs around the head and torso, which are the essential elements of a *hilye* design.

Calligraphy

Calligraphy is perhaps the most widely practiced and appreciated Islamic art form. In its origins, Islamic calligraphy is not formally religious, since it arose in the environment of the courts. Scribal concerns were largely aesthetic, and they developed a number of calligraphic styles intended for use in specific contexts. Over time, the growth of book arts and the centrality of the written words of the Quran meant that calligraphy became associated with religious writing, and it remains so up to the present. In addition to its important place in book arts, calligraphy found a home in architecture, where the use of writing frequently functioned as a visual marker of the religious purpose of buildings or of the spiritual aspirations of the donors who paid for them. In some cases, calligraphy is the dominant feature of the decorative program of a building. This is the case with the Ince Minareli Medrese, a thirteenth-century religious college in the Turkish city of Konya. The facade of the building is almost completely covered by verses from the Quran carved in stone. The writing is clear, if florally intertwined, and one can imagine that it was legible to the teachers and students of the college who would have been well-versed in the Quran. But the calligraphy is on the outside facing the street, and it is certain that the majority of passersby in thirteenth-century Konya would not have been literate in Arabic (the same holds true of contemporary Turkey, since Turkish is written in the Latin script). For them, the calligraphy must have functioned as a visual sign indicating the religious nature and function of the building, among other things. This particular function of calligraphy is important because, as an art form, Arabic calligraphy is visual rather than textual for the

6. Annemarie Schimmel, *And Muhammad Is His Messenger: The Veneration of the Prophet in Islamic Piety* (Chapel Hill: University of North Carolina Press, 1985), 211–12.

majority of Muslim viewers. It indicates religiosity and spirituality, leaving it up to the audience to derive meaning from it aesthetically and cognitively.

Calligraphy is closely linked to painting in many Islamic contexts, since both are very prevalent as book arts. Across western, southern and central Asia, there were rich traditions of miniature painting where the paintings served as illustrations for poetry and stories. Some of these were legends of warriors and heroes, others were romances (frequently religious), while still others were explicitly religious in that they told tales of the prophets. Such works were expensive and rare, and only circulated among narrow circles of the wealthy and powerful. Nevertheless, it is clear from library and palace records that they were highly prized, and some of them—especially religious ones—show wear marks on pages that suggest that images of Muhammad and other holy people were probably kissed when they were encountered.

Religious Arts Today

It is impossible to cover the entire scope of Islamic arts in one short chapter, nor even to provide a comprehensive overview of one particular form, such as miniature painting. In some cases, social and technological changes have caused a decline in art forms. Mass production has had an impact on the role of images that is difficult to measure. Visual representations of all kinds have multiplied in the era of the printing press, making them accessible to broader audiences. This holds true of pictorial images of Muhammad in societies where such traditions exist, as well as of saints, medieval as well as modern. Images such as those of Sufi saints are very popular across South Asia. Cheaply produced and widely available, they are an accessible form of religious art that is hung in homes and places of work with the dual purpose of providing blessings as well as encouraging good behavior and devotion on the part of the viewer. Similarly, religious calligraphy in a variety of mediums is sold in shops and online as home decor. And even cheaply produced miniature paintings are sold in souvenir shops in several countries.

Even in an age of mechanical reproduction, however, dedicated artists remain committed to keeping traditional Islamic arts alive. In particular, this holds true for book arts like miniature painting and calligraphy in the visual arts, but it is also true for other art forms such as music. Book arts are taught as part of the regular curriculum at degree-granting art schools in several countries, and vibrant traditions of private instruction continue to thrive. An example of the preservation and development of calligraphy in the United States is found in the work of Mohamed Zakariya.[7] A noted artist who has received training in several countries, he works

7. Mohamed Zakariya, https://mohamedzakariya.org/.

in traditional as well as modern styles, and has designed the official Eid postage stamps for the US Postal Service. He teaches other calligraphers in a traditional manner, granting his students licenses (*ijāza*) in specific calligraphic styles after they have completed a lengthy apprenticeship. Among these calligraphy students is the respected calligrapher Nihad Dukhan,[8] who has also received two licenses in other styles from the renowned Turkish calligrapher Hasan Çelebi, who was also Zakariya's one-time teacher. Like Zakariya, Dukhan works in traditional and modern styles, and he regularly teaches workshops to introduce people to methods and styles of Arabic calligraphy.

An instance of a small school organized in a very traditional style is the case of New York Islamic Arts.[9] The teacher is a traditionally trained artist from Turkey, Mujgan Baskoylu. An expert in several different arts associated with paper and illumination, she has a small group of students who are themselves accomplished artists specializing in one or more of these techniques, while also learning others. Baskoylu's students study paper preparation, illumination (*tezhip*), miniature painting, calligraphy (*hatt*), and paper cutting (*kati*), spending years perfecting one technique. For example, Behnaz Karjoo started studying illumination with Baskoylu in 2011 and received her *ijāza* in 2016.[10] She continues to be intimately involved in New York Islamic Arts, studying other techniques, including miniature painting.

The stated purpose of New York Islamic Arts is to keep the traditions of Islamic art alive, but Baskoylu and her students also treat their art as a personal practice, immersing themselves in tradition and creativity as a way of life. In important ways, this personal involvement resembles the manner in which audiences engage with traditional and religious arts.

It is difficult to assess the impact of Islamic arts on audiences for a range of reasons: the variety of arts classified as Islamic, the large global population of Muslims, and cultural and religious differences among them make it impossible to make sweeping statements about Muslim attitudes toward the arts. Outside of Muslim-majority societies, many community groups that promote the arts are focused on preserving cultural practices among specific immigrant groups. Few focus specifically on religious arts. In the United States, an example of one of a few such groups focused on religious arts is the Reed Society for the Sacred Arts,[11]

8. Nihad Dukhan (ndukhan.com), Instagram, https://www.instagram.com/nihad.dukhan/?hl=en.

9. New York Islamic Arts, https://www.nyislamicarts.com/.

10. Behnaz Karjoo, www.behnazkarjoo.com.

11. The Reed Society for the Sacred Arts, https://www.reedsociety.org/.

located outside Washington, DC. The Reed Society is committed to understanding and preserving the spiritual processes involved in the study and practice of Islamic arts. The society regularly organizes events and workshops to teach about the Islamic arts (in particular calligraphy and religious music), and to educate audiences in their spiritual dimension. Seeing this society and its audiences as an example, the arts serve a strong, if difficult to define, purpose in the spiritual lives of Muslims.

15

The Process of Spiritualization through Artistic Activity and Training

Faiz A. Hashmi, Alejandro Erut, Zachary Taylor, and Cristine H. Legare

Miniature painting is an ancient artistic tradition with a complex history. Although the term "miniature" first appeared during the colonial period to refer to a diverse array of figurative paintings from Iran, Turkey, and Central and South Asia,[1] the origins of this art form are much more ancient. For example, the early technological and stylistic influences on miniature painting came from the Han dynasty of China (206 BCE–220 CE). Throughout the Middle Ages, this practice was transmitted across Asia, amassing influence from diverse cultures.[2] The art of miniature narrative paintings peaked in popularity between the thirteenth and nineteenth centuries, becoming an emblematic art form of the Mongol, Timurid, Safavid, and Mughal empires.[3]

Originally, miniature paintings illustrated religious texts, poetry, folk tales, and imperial histories of royalty and the elite.[4] Although no longer used to illustrate manuscripts since the invention of book printing,[5] modern miniature paintings continue to depict religious scenes and are used for spiritual instruction and con-

1. Naib Mian, "How Shahzia Sikander Remade the Art of Miniature Painting," *The New Yorker*, June 1, 2022, https://tinyurl.com/mr2bcnuj.

2. Mark Cartwright, "The Art of the Tang Dynasty," *World History Encyclopedia*, October 11, 2017, https://tinyurl.com/5n75j8fe; Guity Novin, "The Art of Miniature Painting in the Medieval East," *Brewminate: A Bold Blend of News and Ideas*, March 5, 2017, https://tinyurl.com/3fnse6pn.

3. D. T. Kuryazova, "From History of Miniature Art," *American Journal of Social Sciences and Humanity Research* 3, no. 2 (2023): 22–29; Novin, "Art of Miniature Painting."

4. "Manuscript and Miniature Painting in South Asia," MAP Academy, April 21, 2022, https://tinyurl.com/242x8h3r.

5. J. L. Propert, *A History of Miniature Art: With Notes on Collectors and Collections* (London: Macmillan, 1887).

templation. For example, *Krishna and the Gopis Take Shelter from the Rain*, a painting from Jaipur, India, was created in the mid-eighteenth century and is currently on display in the New York Metropolitan Museum of Art.[6] This artwork represents a sacred religious story in which Krishna (the Hindu God of protection, compassion, tenderness, and love) protects villagers from Indra (the Hindu God of sky, lightning, weather, thunder, storms, rain, river flows, and war). The cows mimic the cowmaids' (*gopis*) devotion (*bhakti*) to Krishna. The depiction of Krishna's pastoral activity and his relationship with his devotees represent essential aspects of spiritual and religious life. Many paintings in Rajput royal courts depict similar scenes. This painting represents the critical function that miniature painting has traditionally played in preserving and transmitting religious history, tradition, and meaning, both past and present. The content of miniature paintings in India and elsewhere often depicts scenes of what is considered divine, sacred, and holy in the communities that practice this art form.

During imperial rule, Western artistic traditions were prioritized at the expense of traditional art forms, including miniature painting.[7] Miniature painting is still practiced and exhibited in many regions of Asia, including India and Turkey.[8] There has recently been a resurgence of interest in the techniques of miniature paintings.[9] For example, MacArthur "Genius," Pakistani artist Shahzia Sikander applies the techniques of traditional miniature painting, including using paintbrushes made of a few strands of hair from squirrel tails, to reimagine and reinterpret this ancient artistic genre for modern audiences.[10]

In our Art Seeking Understanding (ASU)-funded project, "The Process of Spiritualization through Artistic Activity and Training," we systematically investigated traditional Indian art, primarily focusing on the Indian miniature painting from Rajasthan. Our overarching objective was to examine how the experience of acquiring mastery in miniature painting influences spiritual understanding, reli-

6. *Krishna and the Gopis Take Shelter from the Rain*, 1760, ink, opaque watercolor, and gold on paper, 13 3/4 x 9 3/8 in. (34.9 x 23.8 cm), The Met, NY, https://tinyurl.com/yet9dptz.

7. Mian, "How Shahzia Sikander Remade the Art."

8. G. M. Tanieva and A. G. Tadzhiev, "Art of Miniature in Central Asia and Its Historical Development," *Journal of Look to the Past* 4, no. 8 (2021), http://dx.doi.org/10.26739/2181-9599-2021-8-9; A. Tüzünoğlu and G. Özkara, "Miniature 2.0: Miniature in Contemporary Art," exhibition of miniature paintings, Pera Museum, August 11, 2020–January 24, 2021.

9. Firdavs F. Abdukhalikov, "Interpretation of Rulers in Oriental Miniatures," *International Journal of History and Political Sciences* 3, no. 5 (2023): 23–35; Osman Can Yerebakan, "Women Artists of the Middle East and South Asia Are Reinventing Miniature Painting," Artsy, June 14, 2021, https://tinyurl.com/58uy4c3y.

10. Shahzia Sikander, *Uprooted Order, Series 3, No. 1*, 1997, watercolor on tea-stained wasli paper, Morgan Library and Museum, New York, https://tinyurl.com/9sw2h4du.

gious meaning and practice, and the balance between creativity and conformity in learning and teaching traditional visual art.

Our research sits at the juncture of theological aesthetics and the sciences. We conducted an in-depth analysis of the religious meaning associated with this ancient art form using rigorous research methods. Miniature paintings represent religious and spiritual narratives, depicting deities and sacred rituals. They thus provide unique insight into theological aesthetics, highlighting the profound connection between religious practices and artistic expression. We documented the ritualization of the artistic process, which is a critical feature of acquiring mastery and ensuring the cultural transmission of this art form. We investigated aesthetic and cognitive values associated with Indian miniature painting and surveyed the influence of religious motivation and rituals in the artistic process. We studied the criteria used by gurus during the apprentice selection process, emphasizing aspects like social identity, personality traits, and technical expertise. We explored the cultural transmission of the technical process of learning miniature painting and documented how experts teach novice artists. We also examined the role of this art form in preserving cultural and religious heritage and the extent to which it is adapting to a rapidly changing world.

Indian miniature painting from Rajasthan is more than just an art form; it is a testament to the region's rich cultural tapestry and historical lineage. Over the centuries, these paintings have not only adorned the palatial walls of monarchs but have also captured the imagination of art aficionados worldwide. However, this distinctive tradition remains relatively unexplored despite its widespread acclaim. The limited existing studies primarily focus on its historical aspects.[11] While historical accounts are valuable, they do not examine the lived experience of artists creating these paintings and the role this art form plays in sustaining important religious and cultural heritages in the modern world.[12] We conducted two phases of research: qualitative and quantitative research.

Methods

The initial phase of our research was qualitative. We conducted in-depth, semi-structured interviews with eight prominent figures renowned for their mastery of miniature art. Our interviews allowed for a balance between structure and flexi-

11. B. Lavanya, "Medieval Indian Miniature Paintings: An Overview of the Latest Writings and Trends." *Social Sciences* 11, no. 3 (2022): 188–93; S. Seetharaman and A. K. Chand, "Rajasthani Miniature Painting: A Review," *International Journal of Advancement in Social Science and Humanity* 1, no. 1 (2016): 73–84.

12. Krishna Chaitanya, *A History of Indian Painting: Manuscript, Moghul and Deccani Traditions* (New Delhi: Abhinav, 2013).

bility; preset questions ensured consistency, and open-ended questions allowed us to capture spontaneous insights from the experts.

Each session was video-recorded to document the significance and richness of these conversations. We identified recurring themes, unique insights, and overarching narratives from these conversations. These distilled thematic categories then provided a robust foundation for the subsequent phase of our research. Drawing inspiration from the data obtained, we designed comprehensive survey questions that reflected the realities of miniature artistry. To further enhance the survey's effectiveness, responses were pre-populated based on the findings from the interviews, ensuring that our quantitative phase was deeply rooted in the authentic voices of the experts.

We built a team of eight Rajasthan-based field investigators, supervised by Akash Sharma, to implement the quantitative phase. These investigators underwent rigorous training on the newly designed survey. Following a pilot test and subsequent necessary modifications, we designed a *long survey tool*. This encompassed seven categories, namely:

- **Criteria used in artist recruitment:** Addressed guru-centric selection priorities and the historical unfolding of artist preferences.
- **Pedagogy of miniature painting:** Focused on skill acquisition, guru influence, procedural strictness, and religious motivations.
- **Motivations behind creation:** Examined both religious and secular impetuses behind art creation.
- **Art quality assessment:** Included evaluative methods and criteria for assessing the quality of miniature paintings.
- **Intergenerational changes:** Documented changes in this art form over generations.
- **Rituals and emotions in art making:** Analyzed the role of spirituality and emotion in the creation process.
- **Demographics:** Documented the socioeconomic, educational, religious, and cultural backgrounds of the artists.

In our first round of data collection, we interviewed 184 artists involved in miniature art with varying levels of expertise. Our sample of artists includes 20 internationally recognized experts, 142 experienced artists, and 21 novices. We examined the multifaceted world of miniature art, aiming to unravel its intricate layers and nuances. Our inquiries spanned diverse themes, encompassing the technical intricacies of the art form, the spiritual and religious motifs interwoven with artistic expression, and the sociocultural dynamics that influence its development. We delved into the pedagogical aspects, exploring the pivotal role of gurus in transmitting skills and knowledge to the next generation and the transformative journey of apprentices under their guidance. A significant dimension of our research was understanding the delicate balance between creativity and conformity, especially as artists transition from novices to experts. Additionally, we sought to chart the trajectory of miniature art through the generation of artists, analyzing shifts in interest, changing market dynamics, and the challenges and opportunities these present.

Insights

Ritualization of the Artistic Process

We have documented meticulous detail and procedural rigidity in the production of miniature paintings in Jaipur, India, both characteristics of ritualization.[13] For example, we have examined each step in the painting production process, which includes preparing the canvas, preparing the color from traditional mineral pigments and organic matter, drawing the outlines, filling the colors, adding shadings, finalizing the faces (including eyes) and ornaments, and finishing the art by making the borders. Ritualization serves multiple critical social and psychological functions.[14] It ensures the high-fidelity transmission of socially shared knowledge, skills, and practices. In art, ritualization may also preserve the aesthetics of artistic traditions through careful adherence to process and form. Ritualization is also associated with achieving mastery, a process that takes many decades of practice for miniature artists to achieve. For example, our current research found that the years of training associated with acquiring high-level proficiency can range from forty to sixty years.

There is consensus among artists who range in expertise from apprentices to experts about the steps (and order of the steps) required to complete the artwork, further evidence for the ritualization of the artistic process. Our findings highlight how some steps in the painting process are universally agreed upon, while others allow for more individual interpretation, particularly among more experienced

13. Cristine H. Legare and André L. Souza, "Evaluating Ritual Efficacy: Evidence from the Supernatural," *Cognition* 124, no. 1 (2012): 1–15; Cristine H. Legare and André L. Souza, "Searching for Control: Priming Randomness Increases the Evaluation of Ritual Efficacy," *Cognitive Science* 38 (2014): 152–61.

14. Jennifer M. Clegg and Cristine H. Legare, "Instrumental and Conventional Interpretations of Behavior Are Associated with Distinct Outcomes in Early Childhood," *Child Development* 87, no. 2 (2016): 527–42; Rachel E. Watson-Jones and Cristine H. Legare, "The Social Functions of Group Rituals," *Current Directions in Psychological Science* 25 (2016): 42–46.

artists. This consensus reflects the balance between tradition and personal creativity that characterizes the practice of miniature painting.

The technical and aesthetic criteria for evaluating the quality of Indian miniature paintings also reflect traditional and spiritual values. Over 90 percent of artists prioritize the use of traditional natural colors and gold, while 92 percent emphasize the detailing of human faces. These criteria suggest a strong adherence to established techniques and stylistic elements, which may have roots in spiritual or cultural traditions. The balance between adhering to these crucial traditional elements while allowing for artistic creativity presents a unique challenge that reflects broader tensions between preservation and evolution in cultural practices.

Contributions of Conformity and Creativity to Artistic Mastery

Our study revealed some variation in procedural rigidity within the art-making process as a function of the artist's expertise. We found that novice artists adhere more closely to the chronological order of particular steps in the art creation process than their experienced and expert counterparts. There is a difference in expectations for novice and expert artists within the miniature painting tradition. Novice artists are typically encouraged to replicate established and revered artworks, which helps them learn foundational techniques and internalize traditional styles. This practice ensures that beginners have a solid grounding in the traditional methods before attempting any form of creativity. In contrast, expert artists, who have already mastered the basics, are expected to demonstrate creativity and innovate within the established traditions. This shift from strict adherence to creativity marks the transition from a learner to a master within the miniature painting community, highlighting the evolving role of an artist as they progress in their craft. This expectation is consistent with previous research indicating that novice learners engage in more high-fidelity copying than experts.[15] In addition, when novice artists innovate, they do so in much less systematic ways than experts who utilize their substantial knowledge of the artistic process to create new aesthetic styles.[16] Moreover, experts who innovate often produce works that subtly reinterpret traditional themes, creating a bridge between historical and

15. Cristine H. Legare, "Cumulative Cultural Learning: Diversity and Development, *Proceedings of the National Academy of Sciences* (*PNAS*) 114, no. 30 (2017): 7877–83; Cristine H. Legare and Mark Nielsen, "Imitation and Innovation: The Dual Engines of Cultural Learning," *Trends in Cognitive Sciences* 19 (2015): 688–99; Legare and Souza, "Searching for Control."

16. Ernest Edmonds and Linda Candy, "Creativity, Art Practice, and Knowledge," *Communications of the ACM* 45 (2002): 91–95.

contemporary contexts. This dynamic tension between conformity and creativity shapes the evolution of the art form itself.

Our data revealed that creativity often arises from a deep-rooted comprehension of traditions. What makes this interplay between creativity and conformity particularly striking in the context of miniature painting is the art form's deep religious and cultural significance. Unlike many contemporary art forms that prioritize individual expression, miniature painting traditionally serves as a vehicle for preserving and transmitting sacred narratives and cultural heritage.

Religious and Spiritual Motivations for Creating Art

Miniature artists must learn to effortlessly weave their knowledge of spiritual symbols and motifs with their technical mastery throughout their training. Thus, in addition to acquiring the exquisitely technical skills associated with miniature painting, learning this art form requires mastery of religious and spiritual content, meaning, rituals, and symbolism. Beyond technical mastery, our research reveals how the process of learning and creating miniature paintings facilitates spiritual transmission. The act of painting becomes a form of meditation, with artists reporting deepened spiritual understanding as they engage with religious themes and iconography. This creative process, guided by gurus, not only imparts artistic skills but also cultivates a profound connection to cultural and religious heritage, exemplifying how artistic engagement stimulates spiritual growth and insight.

The use of meticulous artistic techniques and traditional materials to illustrate spiritual content allows the artist to contemplate their spirituality. Most artists we interviewed indicated that gurus integrate religious guidelines into their curriculum. This integration could range from analyzing religious motifs in renowned artworks, to poring over sacred texts, or to dedicating time to prayer and worship. Underpinning these teachings is the emphasis on fostering a relationship of reverence with the guru, highlighting the sanctity of this mentor-mentee bond in the realm of miniature art.

Our findings indicate that religiosity is a strong motivation for mastering miniature paintings. As one young artist Neetu Singh stated, "When I make a painting, and if it's a painting related to religion such as gods and goddesses, I take it very seriously and focus my mind and thoughts because of which I can almost visualize the painting even before it takes any kind of shape." The content of Indian miniature paintings heavily reflects religious themes. Eighty-eight percent of artists report depicting stories from religious scriptures, while 87 percent focus on local deities. This high prevalence suggests that the art form serves as a medium for expressing and preserving religious narratives and iconography. Furthermore,

77 percent of artists create works specifically for temples and prayers, indicating a functional role of art in religious practices.

Artistic Mastery as a Religious Rite

The creative process in miniature painting deeply integrates spiritual elements, with 51 percent of artists reporting that they practice religious customs and rituals while creating sacred art pieces. This fusion of spiritual practices with artistic creation underscores that the process is not merely about producing art but is also an act of religious and spiritual engagement. As Viren Bannu emphasizes, "Prayer and meditation help me clean myself of distracting thoughts before starting my day for painting." This statement highlights how spirituality is woven into every brushstroke, making the act of painting both a devotional practice and an artistic endeavor.

The stages of artistic creation are infused with religious significance, from the preparation of materials to the final touches on the artwork. Such religious rituals encompass acts such as bathing and conducting puja before initiating the artwork, invoking blessings from mentors, abstaining from contacting the art with one's foot, reserving the illustration of deities' eyes for the final stage, and maintaining a state of purity and cleanliness around the art-making area. This integration of spirituality is crucial to understanding the cultural and religious significance of miniature art in communities where it is practiced, as it reflects the artist's connection to their faith and their role in preserving these traditions through their work.

Moreover, the research vividly depicts the artist's emotional and spiritual journey. For many, the creation process transcends the technical realm, morphing into a profoundly spiritual experience. The feelings ranging from joy to a sense of divine connection underscore the power of art as a conduit for profound human experiences. These findings evoke contemplation on art's universal role as a vessel for spiritual expression and self-discovery, regardless of the medium or cultural context.

Cultural Transmission in Indian Miniature Art

Miniature painting demands an exceptionally high level of technical proficiency, requiring artists to master a complex array of skills including the preparation of specialized pigments, intricate brush techniques, and the ability to work on an extremely small scale while maintaining precise detail. In addition, a master miniature painter must have a well-developed spiritual understanding, with deep knowledge of religious symbols and motifs. The careful attention to the divine perspective in miniature paintings is consistent with the precise processes of artistic production. Accordingly, in the Rajasthani tradition of miniature painting, one of the final stages of completing an artwork is painting the eyes of the depicted gods. This final step in the artistic process is thought to infuse the painting with a divine gaze.

Apprenticeship under a seasoned guru is more than mere skill acquisition; it is a journey of profound transformation. In mapping the apprentices' learning trajectory, we identified six to seven critical stages. These encompass the craft of color creation using minerals and organic materials, honing the precision of line drawing, and mastering the intricate details of shading and ornamentation. Central to this learning process is the role of the gurus. They impart technical expertise—like crafting colors, drawing lines, or detailing—and include information about local styles of miniature paintings and nuances of color application within their teachings.

The selection of budding artists or apprentices is a thoughtful and deliberate process, heavily influenced by the guru's discerning eye. A potential artist's lineage and familial ties to established artistic families play a crucial role in their selection, underscoring the significance of intergenerational skill transfer. As Kailash Chand Sharma insightfully noted in one of our interviews, "When a child grows up in this kind of environment, they tend to pick up on things. They see how colors are made, how paintings are made, and the child eventually shows interest in these paintings." This highlights the natural absorption of skills and knowledge within a familial context, where the art form is not just taught but lived and experienced daily.

Cultural Significance and Change

Our findings also reveal the role of Indian miniature painting in broader cultural and religious contexts in Rajasthan. The high percentage of artists incorporating religious elements—ranging from 77 percent to 93 percent across different aspects—indicates that this art form plays a significant role in maintaining and transmitting religious traditions and cultural values. Miniature paintings play a vital role in various religious and cultural ceremonies, serving purposes that extend beyond their aesthetic value. These paintings are often displayed during significant life events, such as weddings, housewarmings, and festivals like Diwali and Holi, symbolizing auspiciousness and religious devotion. In temples, miniature paintings are used as visual aids to narrate stories from Hindu religious texts like the Ramayana, making them an integral part of both private and public worship. The multifunctional role of miniature paintings highlights their importance as both artistic creations and essential components of religious practice and cultural expression.

The evolving dynamics of this unique artistic community raise important questions about the future trajectory of this ancient art form. According to consensus among artists, the interest in learning this traditional art form has declined, largely due to several contributing factors. The most significant of these is the extensive time commitment required to master the intricacies of miniature art. This commitment serves as a deterrent for many aspiring artists. For example, achieving *basic proficiency*, defined as the ability to execute fundamental techniques such as precise line work, color mixing from natural pigments, and the replication of traditional patterns, can require approximately twenty years of dedicated practice. This stage includes mastering the essential skills needed to create works that are faithful to established traditions. In contrast, attaining *a high level of expertise*—characterized by the ability to innovate within the traditional framework, create original compositions, and incorporate complex spiritual and symbolic elements into the artwork—can demand an average of over sixty years. This level of mastery involves not just technical skills but also a deep understanding of the cultural and religious significance of the art form.

With the onset of globalization and technological change, market trends are shifting, which has led to a perceived decrease in demand for this highly specialized art form. Furthermore, the rise of alternative painting styles offers potential artists varied avenues to express their creativity. While the art form has shown adaptability, as evidenced by the introduction of new color palettes and themes, an underlying tension exists between preservation and change. This duality, wherein artists appreciate artistic progression while simultaneously lamenting the erosion of artistic essence, is emblematic of the broader dilemmas many traditional communities face.

In addition to the challenges of time commitment and changing market demands, the artistic journey itself presents significant hurdles. Personal attributes such as discipline, patience, and an unwavering passion for the art are crucial for success. A hands-on approach, demonstrated through technical expertise in painting and crafting natural colors, further distinguishes promising aspirants. However, even with these attributes, the path to mastery is arduous. While a handful of aspirants are inducted into the training fold each year, many falter; nearly half leave their training before achieving mastery. This high attrition rate underscores the challenges faced in preserving and passing on this intricate art form to future generations.

Indian miniature art, deeply rooted in centuries-old traditions, is a testament to the intricate interplay of spirituality, religiosity, cultural transmission, and artistic expression. These artworks, far beyond mere aesthetic endeavors, echo the community's shared values, religious beliefs, and historical tales. They serve as symbolic bridges, linking the past to the present, the divine to the mundane, and weaving narratives of faith, devotion, and cultural identity. Amid the rapid change of societies, this rich canvas of miniature art beckons us to pause and reflect on our origins, collective histories, and the enduring tales of faith and commitment that unite us. Through the lens of miniature art, we are drawn into a profound appreciation of the delicate balance between tradition and change, highlighting an unending journey toward spiritual and artistic enlightenment.

Conclusion

Miniature painting serves as a compass, directing us to the intersections of history, spirituality, and cultural expression. The artists' spiritual journeys, rich with moments of joy, reflection, and divine connection, emphasize the transformative power of art. Their experiences underscore a universal sentiment—art offers a profound medium for human expression regardless of its form.

Miniature paintings play a critical role in cultural preservation. These artworks are reservoirs, ensuring that age-old tales, values, and traditions cascade through generations. Here, the mentorship of art gurus plays an indispensable role. Transmitting skills and stories from generation to generation is crucial for continuity, highlighting the significance of mentorship in cultural transmission. Unlike contemporary technological fields, where knowledge is readily accessible in digital databases, the deep well of wisdom in traditional arts primarily resides with gurus. They are more than mere instructors; they symbolize the living essence of the art's heritage, methodologies, and spirit. This art form's adaptability, while commendable, also raises pressing questions about maintaining its authenticity amid modern influences. Ensuring the future of this art form will require preserving its storied past with the resources of our globally connected present.

16

Thinking about Thinking with Conceptual Art

Taylor Worley

The first and most obvious question concerns our choice of subject. Why conceptual art? Quite simply, if there is one form of contemporary art that uses human cognition as its creative canvas, that form is conceptual art, and its strategies have resourced countless trends in visual art for decades. One particularly astute description of conceptual art relates, "We are being made to think of ourselves thinking."[1] In other words, despite its unorthodox approach, it seems conceptualism actually empowers viewers with a greater degree of imaginative agency through self-reflective thinking *with* art. In this way, perhaps conceptual art functions as a particularly timely, imaginative venue for developing our attention with what Jenny Odell calls "technologies of resistance."[2] For our purposes, such advanced cognitive activity may bear significant parallels to what religious traditions have valued in spiritual contemplation. As Iris Murdoch once said, "Good art which we love can seem holy, and attending to it can be like praying."[3] While austere and elusive, conceptual art provides the least manipulative, non-simulative form of such attentiveness through art.[4] Thus, this project is seek-

1. Tony Godfrey, *Conceptual Art*, Art and Ideas (London: Phaidon, 1998), 142.

2. Resolving a change, she urges: "What I'm suggesting is that we take a protective stance toward ourselves, each other, and whatever is left of what makes us human . . . [and] that we protect our *spaces* and our *time* for non-instrumental, noncommercial activity and thought, for maintenance, for care, for conviviality. And I'm suggesting that we fiercely protect our human animality against all technologies that actively ignore and disdain the body, the bodies of other beings, and the body of the landscape that we inhabit." Jenny Odell, *How to Do Nothing: Resisting the Attention Economy* (Brooklyn, NY: Melville House, 2019), 28.

3. Quoted in David Tracy, *Fragments: The Existential Situation of Our Time: Selected Essays*, vol. 1 (Chicago: University of Chicago Press, 2020), 376.

4. Indeed, a recent text on how to experience contemporary art holds out seven different ways of looking and, for our purposes, chooses to include "Art as Meditation," which is described this way: "This kind of contemplative situation, or 'Art as Meditation,' as I've called it . . . is [not]

ing to rehabilitate the status of conceptualism in empirical aesthetics by discerning the necessary elements to pursue an integrative science of conceptual art.

This project originates from the discourse of theological aesthetics. Thus, it approaches the topic of spiritual knowledge and experience from an intellectual commitment to "divine generosity," as articulated by the Anglican theologian David Brown.[5] This divine generosity, Brown explains, is both mysterious and unsurprising for one who has demonstrated such love for creation as to enter it by means of the incarnation of Jesus Christ.[6] The incarnation, thus, serves as the renewing event for the breadth of human experience, underscoring at the same time the vital place of the human imagination in connecting the sensible world and that which is beyond it.[7] Upon this foundation, a sacramental framework

---

about seeing something that isn't there or posing more thoughts that can only live in your head. It relates to the ability to better appreciate or more deeply engage with a work of art without succumbing to the bite-size nibbles of culture offered elsewhere or having our heads turned this way or that by any number of other tempting distractions." He goes on to relate something of the mystery of such encounters by saying, "At a certain point I felt as though I didn't have to look for the art anymore, that instead it would find me." Ossian Ward, *Ways of Looking: How to Experience Contemporary Art* (London: Laurence King, 2014), 152–54.

5. David Brown, *Tradition and Imagination: Revelation and Change* (Oxford: Oxford University Press, 2004); David Brown, *Discipleship and Imagination: Christian Tradition and Truth* (Oxford: Oxford University Press, 2000); David Brown, *God and Enchantment of Place: Reclaiming Human Experience* (Oxford: Oxford University Press, 2004); David Brown, *God and Grace of Body: Sacrament in Ordinary* (Oxford: Oxford University Press, 2007); David Brown, *God and Mystery in Words: Experience through Metaphor and Drama* (Oxford: Oxford University Press, 2008); Robert MacSwain and Taylor Worley, eds., *Theology, Aesthetics, and Culture: Responses to the Work of David Brown* (Oxford: Oxford University Press, 2012); David Brown, *Divine Generosity and Human Creativity: Theology through Symbol, Painting and Architecture*, ed. Christopher R. Brewer and Robert MacSwain (London: Routledge, 2017); David Brown, *Christian Theology and the Transformation of Natural Religion: From Incarnation to Sacramentality—Essays in Honour of David Brown*, ed. Christopher R. Brewer (Leuven: Peeters, 2018).

6. Brown relates, "Such [direct] experiences would then be appropriately described as sacramental because we have now moved beyond the realm of signs into symbols that themselves always participate in the reality to which they point." David Brown, "A Sacramental World: Why It Matters," in *The Oxford Handbook of Sacramental Theology*, ed. Hans Boersma and Matthew Levering (Oxford: Oxford University Press, 2015), 606.

7. Similar arguments populate the following collection of essays by Brown entitled *Divine Generosity and Human Creativity.* Along similar lines, theologian Natalie Carnes provides a richly embodied account of sacramentality with her theological engagement with Gregory of Nyssa on contemplation (*theoria*): "*Theoria* names a way of seeing that neither excludes the materiality of the object . . . nor reduces sight to the materiality of the object. . . . Describing *theoria* as an 'activity' that does not stop at the sensible suggests the way *theoria* opens up the reality of what is being contemplated. As it does so, it also opens up the reality of the contemplator, and the

for human experience can be discerned, whereby the phenomenology of this gift character in the world (i.e., "divine generosity") makes possible a surplus of meaning in the union of sensory and spiritual experience.[8] Such perspectives inform the theological assumptions behind this project's exploration of a distinct cultural form of visual art like conceptual art.

Of course, it is often the case that these discrete cultures operate with strict rules of engagement, and some narration is required here. Indeed, contemporary art is understood to operate within "an atmosphere of theory," as one prominent philosopher has described it, and this atmosphere makes possible a finely tuned, intellectual ecosystem that allows for the proliferation of meanings that cannot be derived simply from the sensory or material conditions of the artwork.[9] This development stems from a vanguard movement of conceptual art among New York City and London artists during the 1960s and 1970s and currently operates as a highly influential art-making strategy sometimes labeled conceptualism. The level of conceptual (i.e., cognitive, imaginative, aesthetic) engagement required has been likened by its practitioners to a form of mysticism. In the very first of his "Sentences on Conceptual Art," for instance, Sol LeWitt asserts that "conceptual artists are mystics rather than rationalists."[10] Similarly, the art historian Thomas Crow has identified seminal figures like Mark Rothko, Robert Smithson, and James Turrell as demonstrating markedly anti-idolatrous, perhaps even apophatic, impulses in their defining works.[11] Along these lines, this project seeks to better understand the experience of conceptual works of art as promoting imaginative resilience in

---

world she shares with the contemplated." Natalie Carnes, *Beauty: A Theological Engagement with Gregory of Nyssa* (Eugene, OR: Cascade, 2014), 245–48.

8. Of course, this way of thinking is also influenced by the classic text by Lewis Hyde, wherein he professes that "I still believe that the primary commerce of art is gift exchange, that unless the work is the realization of the artist's gift and unless we, the audience, can feel the gift it carries, there is no art." Lewis Hyde, *The Gift: Creativity and the Artist in the Modern World*, 25th anniversary ed. (New York: Vintage, 2007), 356.

9. In his defining 1964 essay "The Artworld," Arthur Danto presented the following thesis: "To see something as art requires something the eye cannot decry—an atmosphere of artistic theory, a knowledge of the history of art: an art world." Republished in Arthur C. Danto, *After the End of Art: Contemporary Art and the Pale of History* (Princeton, NJ: Princeton University Press, 1997), 165.

10. Sol LeWitt, "Sentences on Conceptual Art," in *Conceptual Art: A Critical Anthology*, ed. Alexander Alberro and Blake Stimson (Cambridge, MA: MIT Press, 1999), 3.

11. In this light, the Christian tradition's perennial concerns with idolatry as well as its longstanding celebration of contemplation and the cultivation of a theological imagination emerge as key criteria for engagement with conceptualism. Both might prove surprisingly generative for re-engaging art that resists, in the words of Crow, "both idolatrous figuration and its seeming opposite in the disenchanted materialism" of high modernism's legacy in contemporary art.

viewers and enhancing their capacity for attention and, perhaps, spiritual contemplation.[12] Such understanding, then, necessitates a disciplinary partnership with empirical aesthetics and the resources of experimental psychology of art.

In the first phase of the project, "Thinking about Thinking: Conceptual Art and the Contemplative Tradition" had as its aim to build an interpretive framework for empirical research on the extra-aesthetic nature of conceptual art. Thus, the goal was to support the claim that conceptual art is more effective when the common experience of challenging forms of contemporary art becomes a means to contemplation. The project, then, has worked to decode the art-critical language around conceptual art for more generalized study, identify the causal dynamics that make it fruitful for spiritual contemplation, and outline empirical claims that can be tested. In the second phase, "Art of Attention: Bridge-Building for Field Experimentation on Conceptual Art" has been exploring the way that difficult or challenging experiences with artworks may trigger the imagination in good ways. In summary, the goal has been to explore the psychophysiological nature of audience engagement with examples of conceptual art through field experiments in the authentic setting of the art museum. In this way, we are building a bridge with this pilot study to a fuller program of experimentation on conceptual art.

Toward an Integrative Science of Conceptual Art

"Conceptual Art and the Contemplative Tradition": Research Questions and Design

Despite its cognitive appeal, however, conceptual art has been deemed anti-aesthetic by many scientists and philosophers and thus not eligible for careful study by empirical aesthetics. The enduring influence of conceptualism on so

Thomas E. Crow, *No Idols: The Missing Theology of Art*, Power Polemics (Sydney, Australia: Power Publications, 2017), 85.

12. For instance, Jeffrey Kosky provides a rich and probing discussion of James Turrell's light works as both squarely representative of apophaticism and surprising vehicles for contemplation. He relates the good of contemplative vision thus: "Vision becomes contemplative not when it sees something solid or distinct in the clarity of light, but when it sees in and through distinct, visible objects the indistinct and invisible origin and end that shines darkly in them. In such a vision, the cosmos appears to the human being both as divine light to see (the universe is a theophany of light revealing God who is an invisible light) and light that must be unseen precisely because this light veils the dark light or 'luminous darkness' of the transcendently invisible divine light." Jeffrey L. Kosky, "Contemplative Recovery: The Artwork of James Turrell," *Cross Currents*, 63, no. 1 (2013): 58. Cf. Jeffrey L. Kosky, *Arts of Wonder: Enchanting Secularity: Walter de Maria, Diller & Scofidio, James Turrell, Andy Goldsworthy*, Religion and Postmodernism (Chicago: University of Chicago Press, 2013).

much contemporary art, however, suggests that many museum-goers garner some degree of experiential rewards from it. Instead, a fuller assessment sees conceptual art as extra-aesthetic and acknowledges how these highly contextual artworks subtly direct our attention and integrate cultural meaning. The research design for this project has attempted to take seriously the claims against conceptual art and consider how, in fact, to respond to them.

Background to the Study. While research on the science of art appreciation has flourished in recent years, the field has largely avoided the category of conceptual art because of its apparent anti-aesthetic nature. Where studies have begun to take account of extra-aesthetic properties of art, we find promising developments that lend themselves to more focused research on the nature and function of conceptual art.[13] The initial dismissal of conceptualism, however, should not be overlooked.[14] For instance, in *The Aesthetic Brain*, Anjan Chatterjee includes a brief treatment of conceptual art and seeks to answer this question: "Can scientific aesthetics say

13. Ellen K. Levy, "Enraptured: Art and Attention," in *Perception and Agency in Shared Spaces of Contemporary Art*, ed. Cristina Albu and Dawna L. Schuld (New York: Routledge, 2018), 172–81.

14. For instance, the psychologist Arthur Shimamura develops an exacting set of categories for artworks that demonstrates a genuine sensitivity to the developments of art history. Despite the reliance of his term "meta-art" on classic examples like Marcel Duchamp's *Fountain* and Andy Warhol's *Brillo Boxes* for explaining self-referential and self-questioning art, what results is an unfortunately narrow and reductionist account of conceptualism that understands it to simply be a delivery system for ideas. Shimamura's summary from the introduction:

> In summary, beholders have, over the centuries, approached artistic creations from various perspectives. With a mimetic approach, the beholder interprets an artwork as a window to the world and evaluates the degree to which it succeeds in depicting realistic scenes and events. With an expressionist approach, the beholder seeks an emotional experience, such as beauty or the sublime. With a formalist approach, rather than seeing objects or scenes within an artwork, the raw sensual qualities of colors, lines, and abstract shapes are brought to the forefront. With a conceptual approach, it is the thought or story behind an artwork that is crucial. Today, as we stroll through an art gallery, we may adopt any one or all of these approaches. Thus, anything goes, from interpreting mimetic representations to conceptual meta-art statements. Importantly, these approaches highlight aspects of the beholder's mental processes, such as sensory processes with mimetic and formalist approaches, emotional processes with expressionism, and memory or thought processes with a conceptual approach.

As he explains: "Postmodernism, which some suggest is still with us, intellectualizes the practice of art. It is thus anti-expressionist, anti-formalist, and indeed anti-aesthetic. Issues of beauty, significant form, and other aesthetic (e.g., sublime) experiences give way to conceptual statements about the meaning of art." Arthur P. Shimamura, *Experiencing Art: In the Brain of the Beholder* (Oxford: Oxford University Press, 2013), 14, 12. As an initial rejoinder, however, consider: Gregory Minissale, *The Psychology of Contemporary Art* (Cambridge: Cambridge University Press, 2015).

anything useful about conceptual art?"[15] Due to the complex and layered meanings that constitute conceptual art, Chatterjee rules it out: "The richly textured meaning of individual pieces of art that gives art its power is inherently variable and open to many interpretations and thus closed to neuroscience. . . . Conceptual art, with its emphasis on meaning shaped by culture, is hard to bring under scientific scrutiny."[16] His position is confirmed by multiple voices in the field.[17] This project, however, tries to account for the way in which conceptual art subverts the traditional models of aesthetic pleasure and instead deploys more confrontational or unexpected strategies toward new experiential rewards in meaning making.

Research Questions and Methods. While it is unlikely that all suspicions about conceptual art as anti-aesthetic or its status as less deserving than more traditional forms will dissipate, the goal of this project is to develop a theoretical account of conceptualism that is pliable and innovative enough to begin serious study of this cultural phenomenon and its function. We begin with a process of translation around questions like: If it is the case that conceptual art animates thinking about our thinking, how might we adjust our framework accordingly? What fresh insights from an interdisciplinary set of resources can we draw upon to build such a framework? The conceptual refinement of the research questions involved the following three steps. First, listen to artists and art theorists describe their ambitions for conceptualism. Second, invite colleagues from theology, philosophy, and art history to explore the imaginative value of conceptualism and demonstrate strategies for overcoming the apparent challenges. Third, translate

15. Anjan Chatterjee, *The Aesthetic Brain: How We Evolved to Desire Beauty and Enjoy Art* (New York: Oxford University Press, 2014), 142.

16. Chatterjee, *Aesthetic Brain*, 148–49. Chatterjee explains: "Does science have anything useful to say about meaning in art? The ultimate reach of science is hard to predict, but to my knowledge there has not been any serious attempt to think about the science of conceptual art. Consider the critical aesthetic triad of sensations, emotions, and meaning. Scientists have typically focused on the connection between sensations and emotions. Art, as long as it slides along this sensation–pleasure groove, is amenable to investigation by empirical methods. Scientists can look for hidden stable regularities of light and line and color and form in artwork that are pleasing and relate them to the kinds of neural tuning for which our brains seem to be designed." Chatterjee, *Aesthetic Brain*, 147.

17. Semir Zeki, *Inner Vision: An Exploration of Art and the Brain* (Oxford: Oxford University Press, 1999); Arthur P. Shimamura and Stephen E. Palmer, *Aesthetic Science: Connecting Minds, Brains, and Experience* (Oxford: Oxford University Press, 2012); G. Gabrielle Starr, *Feeling Beauty: The Neuroscience of Aesthetic Experience* (Cambridge, MA: MIT Press, 2013); Eric R. Kandel, *Reductionism in Art and Brain Science: Bridging the Two Cultures* (New York: Columbia University Press, 2016); Susan Magsamen, "Your Brain on Art: The Case for Neuroaesthetics," *Cerebrum: The Dana Forum on Brain Science*, July 19, 2019.

these insights into a viable framework for further empirical study of the basic cognitive operations embedded in experiences of conceptual art.

Thus, the project focused on a modest effort at theorizing how the public experiences conceptual art. Therefore, as the insights of this interdisciplinary study emerge more clearly, our refined understanding of conceptualism can begin to guide more practical explorations around participants' experience, understanding, and processing: How do participants register the effect of works of conceptual art? What remains with them about it after the fact? How do they process these experiences? How does their personal background or past experiences participate in the processing? How do their assumptions about art impact the processing? How do their spiritual beliefs inform the processing? Do these experiences require more or less cognitive effort to process in comparison with other visual art media? These initial efforts to theorize how the public engages conceptual art will contribute to the ongoing refinement of a framework for empirical study.

Learnings. In summary, the first phase concluded the following: The extra-aesthetic nature of conceptualism invites a rich, meaning-making process rather than merely a sensory reaction to visual stimuli. Rather than mere obstacle, conceptual artists employ creative uses of visual dissonance in art as a reward strategy for meaning making. Such complicated interactions surely present challenges for empirical study, but if met conceptual art represents a promising case study for testing aesthetic cognitivism. More specifically, the learnings produced both a map of conceptualism and a preliminary framework for empirical investigation.

A. Mapping conceptualism: For many, conceptual art represents arguably the most influential art-making strategy for contemporary art.[18] For the task of mapping that influence, however, there are both good news and not-so-good news. Conceptualism's influence is quite prolific but at the same time unavoidably diffuse. This means that works of contemporary art cannot simply be classified as conceptual or not. It is more helpful, then, to think of conceptualism in terms of some large categories: *pure conceptualism*, *implanted conceptualism*, and *participatory conceptualism*. Principally, these categories help to name the relationship of a conceptual artwork to its own material conditions.

First, *pure conceptualism* reflects the work of the early innovators that launched and subsequently codified their approach as a discrete movement. Much of the motivation behind the origins of that movement resides in the experience of students at art academies who were seeking to overturn the domineering influence of their instructors, particular figures who were steeped in the formalist traditions of painting and sculpture. In many ways, this diverse group of artists (e.g., the

18. Minissale, *Psychology of Contemporary Art*, xvi.

Art & Language collective, Sol LeWitt, Joseph Kosuth, Robert Barry, Lawrence Weiner, Yoko Ono, Mel Bochner, and Adrian Piper) found in conceptualism an innovative means of expressing their artistic voices and at the same time upsetting the status quo in cultural centers like London and New York. By drawing upon proto-conceptual developments like Marcel Duchamp's *Fountain* and others (e.g., Joseph Beuys, Piero Manzoni, and Robert Rauschenberg), their rebellious efforts adopted a radical stance of ambivalence toward their materials, what Lucy Lippard famously described as the "dematerialization of the art object."[19] Such efforts are well demonstrated in Kosuth's *One and Three Chairs* (1965) in which the artist has displayed an actual wooden folding chair alongside wall hangings of a photo of the same chair and a copy of a dictionary entry for "chair."[20]

The second category of *implanted conceptualism* differs from the first in its incisive approach to embedding concepts within materials. In subsequent generations, artists continued to employ conceptualism as a means of critical inquiry but with a more free and uninhibited deployment of materials. In this way, the conceptual gesture necessitates the careful choice of artistic materials, but the significance of the artwork refuses to be limited to the aesthetic qualities or displayed craftsmanship of its materials.[21] Despite the irreducible materiality of this

19. Lucy R. Lippard, *Six Years: The Dematerialization of the Art Object from 1966 to 1972: A Cross-Reference Book of Information on Some Esthetic Boundaries* (New York: Praeger, 1973).

20. Joseph Kosuth, *One and Three Chairs*, 1965, wood folding chair, mounted photograph of a chair, and mounted photographic enlargement of the dictionary definition of "chair," chair 32 3/8 x 14 7/8 x 20 7/8 in (82 x 37.8 x 53 cm), photographic panel 36 x 24 1/8 in. (91.5 x 61.1 cm), text panel 24 x 30 in. (61 x 76.2 cm), Museum of Modern Art, Manhattan, https://www.moma.org/collection/works/81435. In its variety of display, the artist pokes at our implicit hierarchies of meaning regarding an object, an image, and words. Here, Kosuth questions the relationship of our perceptions of the world and the language we employ to navigate it. Such a gesture, however, is hardly dependent on the specific materials involved; the artwork could be realized again or simultaneously with a different chair entirely. Kosuth himself did not create the object, take the photograph, or write the definition. He merely collected them and organized the installation. In this way, the conceptual nature of artworks remains merely or purely composed of the work's idea. According to the museum's elaborations on the work, art is, for Kosuth, "meaning-making," as opposed to the skillful creation of objects, images, or even words. Perhaps not surprisingly, then, a few of the key leaders of the movement like Kosuth and Terry Smith eventually ceased making artworks and took to writing philosophy and art criticism instead.

21. Take, for instance, Zhang Huan's *Ash Buddha* (2015). Over the course of several years, Huan has executed a series of large-scale sculptural re-creations of a traditional image of the Buddha in international centers like Berlin, Taiwan, and Sydney. Such forms would not be remarkable except for the fact that each one involves approximately twenty tons of incense ash collected from Shanghai temples. Huan utilizes a painstakingly long and careful process wherein studio assistants assemble a sixteen-foot-tall aluminum mold for the shape of the Buddha sculp-

conceptualist category, this is not simply a sly return to a traditional aestheticism, because no matter how precise or happenstance the engagement with materials might be, the significance of the artwork remains stubbornly with its conceptual essence. This category seems the most prevalent in contemporary art today.

Finally, the category of *participatory conceptualism* names a third way in which contemporary artists deploy the creative use of materials toward conceptual ends. In similar ways to the *implanted conceptualism* category, artists here continue to make the material conditions of their artworks subservient to their conceptual goals but in an even more pronounced or exaggerated way. Unlike in other cases, however, artworks in this category involve the interaction of participants with the materials of the artwork in hopes of creating a fresh conceptual link to them. Such efforts display a range of interactive possibilities.[22] Despite its scope, however, the work consistently emphasizes ways in which viewers become participants through interacting with materials, inhabiting curated spaces, or embodying the work in some way.

To be clear, this continuum is merely one of many ways to account for conceptualism's diffuse conditions in contemporary art. Materiality may be, in fact, the most basic aspect to consider. In truth, the sheer breadth of possibility in how contemporary art employs conceptualist strategies is likely much more expansive than our categories could describe.[23] Consider, for instance, the blend of issues represented in the title of Boris Groys's seminal essay of 1979: "Moscow Romantic

---

ture. Once assembled, the hollow form is then filled with the collected incense ash and allowed to sit until the form has settled in the mold. After some time, the mold is removed, along with the supports holding up the shape of the Buddha's face and upraised hand. Without the form and supports, the integrity of sculptural form is lost in a gradual crumbling that begins almost immediately. The artist understands these unruly forms to hold prayers, thoughts, and hopes, and as such, the cyclic formation—as a sculpture—and dissolution—as a pile of ash—reflects well the Buddhist logic of his gesture. In this way, Huan's choice of material here represent a rigorous conceptual effort that cannot be realized apart from the physical characteristics of the materials employed. While Huan's work provides a potent example of this strategy, the category of *implanted conceptualism* can be seen consistently in the work of artists as diverse as David Hammons, Doris Salcedo, Janine Antoni, and Damien Hirst. Learn more about Huan's artwork and see photos at "Zhang Huan's Ash Buddha—20-Ton Incense Sculptures," Public Delivery, last updated September 23, 2024, https://tinyurl.com/58nbaeyp.

22. For instance, the intimate forms of Felix Gonzalez-Torres's shared gifts or Rirkrit Tiravanija's shared gallery meals, the large-scale and often playfully interactive installations of Olafur Eliasson or Carsten Höller, or the way in which artworks by Tino Sehgal or Harrell Fletcher make the pure sociality enacted by the artwork its material substance.

23. Similar continuums could be developed around the issues of site specificity or location, curation, fieldwork and documentation, market dynamics and finance, social-cultural or political impact, institutional context, and emotional poetics. See for instance: Joerg Heiser and Ellen Seifermann, *Romantischer Konzeptualismus = Romantic Conceptualism* (Bielefeld: Kerber,

Conceptualism."[24] Such conditions, however, are not an accident of art history. In fact, the early pioneers of conceptual art refused the term "conceptualism" in hopes of avoiding the formation of another, easily caricatured "-ism" for modern art.[25] By most accounts, their insistence has proved effective for contemporary art, and in light of new media, digital art, and the like, today's possibilities seem limitless. For this reason, it is important to explore the ways that we can better understand the unifying features of conceptualist strategies.[26] In other words, a baseline psychology of conceptualism is needed.

B. A provisional psychology of conceptual art: The experience of conceptual art certainly intersects with many of the perceptual issues that bear on more traditional forms of visual art. The differences, however, represent the most promising areas for further research. Namely, challenging forms of modern and contemporary art involve an experience of what the psychological scientist Robert Solso calls "visual dissonance." He explains: "*Visual dissonance* is defined as a state of psychological tension caused when one experiences a disparity between what one expects to see and what one actually sees. . . . In the case of unfulfilled expectations, the viewer is required to resolve his or her tension, or simply to abandon the piece and consider another."[27] As William Seeley describes it, such work is "visually unrewarding but intellectually stimulating."[28] The confusion that viewers typically experience when encountering works of conceptual art is, then, just the beginning of a more complex and extended cognitive process.[29]

2007); Claire Bishop, *Artificial Hells: Participatory Art and the Politics of Spectatorship* (London: Verso, 2012).

24. Boris Groys, "Moscow Romantic Conceptualism," in *History Becomes Form: Moscow Conceptualism* (Cambridge, MA: MIT Press, 2010). Original work published in the Samizdat magazine 37 (Leningrad, 1979).

25. Terry Smith, *One and Five Ideas: On Conceptual Art and Conceptualism*, ed. Robert Bailey (Durham, NC: Duke University Press, 2017), 117–18.

26. Godfrey, *Conceptual Art*, 4. Relatedly, Godfrey reflects that "because the work does not take a traditional form it demands a more active response from the viewer, indeed it could be argued that the Conceptual work of art only truly exists in the viewer's mental participation." Thus, the strategy of conceptualism was not to dissolve or simply undermine the aesthetic priority of art but to utilize all the cognitive strategies available to render unfamiliar what had become stale in the experience of visual art. Godfrey concludes that "the legacy of Conceptual art is not a historical style, but an ingrained habit of interrogation. It is in the act of questioning that the subject, reader, or viewer becomes himself or herself." Godfrey, *Conceptual Art*, 424.

27. Robert L. Solso, *The Psychology of Art and the Evolution of the Conscious Brain* (Cambridge, MA: MIT Press, 2005), 235.

28. William P. Seeley, *Attentional Engines: A Perceptual Theory of the Arts*, Thinking Art (New York: Oxford University Press, 2020), 27.

29. Minissale, *Psychology of Contemporary Art*, xvi.

Thus, our provisional psychology of that process identifies at least three phases of interaction: confusion, integration, and production. First, viewers experience *conceptual confusion.* This is the initial zone of visual dissonance wherein a viewer encounters a seemingly non-art object within the art-viewing context of other obvious art objects and is faced with a perceptual dilemma. The disorienting quality of the encounter, however, was entirely intended by the artist.[30] At this point, participants must determine whether or not they wish to attempt a cognitive reconciliation of the seemingly out-of-place or anti-aesthetic display. If they choose to persist with the encounter, the viewer is then progressing into the second phase of *conceptual integration.* For this stage, viewers must navigate the dialogical reasoning necessary to balance the artwork's challenge of artistic consistency (e.g., "I have seen seemingly non-art objects in museums before, like perhaps readymades") and artistic innovation (e.g., "This work is unlike any art I have seen before"). Such reasoning continues to draw upon visual perception but also involves a good deal of memory based on prior art encounters.

Once the viewer achieves a level of restored comfort and the cognitive dissonance has been somewhat resolved, they are able to progress into the third and most advanced phase of *conceptual production.* This is the zone of reward, wherein the hard work of holding the aesthetic tension of the encounter and working to integrate the experience receives a payoff in the form of imaginative confidence to engage in fresh meaning making. The viewer has earned the right to collaborate with the artwork on a highly individualized and creative account of the work's ultimate meaning. Here, the cognitive resonance of the artwork within the imagination of the viewer is all that matters, because the object is now seen in a new way—that is, *as* art. The traditional categories of correct or incorrect assessments (i.e., historical, aesthetic, or otherwise) are replaced by new associations imprinted with the participant's personal background and sensibilities. The earned playfulness of this final stage is what, it seems, most artists aim for with conceptual works. Such engaged attentiveness resembles the playful generativity of thought so celebrated in forms of spiritual contemplation.[31] In comparison with other forms of art or

30. Solso, *Psychology of Art*, 235.

31. More recently, Hart's *Contemplation and Kingdom* takes up this question of kingdom by revisiting a historic boundary in the contemplative tradition, and in this way presents a fresh justification for expanding the approved thresholds for contemplation. Namely, *Contemplation and Kingdom* provides a concise exploration of how Aquinas reads Richard of St. Victor on the nature of contemplation. Returning to Richard's *The Mystical Ark*, he endeavors to demonstrate that "we may regard Richard's treatise as an invitation to consider the sheer reach of contemplation in daily life, how each and every aspect of the created world, our intellectual engagement with it, as well as the Creator in his acts and even his essence, offers itself to be tasted and

media, conceptual art challenges the participant at each stage of the encounter, and unlike more manipulative forms, they are not lost in an immersive aesthetic experience but are continually made aware of their own cognitive engagement with the work's conceptual matrix.[32] While this provisional framework remains open to the contemplative nature of aesthetic experiences of conceptual art, more consideration is needed. For instance, pertinent questions remain: What lingering effects can be measured in the experience of conceptual art that parallel and diverge from traditional art forms? And how do these lingering effects contribute to modes of critical cognitive response to the artwork? On this front, recent developments in neuroaesthetics, then, must be supplemented by similar studies on attention and meditation.[33] While these studies set a promising horizon for potential research on conceptual art, it remains to be seen how best to unite such

---

enjoyed." Put more succinctly, Hart asks, "Does contemplation include the Kingdom as well as the King?" In this way, Hart directs readers to passages in Richard's *The Mystical Ark* 4.5 like the following: "Thinking crawls: meditation marches and often runs; contemplation flies around everywhere and when it wishes it suspends itself in the heights." "In thinking there is wandering; in meditation, investigation; in contemplation, wonder." "Thinking is from imagination; meditation from reason; contemplation, from understanding." Kevin Hart, *Contemplation and Kingdom: Aquinas Reads Richard of St. Victor* (South Bend, IN: St. Augustine's Press, 2020), 45, 40.

32. Such a theoretical framework is meant to operate within the parameters of a more comprehensive model, like the "Vienna Integrated Model of Top-Down and Bottom-Up Processes in Art Perception" (VIMAP) developed by Pelowski and colleagues. Matthew Pelowski, Patrick S. Markey, Michael Forster, Gernot Gerger, and Helmut Leder, "Move Me, Astonish Me . . . Delight My Eyes and Brain: The Vienna Integrated Model of Top-Down and Bottom-Up Processes in Art Perception (VIMAP) and Corresponding Affective, Evaluative and Neurophysiological Correlates," *Physics of Life Reviews* 21 (2017): 80–125. The genesis for this model stems from Pelowski's dissatisfaction with the state of psychological aesthetics in which most researchers settle for an account of low-level vision (e.g., symmetry, contrast, clarity) and the reductive target of visual pleasure. Matthew Pelowski and Fuminori Akiba, "A Model of Art Perception, Evaluation and Emotion in Transformative Aesthetic Experience," *New Ideas in Psychology* 29, no. 2 (2011): 80–87. Such basic research interests cannot deal with the level of artistic diversity and sophistication on offer in contemporary art. In response, Pelowski and colleagues have endeavored to develop a model of core stages and broad outcomes for what happens in encounters with visual art. Thus, the VIMAP provides top-down and bottom-up orientations that allow for enough flexibility to adapt the model to a wide range of experiential factors with visual art. Its particular suitability for deeper study of the experience of conceptual art, however, resides in the framework's accounting for checks on schema congruency (i.e., a match between self and expectations to the reality of the world), self-relevance (e.g., "Is this important to myself or my expectations or worldview?"), and coping ability for the viewer (e.g., "Do I continue to interact with this or can I escape?"). Such interrogations are uniquely relevant to the experience of conceptual art.

33. See, for instance, A. Lutz, H. A. Slagter, J. D. Dunne, and R. J. Davidson, "Attention Regulation and Monitoring in Meditation," *Trends in Cognitive Sciences* 12, no. 4 (2008): 163–69.

complementary strands of inquiry and where the most advantageous entry points for experimentation lie.

Project Outputs. The project has generated conversation in multiple forms and in different venues among scholars intrigued by the possibilities of an integrative science of conceptual art. First, the journal *Religions* has hosted a special issue dedicated to a theological exploration of conceptual art, broadly construed. These essays attempt to accomplish three things: (1) provide close readings of conceptual works for the sake of fresh theological insights and connections, (2) demonstrate the power of conceptualism as an artistic strategy for dynamic meaning making in culture today despite its sometimes off-putting appearance, and (3) establish a historical or theoretical connection between what is core to the diversity of conceptual artworks and the particular manifestation of conceptualism in the essay's selection(s).[34]

Second, the topic of art and contemplation was examined through an informal colloquium of scholars from different disciplines and as a conference panel entitled "The Hospitality of Wonder: Art and Contemplation Revisited."[35] The generative connection between art and contemplation was considered in terms of reinvigorated wonder, because at their best, each aspires to access a realm of wonder. In this connection, art and contemplation possess at least three shared concerns in their pursuit of wonder: an anti-idolatrous relationship to human knowing, an orientation to discovery, and anticipations of a transformative effect. Such connections were explored in the fields of poetry, architecture, film, literature, and visual art, and several of the contributions have been published

34. As an online, open-source publication, articles have been published as soon as they are ready. Alex Sosler, "Going to the Morgue with Andres Serrano: Provocation as Revelation," *Religions* 13, no. 6 (2022): article number 562, https://doi.org/10.3390/rel13060562; C. M. Howell, "The Edge of Perception: Gordon Matta-Clark's Hermeneutic of Place and the Possibilities of Absence for the Theological Imagination," *Religions* 13, no. 10 (2022): article number 920, https://doi.org/10.3390/rel13100920; Jonathan A. Anderson, "Conceptual Art, Theology, and Re-Presentation," *Religions* 13, no. 10 (2022): article number 984, https://doi.org/10.3390/rel13100984; Arthur Aghajanian, "The Readymade as Social Exchange: Everyday Tactics of Resistance in Conceptual Art," *Religions* 13, no. 11 (2022): article number 1078, https://doi.org/10.3390/rel13111078; Meaghan Burke, "Art Together, Prayer Together: Relational and Revelatory Practices of Joseph Beuys, Dietrich Bonhoeffer and Leslie Iwai," *Religions* 14, no. 1 (2023): article number 24, https://doi.org/10.3390/rel14010024; Aixin Zhang, "The Neglected Place of 'Totems' in Contemporary Art," *Religions* 14, no. 6 (2023): article number 810, https://doi.org/10.3390/rel14060810; Mark Allen, "The Rothko Chapel: Profane or Sacred Space?" *Religions* 14, no. 7 (2023): article number 853, https://doi.org/10.3390/rel14070853. To date, additional contributions are in production.

35. The panel took place on October 26, 2022, as a part of Baylor University's "Art Seeking Understanding" Symposium on Faith and Culture.

in a special issue on art and spirituality for *Spiritus*, the academic journal of the Society for the Study of Christian Spirituality.[36]

Third, the project has leveraged multiple presentations, conference papers, and consultations toward the development of a white paper dedicated to an integrative psychology of conceptual art.[37] The white paper has been read for feedback by several scholars representing the fields of experimental psychology, philosophy, aesthetics and visual art education, and theology and religious studies.[38] The process for this white paper also helped to generate an article for *The Other Journal* entitled "Art at the Edge of Mourning," which received editorial support and images from the Felix Gonzalez-Torres Foundation.[39] These different venues have provided unique sources of feedback on the main claims of the project and helped to refine the larger research aims.

Assessment. While there are likely many lessons learned, these may be the most significant. First, while the theoretical and philosophical hurdles to engaging conceptual art from a theological vantage point should not be underestimated, there appear to be a growing enthusiasm to engage with contemporary art and an earnest desire to deal well with the especially thick and confusing "atmosphere of theory" that informs so much conceptual art and the significant gap in the larger literature of theology and the visual arts where these unique contributions and imaginative affinities might be explored. In other words, the scholarly strain of theology and the arts possesses the capacity to be much more conversant with the art-critical discourse of contemporary art. Second, the ongoing but encouraging

36. Taylor Worley and Glen G. Scorgie, "Introduction," *Spiritus: A Journal of Christian Spirituality* 23, no. 2 (2023): 187–91; Dennis Kinlaw, "Literary Engagement and the Contemplative Disposition," *Spiritus: A Journal of Christian Spirituality* 23, no. 2 (2023): 192–210; C. M. Howell, "Rhythms of Silence and Space: Contemplation and Architectural Proportion in Dom Hans van der Laan," *Spiritus: A Journal of Christian Spirituality* 23, no. 2 (2023): 211–28; Taylor Worley, "'All Things Visible and Invisible': Conceptual Art and Contemplation," *Spiritus: A Journal of Christian Spirituality* 23, no. 2 (2023): 229–49; Joy Moore, "Before Poetry," *Spiritus: A Journal of Christian Spirituality* 23, no. 2 (2023): 316–30.

37. First, the paper was presented in the form of a public lecture called "Endless Supply: An Exploration of Conceptualism and Contemplation" for the Wheaton College campus sponsored by the art department on September 20, 2022. Next, the paper was presented on October 26, 2022, as a conference paper entitled "I Don't Get It! A Psychology of Conceptual Art" in a session devoted to "Art in Psychology and Medicine," during Baylor University's "Art Seeking Understanding" Symposium on Faith and Culture. Additional presentations were offered at Liberty University, John Brown University, and Dordt University.

38. The white paper is entitled "Thinking about Thinking with Art: Towards an Integrative Science of Conceptual Art" and is available by request to the author.

39. Taylor Worley, "Art at the Edge of Mourning," *The Other Journal* 35: "Vice & Virtue" (Spring 2023): 54–66.

dialogue with colleagues in neuroscience and experimental psychology has provided another surprising and illuminating development. Many voices from these fields find contemporary art fascinating and demonstrate a willingness to navigate its many challenges for the sake of studying it in greater depth. It appears that a range of neuroscientific and related studies could be related to the functions of conceptual art. As more scientists begin to see that much of contemporary art functions like philosophy—probing big questions with new, aesthetic tools—the possibilities for collaboration will make a good deal more sense. Thus, it seems helpful to foreground the philosophizing nature of conceptual art for colleagues that may bring a primarily empirical perspective.

"Art of Attention": Research Questions and Design

By identifying a theoretical model of the basic cognitive operations embedded in experiences of conceptual art, it means we can move beyond conceptual refinement into more ambitious and developed forms of qualitative and quantitative study. The goal of this project is to identify a viable research model to initiate a fuller study on the experience of conceptual art. To that end, the research activities of this project will serve to build upon and extend the ways in which the initial phase established conceptual foundations for the project. First, the project's initial findings will be resourced through extended research on the understandings of practicing visual arts influenced by conceptualism.[40] Second, the project's initial

40. Conceptualism is a vibrant and evolving strategy for art making today, which is diversifying its influence rather than settling into a purely historical category. Thus, the best way to solidify these findings for application to experimental design is to platform the insights and expertise of working artists. In this way, we are resourcing our considerations from the realm of current practice and how artists are deploying these strategies presently. When significant parallels in cognition between the creator and receiver of a conceptual work of art are expected, artistic production should be kept as a significant category of study for conceptual art. Therefore, this project will seek to create space within the research conversation around notions of artistic knowledge, or what education theorists refer to as "craft learning." David Pye, *The Nature and Art of Workmanship*, ed. Ezra Shales (New York: Herbert Press, 2008); Richard Sennett, *The Craftsman* (New Haven: Yale University Press, 2008). Advocates of conceptual art admit that meaning is usually achieved through the creative use of visual dissonance, and the rewards of engagement for the viewer often arrive after an initial reaction of confusion or frustration. Such experiences may represent, here to date, the most creatively exaggerated form of a visual puzzle eliciting "perceptual problem solving," the fifth of Ramachandran and Hirstein's "eight laws of aesthetic experience." Vilayanur Ramachandran and William Hirstein, "The Science of Art: A Neurological Theory of Aesthetic Experience," *Journal of Consciousness Studies* 6 (1999): 15–51. The discussions with artists, then, are exploring the following areas of research interest: (1) Process: How does the language of artists parallel in meaningful ways the description of

findings will be applied to the development and execution of a pilot study to determine feasibility for the design of future experiments. In describing this phase of research, our focus will be on the pilot study.

Research Questions. We have been working on an experimental design that is uniquely suited to engagement with conceptual art and piloting an initial study to explore the viability of this model. Thus, we hope to address the gap in empirical aesthetics where conceptual art resides by focusing on the following research question: What are the autonomic correlates to isolate for in an experimental study of conceptual art? In this way, we are attempting to trace the effects of conceptualism's visual dissonance in the body's stress response. To do so, this pilot study is utilizing the measurement of heart-rate variability (HRV) to derive a psychophysiological picture of how subjects experience challenging encounters with conceptual art.[41] This measure was selected based on the following account of how the cognitive operations prompted by conceptual art might be examined physiologically. If conceptual art is designed to disrupt typical patterns of cognition with art experiences in order to encourage the viewer to a deeper participation with the conceptual aspect of the work, then a potential neurobiological consequence could be the disruption of cognitive homeostasis. The theory of cognitive homeostasis holds that all nervous system function can be modeled on the simple and elegant principle of homeostasis.[42] In short, this model proposes that the nervous system is composed of nested hierarchical homeostatic systems that function in concert to produce human behavior at all levels, from simple

conceptual art as "thinking about thinking?" (2) Intention: How do artists intend for participants to experience works of conceptual art differently than other forms of visual art? (3) Function: Do conceptual artists working today find recognizable the engagement models created by psychology of art? If so, in what ways would artists revise or improve those models? (4) Practice: Do artists possess a value for spiritual contemplation with respect to their artwork? To what degree and in what ways does artistic production in conceptual art involve theories or practices of spiritual contemplation? (5) Reception: How do conceptual artists working today structure their categories for successful and failed works of conceptual art? How do they hope their work will be received and assessed? The aim for this aspect of the larger project is to achieve relative affirmation of our theoretical model of how artists want audiences to conceive of and engage with works of conceptual art.

41. This section is indebted to a previous document called "Why Measure HRV" authored by the project's co-director Nathaniel Thom, who serves as associate professor of biology, chair of biology and health sciences, and director of Wheaton College's neuroscience program.

42. Amol Kelkar, "Cognitive Homeostatic Agents," *arXiv preprint arXiv:2103.03359* (2021), https://doi.org/10.48550/arXiv.2103.03359; J. Scott Turner, "Homeostasis as a Fundamental Principle for a Coherent Theory of Brains," *Philosophical Transactions of the Royal Society B: Biological Sciences* 374, no. 1774 (2019): article number 20180373, https://doi.org/10.1098/rstb.2018.0373.

food-seeking behavior to complex planning and decision-making to very high-level thinking about death and how to live the good life.[43]

If an organism needs to answer these very high-order questions in order to maintain (cognitive) homeostasis, activities that disrupt this process, such as viewing conceptual art, may actually drive the organism toward a deeper state of balance.[44] What remains unknown is what types of stimuli disrupt cognitive homeostasis at a high level, what disruptions to cognitive homeostasis "look like" on a neurobiological level, and what processes occur to promote the re-establishment of high-order cognitive homeostasis after it has been disrupted. Conceptual art could serve as a model to investigate these types of questions by disrupting cognitive homeostasis at the highest levels.

Given the autonomic nervous system's (ANS) involvement in lower-order homeostatic balance, along with growing evidence for ANS involvement in higher-order cognitive functions like interoception, it seems plausible that the ANS may serve a critical role in regulating cognitive homeostasis via the balance between sympathetic and parasympathetic activation.[45] It would be advantageous to measure several indices of nervous system function (e.g., EEG, eye-tracking) in order to converge on a complete picture of ANS activity, but evaluating heart-rate variability (HRV) is a good place to start.[46] Heart-rate variability is an index of ANS

43. More specifically, it is well established that organisms at all levels of complexity use strikingly similar physiological processes to regulate homeostatic parameters as diverse as O_2/CO_2 balance, water/salt balance, nutritional needs, and pH, to name a few. Traditionally, scientists have drawn a distinction between these more basic neurobiological functions and more advanced cognitive functions like memory, language, mood, and complex decision-making involving long-term planning. However, more recently, the concept of cognitive homeostasis has been developed as a way to model the entirety of brain function (Turner, "Homeostasis as a Fundamental Principle"), with the goal of developing more advanced and self-sustaining artificial intelligence (AI) that is not dependent on learning rules for each scenario it might face, allowing it to "live" in real-world environments, interacting seamlessly with humans and other AI (Kelkar, "Cognitive Homeostatic Agents"). The idea is that the entire nervous system can be modeled as nested hierarchical homeostatic functions, thereby allowing very advanced decision-making to be programmed with little constraints on the model besides the parameters necessary for homeostatic balance.

44. The concept of cognitive homeostasis could also be useful for understanding why humans might suppress lower-level homeostatic drives (e.g., nutritional needs) to serve higher-order homeostatic needs, such as well-being, or perhaps even drives that attempt to manage the desire to be prepared for death and the afterlife (Kelkar, "Cognitive Homeostatic Agents").

45. Manos Tsakiris and Hugo Critchley, "Interoception beyond Homeostasis: Affect, Cognition and Mental Health," *Philosophical Transactions of the Royal Society B: Biological Sciences* 371, no. 1708 (2016): article number 20160002, https://doi.org/10.1098/rstb.2016.0002.

46. Marek, J. Malik, Thomas Bigger, A. John Camm, Robert E. Kleiger, Alberto Malliani, Ar-

activity to the heart and can be used to measure parasympathetic influence on the heart in the context of a model of neurovisceral integration.[47] A flexible cognitive system is associated with high levels of HRV and elite performance under extreme stress, whereas low HRV is correlated with a host of maladaptive states such as clinical anxiety and depression.[48] While not directly related to supra-high-level cognitive states like well-being and the contemplation of mortality, if the concept of cognitive homeostasis is indeed a legitimate way to model the entire central nervous system, it is reasonable to expect that measuring HRV would be a viable, field-based, first step toward measuring the changes that occur as a result of disruptions to cognitive homeostasis.[49]

Research Methods. This project is conducting a pilot field study on participants' engagement with conceptual art. Subjects consist of two groups of ten people each: non-experts and experts, as determined by a number of profile factors. They experience real-world museum exhibits consisting of works of conceptual art. Subjects wear Polar heart rate monitors in order to derive HRV responses while experiencing conceptual art. We have predicted that both non-experts and experts will move through a process similar to the one outlined in the Vienna Integrated Model of Top-Down and Bottom-Up Processes in Art Perception (VIMAP) model. More specifically, both groups will initially process the basic perceptual features of the piece. This initial phase will be followed by phases of confusion, integration, and production, analogous to VIMAP's meaning making, affect, and response phases. We predict non-experts and experts will progress through each

---

thur J. Moss, and Peter J. Schwartz, "Heart Rate Variability: Standards of Measurement, Physiological Interpretation, and Clinical Use," *European Heart Journal* 17, no. 3 (1996): 354–81; Julian F. Thayer, Anita L. Hansen, and Bjorn Helge Johnsen, "The Non-Invasive Assessment of Autonomic Influences on the Heart Using Impedance Cardiography and Heart Rate Variability," *Handbook of Behavioral Medicine: Methods and Applications* (New York: Springer, 2010), 723–40.

47. Julian F. Thayer and Richard D. Lane, "Claude Bernard and the Heart-Brain Connection: Further Elaboration of a Model of Neurovisceral Integration." *Neuroscience & Biobehavioral Reviews* 33, no. 2 (2009): 81–88.

48. Julian F. Thayer, Fredrik Åhs, Mats Fredrikson, John J. Sollers III, and Tor D. Wager, "A Meta-Analysis of Heart Rate Variability and Neuroimaging Studies: Implications for Heart Rate Variability as a Marker of Stress and Health," *Neuroscience & Biobehavioral Reviews* 36, no. 2 (2012): 747–56. C. A. Morgan III, Deane E. Aikins, George Steffian, Vladimir Coric, and Steven Southwick, "Relation between Cardiac Vagal Tone and Performance in Male Military Personnel Exposed to High Stress: Three Prospective Studies," *Psychophysiology* 44, no. 1 (2007): 120–27.

49. Interestingly, the exhibition/study *Room to Breathe* at the Manchester City Gallery is also employing HRV as a measure in testing the effect of mindfulness breathing techniques on the quality of public engagement with artworks. See online: https://manchesterartgallery.org/event/room-to-breathe/.

phase differently, both in terms of HRV responses and timing. More specifically, we predict the following: At baseline HRV will not differ between non-experts and experts, and both will move through the baseline period at the same pace. During the initial stimulus processing phase (1) HRV will decrease slightly in both non-experts and experts, reflecting increased sympathetic drive required to engage novelty; (2) Non-experts will spend less time in this phase, due to experts' ability to dedicate more time to basic perceptual processing; (3) This phase is likely to be very brief, making it difficult to assess HRV which requires several minutes of stable signal to mathematically derive and may overlap with the next stage. During conceptual confusion (i.e., the period of visual dissonance) (1) HRV will decrease significantly in both experts and non-experts as cognitive homeostasis is disrupted and therefore sympathetic drive is increased while parasympathetic drive is decreased; (2) it is likely that experts will spend less time in this phase whereas non-experts may linger in this phase longer. During conceptual integration (1) HRV will begin to rise in both groups as the disruption to cognitive homeostasis is resolved. At the end of integration, HRV will rise above baseline levels in experts because the end of this phase will mimic the deep contemplative state analogous to mindfulness meditation; (2) experts will spend more time in this phase whereas non-experts are less practiced in this aspect of the experience. During conceptual production (1) we do not anticipate that the production phase will reliably occur while participants are present in the exhibit; therefore, we do not have any HRV-related hypotheses for this phase; (2) experts may demonstrate time in this phase whereas non-experts will likely not experience it at all.

"During the Exhibition the Gallery Will Be Closed": Reflections on Impact

In the end, it is perhaps its irrepressibly apophatic character that makes conceptual art so difficult to study.[50] Take, for instance, the statement "During the exhibition the gallery will be closed." This seemingly nonsensical assertion delivers the entire content for an infamous 1969 artwork by the conceptual artist Robert Barry. While announcement cards were printed with this sentence and sent out, the three successive galleries that hosted the artwork, indeed, never opened their doors to visitors. The confounding gesture behind this work may have troubled some in its time, but it is also remembered in this way: "In place of a concrete encounter with works of art in an exhibition room, Barry left it entirely to the

50. Rowan Williams, *Understanding and Misunderstanding "Negative Theology"* (Milwaukee, WI: Marquette University Press, 2021).

imagination of the beholder to develop the meaning and form of the artwork."[51] Philosopher William Franke, the compiler of two volumes of ancient and modern apophatic writings, is not at all surprised by the characteristically confounding appearance of such artworks. He surveys artists, poets, writers, and composers and reports, "Throughout the last century the arts have been especially prolific in negative theologies."[52]

Indeed, what makes conceptual art such a potentially generative subject stems from its paradoxical character; it is both eminently mere (in appearance) and yet maximally complex (in associations).[53] Consider, for comparison, what the poet Elizabeth Bishop says about artistic creation: "What one seems to want in art, in experiencing it, is the same thing that is necessary for its creation, a self-forgetful, perfectly useless concentration."[54] Thus, one leading explanation of the paradoxical character of conceptual art maintains that its form retains an undeniably philosophical rigor, the kind that invites contemplative reflection.[55] The philosopher of art and art critic Arthur Danto relates that "history ends with the advent of self-consciousness,

51. Daniel Marzona and Uta Grosenick, *Conceptual Art* (Cologne: Taschen, 2005), 36.

52. William Franke, ed., *On What Cannot Be Said: Apophatic Discourses in Philosophy, Religion, Literature, and the Arts*, vol. 2, Modern and Contemporary Transformations (Notre Dame: University of Notre Dame, 2007), 6. Indeed, he begins his list with the avant-garde Russian Orthodox painter Kasimir Malevech, regarded by many as an intellectual precursor for later conceptualism. Franke offers the following historical explanation for the re-emergence of apophaticism: "At historical moments of crisis, especially of crisis for language, insurgent skepticism, and the collapse of reigning paradigms of discourse, these shadowy traditions show up more prominently because the object of philosophy's contemplation—articulable reality, the *Logos* of being—in its presumptive blinding splendor suddenly darkens. In these circumstances of tottering philosophical confidence, the undercurrents of apophasis resurface. What had gone unheard now clamors for attention and can no longer be suppressed. This has been happening especially in the amazing contortions of culture we are living through at present. It has also enabled the traditions of our past to be re-read in a new light with acute attention to the fundamental apophatic elements that were always there, lurking in the background of the dominant philosophical outlook. These elements are oftentimes nervously ignored, and thereby loomed the more ominously. They are now emerging again into the foreground, as the unspeakable restlessly seethes on all sides round." Franke, *On What Cannot Be Said*, 49.

53. In this way, contemporary art continues to destabilize the definitions of art employed by researchers. Pelowski, Matthew, Gernot Gerger, Yasmine Chetouani, Patrick S. Markey, and Helmut Leder, "But Is It Really Art? The Classification of Images as 'Art'/'Not Art' and Correlation with Appraisal and Viewer Interpersonal Differences," *Frontiers in Psychology* 8 (2017): article 1729, 1–21.

54. Quoted in Lewis Hyde, *A Primer for Forgetting: Getting Past the Past* (New York: Farrar, Straus and Giroux, 2019), 81.

55. For instance, Danto says that "all art is conceptual art (with a small *c*), and always has been." Arthur C. Danto, *Unnatural Wonders: Essays from the Gap between Art and Life* (New York: Farrar, Straus and Giroux, 2005), 18.

or better self-knowledge. . . . Art ends with the advent of its own [embodiment as] philosophy."[56] In this way, works of conceptual art invite a sustained, creative, and integrative kind of beholding that requires more than previous iterations of art history. Along these lines, then, Danto reflects on the dilemmas facing today's museums: "What we see today is an art which seeks a more immediate contact with people than the museum makes possible . . . and the museum in turn is striving to accommodate the immense pressures that are imposed upon it from within art and from outside art."[57] He goes on to describe the museum's audience as the "thirsting millions," relating that "what they thirst for, in my view, what we all thirst for, is meaning: the kind of meaning that religion was capable of providing, or philosophy, or finally art."[58] From this perspective, conceptual art can be seen as an eminently creative attempt to actually protect the experience of meaning in visual art.

Thus, studying conceptual art under such historical conditions has the potential to impact two distinct spheres of academic inquiry: theology and empirical aesthetics. In theology, reckoning with conceptualism serves to address a significant gap in the larger literature of theology and the visual arts. Where there exists a depth of theological reflection on visual art, it rarely—if ever—touches on more recent trends, especially a development as challenging as conceptual art. Where treatments of the relationship between religion and contemporary art feature conceptualism, there is little depth of reflection on its theological value. This project, then, has helped to move theology's consideration of the arts beyond forms of illustration and instrumentalism and toward a more rigorous assessment of the generative methods of contemporary production like conceptualism. Such efforts seek to open theology up to potentially illuminating engagements with current artistic practice. These engagements are all the more strategic because conceptual artists operate with highly reflective and thoughtful modes of artistic practice, which have not featured much in the theoretical accounts of how viewers appreciate art today. In this way, theology stands to gain new channels of understanding in at least both the sphere of sacramental accounts of the world and theological anthropology's assessment of human imagination.

56. Arthur C. Danto, *The Philosophical Disenfranchisement of Art* (New York; Guildford: Columbia University Press, 1986), 107.

57. Danto, *After the End of Art*, 183.

58. Danto, *After the End of Art*, 188. Indeed, the critic Lance Esplund reflects on the experience of today's often mystified public: "Is it any wonder that the art-viewing public is bewildered, even intimidated? What are they to make of the range of possibilities offered in galleries and museums?" In the case of conceptual art, Esplund wonders what the public must think of its "jarring objectlessness." Lance Esplund, *The Art of Looking: How to Read Modern and Contemporary Art* (New York: Basic Books, 2018), 2.

At the same time, empirical aesthetics stands to gain a timely appreciation for the novel imaginative connections that conceptual art affords participants. While the traditional environment of the art museum has evolved in ways that make possible forms of engagement previously unavailable in the history of art, such developments have yet to be analyzed in a thoroughly scientific way. For example, perhaps, what philosophers of art call an "atmosphere of theory" could be integrated into the "predictive processing" models that are emerging for experimental psychology of art.[59] Rather than settling for the basics of visual competency (e.g., symmetry, contrast, clarity) and the reductive target of visual pleasure, conceptual art forces empirical aesthetics to expand its reach beyond the merely sensory and attempt to chart more subtle and sophisticated effects. For instance, conceptual art takes on a contemplative character in the following instances: (1) when it is thoughtful, thought-provoking, and inquisitive, and allows for a distinctly meditative engagement; (2) when it resists an obsessive loyalty to form by stalling immersive effect and negating the dominance of sensation; (3) when it is apophatic in character and renders absence and emptiness meaningful; (4) when it is formative or potentially transformative in seeking to affect or influence its participants by disrupting expectations; (5) when it is plural, diverse, and individualizing in the ways that it invites personal responses that are not simply reciprocating but in fact generative and inimitable; and (6) when it is attentive, critical, and willing to activate responsibility, often through embodied, empathetic participation.

In conclusion, then, we can treat the matter of progress by returning to our opening question: why conceptual art? Conceptualism is the most dramatic development in the visual art of the last century, and its persistence, influence, and adaptability within contemporary art demonstrate its significance for careful study. Along these lines, progress means keeping pace with the dynamic evolution of the arts in our world. In the case of modern visual art, the legacy of the avant-garde has been democratizing and not exclusionary. The efforts aimed at such goals, however, have created ever more elusive forms of art. There is no doubt about that fact, but conceptualism has leveraged its innovations toward the goal of opening new paths for aesthetic cognition. Thus, it falls to the disciplines of interpretation to find pioneering means to not only characterize the failures of such idealistic innovations but more importantly their generative successes as well.

59. Sander Van de Cruys and Johan Wagemans, "Putting Reward in Art: A Tentative Prediction Error Account of Visual Art," *i-Perception* 2, no. 9 (2011): 1035–62.

17

Can Art Be a Bridge to Engagement with the Adversities of Our Time?

Marlene Sophie Altenmüller and Mario Gollwitzer

It has been suggested that artworks have the potential to provide humans with a better understanding of what is happening in the world around (and inside) them:[1] Art might provide new perspectives, raise important questions that prompt further inquiry, or enable us to grasp connections (between beliefs, values, experiences, insights, etc.) that would otherwise be unimaginable. Some forms of such understanding can even be spiritual in the sense that the metacognitive experience of "understanding" provides us with a sense of deeper meaning, which transcends beyond the self.[2] Previous empirical research has suggested that art can indeed provide us with such understanding[3]—but how far can this be pushed? Do we also see such a specific effect of art on understanding even when the artwork itself, its topic, or the experience it creates is aversive and confronts us with tangible and shocking adversities?

Answers to these questions are much needed as such adverse topics reflect the world we live in: the global climate crisis, for example, causes intense droughts, water scarcity, severe fires, rising sea levels, flooding, melting polar ice, and catastrophic storms. This reality is hard to bear, especially when people, other animals, and nature are suffering. Likewise, other current challenges such as war, poverty,

1. Christoph Baumberger, "Art and Understanding: In Defence of Aesthetic Cognitivism," in *Bilder sehen: Perspektiven der Bildwissenschaft*, ed. Mark Greenlee et al. (Regensburg: Schnell & Steiner, 2013), 41–67.

2. Kutter Callaway et al., "Measuring the (Im)Measurable: On the Psycho-Socio-Spiritual Effects of Aesthetic Experiences of Art," *Journal of Psychology and Theology* (2023).

3. See, for example, Matthew Pelowski et al., "Move Me, Astonish Me . . . Delight My Eyes and Brain: The Vienna Integrated Model of Top-Down and Bottom-Up Processes in Art Perception (VIMAP) and Corresponding Affective, Evaluative, and Neurophysiological Correlates," *Physics of Life Reviews* 21 (2017): 80–125.

and migration produce images displaying human and nonhuman suffering to an unbearable extent.

Understandably, many people are overwhelmed by the resulting negative emotions elicited by such images. Their immediate response is avoidance[4] — psychologically and physically "turning away" from what they see or what they are confronted with. Studies suggest that many people avoid watching or reading the news these days because they cannot cope with what they see or hear.[5] Such avoidance and disengagement behaviors might be advantageous for the individual but could lead to a lack of solidarity with others and a lack of concern for problematic issues that can only be addressed by a joint, coordinated effort in which each and every individual is involved.[6] Thus, as understandable as avoidance might be, it is not the answer to the problems and challenges we are facing. What is needed is a proactive, constructive, coordinated approach to tackle these problems. In other words, what we need is understanding, engagement, and a willingness to do something. Can art be a bridge toward such engagement?

The Psychology of Aestheticization

In a series of studies, we put the cognitive, affective, and even behavioral psychological value of art dealing with such adverse topics to the test. More precisely, we experimentally and empirically investigated the effects of aestheticization. We define aestheticization as the conceptualization of an entity (an image, a video, a sound, etc.) as a work of art, created with the intent to satisfy or optimize aesthetic criteria. This implies that one and the same object can be conceptualized—and received—either as "art" or as something else (e.g., a portrayal of objective reality). For example, in one of our studies, we framed the very same war photo-

4. Andrew J. Elliot, "The Hierarchical Model of Approach-Avoidance Motivation," *Motivation and Emotion*, 30 no. 2 (2006), 111–16; Regina Krieglmeyer, Jan De Houwer, and Roland Deutsch, "On the Nature of Automatically Triggered Approach-Avoidance Behavior," *Emotion Review* 5, no. 3 (2013): 280–84.

5. Morten Skovsgaard and Kim Andersen, "Conceptualizing News Avoidance: Towards a Shared Understanding of Different Causes and Potential Solutions," *Journalism Studies* 21, no. 4 (2020): 459–76; Mikko Villi et al., "Taking a Break from News: A Five-Nation Study of News Avoidance in the Digital Era," *Digital Journalism* 10, no. 1 (2022): 148–64.

6. See Russell Golman, David Hagmann, and George Loewenstein, "Information Avoidance," *Journal of Economic Literature* 55, no. 1 (2017): 96–135; Skovsgaard and Andersen, "Conceptualizing News Avoidance: Towards a Shared Understanding of Different Causes and Potential Solutions"; Kate Sweeny et al., "Information Avoidance: Who, What, When, and Why," *Review of General Psychology* 14, no. 4 (2010): 340–53.

graphs either as "artworks" or as "news items."[7] In another study, we contextualized adverse issues either in artistic or informational formats (e.g., as a concert vs. an interview, as a poetry reading vs. a scientific symposium).[8]

Based on prior theorizing,[9] we assume that such aestheticization prompts a psychologically distanced viewing mode, sometimes also interpreted as a "safe space" provided by art.[10] This means that when viewing something people believe is art, their immediate, instrumental response to turn away is attenuated (e.g., fear and anger normally elicit automatic flight or fight responses regarding a potential threat)[11] and their viewing mode shifts to more formalistic features of an object (e.g., style, composition, and color) which, in turn, might enable more engagement, insight (e.g., a sense of meaning, spiritual experiences), and maybe even an increased willingness to act.

In fact, our own and other scholars' previous work suggests that aestheticization might reduce the deterring effect of the depicted content and allow for positive aesthetic enjoyment despite its aversive content.[12] More specifically, our findings suggest that, after initial confrontation with war photography, people who afford higher aesthetic appreciation for these horrible pictures will also report higher emotionalization and a higher willingness to act against the depicted adversity, for example, by donating money or volunteering for anti-war organizations.[13]

Building on the Vienna Integrated Model of Art Perception (VIMAP),[14] we now tried to disentangle the different psychological processes underlying such art ex-

7. Marlene S. Altenmüller and Mario Gollwitzer, "Power of Pictures? Questioning the Emotionalization and Behavioral Activation Potential of Aesthetics in War Photography," *Psychology of Aesthetics, Creativity, and the Arts* (2023).

8. Marlene S. Altenmüller, M. F. Rühl, and Mario Gollwitzer, *Approaching Deterring Art: The Effects of Aestheticization of Adverse Topics*, manuscript in preparation.

9. Gerald C. Cupchik, "The Evolution of Psychical Distance as an Aesthetic Concept," *Culture & Psychology* 8, no. 2: (2002): 155–87; Winfried Menninghaus et al., "The Distancing-Embracing Model of the Enjoyment of Negative Emotions in Art Reception," *Behavioral and Brain Sciences* 20 (2017): article number e347, https://doi.org/10.1017/s0140525x17000309.

10. Stefano Mastandrea, "How Emotions Shape Aesthetic Experiences," in Pablo P. L. Tinio and Jeffrey K. Smith, eds., *The Cambridge Handbook of the Psychology of Aesthetics and the Arts* (Cambridge University Press, 2014), 500–518; Pelowski et al., "Move Me, Astonish Me . . ."

11. Eva Jonas et al., "Threat and Defense," *Advances in Experimental Social Psychology* 49 (2014): 219–86.

12. Altenmüller and Gollwitzer, "Power of Pictures?"; Gernot Gerger, Helmut Leder, and Alexandra Kremer, "Context Effects on Emotional and Aesthetic Evaluations of Artworks and IAPS Pictures," *Acta Psychologica* 151 (2014): 174–83; V. Wagner et al., "Art Schema Effects on Affective Experience: The Case of Disgusting Images," *Psychology of Aesthetics, Creativity, and the Arts* 8, no. 2 (2014): 120–29.

13. Altenmüller and Gollwitzer, "Power of Pictures?"

14. Pelowski et al., "Move Me, Astonish Me . . ."

periences. We identified three stages of engagement with an artwork in which aestheticization and its accompanying psychological distance should be particularly relevant: (1) *pre-confrontation* (e.g., deciding whether to visit an art exhibition); (2) *initial confrontation* (e.g., immediate reactions when actually confronted with an artwork); and (3) *meta-cognitive reflection* (e.g., contemplation of the artwork's meaning). We assume that, depending on observers' psychological experiences during these stages, aestheticization might either help or hinder engagement with the depicted topic. Eventually, engagement should lead to "transformational experiences": feelings of understanding and self-transcendence, spiritual insights, or even attitude and behavior change toward prosocial reactions.[15]

Pre-confrontation: Do People Prefer Aestheticized Formats to Other Formats When It Comes to Adverse Topics?

When making a choice whether to engage with or avoid a negative topic, people find themselves in the *pre-confrontation* stage. Here, we assumed that aestheticization might spark approach instead of avoidance because people anticipate an emotionally "safe space" when seeking out aesthetic experiences—even when the content is highly aversive. To test this idea, we conducted a large, representative online study in Germany in which we asked people about their approach tendencies toward a range of hypothetical aestheticized formats (e.g., graphic art, music, poetry, dance) dealing with highly negative current issues (e.g., war, poverty, famine, environmental destruction) contrasting them with merely informational formats on the same issues.[16] For example, we asked participants how likely they were to listen to a radio program about environmental disasters, varying whether the radio program was introduced as a concert fathoming the topic by means of music (i.e., a highly aestheticized format) or as an expert interview professionally analyzing the topic (i.e., a highly informational, non-aestheticized format).

Surprisingly, our findings do not suggest a clear preference for aestheticization across different adverse topics and formats—it even seems that, on average, people prefer informational to aestheticized formats. However, there was little consensus among our participants; people's willingness to engage with art dealing with adverse topics is highly variable and strongly depends on the specific artistic format and people's predispositions.

More specifically, regarding the format, we found a preference for informational formats for three out of four tested hypothetical formats (i.e., radio pro-

15. Baumberger, "Art and Understanding"; Callaway et al., "Measuring the (Im)Measurable."
16. Altenmüller, Rühl, and Gollwitzer, *Approaching Deterring Art.*

gram: concert vs. interview; stage performance: dance vs. TED-talk; performative meeting: poetry reading vs. scientific symposium)—but the effect was inversed for the format of illustrations where participants preferred the aestheticized variation (i.e., graphic art vs. technical figure). This is noteworthy, since the visual format of illustrations is the format in our study that is most similar to the typically studied stimuli in the literature from this research context. Very often, the studied materials are sourced from the visual arts—paintings, photography, etc.—and, in line with our present findings, previous studies found higher liking for such stimuli when aestheticized (vs. informational).[17]

Speaking for the decisive role of interindividual differences, people's individual affinity for art—for example, how often they like to visit museums—modulated their preference ratings: While people reporting a *low* affinity for art showed a preference for non-aestheticized, informational stimuli, those who reported a *high* affinity for art did not prefer aestheticized over informational formats or vice versa; they showed high approach tendencies for all kinds of formats dealing with adverse topics.

Thus, for the pre-confrontation stage, we find only mixed evidence for art functioning as a kind of bridge between avoidance and engagement with adverse topics. At least compared to non-aestheticized, informational formats, aestheticization does not seem to make a big difference. Importantly, the psychological processes in this pre-confrontation stage (e.g., preferences) might be very different from how people react when they are actually confronted with art (i.e., stages 2 and 3).

Initial Confrontation: How Do People React When Put in Front of Adverse Art?

When *initially confronted* with an actual artwork depicting atrocities, aestheticization might *facilitate* approaching the depicted content because the immediate emotional response—which would normally trigger avoidance—is attenuated. In other words: People do not turn away for good; instead, aestheticization allows them to come closer and take a look at the depicted content. We conducted a highly immersive, 360° virtual reality (VR) experiment to scrutinize this idea.

Virtual reality technology allows us to realistically simulate environments in which one might engage with aestheticized or non-aestheticized stimuli. Specifically, our participants found themselves in a virtual room in which four explicit and gruesome war photographs were put up on isles. They could move freely around, choosing whether and for how long they wanted to look or to not look

17. See, for example, Altenmüller and Gollwitzer, "Power of Pictures?"; Gerger, Leder, and Kremer, "Context Effects on Emotional and Aesthetic Evaluations"; Wagner et al., "Art Schema Effects on Affective Experience."

at these pictures. While the room represented either an art gallery or a news editorial office, the room and the photos looked, in fact, exactly the same in both conditions. The only variation in the environment was lettering on one of the virtual walls reading either "art from all over the world" or "news from all over the world." The experimental framing was introduced by the story surrounding the experiment: participants were told to imagine that they were waiting for a friend who was working for either a big news corporation or a big art publishing house. The friend had either asked them to wait in the editorial office where the most informative pictures for next day's newspaper were selected or the friend had asked them to wait in the art publishing house's exclusive art gallery showing award-winning photographs. The VR technology then allowed us to assess actual physical approach and avoidance behavior in response to the presented adverse stimuli (i.e., the war photography): How close do participants come to the photos? How often and how long do they look at them? Thereby, the VR technology allowed for real-time insights into the initial confrontation stage.

Looking at the results of this VR study, we found that the experimentally varied story frame did, unexpectedly, not make a difference for how participants behaviorally engaged with the war photography. It is likely that choosing such a highly controlled experimental setting (e.g., using the same room as both news- and art-related environment) came at the cost of creating strong enough contrasts between the art and news situation. However, using some data from a subsequent questionnaire, we were able to look at how participants themselves subjectively experienced the VR environment: The more they considered the displayed photographs as artworks rather than as news items, the more they aesthetically appreciated them. And this aesthetic appreciation, in turn, was associated with viewing the photographs longer (but not more often) and moving closer toward them.

Thus, our VR study provides only tentative, correlational evidence regarding the immediate reactions in the initial confrontation stage. While experimentally induced aestheticization did not facilitate direct approach toward horrific war photography, higher aesthetic appreciation of such photos did go hand in hand with approach behavior.

Meta-cognitive Reflection: How Do People Make Sense of Adverse Art?

Finally, we theorized that aestheticization might pave the way for two possible processes when reaching the stage of *meta-cognitive reflection* about a topic. Specifically, aestheticization might either *impede* or *facilitate* further engagement with the depicted content. Due to the initial psychological distance toward the artwork, aestheticization may lead to emotional and cognitive disengagement and, thus, hamper a deeper reflection about the topic. Observers might solely focus on the artistic form, not on the depicted content, appreciating only an artwork's beauty, not its meaning. Maybe aestheticization even offers a form of escapism in which a quick reflection process comes to a disengaging conclusion (e.g., "This is just fictious artwork and has nothing to do with real life").

However, aestheticization and its accompanying distance might also facilitate more productive meta-cognitive reflection. The idea here is that precisely *because* the immediate avoidance reaction is attenuated, perceivers may become emotionally and cognitively more open to a deeper elaboration of the depicted content and, thus, more willing to engage in proactive meaning-seeking, to experience emotional or even spiritual understanding, and to translate these experienced insights into action.

Emphasizing the importance of meta-cognitive reflection, we recently conducted two more experiments,[18] investigating the role of contemplation for the engagement with art. First, we found that presenting the horrific topic of the Holocaust via means of art (i.e., a poem and a painting, taken from the education materials of Yad Vashem, the World Holocaust Remembrance Center) compared to means of information (i.e., an encyclopedia entry) stimulated more reflection about the topic which, in turn, led to less disengagement and less support for historical closure among German participants. Second, in another study dealing with the adverse topic of environmental pollution and climate change, we found that, indeed, the contemplation of an abstract artwork's meaning and message, but not the contemplation of its form and style, was related to a higher willingness to sacrifice for the environment. In other words: an artwork's impact lies not (just) in its aesthetic qualities, but in its message.

Complementing this research, our current VR experiment also allows us to gain further insights into the role of meta-cognitive reflection (vs. disengagement) for achieving transformative art experiences. The more participants reported to have deeply thought about the photographs and their meaning, the more they also experienced transformative outcomes. High levels of reflection and meaning seeking were associated with stronger emotionalization (regarding both positive and negative affect), with deeper understanding and lower disengagement. These high levels of reflection were also associated with stronger anti-war attitudes and a higher willingness to act against the depicted atrocities. Stronger disengagement, by contrast, was correlated with higher positive but lower negative affect, lower understanding as well as lower anti-war attitudes and behavioral intentions.

18. Marlene S. Altenmüller, M. Hollrotter, and Mario Gollwitzer, *Processing Art: Transformation through Reflection*, in preparation.

While our VR study does not allow for any causal conclusions (due to the unsuccessful experimental manipulation as outlined above), the cross-sectionally observed patterns are at least suggestive of possible counteractive effects of metacognitive contemplation and (moral) disengagement when viewing highly adverse (art) stimuli. Importantly, this also means that our VR study cannot fully answer the question whether there are specific benefits of aestheticization compared to other modes of dealing with negatively valent topics (e.g., informational news media). Our results tentatively indicate that, *if* there was a specific, unique value of the arts over and above other contexts as suggested by aesthetic cognitivism,[19] the "aesthetic advantage" is probably not very large and cannot be generalized across different kinds of artistic formats, adverse topics, and people. A much more individualized perspective might be necessary, giving interindividual differences and their possibly modulating effects more consideration.

The Modulating Role of Personality

We assume that the psychological experiences during the different stages of art reception and, ultimately, the outcome of the aesthetic encounter altogether, depend on personality characteristics. To get a better idea about these characteristics, we first conducted a scoping literature review on the role of personality variables for art reception,[20] and then tested some of the traits identified through this review in our virtual reality experiment.

In the review, we found a large body of research in the empirical aesthetics literature investigating traits clustered around openness—one of the so-called Big Five personality traits.[21] The trait *openness for experience* consists of different facets, among them sensitivity to aesthetics and intellectual curiosity, which were particularly relevant for art reception according to the literature. Moreover, traits clustered around empathy (e.g., empathy, emotional contagion, or, inversely, alexithymia) turned out to be relevant.

For the openness cluster, the reviewed evidence suggested predominantly positive associations of openness and the engagement with negatively valent art, but several studies also reported no relationship, leaving the actual connections

19. Baumberger, "Art and Understanding."

20. Marlene S. Altenmüller, C. Sundermann, and Mario Gollwitzer, *(Un)pleasant: A Scoping Review of Person-Related Factors Influencing Engagement with Negative Aesthetic Content*, in preparation.

21. Robert R. McCrae and Paul T. Costa, "The Five-Factor Theory of Personality," in *Handbook of Personality: Theory and Research*, 3rd ed., ed. Oliver P. John, Richard W. Robins, and Lawrence A. Pervin (New York: Guilford, 2008), 159–81.

between openness and art reception a bit unclear. The evidence regarding the empathy trait cluster suggested that highly empathic individuals react strongly toward negatively valent art and might, thus, experience adverse art as more transformational, but likely find no enjoyment in it. One very interesting insight regarding possibly counteractive effects at the different stages of art perception pertained to the trait of sensation seeking. Highly sensation-seeking individuals are constantly looking for strong stimulation and arousal in their environment. This suggests that they might be very much willing to look at repulsive and outright shocking artworks—but once their initial thirst for thrills is saturated, they will not engage further in prolonged meaning seeking and contemplation; therefore, aesthetic experiences have likely no profound, transformative impact on them.

Our VR study corroborates many of these insights. As expected, traits like openness and empathy predicted a sensitive but also serious engagement with the war photographs. These traits were associated with higher initial distance from the horrible pictures and more negative effect—but also with more meaning seeking and reflection, less disengagement, and a higher willingness to act against the displayed atrocities. In contrast, and also in line with the assumptions derived from our review, our VR study revealed that sensation seeking, indeed, is associated with searching for immediate thrills, but not with deep engagement: sensation seekers looked at the presented war photography more often and moved closer to them, but they showed more disengagement later.

Conclusion

In the beginning, we proposed that art might be a "bridge" to engagement with the adversities of our time. While alleviating the immediate deterring impact of highly negative topics, art dealing with horrible content may also invite people in and allow them to reflect and elaborate further on what these topics mean for them and what can be done about them, which may eventually lead to transformative outcomes of their aesthetic experience. Our research set out to put the distinct value of art and aestheticization (compared to non-aestheticized, informational formats) to the test.

Overall, our findings paint a mixed picture. The experimental evidence questions whether artistic formats provide a particular advantage for engaging with adverse issues over and above other forms of dealing with these topics. We theoretically identified three stages of engagement where we assumed to see a specific benefit of aestheticization: pre-confrontation, initial confrontation, and metacognitive reflection. However, barely any of our experimental results support an advantage at any of these stages.

For the pre-confrontation stage, evidence is, at best, mixed, with only the aestheticized illustrations outperforming the informational, non-aestheticized illustrations, while the three other formats were preferred in their non-aestheticized variations. In general, participants' reported approach preferences were quite heterogeneous and dependent on other variables, such as their art affinity. Regarding the actual confrontation and meta-cognitive reflection, our investigation remains inconclusive since the experimental variation in the VR experiment was not sufficiently successful in inducing an aestheticized versus non-aestheticized mode among our participants. Here, we can only look at the cross-sectional, correlational patterns. Interestingly, these associations in our data do indeed suggest that aesthetic appreciation of adverse topics goes hand in hand with deeper reflection and meaning seeking, less disengagement and higher transformative outcomes (e.g., attitude and behavior change).

We thus conclude with a cautiously optimistic outlook: Aesthetic appreciation does co-occur with approach, reflection, meaning seeking, and transformative outcomes. Even if art does not have the potential to build a *unique* bridge toward engagement with the most pressing challenges of our time, our findings suggest an encouraging message for aesthetic cognitivism: Maybe, those of us who perceive the world around us with a keen eye for its aesthetic qualities and can even appreciate the ambivalent beauty of horrible things are also more willing to deeply contemplate these issues and engage with them in a prosocial fashion.

18

A Social-Cognitive Approach to Experiencing Art as Communal Understanding

Bahador Bahrami and Ophelia Deroy

Imagine visitors in an art gallery. The first room presents early sketches, and each person is absorbed in different drawings. The second room, however, presents a renowned painting and all visitors crowd in front of it, their attention collectively taken by the painting. This shared moment of awe is a collective affective experience. It is also a common perceptual experience. How does this communal dimension of experience affect the understanding and cognitive significance of the artwork? Our capacity to address this question is central to understanding art perception, but also to defending aesthetic cognitivism.

The shared aspect we consider here is different from the universal or virtual appeal to others, present for instance in Immanuel Kant's *Critique of Judgment*. According to Kant, when viewing a painting, individuals experience a "disinterested pleasure," a feeling that is not tied to personal desires or interests but to the appreciation of beauty itself. This shared sense of beauty, while personally experienced, has a universal appeal: Kant's idea of the *sensus communis* here suggests an abstract community of taste, where people, despite their subjective experiences, share a common sense of what is (and should be) aesthetically pleasing. By contrast, we are interested in the concrete sharing of an experience when people view a painting together at the same time.

This communal aspect of experience we consider is also distinct from the shared emotion which can follow from viewing a painting with others. Emotional contagion, as well as empathy, can make people responsive to other people's affective states. Instead, we are interested in the perceptual experience itself. This focus may seem intriguing at first given the generally shared idea that perception is an individual state. This idea, however, is what we wish to revisit, by highlighting first the importance of shared attention.

Our proposal is to show that the shared perception in art is not just about parallel individual experiences but that it transforms the perception of the painting by making it part of a common ground and changing our very experience of it.

Viewing Paintings Together: From Joint Attention to Common Ground

Joint Attention

The experience of paintings is often not a solitary experience but is deeply influenced by the presence and reactions of others. Shared or joint attention refers to the shared focus of two or more individuals on an external object or event. It is a crucial component in the development of social cognition, language, and emotional bonding. The phenomenon of joint attention typically emerges in early childhood, around nine to fourteen months of age. It involves not only the ability to focus on an object but also *to understand* that another person is sharing this focus. This shared gaze or attention forms the basis for more complex social interactions and communication skills. For instance, when a child and a caregiver both focus on a toy, and the child recognizes that the caregiver is also interested in the toy, a foundational form of non-verbal communication has been established.

From a developmental perspective, joint attention is essential for language acquisition. It provides a context for children to learn new words and concepts, as they can associate the spoken words with the objects or events they are jointly attending to with others. This shared focus creates a natural opportunity for learning and language development, as children are more likely to understand and remember words that are related to their immediate interests and experiences.

Joint attention also plays a significant role in social and emotional development. Through joint attention interactions, children learn to read and interpret social cues, such as eye gaze, facial expressions, and gestures. This understanding is vital for developing empathy and the ability to infer the intentions and emotions of others. In a shared attention scenario, individuals not only exchange information about the external world but also about their internal states and experience of that world.

In the broader context of social cognition, joint attention is a precursor to theory of mind—the ability to attribute mental states to oneself and others. It helps individuals understand that others have perspectives, desires, and beliefs that may differ from their own. This understanding is fundamental for effective social interaction and communication. Joint attention serves as a training ground for these more complex cognitive skills. Repeated interactions between children during playing or between the child and caregiver provide hundreds of such training opportunities per day.

In art galleries, just as gaze cues in joint attention studies guide the participants' attention, the direction of other observers' gazes can influence how we engage with artworks. Studies in adults like Milliken et al. and Friesen and Kingstone show that gaze-following is automatic and makes us aware of others' perceptual engagement.[1] This skill extends beyond gaze to include body postures, as shown by Azarian et al., showing that eye contact is not necessary and that standing next to someone in a gallery can affect how we attend to art.[2] For example, an observer's body orientation toward a painting or sculpture might draw others' attention to specific parts of that artwork.

Common Ground for Aesthetic Cognitivism

Objects that are jointly attended to by people, meaning those experienced and focused on collectively, are known to result in an "amplification of experience." This concept emphasizes that objects which garner shared attention lead to more intense emotional responses like pleasure or pain, as well as in a higher number of behaviors related to cooperation and the forming of social bonds.[3] More relevant to aesthetic cognitivism, jointly attending to an object also leads to more learning and better memory.

This suggests that artworks that are the focus of joint attention can evoke not just more intense emotional but also cognitive responses. Such shared experiences around a piece of art can significantly deepen its impact on memory,

1. Bruce Milliken et al., "Orienting in Space and Time: Joint Contributions to Exogenous Spatial Cuing Effects," *Psychonomic Bulletin & Review* 10, no. 4 (2003): 877–83; Chris Kelland Friesen and Alan Kingstone, "The Eyes Have It! Reflexive Orienting Is Triggered by Nonpredictive Gaze," *Psychonomic Bulletin & Review* 5, no. 3 (1998): 490–95.

2. Bobby Azarian et al., "Averted Body Postures Facilitate Orienting of the Eyes," *Acta Psychologica* 175 (2017): 28–32.

3. See Erica J. Boothby, Margaret S. Clark, and John A. Bargh, "Shared Experiences Are Amplified," *Psychological Science* 25, no. 12 (2014): 2209–16; Parnia Haj-Mohamadi, Elizabeth H. Fles, and Garriy Shteynberg, "When Can Shared Attention Increase Affiliation? On the Bonding Effects of Co-Experienced Belief Affirmation," *Journal of Experimental Social Psychology* 75 (2018): 103–6; Sasha Nahleen, Georgia Dornin, and Melanie K. T. Takarangi, "When More Is Not Merrier: Shared Stressful Experiences Amplify," *Cognition and Emotion* 33, no. 8 (2019): 1718–25; Pietro Sarasso et al., "Physical but Not Virtual Presence of Others Potentiates Implicit and Explicit Learning," *Scientific Reports* 12 (2022): article number 21205, https://doi.org/10.1038/s41598-022-25273-4; Garriy Shteynberg et al., "Feeling More Together: Group Attention Intensifies Emotion," *Emotion* 14, no. 6 (2014): 1102.

creating a powerful communal reference among viewers. This in turn can also amplify the artwork's role in shaping societal narratives and cultural dialogues. Moreover, the act of jointly attending to an artwork can foster a unique communal experience, where interpretations and reactions are not just individual but also part of a larger social discourse.

Extending Common Ground: The Relevance of Shared Experience of Artworks

Joint attention, as we saw, means that the artwork and its contents are integrated into common ground. Our interactions with others in front of a painting, however, are not limited or constrained by the monitoring of their gaze or body posture. On the one hand, our social interactions can be richer when we are, for instance, discussing the painting with others explicitly communicating social information. On the other hand, our social interactions may be much more minimal, adapting to the mere presence of others aiming to fit in with other visitors in front of a painting.

Social Information

The first category—the rich social interaction—is easier to make sense of, both from an aesthetic and psychological perspective. We are familiar with the idea that social interaction can change and influence our judgment, including about artwork. Seminal research on social conformity, such as the studies by Asch and others, have focused on post-perceptual judgments.[4] In these experiments, participants were placed in a group with actors who were instructed to sometimes give incorrect answers to simple questions about line lengths. Participants were shown a series of cards, each with a standard line and three comparison lines. They were asked to identify which of the three comparison lines matched the standard line in length. While the task was straightforward and the correct answer was obvious, the actors in the group sometimes deliberately gave wrong answers. The key aspect of the experiment was to observe how the real participant would react to the group's incorrect responses. Would they conform to the group consensus despite the evidence of their own eyes, or would they stick to their correct answer? Asch found that a substantial number of participants conformed to the group's wrong answers at least once. This demonstrated the powerful influence of social

4. S. E. Asch, "Effects of Group Pressure upon the Modification and Distortion of Judgments," in *Groups, Leadership and Men: Research in Human Relations*, ed. H. Guetzkow (Oxford: Carnegie, 1951), 177–90; S. E. Asch, "Opinions and Social Pressure," *Scientific American* 193, no. 5 (1955): 31–35.

information on opinion formation. The same idea can be extended to artworks, with people taking into account other people's judgment, eventually even when it contradicts their first-person experience.

These studies traditionally assumed that perceptual experiences or decisions remain unchanged whether a person views stimuli alone or with others. However, recent evidence suggests that this assumption may oversimplify the complex dynamics of co-perception.

Research also indicates that what others say can affect not only our verbal reports of what we see but also our actual perceptual experiences. Germar et al. reveal that social input impacts more than just reporting tendencies, extending to actual perception.[5] In the studies, participants modified a square's mix of orange and blue pixels until they seemed evenly distributed (half orange, half blue). Following this, they were informed about other participants' choices and asked to recalibrate their perception of an equal color mix. The subsequent phase demonstrated that it was perception, not merely reporting, that was influenced by social insights into others' reports.

In another study, Zanesco et al. built up on the classical paradigm first introduced by Moscovici et al. to investigate how social feedback influences perception.[6] In this study, participants initially observed a stimulus with ambiguous color (green-blue) and made a decision on its color. Intriguingly, when participants received information that others perceived the color differently, they were willing to change their initial decision—for instance, switching from "blue" to "green" based on others' perceptions. To delve deeper, Zanesco and colleagues measured the participants' EEG signals to understand the neural underpinnings of this phenomenon. After participants named the color of a patch, they received social feedback that either agreed or disagreed with their decision. Subsequently, they were shown the same color patch again. This setup was crucial to discern whether the social influence was altering merely the verbal reports or also impacting the actual perceptual processing. If the social feedback only affected participants' reports,

5. Markus Germar, and Andreas Mojzisch, "Learning of Social Norms Can Lead to a Persistent Perceptual Bias: A Diffusion Model Approach," *Journal of Experimental Social Psychology* 84 (2019): article number 103801, https://doi.org/10.1016/j.jesp.2019.03.012; Markus Germar, Vinzenz Duderstadt, and Andreas Mojzisch, "Social Norms Shape Visual Appearance: Taking a Closer Look at the Link between Social Norm Learning and Perceptual Decision-Making," *Cognition* 241 (2023): article number 105611, https://doi.org/10.1016/j.cognition.2023.105611.

6. Julie Zanesco et al., "Seeing Is Believing: Early Perceptual Brain Processes Are Modified by Social Feedback," *Social Neuroscience* 14, no. 5 (2019): 519–29; S. Moscovici, E. Lage, and M. Naffrechoux, "Influence of a Consistent Minority on the Responses of a Majority in a Color Perception Task," *Sociometry* 32, no. 4 (1969): 365–80.

the neural processing for both viewings of the color patch would be expected to remain consistent. However, the study found that following disagreeing social feedback, the neural processing of the same color patch altered, as evidenced by changes in the event-related potentials in early visual brain areas. This outcome suggests that the social feedback did indeed influence the perceptual processing, not just the verbal reports. The fact that the stimuli were identical in both viewings implies that these perceptual changes were not due to the physical features of the object but resulted from the social influence on perception.

The underlying mechanism for this influence raises intriguing questions. One possibility is that the positive reinforcement associated with social agreement plays a role, as prior research like that by Takagaki and Krug has shown, in proving that rewards can influence perceptual processing.[7] However, normative conformity, which refers to the influence of social norms and the desire to fit in, is not the only potential factor. Informational conformity, where individuals adjust their perceptions based on the information provided by others, could also be at play, suggesting multiple pathways through which social influence can affect perception (as discussed in studies by Mahmoodi et al.).[8]

Mere Social Presence

Independently of discussions, the mere presence of others can also influence our perception of the spatial and structural aspects of an environment. As discussed above, when individuals find themselves in the company of others, their perception is influenced by the non-verbal cues of those around them, such as eye direction or body movements and posture. More minimally, their perception can also be influenced by the mere spatial positioning of another stranger with whom they do not coordinate attention. This phenomenon is evident in various studies that highlight the involuntary assimilation of another person's perspective.

Research focusing on vision aspects, such as studies conducted by Azarian et al. and Hietanen et al., reveals how people unconsciously integrate the viewpoints of others based solely on their body orientation.[9] For example, in experiments where participants are shown dots on different sides of a room and a virtual co-

7. Kentaroh Takagaki and Kristine Krug, "The Effects of Reward and Social Context on Visual Processing for Perceptual Decision-Making," *Current Opinion in Physiology* 16 (2020): 109–17.

8. Ali Mahmoodi et al., "Distinct Neurocomputational Mechanisms Support Informational and Socially Normative Conformity," *PLoS Biology* 20, no. 3 (2022): article number e3001565, https://doi.org/10.1371/journal.pbio.3001565.

9. Bobby Azarian et al., "Averted Body Postures Facilitate Orienting of the Eyes," *Acta Psychologica* 175 (2017): 28–32; Jari K. Hietanen et al., "Automatic Attention Orienting by Social

perceiver looking in a specific direction, participants demonstrate quicker responses in identifying the number of objects when their perspective aligns with that of the co-perceiver. This contrast between jointly perceived and individually perceived objects is evident in studies by Becchio, Bertone, and Castiello and Nuku and Bekkering.[10] Ward, Ganis, and Bach further illustrate this effect in regard to the orientation of objects.[11] Participants often subconsciously adopt the perspective of their co-perceiver, even when it's not directly relevant to the task at hand. For instance, in judging the tilting angle of an object, participants' perceptions are influenced by the direction of another person's gaze.

Beyond spatial relationships, neurophysiological evidence from EEG studies, like those by Böckler and Zwickel, shows that the presence of another person with a different spatial perspective impacts facial processing.[12] When participants view a face while another person is present, there is increased neural activity, indicative of the brain encoding and maintaining both perspectives.

Numerous investigations have raised doubts about the strictly social nature of direction-inducing effects attributed to gaze or bodily orientations. It's been noted that non-social symbols like arrows and words indicating direction can also effectively direct attention, as highlighted in various studies.[13] The underlying processes for the influence of gaze and arrow cues differ significantly: gaze cues lead to concentrated activation associated with improved visual processing, whereas arrow cues involve a wider range of brain areas, encompassing those linked to intentional orienting.[14] Directional symbolic cues exert less impact than those

---

and Symbolic Cues Activates Different Neural Networks: An fMRI Study," *NeuroImage* 33, no. 1 (2006): 406–13.

10. Cristina Becchio, Cesare Bertone, and Umberto Castiello, "How the Gaze of Others Influences Object Processing," *Trends in Cognitive Sciences* 12, no. 7 (2008): 254–58; Pines Nuku and Harold Bekkering, "Joint Attention: Inferring What Others Perceive (and Don't Perceive)," *Consciousness and Cognition* 17, no. 1 (2008): 339–49.

11. Eleanor Ward, Giorgio Ganis, and Patric Bach, "Spontaneous Vicarious Perception of the Content of Another's Visual Perspective," *Current Biology* 29, no. 5 (2019): 874–80.

12. Anne Böckler and Jan Zwickel, "Influences of Spontaneous Perspective Taking on Spatial and Identity Processing of Faces," *Social Cognitive and Affective Neuroscience* 8, no. 7 (2013): 735–40.

13. Bernhard Hommel et al., "Symbolic Control of Visual Attention," *Psychological Science* 12, no. 5 (2001): 360–65; Jelena Ristic, Chris Kelland Friesen, and Alan Kingstone, "Are Eyes Special? It Depends on How You Look at It," *Psychonomic Bulletin & Review* 9, no. 3 (2002): 507–13; T. L. Taylor and R. M. Klein, "Visual and Motor Effects in Inhibition of Return," *Journal of Experimental Psychology: Human Perception and Performance* 26, no. 5 (2000): 1639–56; Jason Tipples, "Eye Gaze Is Not Unique: Automatic Orienting in Response to Uninformative Arrows," *Psychonomic Bulletin & Review* 9, no. 2 (2002): 314–18; Jason Tipples, "Negative Emotionality Influences the Effects of Emotion on Time Perception," *Emotion* 8, no. 1 (2008): 127–31.

14. Hietanen et al., "Automatic Attention Orienting"; Ristic, Friesen, and Kingstone, "Are Eyes Special?"

emanating from human-like figures.[15] Furthermore, the extent of social influence is contingent on the level of engagement of the agent[16] and their perceived or actual ability to perceive the object.[17]

This body of research collectively underlines that a shared experience of an artwork is perceptually different. When two people perceive the same objects, their shared view leads to congruence in perception. Conversely, discrepancies in perspectives can cause incongruence in what is perceived. When applied to the context of art viewing, this suggests that the presence of others can alter our perception of the artwork, further influencing our overall experience.

Case Studies and Experiments in Joint Perception of Art

Our case studies and experimental findings illustrate the impact of the social context not just on the perceptual appreciation of art. These studies help to demonstrate the practical implications of joint attention and shared experiences.

Both concepts involve mutual engagement with the environment, but joint perception generally covers a wider range of experiences than joint attention. Take, for example, a visit to a museum where two individuals are looking at the same painting. In this context, they are engaged in joint perception of the artwork, even if their focus might be on different aspects or details of the painting at any given moment. It's possible for them to be paying attention to separate features or even missing some parts of the painting entirely, yet they still share a perceptual experience of the entire artwork. Attention is a fluid and often shifting state, intricately linked to specific actions such as where the eyes move or what details are momentarily focused on. Consequently, the aspects of the painting that are jointly attended to constitute only a subset of the painting that is jointly perceived.

In practical terms, what is often believed to be joint attention in a spatial context may, in reality, be an instance of shared perception. This broader scope of joint perception, compared to the more focused and transient nature of joint attention, is what our current research program on artworks in a gallery setting is exploring.

15. Cristina Becchio et al., "In Your Place: Neuropsychological Evidence for Altercentric Remapping in Embodied Perspective Taking," *Social Cognitive and Affective Neuroscience* 8, no. 2 (2013): 165–70; Maria Kragh Nielsen et al., "Inclined to See It Your Way: Do Altercentric Intrusion Effects in Visual Perspective Taking Reflect an Intrinsically Social Process?" *Quarterly Journal of Experimental Psychology* 68, no. 10 (2015): 1931–51.

16. Xuan Zhao, Corey Cusimano, and Bertram F. Malle, "In Search of Triggering Conditions for Spontaneous Visual Perspective Taking," *CogSci* 2015: 6.

17. For examples, see Tiziano Furlanetto et al., "Altercentric Interference in Level 1 Visual Perspective Taking Reflects the Ascription of Mental States, Not Submentalizing," *Journal of Experimental Psychology: Human Perception and Performance* 42, no. 2 (2016): 158.

In our work, we use wearable, head-mounted eye tracking devices to measure the visitors' first-person experience and their focus of attention as they walk through the art gallery and examine the art works and join others and break away from them. This new technology, which is now available at a reasonable price in the market, has the capacity to revolutionize the academic study or perception and appreciation of art both for those interested in behavioral sciences as well as those interested in visitor experience for artists, architects and curators who create the artistic exhibitions and museum spaces and art objects.

Our findings so far point to several key directions. Using head-mounted, free-moving eye tracking, we see substantial diversity in individual experiences even when people examine the same artwork in the same gallery context. Interestingly, when we collapse the gaze-tracking data from a large group of visitors into one big sample, it looks like the population has successfully found and paid attention to all the important components of the artwork. However, when we look at the data from each individual member of that population, we realize that in fact, each observer's personal experience is extremely idiosyncratic and consists of a somewhat arbitrary subsample of those elements. Most individual observers, we found, miss important elements of a given artwork and move on to the next item having, perhaps, encountered and experienced less than 50 percent of the actual content of the artwork. Observers who watched the artworks together, however, spent more time examining the paintings and gaze-tracking data showed that they captured a larger number of elements of the artworks than did the individuals. Compared to individuals, the recorded experiences of the pairs were more similar to the population level average that—as mentioned above—captured the canonical elements of the artworks. These are, at this stage, preliminary data and need to be confirmed in larger-scale experiments across different cultures and art categories but they do suggest that using wearable eye tracking can pave the way to examining the role of social context in aesthetic cognitivism.

Conclusion

Our study highlights the transformative effect of joint attention and shared perception on art appreciation. Through wearable eye-tracking devices, we reveal that communal viewing enriches individual experiences by capturing more artwork elements. This suggests the significance of social context in enhancing both emotional and cognitive engagement with art.

19

Knowledge, Perception, and the Prospects of Criticism

Guy Dammann, Elisabeth Schellekens, and John Gibson

Art seeks understanding. From the paintings which have lain concealed for many millennia in the dark caves at Lascaux, to the urban detritus littering Jesse Darling's 2023 Turner Prize–winning exhibition at the Towner Gallery, the impulse that leads human beings to create and experience art remains in many respects shrouded in mystery. All art, perhaps, retains some aspect of mystery around it. And yet one universal feature of art seems clear enough. Works of art, irrespective of the myriad forms they take, seek understanding from those who encounter them. Indeed, whether by attracting us with pleasing arrays of colors, sounds, images, or challenging us with puzzles and questions, they seem quite clearly to constitute a demand on us that we engage with them and try to understand them. The desire both to create and experience works of art seems bound up with the perhaps uniquely human urge to make sense of our world and our place in it.

If this seems in some fundamental way self-evident, then it is all the more surprising that contemporary discussions of art seem so often to focus on everything but this matter of understanding. In popular culture, this can be seen in the widespread elision between the concepts of art and entertainment, and the resulting notion that art can be adequately understood, at best, as a pleasant diversion from everyday life. In philosophy, too, a rise in hedonistic accounts of aesthetic value marks a retreat from the once unquestioned focus on the spiritual, moral and cognitive value that dominated aesthetics.[1] Likewise, the significant and in many

1. For historical overviews of the role of pleasure in aesthetics, see, e.g., Paul Guyer, *Values of Beauty: Historical Essays in Aesthetics* (Cambridge: Cambridge University Press, 2005); Christopher Butler, *Pleasure and the Arts: Enjoying Literature, Painting, and Music* (Oxford: Oxford University Press, 2004); Daniel Herwitz, "Pleasure," in *Encyclopedia of Aesthetics*, 2nd ed., ed. Michael Kelly (Oxford: Oxford University Press, 2014). For more on current versions of aesthetic

ways extremely positive increase in research into art and aesthetic experience in the natural sciences has tended overwhelmingly and often exclusively to focus on aesthetic pleasure.[2]

As contemporary Western concepts of art become increasingly dominated by the pleasure principle, then, questions concerning what we learn and understand from our experiences of art, or whether we seem to understand them well or not, fade out of focus and become eclipsed by the much easier but perhaps largely arbitrary question whether we enjoy them or not. Consequently, art loses its unique standing and simply becomes one form of entertainment among many. Understood principally in terms of subjective pleasure, in other words, art begins to lose its hold on us and, in that sense, forgoes much of its power both to generate meaning and to bind our communities and wider cultures together.[3]

Templeton Religion Trust's initiative to foster a community of scholars in the empirical sciences, philosophy, theology, the arts, and humanities under the umbrella of "Art Seeking Understanding" therefore represents a welcome and much-needed effort to redress this trend.[4] With its focus on the idea of aesthetic cognitivism—a set of claims to the effect that our experience of art and the aesthetic is intimately and perhaps essentially bound up with knowledge and understanding—and on experimental strategies to test these claims empirically, the initiative constitutes a vital effort to remind and prove to ourselves what we once took for granted. Namely, that the value of art, and its role in generating and regenerating cultures and communities of practice, is deeply bound up with the way in which it helps us make sense of our world. Or, simply put, the program reminds us that just as art seeks understanding, so too have we always sought out aesthetic experience for the understanding of our world that it can provide.

---

hedonism, see e.g., Rafael De Clercq, "Aesthetic Pleasure Explained," *Journal of Aesthetics and Art Criticism* 77, no. 2 (2019): 121–32; Jerrold Levinson, "Pleasure and the Value of Works of Art," *British Journal of Aesthetics* 32, no. 4 (1992): 295–306; Jerrold Levinson, *The Pleasures of Aesthetics: Philosophical Essays* (Ithaca, NY: Cornell University Press, 1996).

2. See, e.g., Denis Dutton, *The Art Instinct: Beauty, Pleasure, and Human Evolution* (Oxford: Oxford University Press, 2009); Mohan Matthen, "The Pleasure of Art," *Australasian Philosophical Review* 1, no. 1 (2017): 6–28; Mohan Matthen, "New Prospects for Aesthetic Hedonism," in *Social Aesthetics and Moral Judgment: Pleasure, Reflection and Accountability*, ed. Jennifer McMahon (London: Routledge, 2018), 13–33; V. S. Ramachandran, "The Science of Art: A Neurological Theory of Aesthetic Experience," *Journal of Consciousness Studies* 6 (1999): 15–51.

3. See, e.g., Dominic McIver Lopes, "Beyond the Pleasure Principle: A Kantian Aesthetics of Autonomy," *Estetika: The European Journal of Aesthetics* 57/14, no. 1 (2021): 1–18; Servaas van der Berg, "Aesthetic Hedonism and Its Critics," *Philosophy Compass* 15, no. 1 (2020).

4. See https://tinyurl.com/364376hp.

Aesthetic Cognitivism and Art Criticism

The idea of aesthetic cognitivism amounts to the claims that (1) our aesthetic experiences, and most notably our experiences of art, are cognitively productive, and (2) that this cognitive dimension of art contributes to how and why we value art and aesthetic experience.[5] For our research group the notion is thus fundamentally (although not exclusively) understood as a philosophical one, inviting a conceptual analysis of what aesthetic experience and value amount to, how they relate to and differ from other kinds of experience and value, and of what cognitive productivity in art consists of. If art yields understanding, how is the concept of understanding best formulated? Does art furnish us with understanding in ways that are particular to aesthetic experience and unique to art? If so, how does that understanding relate to traditional concepts of knowledge as applied to the cognitive gains furnished by, say, the natural sciences?

At our project's heart, then, is a set of interlocking questions about aesthetic cognitivism and its suitability as a model for explaining how and why we value art and the experience it affords. However, in so far as these questions begin with the methods of philosophical aesthetics, they do not end with them. Accordingly, our approach in the initial stage of our project has been to explore points of contact with research in empirical psychology, digital humanities, theology and the arts. Our aim in this has been to map out how our basic research questions can extend in ways that can be applied in different methodological environments.

A particular focus for the project has been the practice of art criticism. Once central to philosophical aesthetics,[6] the domain of art criticism in some respects nowadays occupies a largely nominal place in the discipline. It is also largely neglected in most empirical research. This neglect is understandable because art

5. For recent and influential elucidations and defenses of aesthetic cognitivism, see Christoph Baumberger, "Art and Understanding: In Defence of Aesthetic Cognitivism," in *Bilder sehen: Perspektiven der Bildwissenschaft*, ed. Mark Greenlee et al. (Regensburg: Schnell & Steiner, 2013), 41–67; Berys Gaut, "Art and Knowledge," in *The Oxford Handbook of Aesthetics*, ed. Jerrold Levinson (Oxford: Oxford University Press, 2003), 439–41; John Gibson, *Fiction and the Weave of Life* (Oxford: Oxford University Press, 2007); John Gibson, "Cognitivism and the Arts," *Philosophy Compass* 3, no. 4 (2008): 573–89; Gordon Graham, "Learning from Art," *British Journal of Aesthetics* 35 (1995): 26–37; Gordon Graham, *Philosophy of the Arts: An Introduction to Aesthetics* (London: Routledge, 1997); Eileen John, "Reading Fiction and Conceptual Knowledge: Philosophical Thought in Literary Context," *Journal of Aesthetics and Art Criticism* 56, no. 4 (1998): 331–48.

6. Even to the extent that philosophical aesthetics was frequently identified with the philosophy of art criticism. See, e.g., Monroe Beardsley, *Aesthetics: Problems in the Philosophy of Criticism*, 2nd ed. (Indianapolis: Hackett, 1980); Arnold Isenberg, *Aesthetics and the Theory of Criticism* (Chicago: University of Chicago Press, 1973).

criticism is usually considered too extensive, complex, and perhaps also too subjective to be deployed effectively in experimental environments. Furthermore, art criticism is often misconceived in terms of personal testimony and preference, and thus construed as either fundamentally irrelevant or unhelpful when measuring responses to art and generating shared insights in such contexts. In our view, however, criticism can be considered a crucial resource for developing a well-grounded account of the ways in which the cognitive, moral, and spiritual value of the arts has been articulated, rationalized, and communicated.

In relation to the idea of aesthetic cognitivism, the value of criticism can be expressed in two key contexts. The first relates to the form that the cognitive productivity of aesthetic experience takes. Simply put, when we ask what kinds of knowledge and understanding we have derived from our experience of art, a good if partial answer is that this includes the knowledge and understanding recorded in art criticism. Here, in other words, we have an extensive corpus of texts within which is recorded a wide range of historical and contemporary formulations about what artworks represent, what they mean, and why that meaning is valuable.

The second respect in which art criticism is important for our project emerges when we consider not merely what criticism contains in the way of knowledge and understanding, but what effect it has both on art and those who engage with it. This agency extends in two directions. On the one hand, it reaches back into art and its traditions—informing the way artists themselves have understood their intentions, possibilities, and expressive creativity. Criticism, in this respect, is an inalienable part of the history of art. On the other hand, criticism affects the way all of us experience works of art, by determining the contexts appropriate for its appreciation, and showing us where and how to look, listen, and read, and what to look, listen, and read for. In this sense, art criticism can be understood in terms of that which shapes and reshapes the cognitive and perceptual pathways through which our aesthetic and cognitive experience of art takes place. And, by extension, to the extent that art criticism helps us make sense of art and aesthetic experience, it can also be shown to be part of what allows art and aesthetic experience to make sense of the world for us.

Our core questions are thus the following: How do the cognitive and perceptual pathways through which we engage with art come about? What role(s) do(es) art criticism play in this process? When subjects are equipped with the appropriate cognitive and perceptual pathways, do their experiences of art lead to new or deeper understanding? In confronting these questions, we seek to establish robust grounds for the case that artworks, in tandem with the critical practices that arise around them, convey and elicit epistemically significant forms of understanding.[7]

7. Our conception of the forms of understanding by and large follows that laid out in Baumberger, "Art and Understanding."

Knowledge, Perception and the Prospects of Criticism

The work undertaken in the initial phase of the project (May 2022–August 2023) can be understood in terms of a process of refining these central questions in order to prepare the ground for a larger-scale program of research during which they can be put to the test, empirically, historically, and philosophically. Our activities can be divided into the following categories: (1) philosophical analysis; (2) gathering perspectives and building networks; (3) conducting a pilot project in digital humanities and applied aesthetics; (4) preparing experimental frameworks within empirical psychology; and (5) outreach. We will discuss each of these in turn.

Philosophical Analysis

Much of our work so far has taken the form of philosophical investigations into the key concepts. In the article on "Aesthetic Understanding and Epistemic Agency in Art,"[8] Dammann and Schellekens assess some of the main, recurring objections to the claims of cognitivism, namely that the knowledge yielded by our experience of artworks seems typically trivial, vague, and lacking in the kind of logical underpinnings that characterize, say, scientific work.[9] In our discussion, we show these arguments to be less robust than commonly supposed. On the one hand, we showed that the logical underpinnings of the knowledge and understanding we gain from, for example, fictional works are less dissimilar to those which obtain in non-fiction cases: both can be confirmed through a combination of empirical means—through application to comparable real-life situations—and contextual methods, where beliefs are confirmed through reference to other textual sources. We argued that much progress can be made by distinguishing between "subtractive" and "cumulative" conceptions of the cognitive yield of art, where important differences obtain between a subtractive model where we seek merely to "take away" discrete beliefs from our reading of literature, and a cumulative one in which the lessons of literature are acquired progressively, informing the cognitive perspective through which we engage with the real world.

An important question for aesthetic cognitivism relates to putative parallels between our aesthetic experience of art and our aesthetic experience of other "intellectual pursuits," such as scientific research, where the relation to the acquisition of knowledge and understanding is considered relatively unproblem-

8. Guy Dammann and Elisabeth Schellekens. "Aesthetic Understanding and Epistemic Agency in Art," *Disputatio* 13, no. 62 (2022): 265–82.

9. See, for example, Gregory Currie, *Imagining and Knowing: The Shape of Fiction* (Oxford: Oxford University Press, 2020).

atic. When the proof of a mathematical theorem, for example, is experienced as something beautiful, is that beauty of the same kind as the beauty we find in our experiences of music and painting? In her paper "Aesthetic Experience and Intellectual Pursuits,"[10] Schellekens argues that when we ascribe beauty in non-artistic, intellectual cases (and even non-standard artistic cases, such as conceptual art), the phenomenological, affective, and epistemic structures of the corresponding judgments are more similar to standard artistic cases than is often assumed.[11] The contrast between artistic and non-artistic cases is instead to be found in the epistemic outcome of the judgment, where in the former the judgment reverts back to our experience of the work of art, while in the latter it typically turns outward toward the world. This being the case, the traditional arguments for maintaining a robust distinction between aesthetic and cognitive judgments, such that genuine aesthetic judgments are partly defined by the absence of any discrete cognitive yield, seem much weaker, and the grounds for aesthetic cognitivism much stronger than is often supposed.

In view of our focus on art criticism, our research team has also written two articles on the philosophy of criticism as part of our preparations for the more empirical work we intend to pursue on this subject. The first shows that the relationship between criticism and the works of art it takes as its subject is a more fluid one than emerges from traditional philosophical conceptions in which the practice of criticism is understood to fulfill a specific function in relation to art (typically one of description, interpretation, or evaluation, or a mixture of the three).[12] By contrast, we advance a model where the mark of successful criticism lies in its propensity to bind itself to the work(s) of art it is about. Thus, to the extent that a critic succeeds in showing something to be valued in the work—regardless of whether this value is primarily aesthetic, art-historical or more straightforwardly epistemic—this value can become part of what a community expects to find in the work, and thereby become normative for that community's experience and evaluation of it. Criticism, in this sense, doesn't stand outside of the work of art, as if were in judgment, but participates in it. The advantage of this model is that

10. Elisabeth Schellekens, "Aesthetic Experience and Intellectual Pursuits," *Aristotelian Society Supplementary Volume* 96, no. 1 (2022): 123–46. See also Elisabeth Schellekens, "Aesthetic Experience as Explorative Thought: The Noetic Conception of the Aesthetic," *Journal of Aesthetics and Art Criticism* (forthcoming, 2024).

11. For example, Cain Todd, "Fitting Feelings and Elegant Proofs: On the Psychology of Aesthetic Evaluation in Mathematics," *Philosophia Mathematica* 7 (2017).

12. Guy Dammann, "Criticism in Crisis," *The Times Literary Supplement* (forthcoming). For functional conceptions of criticism, see, for example, Noël Carroll, *On Criticism* (New York: Routledge, 2009); and James Grant, *The Critical Imagination* (Oxford: Oxford University Press, 2013).

it not only provides a better understanding of how criticism in fact works, but also helps us see how the cognitive yield of criticism can be understood in the way it forms and informs the norms and habits we rely on to engage with art, to realize its values and ascribe it with meaning.

In the second paper, we further develop this model to advance an account of critical cognitivism.[13] The argument here concerns the idea that incorporating a philosophically refined view of critical practices, and their role in informing the cognitive and perceptual pathways through which our experience of art is realized, considerably strengthens accounts of aesthetic cognitivism according to which works of art not only bear genuine cognitive value, but where this cognitive value is encoded in what we take to be the intuitively "art-making" features of the work (i.e., those features, such as its aesthetic and art-historical features, which are responsible for making it a work of art). Our idea of critical cognitivism turns on identifying the sensemaking practices at the heart of both art and art criticism, and showing how art helps us make sense of—that is, understand—the world around us.

Gathering Perspectives and Building Networks

A significant part of our activities during the initial grant phase has been concerned with building up a multidisciplinary network of researchers. Our principal forum for this has been the series of tri-weekly seminars, held between May 2022 and June 2023.[14] Our speakers have included scholars from our official research network of philosophers, theologians, art and literature scholars, as well as other researchers and professional art critics.

The papers and subsequent discussions encompassed a number of recurring themes central to our program of research, including aesthetic cognitivism in critical, political, and even gustatory contexts;[15] art education;[16] aesthetic appre-

13. Guy Dammann, John Gibson, and Elisabeth Schellekens, "Critical Cognitivism about Art," in preparation.

14. Aesthetic Cognitivism and the Prospects of Criticism, www.aestheticcognitivism.com.

15. Critical contexts: Rob Chodat, "Knowledge, Perception, Criticism: Seminar with Rob Chodat" (September 19, 2022); Tzachi Zamir, "Knowledge, Perception, Criticism: Seminar with Tzachi Zamir" (June 28, 2022); Guy Dammann, "Knowledge, Perception, Criticism: Seminar with Guy Dammann" (May 31, 2022). Political contexts: Jonathan Neufeld, "Knowledge, Perception, Criticism: Seminar with Jonathan Neufeld" (October 26, 2022). Gustatory contexts: Ole Martin Skilleås, "Knowledge, Perception and the Prospects of Criticism: Ole Martin Skilleås" (April 20, 2023), www.aestheticcognitivism.com/events.

16. John Haldane, "Knowledge, Perception and the Prospects of Criticism: John Haldane" (March 23, 2023), www.aestheticcognitivism.com/events.

ciation and disagreement;[17] religious experience;[18] and the application of artificial intelligence techniques to cultural heritage.[19] Our discussions with the arts critics Alex Ross, Laura Cumming, and Noël Carroll were designed to show how the practice of criticism, and the intuitions, beliefs, and expertise of professional critics, map onto the philosophy of criticism as we understand it.[20] These contributions have been significant both in the development of our own ideas about aesthetic cognitivism and the concept of criticism, as well as in growing a community of scholars and scholarship with a critical interest in our project. The seminars also bore fruit in the symposium we held in Uppsala in June 2023, at which members of our research network and other scholars presented work addressing our project's central questions.[21] All those involved expressed a firm commitment to continue to engage with our project in the event of its continuation.

Pilot Project in Digital Humanities

An important strand of our research has been exploring the opportunities offered by methods in the digital humanities, and we have developed a strong working relationship with Uppsala's groundbreaking Centre for Digital Humanities, the director of which was part of our research network for the project's initial phase and who will also be more formally involved in the program stage of our project.

The main strand of our collaboration with the Centre revolved around a pilot project designed to assess the viability of a larger-scale study about the formation and transformation of critical concepts. The philosophical basis of this study relates to our argument that criticism, and thus the critical concepts and terms used by critics to describe, interpret and evaluate works of art, come to be reflected in

17. Aesthetic appreciation: Irene Martinez Marin, "Knowledge, Perception and the Prospects of Criticism: Irene Martinez Marin" (March 2, 2023). Disagreement: Eileen John, "Knowledge, Perception and the Prospects of Criticism: Eileen John" (May 4, 2023), www.aestheticcognitivism.com/events.

18. Andrew Huddleston, "Knowledge, Perception, Criticism: Seminar with Andrew Huddleston" (January 17, 2023), www.aestheticcognitivism.com/events.

19. Anna Foka, "Knowledge, Perception, Criticism: Seminar with Anna Foka" (December 1, 2022), www.aestheticcognitivism.com/events.

20. Alex Ross, "Knowledge, Perception and the Prospects of Criticism: Alex Ross" (February 9, 2023); Laura Cumming, "Knowledge, Perception, Criticism: Seminar with Laura Cumming" (October 13, 2023); Noel Carroll, "Knowledge, Perception, Criticism: Seminar with Noel Carroll" (September 1, 2022), www.aestheticcognitivism.com/events.

21. "Knowledge, Perception, and the Prospects of Criticism," Uppsala, June 2023. Non-network speakers included Ryan Doran, David Davies, Vid Simoniti, Hannah Kim, Rebecca Wallbank, and Nils-Hennes Stear.

our experience. That being the case, the development and proliferation of critical concepts and vocabularies could prove crucial to understanding how this process has worked in practice, and also provide us with a valuable map of the history of aesthetic experience.

Our pilot project limited itself to critical responses to Beethoven's piano sonatas, a body of work that arguably had a profound transformative effect on Western culture's aesthetic and emotional expectations in respect to solo piano music. Beethoven's sonatas intentionally challenged not just their players (the sonata genre had traditionally been associated with the amateur, private sphere, but Beethoven's contributions necessarily exceeded that environment) but also their listeners, eliciting a depth of emotional response previously reserved for liturgical and dramatic music. At the same time, Beethoven's career coincided (though not, perhaps, coincidentally) with an exponential growth in the field of music criticism in Europe, both in general interest newspapers as well as specialist musical publications. These considerations suggested to us that a corpus drawn from music criticism about Beethoven sonatas should provide sufficient variation in its critical language for us to apply techniques from natural language analysis to study the distribution, frequency, and development of particular critical concepts.

Our corpus was drawn from three existing databases (C19, Internet Archive, and The Times Digital Archive) chosen for compatibility with the data extraction techniques of our research engineer, encompassing around twenty publications (including the London *Times*, *The Musical Times*, *The Musical Standard*) from which we extracted all critical review articles mentioning Beethoven's sonatas dating from 1820 to the present day. From these we extracted each paragraph or passage specifically about the sonatas. After submitting the resulting corpus to quality controls and standard natural language analysis techniques in order to normalize and regularize occurrences, we compiled a list of 223 aesthetic concepts linked to adjectives and adjectival phrases.

The results of the pilot study were presented at the symposium and can be interpreted in two ways.[22] First, we succeeded in showing how the usage of certain aesthetic descriptive concepts such as "beautiful," "brilliant," and "elegant" decreases over time, while others, such as "romantic," "imaginative," and "emotional," increase over time. Others, such as "profound," "poetic," and "powerful," while unusual before the timescale encompassed by the project, remain relatively constant. Second, we succeeded in developing a functioning model for natural language analysis applied to a corpus of art-critical texts which lends itself to

22. Guy Dammann, "Playing with Words: Critical Language and Beethoven's Sonatas" (paper presented in Uppsala, Sweden, June 2023).

expansion in several directions. These include (1) significantly increasing the size of the corpus to allow for a much greater range of application, (2) incorporating machine-learning techniques to identify extracts as instances of arts reviews or aesthetic-critical language, (3) using similar techniques to identify a wider category of expressive functions for critical concepts, such as metaphors, and (4) incorporating a conceptual map linking concepts to each other and to the artworks and artists they are applied to.

Such an expanded study, we believe, would have immense value, both for our wider project and for scholarship in the arts and humanities in general. In terms of its importance to the wider community of arts and humanities scholarship, the resulting database could provide an invaluable resource for research in the genealogy of critical concepts and reception studies.

For our project, the value would consist more specifically in the way the data acquired could complement our account of aesthetic cognitivism and art criticism, potentially showing how specific critical concepts do not merely describe aspects of our aesthetic experience, but rather make them both possible and cognitively valuable. That is, in helping to form the cognitive and perceptual pathways through which our aesthetic experiences are formed, critical concepts can also be shown to provide important evidence for the key tenets of aesthetic cognitivism as formulated in our project. In this way, our model according to which art criticism not only makes sense of art and aesthetic experience, but also helps us see how art and aesthetic experience make sense of the world, will be significantly strengthened by being mapped onto a large data set showing how this process has taken shape historically.

Experimental Frameworks

During the initial phase of our research, in addition to strengthening our philosophical accounts of aesthetic cognitivism and art criticism, and the twofold relation between them, we have also sought advice from colleagues from experimental psychology to conceive of ways in which this model can be tested. After consulting widely in the field, including within the Art Seeking Understanding community of scholars,[23] we have worked with Emily Holmes, of the University of Uppsala, whose expertise in both clinical and experimental psychology of art will prove invaluable in realizing the experimental potential of our research.

23. We had meetings with, among others, Anjan Chatterjee, principal investigator on the Templeton- funded project "Coming to Terms with Art," and Ryan Doran, researcher on "Measuring the Effect of Aesthetic Experiences."

Our hypothesis is that access to good art criticism results in an increase among viewers, listeners, and readers of the cognitive and affective depth, and intensity, of their aesthetic experience, as well as an increase in the degree of applicability of the understanding gained from this experience.

The hypothesis breaks down into two parts, which mirror our twofold conception of criticism as both enabling our cognitive access to art and facilitating the degree to which our aesthetic experience yields enhanced cognitive access to the world. The first part holds that incorporating the reading of art criticism into our experience of three core areas of aesthetic experience—listening to instrumental (i.e., non-vocal) music, looking at conceptual art, and reading poetry—results in significant alterations and enhancements to that experience. In particular, our hypothesis holds that criticism amplifies both the intensity and affective depth of aesthetic experience, while altering the range of associated cognitive gains. Our model here draws on Holmes's field-defining experimental studies on the human experience of internal mental imagery.[24] The second part relates to the idea that when our aesthetic experience is amplified and intensified in these ways, it can enhance our preparedness to apply the associated cognitive gains in real-world situations. This effect can be understood in the way in which critically enhanced aesthetic experience might not merely affect our behavioral responses in certain social contexts, but also expand the range of possible actions and responses associated with these contexts. Together with Holmes, we have made significant progress in developing an experimental framework which will allow both strands of our hypothesis to be tested empirically.

Outreach

The subject of the cognitive benefits of art and aesthetic experience is of interest not simply to scholarship, but to the public at large. For this reason, we have pursued several strategies to increase the accessibility of our research.

First, through our project website we have made our seminar series available online, and by inviting well-known art critics to participate in the series, we have

24. Emily A. Holmes et al., "The Causal Effect of Mental Imagery on Emotion Assessed Using Picture-Word Cues," *Emotion* 8, no. 3 (2008): 395; Emily A. Holmes et al., "Mental Imagery as an Emotional Amplifier: Application to Bipolar Disorder," *Behaviour Research and Therapy* 46, no. 12 (2008): 1251–58; E. A. Holmes and A. Mathews, "Mental Imagery in Emotion and Emotional Disorders," *Clinical Psychology Review* 30, no. 3 (2010): 349–62; Emily A. Holmes, Ella L. James, and Simon E. Blackwell, "They Flash Upon That Inward Eye," *Applied Cognitive Psychology* 24, no. 3 (2011): 338–50; Emily A. Holmes et al., "Emotional Mental Imagery as Simulation of Reality: Fear and Beyond—A Tribute to Peter Lang," *Behavior Therapy* 47, no. 5 (2016): 702–19.

hoped to increase the interest in this material. Second, in connection with the symposium held in Uppsala in June 2023, we invited a number of high-profile editors, critics, and public academics to participate in a series of panel discussions, approaching the subject of "Criticism in Society" from different angles. Open to the public, the event was well attended and was subsequently also made available through our website.[25] Third, thanks to the partnership between the Art Seeking Understanding program and Grey Matter Group, a marketing agency based in Grand Rapids, Michigan, our project's principal and co-principal investigators were interviewed for a short film, which also featured material from the symposium and public event. The film is now available on the Templeton Religion Trust website,[26] as well as via our own project website. Finally, we have also written a commentary article for the *Times Literary Supplement* which makes the case for our account of criticism and aesthetic cognitivism in accessible language.[27]

Conclusion

Our research efforts are best understood in terms of a comprehensive preparation for the second phase of our research program, which began in June 2024. Our main focus here will be on pursuing the empirical directions sketched above, and then on feeding the results of these studies back into our philosophical research. At the same time, we intend to continue our general line of collaboration and consultation both with our own research network, and with the ASU community, and to increase the visibility of our research through a variety of outreach activities. In the longer term, we hope in addition to make our digital humanities database available as a publicly accessible internet resource.

That said, the research undertaken during the initial phase of the project already constitutes significant progress. Compared with when we began the project in spring 2022, our philosophical accounts of aesthetic cognitivism and art criticism are much more sharply focused, and we have been gratified by the enthusiasm that our ideas have met from colleagues from our research network and beyond. At the same time, we also have a much clearer idea of how the philosophical theory can be applied in more empirical research environments, in particular those of digital humanities and experimental psychology. Another aspect has been the gratifying enthusiasm that our focus on art criticism has held for colleagues both within our research network and within the larger ASU

25. Online: www.aestheticcognitivism.com/criticism-in-society.

26. Online: https://templetonreligiontrust.org/explore/how-critical-language-lets-us-see/.

27. Guy Dammann, "Criticism in Crisis," *The Times Literary Supplement* (forthcoming).

community, where the view that focusing on the role of art criticism in realizing the cognitive values of art and strengthening the philosophical claims associated with aesthetic cognitivism fills an important gap in contemporary approaches to the subject.

In this respect, we believe that our project, both in its initial phase and particularly in the larger program envisaged as a result of our initial phase research, squarely addresses and stands to provide answers to three of the central questions posed by the Art Seeking Understanding Request for Proposals.[28]

With respect to the question "Is there an empirically demonstrable connection between art and understanding?," we believe that the connection between art and understanding, as formulated in our philosophical research, can be adequately tested using a combination of complementary methods from experimental psychology and digital humanities, such that we can provide an account that encompasses both the responses of contemporary living subjects and the historical literature of art criticism. Our empirical framework will make use of statistical (online questionnaire-based) and natural field (measuring responses in standard, real-life environments) methods, the design in each case guided by data acquired from our digital humanities research, building on the hypothesis that access to good criticism increases cognitive gains in normal subjects during and after their experience of art. These putative cognitive gains will relate both to how subjects understand and engage with the work in question, but also to how that engagement may yield understanding or knowledge of the world beyond the artwork. In this way, an informed experience of the work may be said to yield genuine understanding of a kind that can be applied in real-world practical and theoretical contexts.

Another central question for the overall program relates to which distinctively cognitive values are generated by engagement with the arts. Our belief is that, by drawing on the complementary methodological strands sketched above, we will be able to support the claim that the cognitive value generated by the arts has for centuries been partly realized in the form of art criticism. Our research will show art criticism to be a reason-saturated, sense-making practice that acts in two directions. On the one hand, it enables and informs our aesthetic experience, and our ability to "make sense" of the artworks we engage with, by helping readers, listeners, and viewers discern, perceive, and understand the features of works of art which render them cognitively valuable. On the other hand, art criticism acts by giving rationally articulated assessments and interpretations of how works of art make sense of the world beyond them. In these respects, art criticism should

28. See "Questions We're Exploring," https://tinyurl.com/364376hp.

not be understood as a mere report of subjective impressions, but rather as a significant objective contribution to the traditions of thinking and feeling which exist in relation to art.

The third of the overall program's central research questions relates to the ways in which participation in artistic activities might encourage or stimulate spiritual understanding and insight. Our research is intended to show how criticism can be transformative of our epistemic and aesthetic experiences. Building on our empirical work, we would hope to be able to provide a philosophical analysis of this idea through the concept of transcendence. By transcendence we mean specifically the way in which aesthetic experiences can lead us out of our habitual nexus of perspectives and affective responses and equip us with new epistemic perspectives and phenomenal knowledge, and that these, in turn, can lead us to see features of our environment in a new way.[29] Armed with the results of our empirical research, we will be able effectively to link measurable epistemic changes to the wider and more obvious spiritual concept of transcendence as it is used in art-critical literature, resulting in a clearly defined sense in which our criticism-enabled artistic experiences can lead to spiritual growth and increased self-insight.

29. See Baumberger, "Art and Understanding"; John Gibson, "An Aesthetics of Insight," in *Beauty: New Essays in Aesthetics and the Philosophy of Art*, ed. Wolfgang Huemer and Ìngrid Vendrell Ferran (Munich: Philosophia, 2019), 277–306; Graham, "Learning from Art"; Dustin Stokes, "Mental Imagery and Fiction," *Canadian Journal of Philosophy* 49, no. 6 (2019): 731–54.

20

Light Variation and the Perception of Religious Stained Glass

David Shepherd, Kate Nevin, Elizabeth Mason, and Fiona Newell

Given the extraordinary beauty, rich iconography, and long history of stained glass windows found in churches and other religious buildings around the world, it is not surprising that the medium has attracted the attention of art historians.[1] As has long been recognized, one of the features of stained glass which differentiates it from most other forms of visual art is that the medium does not merely reflect or absorb light, but transmits it to viewers in spectacular fashion. While this unique dependence on changing external light conditions is one of the most captivating features of stained glass, it also offers a rich and previously unexplored area for research in the field of empirical aesthetics. Accordingly, we undertook to begin this exploration by testing the ways in which light variation impacts how people appreciate, attend to, remember, and experience a sense of awe when viewing religious imagery in stained glass windows.

Light in the Judeo-Christian Religious Tradition and Stained Glass

The association of the divine with light in Western religion has its origins in the Hebrew Bible, where God creates light to both illuminate the day and dispel the darkness (Gen. 1:3–5, 14–18).[2] Yet the book of Numbers insists that light is not merely a created "good," but a characteristic of God himself: "the LORD make his face to shine upon you, and be gracious to you" (Num. 6:24–25).[3] Indeed, radiance

1. E.g., Robert Sowers, *The Language of Stained Glass* (Forest Grove, OR: Timber, 1981); Sarah Brown, *Stained Glass: An Illustrated History* (London: Bracken, 1994).

2. Leland Ryken, James C. Without, and Tremper Longman III, eds., *Dictionary of Biblical Imagery* (Downers Grove, IL: InterVarsity Press, 1998), 509–12.

3. Translations of Scripture in this chapter are from the New Revised Standard Version.

as a feature of the divine in ancient Judaism explains in part the subsequent Christian identification of Jesus with light ("I am the light of the world," John 9:5) and the recollection of his revelation to Saul/Paul as a "light from heaven" on the road to Damascus (Acts 9:3).

Persisting into late antiquity,[4] the theological significance of "light" eventually finds full expression in the works of Dionysius the Areopagite, the translation and interpretation of which by John Scotus Eriugena almost certainly influenced the famous renovation of the Cathedral of St. Denis, instituted by Abbot Suger.[5] Perhaps persuaded by the historical conflation of Dionysius with St. Denis, the third-century patron saint of France, Suger set about transforming the architecture of the cathedral in keeping with an understanding of light as a symbol of revelation and illumination, expressing his desire that minds should be brightened and allowed to travel through the "lights" (windows) to the "true light" of Christ.[6]

The means by which this illumination takes place for Suger and his contemporaries is well described a century later by William Durandus, bishop of Mende: "The glass windows in a church are Holy Scriptures, which expel the wind and the rain, that is, all things hurtful, but transmit the light of the true Sun, that is, God, into the heart of the faithful."[7] Along with an awareness of the windows' architectural function, we find an identification of the light with the Holy Scriptures emitted by the "True Sun," with its conflation of the natural and the theological. By Durandus's time more than eighty cathedrals inspired by Suger's "Gothic" style had been built in France alone, underpinned by the assumption that the light admitted by these windows would reveal to worshipers "transcendent realities by captivating their senses."[8]

Reflecting in the 1930s on the impact of light on these windows, Charles Connick, the great craftsman of the American Gothic revival, recalls what he wished he had said when overhearing a tour guide's indifference to Chartres Cathedral's famed Belle-Verrière window: "Its moods are as various as the changing light that plays through it. See it later in the day and note its smoldering somber glow. See it at an early mass in autumn and mark the glory of shifting sunlight as it plays

4. Jaroslav Pelikan, *The Light of the World: A Basic Image in Early Christian Thought* (New York: Harper, 1962).

5. Felipe de Azevedo Ramos, "The Metaphysics of Light in the Aesthetics of Suger of Saint-Denis," *Dionysius* 32 (2014): 116–39.

6. Erwin Panofsky and G. Panofsky-Soergel, eds., *Abbot Suger on the Abbey Church of St.-Denis and Its Art Treasures* (Princeton: Princeton University Press, 1946), 47–48.

7. William Durandus, *Rationale Divinorum Officiorum* 1.1.24, trans. J. M. Neale and B. Webb, *The Symbolism of Churches and Church Ornaments* (New York: Scribner's Sons, 1893), 23.

8. Ramos, "Metaphysics of Light," 128.

around the heavy guard of buttresses that almost surrounds it."[9] He continues in relation to the "Tree of Jesse Window": "Any windows should have several illustrations to give an adequate suggestion of its actions in volatile light. That action is the essential truth which determines its genuine value, and it is almost always neglected."[10] Connick's comments reflect the fact that stained glass, unlike other art forms, primarily transmits light rather than reflecting it. However, Connick also points toward the possibility that light variation is not merely incidental, but essential to a viewer's appreciation of stained glass. Together with the reflections of Suger and his contemporaries at the dawn of the Gothic movement, Connick's comments toward the end of the Gothic revival on the neglect of light variation in the study of stained glass highlight the need for an assessment of how it impacts the way in which viewers experience the religious imagery in stained glass windows. Thankfully, empirical psychology has developed various tools and methods for studying perception, light and art.

Psychology, Art, and Light

Since first proposed by Gustav Fechner,[11] aesthetics has been informed by empirical investigation within psychology and neuroscience, especially with the emergence of the subdiscipline known as neuroaesthetics. Along with other findings, studies within neuroaesthetics have shown that aesthetic judgments can be underpinned by cognitive functions, including learning, attention, perception, and memory, and their associated neural mechanisms.[12] Nevertheless, while the field of neuroaesthetics has provided important insights into the behavioral and brain bases of aesthetic judgments, most, if not all, of this research is based on portraits, other paintings or sculpture[13] and has not considered stained glass. The unique properties of stained glass in transmitting rather than reflecting light are likely to have associated perceptual and cognitive effects that are not shared by other art media. For example, light transmission would have the effect of increasing the hue of glass whereas light reflected on a surface may decrease its hue, as is clearly

9. Charles J. Connick, *Adventures in Light and Color: An Introduction to the Stained Glass Craft* (New York: Random House, 1937), 10.

10. Connick, *Adventures in Light and Color*, 33.

11. G. T. Fechner, *Vorschule der Aesthetic*, vol. 1 (Leipzig: Breitkopf & Härtel, 1876).

12. E.g., Marcus T. Pearce et al., "Neuroaesthetics: The Cognitive Neuroscience of Aesthetic Experience," *Perspectives on Psychological Science* 11, no. 2 (2016): 265–79.

13. See, e.g., Di Dio Cinzia and Gallese Vittorio, "Neuroaesthetics: A Review," *Current Opinion in Neurobiology* 19, no. 6 (2009): 682–87; Anjan Chatterjee and Oshin Vartanian, "Neuroaesthetics," *Trends in Cognitive Sciences* 18, no. 7 (2014): 370–75.

seen from specular highlights.[14] Furthermore, the direction of light through the glass toward the observer may be processed by means of more egocentric than allocentric mechanisms, which may lead to different cognitive (and emotional) responses to the content of the stained glass that are not yet fully understood.

As recently noted by Callaway et al., the study of art by psychologists has also attended to a variety of dimensions of the perceptual event including framing (e.g., art or non-art, forgery or original etc.), time (e.g., duration, both perceived and actual, frequency and number of viewings, etc.), attention (location of objects, gaze-cuing, etc.) and context (e.g., museum, church, lab). An additional contextual variable is light. While some studies have considered how variation in gallery lighting affects the appreciation of art within museum contexts,[15] this previous research has again focused on reflected light rather than transmitted light and does not include stained glass. Indeed, even where light variation in stained glass has been studied, the focus has been on light transport properties in order to allow for the simulation of transmitted light variation of stained glass.[16] While useful for our purposes, such a study does leave unanswered our question of how light variation impacts viewers' appreciation of stained glass.

That the perception of light variation might induce a sense of awe was first suggested explicitly in the middle of the eighteenth century by a former student of Trinity College Dublin, Edmund Burke, in his famous treatise on the sublime and the beautiful: "Light . . . if it moves with great celerity, has the same power; for lightning is certainly productive of grandeur, which it owes chiefly to the extreme velocity of its motion. A quick transition from light to darkness, or from darkness to light, has yet a greater effect."[17] Indeed, in a study which has proven seminal for the empirical study of awe in the last two decades, Keltner and Haidt cite the conversion of Paul (mentioned above) as an early example of the transformative power of awe induced by the sudden appearance of divine light.[18] Moreover, some

14. Richard F. Murray and Wendy J. Adams, "Visual Perception and Natural Illumination," *Current Opinion in Behavioral Sciences* 30 (2019): 48–54.

15. E.g., Matthew Pelowski et al., "Does Gallery Lighting Really Have an Impact on Appreciation of Art? An Ecologically Valid Study of Lighting Changes and the Assessment and Emotional Experience with Representational and Abstract Paintings," *Frontiers in Psychology* 10 (2019): article number 2148, https://doi.org/10.3389/fpsyg.2019.02148.

16. Niranjan Thanikachalam et al., "VITRAIL: Acquisition, Modeling, and Rendering of Stained Glass," *IEEE Transactions on Image Processing* 25, no. 10 (2016): 4475–88.

17. Edmund Burke, *A Philosophical Enquiry into the Origin of Our Ideas of the Sublime and Beautiful* (London: R. & J. Dodsley, 1757), sec. 16.

18. Dacher Keltner and Jonathan Haidt, "Approaching Awe: A Moral, Spiritual, and Aesthetic Emotion," *Cognition and Emotion* 17, no. 2 (2003): 298–99.

very recent empirical research suggests that light variation is one of a variety of stimuli which elicit a sense of awe.[19]

In view of this and the uniqueness of stained glass as an artistic medium which is radically dependent on transmitted light and its variation, it is remarkable how little is known about the effect of the latter on cognitive processes, such as spatial attention, perception, and memory as well as the perception of a sense of awe. Our recent project offered a preliminary empirical investigation of this specific feature of stained glass on cognitive processes and the role of light variation on aesthetic judgments.

Research Questions and Hypotheses

Connick notes above, in passing, that the brightness, tone, and color of light transmitted by stained glass may be impacted by the time of day, season, and shadows caused by external architectural features. Indeed, natural light variability experienced by interior viewers of stained glass may be caused by directional orientation (north, south, etc.), angle of sunlight as a function of season and time of day, weather conditions (e.g., persistent or passing cloud cover), seasonal variation of foliage on trees planted nearby, and potentially even external artificial lighting in evening hours. External viewing of stained glass in the darkness of evening hours may also be subject to light variation caused by internal lighting (e.g., candles, etc.).

The potential relevance of such light variation on the perception of stained glass becomes clear when it is recognized that the daily, weekly, and monthly rhythms of individual and corporate worship within church buildings mean that windows are viewed under a wide range of lighting conditions. Indeed, Connick's contrasting of the "somber glow" of the window in the evening with the "glory of shifting sunlight" during an "early mass" points to the ways in which light variation might impact viewers at worship. Given that like other art in places of worship, stained glass was intended to nurture piety and enhance religious knowledge and given that these might be facilitated by the window's imagery, memorability, and capacity to elicit wonder/awe, our basic research question was, How does light variation impact the way in which people appreciate, attend to, remember, and experience a sense of awe when viewing religious imagery in stained glass windows?

Accordingly, our hypotheses were that

19. Jialin Ke and JungKyoon Yoon, "Design for Breathtaking Experiences: An Exploration of Design Strategies to Evoke Awe in Human–Product Interactions," *Multimodal Technologies and Interaction* 4, no. 4 (2020), 81.

1. greater intensity in transmitted light will correlate to increased attention, duration of viewing, and memory;
2. dynamic light variation of entire windows, or parts of them, will correlate to increases in attention, duration of viewing, and memory; and
3. greater light intensity and variation will correlate to increases in a sense of awe.

Methods and Studies

In order to test the above hypotheses, we had to first create a visual asset database of images and animations of stained glass windows which reflected and simulated static and dynamic variations in transmitted light. We are currently conducting lab-based experiments to measure the effect of static and dynamic variations in light transmitted by stained glass on cognition, aesthetic judgments, and emotional responses. The following sections outline the preliminary findings from our studies to date. Although this work is still ongoing, these early findings are promising and will help guide and shape future research questions and studies.

Selecting Images for Our Studies

The initial stages of our current research activities were focused specifically on identifying a suitable database of images of stained glass windows and characterizing their properties within the criteria of interest for our studies. To that end, we performed an online rating study to determine participants' perception of images of windows. First, a researcher (Stephen Huws) currently undertaking a study of religious iconography in stained glass in the greater Dublin area provided the research team with access to his large set of images of stained glass windows taken from various churches. From that set, an initial database of 160 images was selected which avoided distinguishable text or internal obstructions. We surveyed a large group of participants regarding their familiarity with these windows. We also asked a number of questions about their perception of the visual complexity (in terms of colors and segments) of these windows, their scale, and extent of light distribution. These results helped identify ideal images to use in our research by allowing us to avoid high levels of familiarity, perceptions of unusual scale, and the perceived non-uniform distribution of brightness in the image. Following the selection of stimuli, scientists from Trinity's School of Computer Science and Statistics, Professor John Dingliana and his doctoral student, Priyansh Jalan, worked with the research team to create 2D simulations of static and dynamic light variation, allowing us to proceed with investigations of the role of dynamic lighting.

The Impact of Light Variation on Attention and Memory Performance

Our initial experiments explored to what extent light variation as a peculiar visual property of stained glass might begin the process of acquiring new knowledge. In particular, we tested the hypothesis that light variation across images of entire windows, or parts of them, is associated with shifts in attention and improved memory for those features. To this end, we used a Tobii eye tracker to measure the allocation of attention during free viewing of stained glass windows, followed by a memory task, which allowed us to link visual recall performance to attention.

Specifically, three types of light variation were explored, based on twenty-nine individual images of windows: diffuse light, a light patch on a foreground feature, and a light patch on a background feature (eighty-seven images in total). Participants were presented with a study image and instructed to memorize the window while we measured their eye movements. Subsequently, they engaged in a two-alternative forced-choice (2AFC) task to choose the correct match to the image previously viewed. Participants' number of fixations and gaze time on the foreground and background features during each trial were recorded. The total duration of time spent attending to these features was also documented. Response times and accuracy were measured as participants completed the memory task. Although this study is ongoing, our initial results suggest that static light variation does not specifically draw attention, as measured in eye fixation patterns distributed across the image, although accuracy responses to a memory task suggest a benefit for lighting on memory.

Individual Differences and the Impact of Light Variation on Emotional Responses

A second study was designed to test the hypothesis that dynamic variation of light through stained glass would elicit awe and also be associated with a greater sense of awe than diffuse lighting. We also tested if this may be dependent on the complexity of the window (i.e., the variation of colors and number of different sections in each image). In addition, we were specifically interested in the impact of the observer's disposition on these effects as well as on the emotional response and aesthetic judgment of stained glass windows. Thus, our aim was to recruit participants with high self-reported religiosity, as well as experts in the art form of stained glass. Our initial study also allowed us to begin to explore the way in which expertise and religiosity might influence the ways in which people experience a sense of awe when viewing stained glass.

To examine these effects, we used pupillometry as a physiological response to awe experiences. We also solicited responses to a series of different questions relating to viewers' assessment of stained glass windows in terms of beauty, familiarity with the image, perceived scale of the window, and awe experiences. To date, we have tested experts and non-experts in the production of stained glass. Our preliminary analyses suggest an interesting difference across expert groups, with experts having a larger pupil dilation when viewing images of windows than the non-expert participants. Interestingly, across all participants, we found a significant correlation (R) of 0.569 between ratings of awe induced when viewing the images of stained glass and pupil dilation. The results suggest a role of expertise in eliciting awe and call into question previous models of complexity on aesthetic judgments, such as Berlyne's optimal complexity theory.[20]

Further Questions and Future Studies

Given that no previous work had been conducted on stained glass from an empirical aesthetics perspective, the results of our current studies are incomplete and therefore suggestive rather than conclusive. Thus, it is worth reflecting on what questions remain to be explored in light of our initial studies. These reflections may be framed in relation to three general questions posed by scientists investigating aesthetic cognitivism:[21] (1) How do contextual factors increase the likelihood of knowledge and understanding being enhanced by stained glass? (2) How does stained glass function to enhance various kinds of knowledge and understanding? (3) What makes some people more likely to have their knowledge and understanding enhanced by stained glass?

How do contextual factors increase the likelihood of knowledge and understanding being enhanced by stained glass? While our preliminary studies explored to what extent light variation as a peculiar visual property of stained glass might begin the process of gaining new knowledge, it is clear that further work is needed to deepen our understanding of the visual feature of light variation and additional contextual factors. For instance, questions remain regarding the validity of our experiments given that they were undertaken in a laboratory setting with 2D images on computer monitors. To address these remaining questions, future studies might employ virtual reality experimental environments to simulate light variations in more ecologically valid ways and study the influence of key contextual factors, such as scale and height,

20. D. E. Berlyne, *Studies in the New Experimental Aesthetics: Steps toward an Objective Psychology of Aesthetic Appreciation* (Washington, DC: Hemisphere, 1974).

21. Cf. A. P. Christensen, E. R. Cardillo, and A. Chatterjee, "Can Art Promote Understanding? A Review of the Psychology and Neuroscience of Aesthetic Cognitivism," *Psychology of Aesthetics, Creativity, and the Arts* (2023).

associated with awe and wonder in previous studies. In addition, where possible, it would be helpful to test the validity of our initial findings by undertaking studies of the impact of light variation on the perception of stained glass windows in the physical environment in which they are located (e.g., a church). Such experiments would deepen our understanding of how different lighting conditions (especially diurnal and seasonal variation) impact memory of features and aesthetic features of stained glass windows. Additionally, the research team is conscious of the potential relevance of the additional contextual variable of sound. Stained glass windows are rarely viewed in silence (especially in worship); therefore, future studies should explore the role of the ambient sounds of a church environment (e.g., choir music) on cognitive and emotional responses when viewing a stained glass window.

How does stained glass function to enhance various kinds of knowledge and understanding? Our initial studies sought to evaluate the extent to which experiences of stained glass might generate a sense of awe in viewers, and more work clearly needs to be done to test the potential impact of scale and height on experiences of awe and wonder (see above). However, future studies might also consider how stained glass enhances other kinds of knowledge and understanding. For instance, it would be both useful and interesting to empirically test whether a stained glass window's illustration of a particular narrative event or episode within a religious story makes that specific event more memorable for viewers than other events within that same story. Alternatively, the depicted event may generalize to other events and facilitate memory of the entire story. Future studies might seek to evaluate the capacity of stained glass to shape a viewer/hearer's understanding of foundational religious texts and stories (narrative). Additionally, various claims have been made for the spiritual value of art making.[22] While our initial research created opportunities for engagement with communities focused on the creation of stained glass, questions remain about the extent to which knowledge of the properties of windows and contemporary production of stained glass, as a historically and predominantly religious art form, may enhance spiritual self-understanding. Future studies might well be devoted to exploring and answering these questions empirically.

What makes some people more likely to have their knowledge and understanding enhanced by stained glass? While a variety of factors have been suggested as making people more susceptible to gaining understanding by experiencing art, several studies suggest disposition is not inconsequential.[23] Our initial studies allowed

22. Beyza Kirca, "Spiritual Dimension in Art Therapy," *Spiritual Psychology and Counseling* 4 (2019): 257–74.

23. K. Fayn et al., "Confused or Curious? Openness/Intellect Predicts More Positive Interest-

us to begin to investigate how religiosity might influence the ways in which people experience an emotional response and sense of awe when viewing stained glass. In this connection, it is worth noting that the vast majority of religious stained glass in Ireland and much beyond is situated in places of worship associated with the Christian tradition. It is also true that within this Christian tradition, Protestant, Catholic, and Orthodox Christian traditions have displayed historically differentiated attitudes toward religious art, including stained glass. Accordingly, it would be useful for future studies to explore the extent to which such differences moderate how viewers experience awe when viewing stained glass and how the religious content of these windows shapes the interpretation of the stories from which this content is derived. Such research would build on and complement recent and current work on how the iconography of stained glass may be differentiated within Catholic and various Protestant traditions here in Ireland, a place in which the interplay of these traditions is rich and not inconsequential.

Through a Glass Brightly and Aesthetic Cognitivism

Aesthetic cognitivism claims that art has the potential to change what and how we think. In order to test these claims, researchers have been exploring how contextual factors influence art's ability to enhance knowledge, how art can enhance different types of understanding and whether some are more disposed to this enhancement than others.[24] Our project has broken new ground by exploring how light variation—a key contextual variable in the appreciation of stained glass—impacts the way that viewers attend to and remember stained glass windows. With respect to different types of understanding, our study has deployed novel methods (including pupillometry) to assess the ability of art (including stained glass) to elicit aesthetic emotions like awe and wonder. Finally, in relation to disposition, the project continued the study of the role of expertise and religion on the aesthetic appreciation of art. In making these contributions, the project has not only paved the way for further study of stained glass through the lens of empirical aesthetics, but also contributed to the wider testing of the claims of aesthetic cognitivism.

Confusion Relations," *Journal of Personality and Social Psychology* 117, no. 5 (2019): 1016–33; P. J. Silvia, "Confusion and Interest: The Role of Knowledge Emotions in Aesthetic Experience," *Psychology of Aesthetics, Creativity, and the Arts* 4, no. 2 (2010): 75–80; P. J. Silvia, "Interested Experts, Confused Novices: Art Expertise and the Knowledge Emotions," *Empirical Studies of the Arts* 31, no. 1 (2013): 107–15.

24. Cf. Christenson, Cardillo, and Chatterjee, "Can Art Promote Understanding?"

21

The Cognitive Processes Promoted by Exposure to Art

Madeleine E. Gross and Jonathan W. Schooler

Art possesses the remarkable capacity to expand our cognitive boundaries, prompting us to perceive and engage with our surroundings in novel ways. While such virtues are intrinsically cognitive, existing research has primarily explored the emotional repercussions of art, leaving its epistemic value largely to critical theory. Indeed, the bulk of prior studies has focused on immediate responses to art, such as emotional reactions or aesthetic evaluations,[1] with little attention paid to art's downstream influence on cognitive outcomes. Our research program pioneered one of the first extensive empirical initiatives to bridge this void, adopting a comprehensive methodology that concurrently addresses individual-specific and art-specific variables.

The present research followed from a recent study in our lab revealing that exposure to art can temporarily broaden individuals' conceptual boundaries.[2] This study used two film genres: conventional, which employed a linear narrative and traditional film techniques, and avant-garde, which employed a non-narrative style and contained unconventional methods and visuals. The impact of these two film genres was examined with respect to their ability to promote what's known as overinclusive thinking.[3] Overinclusive thinking is a state of cognitive

1. E.g., Helmut Leder et al., "What Makes an Art Expert? Emotion and Evaluation in Art Appreciation," *Cognition and Emotion* 28, no. 6 (2014): 1137–47; Matthew Pelowski, and Fuminori Akiba, "A Model of Art Perception, Evaluation, and Emotion in Transformative Aesthetic Experience," *New Ideas in Psychology* 29, no. 2 (2011): 80–97; Paul J. Silvia, "Emotional Responses to Art: From Collation and Arousal to Cognition and Emotion," *Review of General Psychology* 9, no. 4 (2005): 342–57.

2. Madeleine E. Gross, Daniel Martini, and Jonathan W. Schooler, "Can Viewing Films Promote Creative Thinking Styles? Examining the Complex Roles of Personality and Meaning-Making," *Creativity Research Journal* 35, no. 2 (2022): 154–68.

3. Hans J. Eysenck, "Creativity as a Product of Intelligence and Personality," in *International*

expansiveness assessed by one's willingness to endorse nontraditional exemplars as belonging to predefined categories, such as classifying a camel or feet as transportation. By blurring categorical boundaries, this state promotes accessibility to remote ideas and enables connections between ostensibly unrelated concepts—key processes in the generation of creative insights. For instance, few would link a falling apple to planetary motion, yet Newton did, resulting in his revolutionary insight into the nature of gravity. In line with this, conditions that promote overinclusive thinking have been found to promote creative performance.[4]

We found that exposure to artistic films could similarly encourage conceptual expansiveness as well as feelings of creative inspiration. Yet, the extent to which individuals were impacted varied based on their levels of magical ideation—a personality trait characterized by uninhibited perceptual focus (e.g., decreased latent inhibition),[5] openness to mystical beliefs, and artistic creativity.[6] Specifically, those with higher levels of magical ideation showed increased conceptual expansiveness following exposure to avant-garde film, whereas the conventional film had an effect on both conceptual expansiveness and creative inspiration for those with lower levels of magical ideation.

These preliminary findings illustrate several important points. First, art's efficacy may depend on the fit between the audience's traits and the artistic style of the work they are viewing. Second, art has demonstrable impacts on human thinking, especially toward more expansive, associative modes of thought. More generally, this implies that art has the potential to redefine the cognitive landscape where understanding evolves, enabling the emergence of new ideas and the integration of new perspectives. This expanded cognitive realm may be essential for cultivating elements of our "Spiritual Reality," as envisioned by Sir John Temple-

Handbook of Personality and Intelligence, ed. Donald H. Saklofske and Moshe Zeidner (Boston: Springer, 1995), 231–47.

4. Lixia Wang et al., "High Schizotypal Individuals Are More Creative? The Mediation Roles of Overinclusive Thinking and Cognitive Inhibition," *Frontiers in Psychology* 9 (2018): article number1766, https://doi.org/10.3389/fpsyg.2018.01766; F. C. Chiu, "Improving Your Creative Potential without Awareness: Overinclusive Thinking Training," *Thinking Skills and Creativity* 15 (2015): 1–12; D. D. Ottemiller, C. S. Elliott, and T. Giovannetti, "Creativity, Overinclusion, and Everyday Tasks," *Creativity Research Journal* 26, no. 3 (2014): 289–96.

5. V. Kumari and U. Ettinger, "Latent Inhibition in Schizophrenia and Schizotypy: A Review of the Empirical Literature," *Latent Inhibition: Cognition, Neuroscience, and Applications to Schizophrenia* (2010): 419–47.

6. Giles St J. Burch et al., "Schizotypy and Creativity in Visual Artists," *British Journal of Psychology* 97, no. 2 (2006): 177–90; Selcuk Acar and Sedat Sen, "A Multilevel Meta-Analysis of the Relationship between Creativity and Schizotypy," *Psychology of Aesthetics, Creativity, and the Arts* 7, no. 3 (2013): 214.

ton, including heightened creativity, emotional intelligence, and humility. These early results also support core assertions of aesthetic cognitivism: that artworks serve cognitive purposes—the epistemic claim—and that these cognitive functions partially dictate their artistic worth—the aesthetic claim.[7]

In the present research, we explored the epistemic value of art by investigating how engagement with art expands individuals' usual way of thinking, as well as the individual-specific nature of these effects. The central mission of Art Seeking Understanding (ASU) centers on empirically testing the tenets of aesthetic cognitivism (AC). We aimed to test AC's chief assertion—the cognitive claim—by examining the diverse ways art may promote observable cognitive shifts. In particular, we examined the effect of art on five interrelated outcomes associated with cognitive openness: creative thinking, curiosity, humility, empathy, and transliminality (i.e., the boundary between conscious and subconscious processes). As our overarching goal was to understand the influence of art on cognition, we chose an empirical approach that reflects the core principles of empirical aesthetics. The ASU program strategy further poses specific queries, such as identifying any tangible links between art and understanding, determining the unique cognitive benefits arising from engaging with the arts, and examining the circumstances under which artistic activities can enable spiritual insight, understanding, or development. Our research tackled these questions head-on, exploring how art informs understanding across five socio-epistemic realms while determining the person-specific conditions needed for art to have demonstrable effects.

Summarized Objective and Hypotheses

Our first experiment examined how art influences categorical expansiveness and creativity. Based on our preliminary findings investigating the impact of viewing film clips[8] we hypothesized that art may effectively blur the perceived boundaries around categories, enabling associations that would not otherwise be made, and thereby facilitating creativity. Our next experiment examined whether art can stimulate curiosity. We predicted that exposure to art would increase epistemic feelings and motivate information-seeking behavior. The next study explored the hypothesis that exposure to art provides an opportunity for experiencing alternative perspectives that in turn may foster greater intellectual humility. Next, we

7. Christoph Baumberger, "Art and Understanding: In Defence of Aesthetic Cognitivism," in *Bilder sehen: Perspektiven der Bildwissenschaft*, ed. Mark Greenlee et al. (Regensburg: Schnell & Steiner, 2013), 41–67.

8. Gross, Martini, and Schooler, "Can Viewing Films Promote Creative Thinking Styles?"

aimed to determine whether art's capacity to invoke an appreciation of the experience of the artist may foster a greater capacity for empathy, and in particular for recognizing the emotions of others. Finally, we aimed to explore whether art can enhance the permeability between conscious and nonconscious thoughts, potentially increasing individuals' access to information that is presented subliminally. In every study we additionally investigated the potentially differential impact of art as a function of assorted personality traits (e.g., openness). By examining the relationship between personality differences and art we may begin to understand how different forms of art may uniquely enhance the understanding of different kinds of people.

General Methods

Design

Each of the studies consists of a two-condition between-subjects design in which participants were randomly assigned to either an art-viewing condition or a control condition; see further details about the stimuli used in these conditions in the following section.

Artistic Stimuli

The art condition we used involved exposure to short animated films, i.e., films that use traditional (hand drawn) animation, computer animation, stop motion, claymation, etc. The use of animated film as our prototype art form was based on several empirically and theoretically grounded principles. First, animated films are multifaceted art forms that incorporate visual art, storytelling, and music to create an absorbing and richly aesthetic experience. Second, unlike in live action film, the entire visual world (e.g., characters, sets, and props) is created by an artist, thereby maximizing the presence of an artistic voice. Third, short films provide an excellent fit for testing the effects of exposure to art in tightly controlled, laboratory experiments delivered via a computer. Conversely, static art (e.g., paintings, sculptures, and other visual art works) cannot be rendered in their entirety via a computer as essential elements such as scale and texture are lost; such art forms must instead be studied in museums or galleries, which presents several difficulties including the inability to control for confounding aspects of the museum-going experience, challenges involving participant travel or live recruitment, and the substantial increase in experimental resources (time and cost). Finally, we have found significant and reliable effects using short films as the artistic medium in our previous work,[9] reinforcing the argument for its value in aesthetics research.

To select the short films, various film curation platforms were used (e.g., *shortoftheweek.com*). The films were all created by professional filmmakers from varied cultural backgrounds, many of whom have had their films recognized by awarding agencies in the field. For example, the short entitled *I'm OK*—one of the films included in our experimental condition—was nominated for a prestigious British Academy of Film and Television Arts award in the UK and was created by Elizabeth Hobbs, a London-based artist.

Due to the amorphous nature of what defines "art," selecting stimuli that are universally recognized as "non-art" for control conditions poses a challenge. To approach this challenge, we chose control materials that typically fall outside the traditional category of art. For this, we used compilations of humorous home videos, such as domestic pets' mischievous behaviors and domestic bloopers/pranks, which were largely created/compiled by the YouTube channel *FailArmy*.[10] Several pilot tests were conducted to confirm that both the artistic and control stimuli were generally considered equally entertaining but could be consistently identified as art or non-art, respectively, based on the consensus of our research assistants. Both the experimental (art) and control films were also matched in length, being approximately six to seven minutes long.

Personality Measures

A wealth of research in neuroaesthetics and personality psychology suggests that artistic preferences can be predicted by personality type.[11] The vast majority of this existing research has focused on the relationship between personality and art appreciation or preferences for different artistic styles (e.g., abstract vs. representational); on the other hand, very little research has examined if or how personality-dependent aesthetic responses play a role in facilitating downstream effects on cognition. This is a critical consideration for examining aesthetic cognitivism, particularly the epistemic and aesthetic claims, as some art forms or artistic styles may facilitate cognitive benefits only for individuals who value art in general, or the art form in particular. Indeed, based on past research,[12] certain

9. E.g., Gross, Martini, and Schooler, "Can Viewing Films Promote Creative Thinking Styles?"

10. FailArmy (n.d.), *FailArmy*, YouTube, https://www.youtube.com/@failarmy.

11. Tomas Chamorro-Premuzic et al., "Who Art Thou? Personality Predictors of Artistic Preferences in a Large UK Sample: The Importance of Openness," *British Journal of Psychology* 100, no. 3 (2009): 501–16.

12. Małgorzata A. Gocłowska et al., "Why Schema-Violations Are Sometimes Preferable to

art forms may have the strongest impact on some individuals, while having a weak or even detrimental effect on others.[13] In order to account for this variability, the studies described included a battery of personality tests that have previously been found to be associated with artistic preferences. The following personality traits were of particular interest: openness to experience, magical ideation (i.e., schizotypy), and curiosity.

Art and Creativity

Engaging with art encourages individuals to think beyond established norms and consider unconventional perspectives and ideas. This process may promote creativity, which similarly relies on the ability to think from multiple perspectives in order to generate a wide range of possible ideas or solutions to a given problem. Although rigorous, laboratory-controlled studies are lacking, existing research efforts underscore the potential for art to promote creative outcomes. For example, previous research has examined the impact of arts-based education on creativity in pedagogical contexts.[14] Such work emphasizes the potentially diverse benefits art exposure may have for enhancing creative thinking and expression. However, existing findings are limited given that most studies to date have relied on longitudinal study designs and lack true experimental control. This shortcoming limits our ability to understand the unique contribution of *art* with respect to other entertaining or interesting stimuli.

Therefore, our approach for examining the downstream consequences of art used a laboratory-controlled experimental design. A central objective of our first study was to extend our previous findings, in which we observed an effect of artistic film on conceptual expansion,[15] by replicating this effect using different materials and a control condition, while further exploring the potential for artistic film to promote creativity. Participants were randomly assigned to watch either one of

---

Schema-Consistencies: The Role of Interest and Openness to Experience," *Journal of Research in Personality* 66 (2017): 54–69; D. V. Wiersema, J. Van Der Schalk, and G. A. van Kleef, "Who's Afraid of Red, Yellow, and Blue? Need for Cognitive Closure Predicts Aesthetic Preferences," *Psychology of Aesthetics, Creativity, and the Arts* 6, no. 2 (2012): 168.

13. Travis Proulx, Steven J. Heine, and Kathleen D. Vohs, "When Is the Unfamiliar the Uncanny? Meaning Affirmation after Exposure to Absurdist Literature, Humor, and Art," *Personality and Social Psychology Bulletin* 36, no. 6 (2010): 817–29.

14. E.g., Marie Briguglio, Leonie Baldacchino, and Margaret Mangion, "Assessing Creativity in Secondary Schools: A Focus on the Impact of an Arts-Based Intervention," *Journal of Creative Behavior* 56, no. 4 (2022): 501–20.

15. Gross et al., "Can Viewing Films Promote Creative Thinking Styles?"

five artistic shorts in the experimental condition, or one of five humorous home videos in the control condition (see "Artistic Stimuli" for more details). To assess conceptual expansion (i.e., overinclusive thinking), participants completed a categorization task after viewing the film.[16] The task gauges how individuals classify different concepts. Typically, items are rated based on how strictly they fit within traditional categories; for example, *car* is generally rated highly as belonging to the category of *transportation*. But we anticipated that after watching an artistic short film, participants might broaden their categorization perspectives, leading them to rate even unconventional items, like *feet* or *camels*, more highly as potential transportation options.[17] Participants also completed a creative writing task[18] post-film viewing in which they were asked to generate a short story based on three given words. The creative story that participants generated was scored in two ways: (1) using an automated platform that analyzes semantic distance in natural language (SemDis),[19] resulting in ratings of semantic divergence, and (2) using subjective ratings of creativity based on two trained raters, blind to condition.

Our findings revealed that artistic films promote individuals' capacity to think outside the box,[20] as evidenced by greater conceptual expansiveness and verbal creativity. After watching an artistic film, participants in the experimental condition were more likely to endorse unconventional items as belonging to traditional categories and the stories they generated were significantly more original than those in the control group. This originality was evident in both the creativity scores assigned by raters and by marginally higher scores based on automated semantic analysis. Collectively, these findings suggest that artistic films can potentially broaden an individual's mental horizons and encourage them to think beyond established boundaries. In other words, artistic films may serve as a catalyst for creativity, encouraging individuals to think and express themselves in original ways.

16. Alice M. Isen and Kimberly A. Daubman, "The Influence of Affect on Categorization," *Journal of Personality and Social Psychology* 47, no. 6 (1984): 1206, https://psycnet.apa.org/doi/10.1037/0022-3514.47.6.1206; revised by Chiu, "Improving Your Creative Potential without Awareness: Overinclusive Thinking Training," *Thinking Skills and Creativity* 15 (2015): 1–12, https://doi.org/10.1016/j.tsc.2014.11.001.

17. As observed in Gross et al., "Can Viewing Films Promote Creative Thinking Styles?"

18. Ranjani Prabhakaran, Adam E. Green, and Jeremy R. Gray, "Thin Slices of Creativity: Using Single-Word Utterances to Assess Creative Cognition," *Behavior Research Methods* 46 (2014): 641–59.

19. Roger E. Beaty and Dan R. Johnson, "Automating Creativity Assessment with SemDis: An Open Platform for Computing Semantic Distance," *Behavior Research Methods* 53, no. 2 (2021): 757–80.

20. Madeleine E. Gross and Jonathan W. Schooler, "Standing Out: An Atypical Salience Model of Creativity," *Trends in Cognitive Sciences* 28, no. 7 (2024): 597–99.

Art and Curiosity

Do aesthetic processes promote epistemic outcomes? Art has long been theorized to confer epistemic benefits which may be driven by feelings of curiosity aroused following art viewing. The incongruity theory of curiosity suggests that when individuals face information that contradicts their current understanding, curiosity is sparked.[21] Such intellectually challenging elements have long been linked to art.[22] Indeed, it's believed that art's potential to prompt personal and even broader societal shifts arises from its tendency to challenge established beliefs.[23] Yet, the epistemic impact of art remains largely unexplored.[24] To fill this void in existing literature, the next study sought to determine whether art exposure fosters different forms of knowledge-driven curiosity.

Knowledge-driven curiosity, also known as epistemic curiosity, can be broken down into two types—interest curiosity and deprivation curiosity—which vary based on their antecedents, emotional character, and consequences. Interest curiosity is characterized by a joyous appetite for new information, driving one to explore widely, while deprivation curiosity reflects that itch one gets when they feel they're missing a piece of the puzzle, driving one to zoom into a specific topic. Art, particularly art forms that delight the imagination while resisting straightforward interpretation, may provoke either, or both, of these types of curiosity due to its intellectually and perceptually stimulating nature.[25] To test these possibilities, two novel state-based measures were developed which capture self-reported feelings of interest- and deprivation-based epistemic curiosity.[26]

Curiosity also acts as a drive-state that propels learning and problem-solving. Despite this active nature, there's a lack of tools available to capture behavioral manifestations of curiosity in real time.[27] While prior research has linked stable

21. Gregory Berns, *Satisfaction: The Science of Finding True Fulfillment* (New York: Macmillan, 2005).

22. Judy Ann Rollins, "Arousing Curiosity: When Hospital Art Transcends," *HERD: Health Environments Research & Design Journal* 4, no. 3 (2011): 72–94.

23. Aleksandra Sherman and Clair Morrissey, "What Is Art Good For? The Socio-Epistemic Value of Art," *Frontiers in Human Neuroscience* 11 (2017): 411.

24. Yoed N. Kenett, Stacey Humphries, and A. Chatterjee, "A Thirst for Knowledge: Grounding Curiosity, Creativity, and Aesthetics in Memory and Reward Neural Systems," *Creativity Research Journal* (2023): 1–15; Sherman and Morrissey, "What Is Art Good For?"

25. Kenett et al., "Thirst for Knowledge."

26. Madeleine Gross, "Perceptual, Phenomenological, and Behavioral Processes Underpinning State and Dispositional Curiosity" (PhD dissertation, University of California Santa Barbara, 2022).

27. Madeleine E. Gross, Claire M. Zedelius, and Jonathan W. Schooler, "Cultivating an Un-

curiosity traits with patterns of information-seeking behavior,[28] there's a notable gap in instruments that are capable of capturing momentary fluctuations, or *state* shifts, in curiosity. Addressing this, we developed a novel measure that tracks real-time changes in curiosity-induced information-seeking behavior.[29] The measure we developed captures participants' choices to read a variety of articles (indicating a boost in curiosity) or complete word search puzzles (the less curious alternative). Our previous findings support the efficacy of this method for capturing states of curiosity.[30]

We hypothesized that art might have the potential to promote information-seeking behavior, as well as interest and deprivation curiosity. Our findings supported this hypothesis, revealing that exposure to artistic shorts promotes all three manifestations of curiosity, which may represent an optimal condition for intrinsically motivated, exploration-based learning. The ability for art to increase information-seeking behavior suggests that art doesn't just arouse passive feelings of interest, but rather promotes an active, drive state in which individuals are motivated to seek out new knowledge and learn about topics that are interesting to them. This result has exciting implications for applied settings, such as learning and intrinsically motivated exploration in pedagogical and workplace contexts. Beyond this, our results suggest that art has the unique capacity to promote both interest and deprivation facets of epistemic curiosity. Most experiences that pique our curiosity usually only hit one of these buttons at a time, or if they hit both, they might wind down one as they crank up the other. But art seems to reflect a sweet spot in which both interest and deprivation facets of curiosity are promoted simultaneously. This could be envisioned as the perfect balance of wanting to roam freely and explore, mixed with the tenacity to dive deep and get the details when something grabs your attention—a "Goldilocks zone" of curiosity.

We also explored the relationship between curiosity and mood. Consistent with previous research, interest curiosity correlated with positive emotions, while deprivation curiosity, driven by a sense of uncertainty, was tied to negative emotions. This highlights the unique ability of art to simultaneously evoke effectively opposed states. The unusual relationship between art reception and emotion is evident in the popularity of tragic narratives in theater and literature, as well as individuals'

---

derstanding of Curiosity as a Seed for Creativity," *Current Opinion in Behavioral Sciences* 35 (2020): 77–82.

28. David M. Lydon-Staley et al., "Hunters, Busybodies, and the Knowledge Network Building Associated with Deprivation Curiosity," *Nature Human Behaviour* 5, no. 3 (2021): 327–36.

29. C. M. Zedelius and J. W. Schooler, unpublished data, University of California, Santa Barbara; Gross, "Perceptual, Phenomenological, and Behavioral Processes."

30. Gross, "Perceptual, Phenomenological, and Behavioral Processes."

affinity for melancholic or somber music. Such observations have led theorists to propose that art possesses a distinctive capability to render negative emotions enjoyable.[31] This unique quality of art may be the key to its ability to simultaneously foster both forms of epistemic curiosity we examined in this study.

Our findings challenge and inform current psychological theories of curiosity by showing that art can induce a powerful desire for knowledge. Most existing experimental techniques for inducing curiosity involve withholding specific, well-defined information, such as not providing an answer to a trivia question. Such methods have informed theoretical work which suggests that curiosity is only evoked by such concrete information gaps;[32] however, we discovered a unique method to stimulate states of curiosity: exposure to art. With its thought-provoking qualities, art seems to have the potential to promote a knowledge-hungry state, driving curiosity-driven behaviors.

Art and Humility

Intellectual humility refers to the fundamental capacity of individuals to admit to their own limitations and display an openness to differing viewpoints, beliefs, and perspectives.[33] Dual process accounts of humility suggest that either intelligence or cognitive flexibility—the ability to adapt to changing environments and circumstances—alone is sufficient for predicting scores on this trait.[34] Though there is limited research examining methods for inducing intellectual humility directly,[35] cognitive flexibility can be promoted through environmental enrichment and diversifying experiences.[36] This suggests that exposure to stimuli that offers opportunities for deep engagement, exploration, and alternative perspectives may

31. Jerrold Levinson, ed., *Suffering Art Gladly: The Paradox of Negative Emotion in Art* (Hampshire: Palgrave Macmillan, 2013); Winfried Menninghaus et al., "The Distancing-Embracing Model of the Enjoyment of Negative Emotions in Art Reception," *Behavioral and Brain Sciences* 40 (2017): article number, e347, https://doi.org/10.1017/s0140525x17000309.

32. A. Markey and G. Loewenstein, "Curiosity," in *International Handbook of Emotions in Education*, ed. Reinhard Pekrun and Lisa Linnenbrink-Garcie (New York: Routledge, 2014), 228–45.

33. Mark R. Leary et al., "Cognitive and Interpersonal Features of Intellectual Humility," *Personality and Social Psychology Bulletin* 43, no. 6 (2017): 793–813.

34. Leor Zmigrod et al., "The Psychological Roots of Intellectual Humility: The Role of Intelligence and Cognitive Flexibility," *Personality and Individual Differences* 141 (2019): 200–208.

35. E.g, Julia Ernesta Romanowska, Gerry Larsson, and Töres Theorell, "An Art-Based Leadership Intervention for Enhancement of Self-Awareness, Humility, and Leader Performance," *Journal of Personnel Psychology* 13, vol. 2 (2014): 97.

36. S. M. Ritter et al., "Diversifying Experiences Enhance Cognitive Flexibility," *Journal of Experimental Social Psychology* 48, no. 8 (2012): 961–64; Francesca Gelfo, "Does Experience Enhance

promote cognitive flexibility, a key antecedent to humility. We therefore predicted that exposure to art may enhance intellectual humility.

To examine this, participants were given a behavioral intellectual humility task in which they were given the opportunity to learn more about opposing views, and a self-reported General Intellectual Humility Scale.[37] Unfortunately, a valid behavioral measure of intellectual humility does not exist, particularly one that has been rigorously tested and found to predict theoretically associated outcomes.[38] However, in our commitment to not rely solely on self-report questionnaires, we included a measure which has previously been found to be associated with intellectual humility and has been shown to be sensitive to change via a manipulation.[39] In this task, participants are asked their position on a controversial topic (e.g., gun control). They are then given the choice to read through views on the topic—ostensibly given by other participants—that are for or against their own position on the topic. They may also choose to skip ahead to the next part of the study at any time. The proportion of times that participants chose to read an opposing view versus one congruent to their own was used as an operationalization of state intellectual humility. We found that art promotes self-reported feelings of intellectual humility; however, we did not find behavioral changes in humility using this choice-based behavioral task. It is important to note we also did not find a correlation between the self-report and behavioral task which may indicate the behavioral measure was not a valid way to capture this construct. Future research should continue to explore the potential of art to promote behavioral manifestations of intellectual humility based on our promising initial findings supporting its effect on self-report measures.

The abstract, multifaceted, or unfamiliar perspectives present in art may challenge viewers to question their existing beliefs and biases leading to an openness to consider alternative viewpoints. Furthermore, intellectual humility is based on the understanding that there's always more to learn. Thus, similarly to our above findings regarding curiosity and art, exposure to films may make individuals more receptive to new information and strive to seek new knowledge. The finding that artistic short films foster self-reported intellectual humility not only elevates the value of such art but also emphasizes the profound impact of art on personal and

---

Cognitive Flexibility? An Overview of the Evidence Provided by the Environmental Enrichment Studies," *Frontiers in Behavioral Neuroscience* 13 (2019): 150.

37. Leary et al., "Cognitive and Interpersonal Features."

38. Tenelle Porter et al., "Predictors and Consequences of Intellectual Humility," *Nature Reviews Psychology* 1, no. 9 (2022): 524–36.

39. Tenelle Porter and Karina Schumann, "Intellectual Humility and Openness to the Opposing View," *Self and Identity* 17, no. 2 (2018): 139–62.

societal growth. The ripple effects of intellectual humility can lead to more open, inclusive, and growth-oriented individuals and communities.

Art and Transliminality

Next, we aimed to examine whether art can broaden the landscape of individuals' minds via perceptual expansion. Visual perceptions are inherently filtered and restricted—a significant portion of our surrounding visual environment escapes our notice. However, new research suggests that there's variation in how quickly individuals process specific visual data. In other words, some people might detect sensory details faster than others.[40] This idea relates closely to the concept of transliminality, which describes how psychological content crosses into our conscious awareness.[41] A prime example of this phenomenon is hypnagogia—a phase where individuals experience vivid visions as they drift from wakefulness to sleep. Previous research suggests that those predisposed to such transliminal states often exhibit enhanced creativity and a tendency to recall profound dreams.[42]

Despite these intriguing findings, current methods for measuring transliminality face limitations. Existing measures often capture related concepts, like creative thinking, instead of transliminality directly (e.g., the Revised Transliminality Scale).[43] They also largely depend on self-reports, which can be unreliable or influenced by confounding factors. Moreover, existing tools capture stable individual differences, or traits, rather than transient fluctuations, or states.

To address these issues, we began this line of research by developing novel methods for measuring transliminality within laboratory-controlled settings. Our first objective was to assess the relationship between transliminality and unconscious information leakage through intuitive thinking tasks.[44] Our results indicated that while transliminality showed a strong association with magical

40. Assail Y. Sklar et al., "Did You See It? Robust Individual Differences in the Speed with Which Meaningful Visual Stimuli Break Suppression," *Cognition* 211 (2021): article number 104638, https://doi.org/10.1016/j.cognition.2021.104638.

41. M. A. Thalbourne and P. S. Delin, "Transliminality: Its Relation to Dream Life, Religiosity, and Mystical Experience," *International Journal for the Psychology of Religion* 9, no. 1 (1999): 45–61.

42. M. A. Thalbourne, "Transliminality and Creativity," *Journal of Creative Behavior* 34, no. 3 (2000): 193–202; Thalbourne and Delin, "Transliminality."

43. Rense Lange et al., "The Revised Transliminality Scale: Reliability and Validity Data from a Rasch Top-Down Purification Procedure," *Consciousness and Cognition* 9, no. 4 (2000): 591–617.

44. J. R. Ortega, M. E. Gross, and J. W. Schooler, "Intuitive, Creative, or Transliminal? Crossing the Threshold from Intuition to Convergent Thinking," poster presentation, Annual Meeting of the Society for the Neuroscience of Creativity (SfNC), San Francisco, March 24, 2023.

ideation, it wasn't closely tied to intuition. This suggests that the current primary measure, the Revised Transliminality Scale, may be confounding a result of transliminality, like magical ideation, with the actual process of transliminality. Interestingly, we observed a link between intuition and overinclusive thinking, which our previous studies have associated with enhancement from art exposure. These findings indicate that to truly understand art's potential to induce genuine transliminal states, we need to employ novel, direct methods of measuring transliminality.

In another line of this research, we examined the phenomenology of waking thoughts as potential indicators of transliminality.[45] Given that transliminality is theorized to involve unconscious content seeping into consciousness, we reasoned that trait differences in transliminality might influence an individual's day-to-day thoughts, making them resemble dreamlike states. By having participants report on their thoughts' qualities during daily life, we discovered that those with higher levels of transliminality reported thoughts that were more bizarre, novel, and interesting—qualities that tend to be characteristic of dreaming and dream thoughts. These results open up the intriguing possibility that engaging with art could influence certain thought patterns due to its capacity to induce transliminal states. Equipped with these new methodological insights, we're poised to explore art's impact on these new measures of transliminality in upcoming research.

Art and Empathy

Art has the potential to facilitate a strong emotional connection with the artist's experience, thereby potentially heightening individuals' empathy. Expounding on this notion, Baumberger suggests that when one becomes deeply familiar with both sensory and emotional elements, it can enhance their understanding by providing an intimate viewpoint into another's lived experience.[46] In our pursuit to examine this hypothesis, we will apply methodologies similar to those in our previous investigations. Our approach will integrate scientifically recognized tools tailored to gauge empathy—often described as emotional intelligence—based on observed behavior. In particular, we are interested in tools that focus on the ability to interpret individuals' emotional states. We are currently in the process of fine-tuning our empathy measure and anticipate that exposure to art will bolster

45. J. R. Ortega, M. E. Gross, and J. W. Schooler, "When Life Is but a Dream: Transliminality Predicts Continuity in Bizarreness across the Sleep-Wake Cycle," *Philosophy and the Mind Sciences*, special issue, submitted.

46. Baumberger, "Art and Understanding."

performance on this behaviorally measured task—though the influence of art might again be contingent on individual personality traits.

Discussion

In observing the intricate facets of human development, Sir John Templeton coined the term "Spiritual Reality," a term used to capture the foundational elements that drive human advancement and well-being. Our research aimed to understand how individuals can use the transformative power of art to connect with this "Spiritual Reality." We found that art acts as a conduit for fostering creativity, conceptual expansiveness, humility, curiosity, and a drive for acquiring knowledge.[47] All of these outcomes echo a common theme: a general state of cognitive openness. In this state, individuals are not only receptive of, but actively engage with, diverging perspectives, ideas, and concepts.

These exciting findings open up significant areas for further inquiry. First, an open question from our research is whether there is domain generality in art's influence on creativity. Our research focused on artistic films given that this mode of art comprises narrative, visual, and musical features in one. However, the use of this multifaceted art form raises the question whether similar effects would be observed following exposure to art forms that include just one of these facets, such as purely visual works (e.g., painting or sculpture). Each art form may engage the human mind in unique ways. Similarly, creativity itself is multifaceted. Beyond verbal creativity, creative outcomes can include problem-solving, artistic expression in various mediums, and mathematical or scientific innovation—these variants of creative expression should also be explored as potential outcomes to art exposure. It is further possible that a congruency between the art form and the type of creative expression may amplify the effects we observed; for instance, verbal art (e.g., poetry) may have a bigger impact on verbal creativity than auditory art (e.g., music). Further research is necessary to determine whether exposure to art enhances creativity more broadly or if the effects are confined to the specific interrelations between the art and the type of creativity being measured.

Given that artistic films, a non-written art form, led to enhancements in creative writing, we suggest that art's influence might be domain general, impacting creative outputs across various forms. Based on our creativity-related findings, as well as the observed impact of art on other forms of open-mindedness, we further put forward a novel theory of aesthetic processing that suggests that art leads to

47. Gross et al., "Can Viewing Films Promote Creative Thinking Styles?"; Gross and Schooler, "Standing Out."

a general state of cognitive openness in which individuals take on qualities that are characteristic of the personality trait openness to experience. This trait has been linked with a broad range of virtues reflecting an explorative and receptive mindset, including aesthetic sensitivity and novelty seeking. Importantly, many of the very same virtues that are linked to trait openness to experience were also found to be influenced by art, including creativity, humility, and curiosity. We therefore suggest that art may have the capacity to temporarily promote this facet of human personality. Furthermore, given that one of the qualities of openness to experience is an appreciation of art, our research suggests a reciprocal relationship; not only does openness to experience lead to an appreciation of art, but appreciating art leads to a state akin to openness to experience. We fleshed out the neurobiological basis and behavioral implications for this working hypothesis in a recent theoretical publication.[48]

Our research further revealed that the impact of art is often amplified by specific personality traits. For example, we found that those predisposed to magical ideation experienced a heightened impact of art on creativity, while those with a naturally curious nature showed greater epistemic feelings and information-seeking behaviors in response to art. While it might seem that art primarily benefits individuals with certain personality characteristics, recent studies show that personality traits can be fluid, changing in response to specific moments or situations rather than being fixed aspects of our identity. This presents an exciting possibility: if we can temporarily promote traits like curiosity or openness in individuals, we might amplify their responsiveness to art. Our team is currently exploring ways to boost curiosity;[49] future studies could use these techniques to see if such induction methods amplify the effects of art. Besides personality, people also differ in terms of their cognitive styles, educational backgrounds, and cultural experiences, all of which may shape their interaction with art. How these individual differences influence the relationship between art exposure and creativity could provide much-needed nuance into our observed effects.

The mechanisms through which art exposure influences facets of openness also need to be further explored. It is possible that art influences cognitive capacities related to open-mindedness—like mental flexibility. Art may also promote emotional states that are particularly conducive to openness. Yet another possibility is that art triggers more associative thinking, wherein one idea or concept triggers a related or seemingly unrelated idea. This associative style of thinking may offer a fertile ground for creative connections or help promote visual imag-

48. See Gross and Schooler, "Standing Out."

49. Gross, "Perceptual, Phenomenological, and Behavioral Processes."

ery in one's writing or visual art. Art often portrays beautiful or fantastical scenes which may also spark one's imagination, making them more inclined to engage in imaginative play and storytelling. Art may also offer individuals a sense of freedom to express themselves without judgment. This reduction in self-censorship may further encourage exploration, humility, and creative expression. For example, viewing unconventional or avant-garde art may lead individuals to engage with unconventional ideas in their own beliefs, ideas, or creative work. And finally, as our results suggest,[50] art may generally loosen conceptual boundaries, allowing increased flow and cross-pollination between distantly related ideas and concepts. All of these possible mechanisms should be examined in future research. Once these mechanisms are understood, it opens the possibility of using art in more intentional ways. For instance, educational institutions might integrate art into curricula to enhance students' engagement with challenging or controversial subjects.

The interdisciplinary nature of this work opens a host of future research avenues within various disciplines. Our findings sit at the intersection of art, psychology, and cognitive science with implications for philosophy, art theory, and sociology. By examining the underlying mechanisms central to various cognitive states, this research moves empirical aesthetics into the mainstream arena of cognitive and general psychology. We've examined how art impacts human thought processes, behavior, and emotional comprehension, which represent core concerns of both cognitive science and general psychology disciplines. Additionally, by linking the effects of art to personality traits, our findings offer relevant insights to personality psychology, a branch of psychology concerned with how different stimuli impact individuals based on their personality structures. This research doesn't just use art as a stimulus; it also seeks to understand the role and impact of art, making the research relevant to disciplines focused on art theory and criticism. In exploring how art might fan the flames of curiosity and enhance learning, the research also touches on educational theory—how do we learn, what enhances that learning, and how can various disciplines (like art) be used pedagogically? When considering aspects like the permeability between conscious and nonconscious thoughts, the research borders on philosophical questions of human consciousness. And finally, by examining art's differential impact based on individual differences and its role in fostering empathy and humility, this work speaks to sociological topics, particularly when considering group behaviors and societal impacts. For example, although many advocate for more funding in arts

50. Gross et al., "Can Viewing Films Promote Creative Thinking?"; Gross and Schooler, "Standing Out."

education, these policies are increasingly contingent on tangible, empirical evidence. By integrating methods, theories, and concepts from each discipline, our project doesn't just borrow from various areas of study—it contributes back to them, potentially offering new insights or methodologies that are relevant within the context of each field.

In summary, our research contributed numerous methodological and theoretical advances as well as revealed the positive effects of artistic films on certain types of creative thinking, curiosity, and humility. As exciting as these initial findings are, we also uncovered a frontier of unknowns. Our research invites further investigation into whether different forms of art similarly influence these outcomes, what underlying cognitive processes might underpin these effects, and how various individual differences may amplify or diminish the effects we observed. Understanding the full scope of art's impact on the human mind, therefore, remains an exciting and open venture in cognitive research.

22

Imagination and Perspective in Film

Stacie Friend

According to aesthetic cognitivism, artworks can be valuable sources of understanding. But this claim leaves open many questions: Which kinds of art facilitate which kinds of understanding? In virtue of which features? Under what conditions? And for whom? These questions are both conceptual and empirical. However, there has been little interaction between the arts and humanities on one hand, and the empirical sciences on the other, in answering them. Consequently, experimental results often appear irrelevant to theoretical positions, while those positions cannot easily be tested. What is needed is a genuinely interdisciplinary approach, of just the kind that the Art Seeking Understanding program is designed to support.

It is within this context that colleagues and I have undertaken the project "Art Opening Minds: Imagination and Perspective in Film," which I direct. I am a philosopher of art and aesthetics, and my team includes a cognitive psychologist (Heather Ferguson, University of Kent), a developmental psychologist (Angela Nyhout, University of Kent), and a researcher in both film studies and philosophy (Murray Smith, University of Kent). It is a thoroughly interdisciplinary project, which might be described as *philosophically framed empirical aesthetics*. As such, the project involves philosophy, the sciences, and arts research, but it also touches on issues in theology and religion, especially spirituality and self-transcendence.

Philosophers and others have proposed many ways in which art can be cognitively valuable, from offering insight into human nature[1] to generating vicarious

1. E.g., Oliver Conolly and Bashar Haydar, "Literature, Knowledge, and Value," *Philosophy and Literature* 31, no. 1 (2007): 111–24.

experiences,[2] from reconfiguring concepts[3] to enhancing moral capacities,[4] from exercising imaginative and emotional skills[5] to fostering virtues such as open-mindedness.[6] These arguments, though plausible, typically proceed with little attention to empirical evidence. Yet the claim that art is a source of one or another kind of understanding surely demands empirical investigation.

At the same time, there is now a body of psychological research examining the effects of engaging with art and media on (for example) beliefs and attitudes, affective empathy, and the understanding of others' mental states (theory of mind). Results from these studies are mixed, however, and several have not been replicated.[7] Moreover, psychologists have generally approached the study of art without attention to the dimensions that matter most to aesthetic cognitivists in other disciplines, like the relationships between different kinds of value.

A consequence of this disciplinary siloization is that empirical results have often failed to address concerns of scholars in the arts and humanities, while those scholars have defended positions that are difficult to evaluate empirically. This is why we have adopted an interdisciplinary approach.

With that in mind, our project examines a common cognitivist claim which had not previously been explored empirically: that works of art can "open our minds" and "expand our horizons." Open-mindedness is typically recognized as a paradigmatic intellectual or epistemic virtue,[8] and efforts to instill it are often fundamental to education.[9] Because artworks engage us imaginatively, challeng-

2. E.g., David Novitz, *Knowledge, Fiction, and Imagination* (Philadelphia: Temple University Press, 1987).

3. E.g., Eileen John, "Reading Fiction and Conceptual Knowledge: Philosophical Thought in Literary Context," *Journal of Aesthetics and Art Criticism* 56, no. 4 (1998): 331–48.

4. E.g., Martha C. Nussbaum, *Love's Knowledge: Essays on Philosophy and Literature* (New York: Oxford University Press, 1992).

5. E.g., Jenefer Robinson, *Deeper Than Reason: Emotion and Its Role in Literature, Music, and Art* (Oxford: Oxford University Press, 2005).

6. Dominic M. Lopes, *Sight and Sensibility: Evaluating Pictures* (Oxford: Clarendon, 2005); John Gibson, "Cognitivism and the Arts," *Philosophy Compass* 3, no. 4 (2008): 573–89.

7. See Lena Wimmer et al., "The Effects of Reading Narrative Fiction on Social and Moral Cognition: Two Experiments Following a Multi-Method Approach," *Scientific Study of Literature* 11 (2022): 223–65.

8. E.g., Wayne Riggs, "Open-Mindedness," *Metaphilosophy* 41, nos. 1–2 (2010): 172–88; Jason Baehr, *The Inquiring Mind: On Intellectual Virtues and Virtue Epistemology* (Oxford: Oxford University Press, 2011).

9. E.g., Jason Baehr, "Educating for Intellectual Virtues: From Theory to Practice," *Journal of Philosophy of Education* 47, no. 2 (2013): 248–62; Rebecca M. Taylor, "Open-Mindedness: An Epis-

ing us to see the world in different ways, they seem to have significant potential to enhance open-mindedness.

Our primary research question is: In what ways can art enhance open-mindedness, and how does this contribute to its cognitive value? To address this question, we decided to focus on film (broadly construed, including video and other moving-image media) because it is a widely accessible art form, and one whose cognitive effects have been understudied relative to literature. With respect to film, our subsidiary empirical questions are:

- How does watching film influence different characteristics of open-mindedness?
- How do specific features of film or differences in audience predict and/or modulate these effects?
- Can effects be traced to the attentional and/or affective responses elicited by film in real-time?

We have contextualized these questions within a philosophical approach to open-mindedness as an intellectual virtue, so that the answers can feed into an account of open-mindedness as a cognitive value of film as art. In this way we aim to demonstrate the value of cutting-edge interdisciplinary research in making progress on aesthetic cognitivism.

To address these questions, we first had to analyze and operationalize the concept of open-mindedness. Most philosophical accounts that treat it as an intellectual virtue focus on the role of open-mindedness in seeking true beliefs. However, this approach is too restrictive when it comes to the kinds of open-mindedness frequently attributed to engagement with art. We therefore construe open-mindedness broadly, breaking it down into a variety of different facets: creativity, imagination, cognitive flexibility, openness to new evidence, self-transcendence, and receptiveness to experiences, for each of which there are established measures:

a. For creativity, the Alternative Uses Test[10] in which participants think of as many uses as possible for a common object (e.g., paper clip, brick); responses are coded for number and originality.
b. For imagination, an exercise in which participants are asked to imagine vivid scenes in their mind's eye and describe them out loud.[11] The descriptions are

---

temic Virtue Motivated by Love of Truth and Understanding," *Philosophy of Education* 69 (2013): 197–205.

10. J. P. Guilford, "Creativity: Yesterday, Today and Tomorrow," *Journal of Creative Behavior* 1 (1967): 3–14.

11. Demis Hassabis, Dharshan Kumaran, and Eleanor A. Maguire, "Using Imagination to

coded on dimensions including the number of people/objects mentioned, sensory descriptions, and mental states described, to create an imagination index.

c. For cognitive flexibility, the Wisconsin Card Sorting Task[12] in which participants are asked to sort cards according to one of three classification rules: color, shape, or number of symbols. The sorting rule changes throughout the task; the number of perseverative errors (times participants persisted with an incorrect sorting rule) is measured.
d. For openness to new evidence, a trait hypothesis-testing task,[13] in which participants are presented with initial biasing evidence about an individual. They are then given a list of questions to pose to the individual, including hypothesis-confirming and -disconfirming items. A higher proportion of hypothesis-disconfirming questions indicates greater openness.
e. For self-transcendence, an adapted version of the Self-Disillusionment scale,[14] in which participants rate their agreement with statements such as "I felt a sense of union with the film characters" and "I felt far less absorbed by my own issues and concerns."

In addition to measures A–E, we included the following measure in all studies, to be used as a predictor in the statistical models:

f. Openness to experience, an assessment using the openness subscale of the International English Big-Five Mini-Markers,[15] in which participants self-report how accurately adjectives describe them using a five-point scale.

We have been running a series of experimental studies deploying these measures to examine how different features of film—specifically genre, formal complexity, and perspective shifting—interact with features of audiences in influencing characteristics of open-mindedness. Participants include both adults and chil-

Understand the Neural Basis of Episodic Memory," *Journal of Neuroscience* 27 (2007): 14365–74, https://doi.org/10.1523/jneurosci.4549-07.2007

12. A. Miyake et al., "The Unity and Diversity of Executive Functions and Their Contributions to Complex 'Frontal Lobe' Tasks: A Latent Variable Analysis," *Cognitive Psychology* 41 (2000): 49–100.

13. Adam D. Galinsky and Gordon B. Moskowitz, "Perspective-Taking: Decreasing Stereotype Expression, Stereotype Accessibility, and In-Group Favoritism," *Journal of Personality and Social Psychology* 78 (2000): 708–24.

14. Matthew M. Nour et al., "Ego-Dissolution and Psychedelics: Validation of the Ego-Dissolution Inventory (EDI)," *Frontiers in Human Neuroscience* 10 (2016): article number 269, https://doi.org/10.3389/fnhum.2016.00269

15. Edmund R. Thompson, "Development and Validation of an International English Big-Five Mini-Markers," *Personality and Individual Differences* 45 (2008): 542–48.

dren (ages eight–twelve), and in one study we have also measured the moment-by-moment attentional and affective responses of audiences watching films, to identify specific mechanisms by which aesthetic experience can influence characteristics of open-mindedness.

Study 1: Formal Complexity

Consistently with aesthetic cognitivism, we typically take artworks that are more profound, thought-provoking, and challenging to be better as art. This view aligns with the claim that a core characteristic of art is "defamiliarization"—rendering the familiar strange, or presenting the experience of those remote from us, thereby opening our minds to new aspects of the world.[16] One dimension of complexity standardly regarded as central to defamiliarization in film is narrative order. Films presenting narrative events in non-linear form are thought to offer a greater challenge to understanding and a greater reward in exercising imagination.

In this study, which was adults only, we tested the hypothesis that increasing formal complexity would enhance many characteristics of open-mindedness. However, based on psychological research showing that films with higher complexity make greater processing demands and deplete cognitive resources,[17] we predicted that performance on the cognitive flexibility task would be negatively impacted, particularly among participants with lower expertise in film.[18] In this study, the two experimental groups watched different versions of the Christopher Nolan film *Memento*, either the original (in which scenes are in a non-linear temporal order) or an alternate version created by Nolan, with scenes in chronological order. A control group completed the measures without watching any film. In addition to openness to experience (F. above), this study included a second measure as a predictor in the statistical models: need for cognitive closure, assessed using the Need for Closure Scale.[19] Participants rate on a six-point scale the extent to which they agree with statements reflecting a preference for or aversion to closure.

16. Viktor Shklovsky, *Theory of Prose*, trans. Benjamin Sher (Elmwood Park, IL: Dalkey Archive, 1991).

17. S. Geiger and B. Reeves, "The Effects of Scene Changes and Semantic Relatedness on Attention to Television," *Communication Research* 20 (1993): 155–75.

18. Todd Berliner, *Hollywood Aesthetic: Pleasure in American Cinema* (New York: Oxford University Press, 2017).

19. A. W. Kruglanski, D. M. Webster, and A. Klem, "Motivated Resistance and Openness to Persuasion in the Presence or Absence of Prior Information," *Journal of Personality and Social Psychology* 65 (1993): 861–76.

Study 2: Perspectives

Aesthetic cognitivists often argue that art is valuable insofar as it provides new perspectives, reframing and reshaping our experience and perception of the world.[20] Films depict story worlds from the perspectives of characters and narrators; they prompt us not merely to imagine that certain events occur, but to imagine experiencing such events.[21] Artworks invite us imaginatively to adopt the mindsets of a wider and more diverse array of agents than we are ever likely to encounter directly.[22] Such works may thereby "encourage us to consider and to become open to people, dilemmas, and states of affairs we might otherwise have dismissed out of hand."[23]

In this study, run separately with both adults and children, we tested the hypothesis that narrative films embodying multiple perspectives on the same events would enhance characteristics of open-mindedness relative to works embodying a single, dominant perspective. This claim is implicit in the tradition of modernist experimentation, particularly through the influential writings of Brecht,[24] and echoed in the psychological literature on narrative "transportation," which suggests that immersion in a single perspective inhibits the ability to perceive and weigh other perspectives.[25] Adult participants in the experimental groups watched different versions of the final sequence of Quentin Tarantino's *Jackie Brown*, while child participants watched different versions of a segment of the animated film *Hoodwinked!* The groups watched either a version that presented the events leading up to a final scene from multiple perspectives (as in the original films) or a version that was edited to restrict the perspective to a single character

20. E.g., Stacie Friend, "Narrating the Truth (More or Less)," in *Knowing Art: Essays in Aesthetics and Epistemology*, ed. M. Kieran and D. M. Lopes (Cham: Springer, 2006): 35–50; Christoph Baumberger, "Art and Understanding: In Defence of Aesthetic Cognitivism," in *Bilder sehen: Perspektiven der Bildwissenschaft*, ed. Mark Greenlee et al. (Regensburg: Schnell & Steiner, 2013), 41–67.

21. Richard Wollheim, *Painting as an Art* (London: Thames & Hudson, 1987); Kendall L. Walton, *Mimesis as Make-Believe: On the Foundations of the Representational Arts* (Cambridge, MA: Harvard University Press, 1990).

22. Murray Smith, *Engaging Characters: Fiction, Emotion, and the Cinema*, 2nd ed. (Oxford: Oxford University Press, 2022).

23. Matthew Kieran, "Art, Imagination, and the Cultivation of Morals," *Journal of Aesthetics and Art Criticism* 54, no. 4 (1996): 337–51.

24. Murray Smith, "The Logic and Legacy of Brechtianism," in *Post-Theory: Reconstructing Film Studies*, ed. David Bordwell and Noël Carroll (Madison: University of Wisconsin Press, 1996), 130–48.

25. Melanie C. Green and Timothy C. Brock, "The Role of Transportation in the Persuasiveness of Public Narrative," *Journal of Personality and Social Psychology* 79 (2000): 701–21.

before the same final scene. In this study we also recorded "online" measures while participants watched the final scenes, using eye-tracking and heart-rate measurements. By combining multiple measures to identify attentional and affective responses in both adults and children, and whether/how they predict changes in open-mindedness, we aimed to go beyond previous research in providing insights into the mechanisms through which film influences aesthetic experience. We hypothesized that attentional/affective responses would differ when single versus multiple perspectives have been presented, and that these responses would predict differences in our open-mindedness measures.

Study 3: Realistic and Fantastic

The imagination plays a significant role in discussions of aesthetic cognitivism. On one hand, the fact that art traffics in the imaginary is sometimes highlighted by skeptics of its educative potential; on the other, the contribution of imagination is thought to be key to art's distinctive cognitive value.[26] For example, fictions are often compared to thought experiments in philosophy and science, which forward understanding by prompting us to imagine counterfactual scenarios.[27] Baumberger, who argues that "literary fictions are thought experiments," suggests that fictions thereby prompt us to adopt new perspectives, ask new questions, and develop new categories.[28]

In this study, which is ongoing at the time of writing and includes both adults and children, we test the hypothesis that films inviting more significant leaps of imagination will have a greater influence on many characteristics of open-mindedness than relatively realistic films. This prediction draws on findings in psychology indicating that situating events in fantastical/far-off worlds helps children reason more logically,[29] and engaging in counterfactual thinking increases adults' openness to alternative possibilities.[30] Intriguingly, recent research has reported negative effects of watching films with fantastical content:[31] Children's

26. E.g., Gordon Graham, *Philosophy of the Arts: An Introduction to Aesthetics*, 3rd ed. (London: Routledge, 2005).

27. Catherine Z. Elgin, *True Enough* (Cambridge, MA: MIT Press, 2017).

28. Baumberger, "Art and Understanding," 41–67.

29. E.g., M. G. Dias and P. L. Harris, "The Effect of Make-Believe Play on Deductive Reasoning," *British Journal of Developmental Psychology* 6 (1988): 207–21.

30. E.g., Adam D. Galinsky and Gordon B. Moskowitz, "Perspective-Taking: Decreasing Stereotype Expression, Stereotype Accessibility, and In-Group Favoritism," *Journal of Personality and Social Psychology* 78 (2000): 708–24.

31. Sinéad M. Rhodes, Tracy M. Steward, and Margarita Kanevski, "Immediation Impact of

cognitive flexibility was poorer compared to watching reality-based clips, perhaps because keeping track of unexpected content depleted cognitive resources; so we predicted that we would find cognitive flexibility negatively impacted, at least for children. For this study, we are using clips from films that include both realistic and fantastic segments, with adult and child participants randomly assigned to watch clips that have been edited to present either exclusively realistic content or both realistic and fantastic content, from *Coco*, *Soul*, *Luca*, or *Encanto*.

We have now completed data collection for two of the three studies (totaling N = 250 adult participants and N = 150 child participants, where N is the sample size for each experiment), including the real-time measures of eye movements and heart rate. Coding and analysis are complete for the adult data in studies 1 and 2, and we are on track to complete coding and analysis of the child data in study 2 before the project end date. Study 3 materials have all been prepared (including newly edited film clips) and the study preregistration has been submitted; data collection began in September 2023.

From data collection so far, we have not found effects on our measures of open-mindedness, nor have all the measures we used correlated systematically. Although this is a negative result, it has prompted us to recognize a need for a new concept of open-mindedness that can apply to the arts, which we have begun developing; we have also made plans to develop a new measure for the concept, if we can obtain further funding. At the same time, we did find differences between the two experimental groups in study 2 with respect to our "online" measures of eye-tracking and heart-rate monitoring, which we are in the process of analyzing. The full data sets, once coded and posted on our Open Science Framework project page, will be available to researchers for further research and will thus be a major legacy of the project.

Although the project is not yet completed, it has already generated a number of papers on aesthetic cognitivism, including several that are forthcoming. For example, the lead researchers on the team (Stacie Friend, Angela Nyhout, Murray Smith, and Heather Ferguson) have coauthored "Moral Understanding and Media: Meeting the Challenges of Interdisciplinary Research," which is now published in a special issue of *Journal of Media Psychology* on media and moral understanding (vol. 36, 2024). In this article we propose a framework for interdisciplinary research, focusing on how media can influence moral understanding. We first out-

---

Fantastical Television Content on Children's Executive Function," *British Journal of Developmental Psychology* 38 (2019): 268–88; but see Claire Essex et al., "Understanding the Differential Impact of Children's TV on Executive Functions: A Narrative-Processing Analysis," *Infant Behavior and Development* 66 (2022): article number 101661, https://doi.org/10.1016/j.infbeh.2021.101661.

line the challenges that must be met for such research to be successful, including clarifying and operationalizing concepts, measuring moral understanding, and applying empirical methods to media and the arts. We then describe the advantages of interdisciplinary collaboration for meeting these challenges, in the context of some recent examples of interdisciplinary projects on related themes.

Furthermore, three theoretical papers have been published recently or are due to be published in the near future. In the first,[32] I offer an overview of theories of fiction in philosophy and related disciplines, while considering reasons to be skeptical that fiction can be defined by the contrast between imagination and belief. I conclude by considering the implications for learning from fiction. In the second,[33] I argue that the way we learn facts from fiction is essential to explaining several other cognitive values often attributed to fictions. I further suggest that truth and accuracy may contribute, not just to the cognitive value of a work of fiction, but also to its value as fictional literature. In the third,[34] Murray Smith elaborates the connections between filmmaking, creativity, and imagination. Noting that filmmaking is not restricted to artistic production but has diverse uses as a medium of representation, Smith addresses the question whether creativity arises uniquely in relation to aesthetic and artistic uses of film, or in fact to a much wider array of filmmaking.

In addition to these papers, empirical papers reporting results from our studies are in progress. The lead author on these papers is a postdoctoral research associate on the project, Francesca Carbone (another research associate, Abigail Pitt, also contributed, along with the rest of the research team). The first paper, currently under review, is "Art Opening Minds: An Experimental Study of Film Complexity and Perspectives on Open-Mindedness." This paper presents results from the adult participants in studies 1 and 2, concerning formal complexity and perspectives. The second article, "Single vs. Multiple Perspectives in Films: The Impact on Children's Open-Mindedness," will present the results of study 2 on children. These two papers include data from both the open-mindedness and the online measures. We plan a third paper reporting the results of study 3, "Art Opening Children and Adults' Minds: Realistic vs. Fantastic in Film."

32. Stacie Friend, "Belief, Imagination, and the Nature of Fiction," in *The Routledge Handbook of Fiction and Belief*, ed. Alison James, Akihito Kubo, and Françoise Lavocat (New York: Routledge, 2023), 15–27.

33. Stacie Friend, "Fiction, Belief, and Understanding," in *Proceedings of the European Society of Aesthetics*, vol. 15, ed. V. Moura and C. Vaughan (Fribourg: European Society for Aesthetics, 2023), 185–204.

34. Murray Smith, "Imagination, Creativity and Film," in *The Oxford Handbook of Imagination and Creativity*, ed. Amy Kind and Julia Langkau (Oxford: Oxford University Press, 2024).

Finally, two of the lead researchers on the project have contributed to a meta-analysis of studies examining the social and cognitive effects of reading fiction, a closely related topic within aesthetic cognitivism. In that article,[35] we present one meta-analysis synthesizing results from experimental studies (meta-analysis 1) and another synthesizing results from correlational studies (meta-analysis 2). The results of both provide evidence of a small-sized but positive relationship between reading fiction and cognitive benefits.

As this overview indicates, the project has been successful in several respects, not least in demonstrating the value of interdisciplinary research in investigating aesthetic cognitivism. The team developed and improved skills in manipulating films to test specific features and more generally in effectively designing empirical studies guided by theoretical frames from philosophy and film. In addition, the online measures of eye-tracking and heart-rate monitoring generated a rich mine of data that we expect to lead us in new directions.

That said, we would make some changes in any continuation of the project. First, we would raise the age range of the child participants in our studies (which was eight to twelve years). We chose this range due to evidence indicating that this was when children had developed an understanding of the formal features of film; however, the younger children in our studies have had difficulty remaining attentive to the film clips. Second, we could consider using other online measures to examine the real-time processes that are active while observers are engaging with arts. For example, neuroimaging methods would offer novel insights into the brain's distinctive responses to film. Third, we would aim to develop a new measure of open-mindedness. We are motivated by the fact that we did not detect effects on the measures we used even though there were interesting differences between viewers watching a scene after exposure to single versus multiple perspectives. In this respect, our research has raised a key question, namely: *How can we best measure open-mindedness? In particular, how can we best measure the effects of artworks that we typically describe as "opening our minds" and "expanding our horizons"?*

As noted above, we are currently developing a new concept of open-mindedness. We take as our starting point Jason Baehr's proposal that open-mindedness essentially involves the transcendence of one's own perspective.[36] However, we broaden this beyond its role in acquiring true beliefs and associate it

35. Lena Wimmer et al., "Cognitive Effects and Correlates of Reading Fiction: Two Pre-Registered Multi-Level Meta-Analyses," *Journal of Experimental Psychology: General* 153, no. 6 (2024): 1464–88.

36. Jason Baehr, *The Inquiring Mind: On Intellectual Virtues and Virtue Epistemology* (Oxford: Oxford University Press, 2011).

with experiences of spirituality and insight. We also distinguish open-mindedness in this sense from close cousins including intellectual humility, gullibility, and epistemic curiosity, and from opposing vices such as dogmatism and cognitive rigidity. Psychologists have developed measures of related traits, for instance "openness" as a Big Five personality trait,[37] as well as a flurry of recent measures of intellectual humility.[38] But there is no measure of open-mindedness that can plausibly capture this potential effect of engagement with art.

The project has prompted other new research questions, in addition to the question of how best to conceptualize and measure open-mindedness in relation to art. The questions we would pursue if we obtained funding for a longer research program include:

To what extent does post-viewing reflection or discussion make a difference to film's influences on open-mindedness? We are inspired to raise this question by the Art Seeking Understanding program "Character Engagement and Moral Understanding in Screen Stories," in which the investigators postulate that such post-viewing experiences likely impact moral understanding. We are interested in distinguishing between the effects of watching films with and without individual reflection, and with and without group discussion, as well as considering what sorts of discussions might have the most impact.

How much difference does it make to the real-time experience and to the cognitive effects of film whether one watches alone or together? Due to constraints of time and equipment, in our project we were able to measure the effects only on individuals watching a film. However, recent research has demonstrated that inter-brain couplings are crucial for building a shared social world,[39] and this method is increasingly being used to study real-life social interactions.[40] We would therefore be eager to deploy new technologies to compare effects while watching film in different social contexts.

In what ways do spirituality and religiosity mediate changes in open-mindedness? Although open-mindedness is typically considered an intellectual

37. See Thompson, "Development and Validation," 542–48.

38. E.g., Elizabeth J. Krumrei-Mancuso and Steven V. Rouse, "The Development and Validation of the Comprehensive Intellectual Humility Scale," *Journal of Personality Assessment* 98 (2016): 209–21; Mark R. Leary et al., "Cognitive and Interpersonal Features of Intellectual Humility," *Personality and Social Psychology Bulletin* 43 (2017): 793–813; Tenelle Porter and Karina Schumann, "Intellectual Humility and Openness to the Opposing View," *Self and Identity* 17 (2018): 139–62.

39. Uri Hasson et al., "Brain-to-Brain Coupling: A Mechanism for Creating and Sharing a Social World," *Trends in Cognitive Sciences* 16 (2012): 114–21.

40. See Artur Czeszumski et al., "Hyperscanning: A Valid Method to Study Neural Inter-Brain Underpinnings of Social Interaction," *Frontiers in Human Neuroscience* 14 (2020): article number 39, https://doi.org/10.3389/fnhum.2020.00039 for a review.

virtue, this assumption has been challenged. As noted above, one concern is distinguishing open-mindedness from gullibility. Being open to any beliefs or perspectives whatsoever is more likely to be damaging than otherwise, especially in the current climate of disinformation and polarization. Another concern is how open-mindedness can be compatible with deeply held convictions, including religious convictions. Furthermore, some studies indicate that people who self-identify as spiritual (i.e., personally engaged with sacredness) score high on openness as a Big Five personality trait, whereas people who self-identify as religious (i.e., adhering to a particular creed or practice) score lower.[41] We suspect that the contrast arises, at least in part, from an overly narrow conception of open-mindedness that does not capture the potential effects of engagement with art and film.

How might watching film in an educational context influence the effects of film on children's open-mindedness? The restriction of our research so far to individuals watching films alone extends to the child participants in our studies. But children are often exposed to film and other media together, in school and related contexts, where this is typically accompanied by discussion. Moreover, as noted above, educating for open-mindedness is often an explicit pedagogical goal. We would be interested in studying the effects of film outside the lab, moving our research into schools where we think films may have a greater impact.

Does the study of the arts have a long-term impact on open-mindedness? Like most experimental work in psychology, the studies we have undertaken in our current project have tested the effects of one-off interventions. However, it is plausible that any long-term effects on open-mindedness require cumulative experience rather than one exposure to (part of) a film. Moreover, there may be differences between those who engage with the arts as casual spectators and those who engage with them either as producers or as serious objects of study. To examine these questions, longitudinal comparisons of students in different disciplines would be ideal.

Taking stock: Thus far we have not been able to empirically demonstrate a connection between cinematic art and open-mindedness. However, we have made progress in developing a better concept of open-mindedness and in identifying further methods of research, which we believe are more likely to illuminate the cognitive values of engaging with the arts. By deploying these methods, we can make progress on the mission of the ASU strategy, to determine the conditions

41. E.g., H. Streib, C. Klein, and R. W. Hood, "Personality Dimensions and Versions of 'Spirituality,'" in *Semantics and Psychology of Spirituality: A Cross-Cultural Analysis*, ed. H. Streib and R. W. Hood (Cham: Springer, 2016), 189–203; John W. Lace et al., "Five-Factor Model Personality Traits and Self-Classified Religiousness and Spirituality," *Journal of Religion and Health* 59, no. 3 (2020): 1344–69.

under which engagement with the arts stimulates spiritual understanding, insight, or growth. Specifically, we can explore the ways in which engaging with film can encourage people to transcend their own limited, self-oriented perspectives, opening them to new experiences and a greater understanding of reality, both visible and spiritual. By gathering more comprehensive data concerning people's real-time experiences of film, we can also make progress on the question of how artworks have these effects. For example, we can identify those moments in films that generate attentional and affective response and see how these relate to effects on open-mindedness. Making this kind of progress would fulfill the promise of interdisciplinary research into aesthetic cognitivism.

23

A Cognitive Exploration of the Arts and Empathy

Kelly James Clark

When I was a little boy in the early '60s, my father directed the Community School at Lincoln Elementary School in Kalamazoo, Michigan. Lincoln School was in Kalamazoo's Black north side, literally just over the tracks from Kalamazoo's White south side. My brother and I spent a lot of time at Lincoln School—every weekday in the summers and, during the school year, at least one evening a week and most Saturdays. We played basketball, raced around, took swimming lessons, and just hung out with Charlie and Leroy and Debbie and Jimmie and Earl and Curtis and countless others. It was a magical place to grow up.

While I could easily see the substantial White-Black differences in housing and clothing, I wasn't aware that all US cities were segregated, ensuring generational poverty for most Black people. On the White side, I would hear that the north side was the ghetto. I recall hearing, again on the White side of the tracks, a host of dehumanizing names (you know them), names that "justified" White people's historic mistreatment of Blacks.

I remember taking a Boy Scout camping trip to northern Michigan and having to drive through the north side (the ghetto). Before we crossed the tracks into the north side, our driver, one of the dads, insisted that we roll up our windows and lock our doors and not look anyone in the eye because, he said, you don't know what they might do. I recall his relief when we had safely passed through the threatening north side. I remember thinking, "How can he say this? He doesn't know Charlie and Leroy and Debbie and Jimmie and Earl and Curtis, and countless others."

Charlie, by the way, would go on to earn his PhD and become Magic Johnson's agent; Leroy would become a prominent educator, and Jimmie a distinguished Navy veteran. Debbie went to a formerly all-White university, and then was a devoted teacher of young children. Earl would become Vice President of Upjohn (Pfizer), and Curtis a boxing coach who teaches impoverished children discipline and success. And countless others.

But not without the Civil Rights Act, passed when American congressional leaders united together to overcome fear and ferocious opposition. The Civil Rights Act offered legislation that prohibited discrimination on the basis of race. I remember the north side's joyous celebration when the US finally passed the Civil Rights Act in 1964.

Fear closed my driver's windows and doors, preventing him from seeing Charlie and Leroy and Debbie and Jimmie and Earl and Curtis and countless others as individual human beings *like him* with hopes and dreams for a better future. He saw Charlie and Leroy and Debbie and Jimmie and Earl and Curtis and countless others as "one of them"—less than fully human, living in their self-imposed ghetto.

But he is not alone. Fear, I've come to learn, does that to all of us. It not only makes us think the worst of others, it makes us blame and scapegoat others. And if we can blame "them" for crime, say, or drugs or rape or theft, then we can "justify" disadvantaging and even harming them.

Sadly, though it is four-plus decades since the Civil Rights Act, we continue to harm Black people with racially-biased police, juries, prisons, sheriffs, schools, and vigilantes. Blacks, indeed all people we deem as less human than ourselves, get harsher jail sentences, more frequent death penalties, worse jobs, and lower pay. Why, after centuries of slavery and decades of discrimination, did the US determine that, as a matter of law and principle, Blacks and Whites are equal?

I don't know the exact numbers but, during the time of slavery, most White people in the south and many Whites in the north considered Blacks to be both deficient in rationality and superior in strength; as such, Blacks are by nature suited to slavery. Whites could and would probe a potential slave's body as they might that of a cow, sizing up their hocks and checking their teeth. Whites could and would then bid without blinking on a husband but not a wife—disrespecting both their humanity and the sanctity of marriage. White slave owners would beat their slaves, whom they owned, into submission as they might a stubborn donkey. I could go on, but you get the point. White slave owners dehumanized slaves in ways that made owning them and treating them like animals seem right and good. What the owners lacked, so it seems, was empathy—the ability to feel their pain or understand their plight and, then, to seek to relieve it.

How, one might wonder, after centuries of treating Blacks as sub-humans did people in the US pass a law requiring the treatment of Blacks with respect and all of the human rights that entails?[1] While I suspect that enacting the Civil Rights

1. I assume that "treating Blacks with respect and all of the human rights that entails" is a work in progress.

Act was motivated by increasing human empathy (among Whites, the majority power) in ways that moved White people to create laws that would (in principle) permit the full and equal flourishing of Blacks, I still don't fully understand *how* and *why* there was an increase in empathy at the time (about 60 percent of Americans supported the Civil Rights Act in 1964).

There was, of course, the civil rights movement of the 1950s and '60s, which aimed at erasing the lingering and debilitating effects of racism (discrimination, Jim Crow Laws, segregation) since the abolition of slavery. Post-slavery Blacks were mostly low-wage farm or factory workers, forbidden from entering the same facilities (from restaurants to restrooms) or neighborhoods or schools as privileged White people. Although countless Blacks fought bravely for freedom in WWII, they returned to the USA to find their freedoms curtailed. So, Blacks—from Rosa Parks to Stokely Carmichael to Martin Luther King Jr.—peacefully fought just as bravely for the full and flourishing freedom of the USA's Black citizens. But the rising up of "uppity" Blacks was met with a great deal of resistance and resentment, especially in the South. So there must be more to the story than just the civil rights movement (crucial as it was).

I know this—a lot of White youth, including myself, sang along to a lot of catchy songs that raised awareness of and spoke against racial, social, and economic injustice and inequality. Maybe after singing a song over and over and over again, the words and tunes worked their way into our bones, changing our feelings and thoughts toward the oppressed and dispossessed. Maybe such songs generated such a profound understanding of and feeling for the plight of Blacks that it engendered actions aimed at racial and social equality (empathy producing justice).

Let me take a moment to consider just a few of those songs. In "Inner City Blues (Makes Me Wanna Holler)," Marvin Gaye speaks out against the misplaced priorities of a society which spent money on "rockets, moon shots" instead of "spend[ing] it on the have nots"; rich politicians take our money, "money, we make it," and "fore we see it you take it" to spend on a war which was disproportionately fought by the impoverished ("send that boy off to die"). Gaye also laments "trigger happy policing" in response to increasing inner-city crime caused by desperate people doing desperate things to resolve their desperate economic circumstances.

We not only sang along with Black soul singers we also sang along with White folk singers. Pete Seeger's "We Shall Overcome" was one of the civil rights movement's most popular songs. Sung as a gospel song its refrain—

Deep in my heart,
I do believe
We shall overcome, someday[2]

—echoed from Montgomery, Alabama to Washington, DC. The song was quoted by President Lyndon Johnson to Congress and sung to 300,000 by Joan Baez at the Lincoln Memorial. Every school child in the nation likely joined in on its clarion call for peace:

We shall live in peace,
We shall live in peace,
We shall live in peace, someday.[3]

I suspect that more American children could sing "We Shall Overcome" than recite the Pledge of Allegiance.

Although Bob Dylan never explicitly mentions race in "The Times They Are A-Changin'," it was nonetheless an anthemic warning against racial bigotry:

How many roads must a man walk down
Before you call him a man?

To congressmen and senators:

The battle outside ragin'
Will soon shake your windows
And rattle your walls.[4]

The times they are a-changin' and Dylan sought to inspire us to be agents of that change.

Nina Simone wrote the wrenching, angry lyrics to "Mississippi Goddam" after she learned of the murder of four young Black girls in the bombing of the 16th Street Baptist Church in Birmingham, Alabama on September 15, 1963. After lamenting the sorry and savage treatment of Blacks in the Deep South, Simone cries out

2. Pete Seeger, "We Shall Overcome," Lyrics.com, https://tinyurl.com/bdzdbar6.
3. Pete Seeger, "We Shall Overcome."
4. Bob Dylan, "Blowin' in the Wind," Genius.com, https://tinyurl.com/2b8hr55p.

> All I want is equality
> For my sister, my brother, my people, and me.[5]

Billie Holiday's "Strange Fruit" is likewise rooted in a characteristically savage and all-too-common treatment of post–Civil War Blacks (although they could no longer enslave Blacks, southern Whites were determined to terrorize/control them, sometimes through lynchings); the song portrays the horrors of lynching as a form of racial terrorism, comparing the victims' bodies to a "strange and bitter crop." The song begins,

> Southern trees bear a strange fruit
> Blood on the leaves and blood at the root
> Black body swinging in the Southern breeze
> Strange fruit hanging from the poplar trees.[6]

It goes downhill from there.

Did music, does music, create the empathy that motivates justice (in this case, the Civil Rights Act of 1964)?

A Summing Up

I have so far written a non-fiction narrative, mostly a sort of autobiography, bringing in mini-stories of other people along the way. I also inserted narrative songs in my non-fiction narrative, songs of pain and revolt and hope and peace. I used narratives because, although I am trained in the way of argument, I have learned that offering evidence against a position moves people more to extremes *and* makes them more dogmatic.[7] If you really want someone to change their minds, narrative is vastly more effective. My narrative aimed at getting the reader not only to think sympathetically about the importance of the Civil Rights Act of 1964 but also to begin getting the reader to think (realize?) that the dehumanization of Blacks in pre–Civil War and Jim Crow America, the dehumanization that engendered their tragic mistreatment, was rooted in a lack of empathy. Finally, I used narrative to motivate the suggestion that songs—narratives set to music—may

5. Nina Simone, "Mississippi Goddam," Genius.com, https://tinyurl.com/2sftzt76.

6. Billie Holiday, "Strange Fruit," Genius.com, https://tinyurl.com/22pdan82.

7. Eleanor Gordon-Smith, *Stop Being Reasonable: How We Really Change Minds* (New York: Public Affairs, 2019); Lee C. McIntyre, *How to Talk to a Science Denier: Conversations with Flat Earthers, Climate Deniers, and Others Who Defy Reason* (Cambridge, MA: MIT Press, 2021).

have contributed to the cultivation of empathy in ways that led the majority of Americans to a change in their beliefs and affections, a change so dramatic, they began to see Blacks as fully human and, thus, fully deserving of human rights. The narrative arts were deliberately used instead of argument to generate sympathetic understanding. But what if I had been able to set the narrative to music?

So, I ask directly: does music create empathy, empathy across deeply troubled divides, empathy of the sort that moves people to act justly?

The Arts and Empathy

I directed an eighteen-month Templeton Religion Trust (TRT)–funded research project seeking to answer the more general question—do the arts create empathy, empathy across deeply troubled divides, empathy of the sort that moves people to act justly? Our team included mostly social and cognitive scientists but also philosophers and theologians; it included visual artists, writers, and a professional musician; it included both theoreticians and people actively involved in conflict resolution, one in Israel-Palestine; finally, our Muslim or Christian or Jewish or atheist or agnostic team members hailed from Israel, Jordan, Turkey, the Netherlands, India, the USA, and England. We discussed together the state of social and neuroscience studies on the arts and empathy/justice, and then we worked on developing empirical studies which would advance the science of the arts and empathy/justice across religiously troubled divides. We then conducted pilot projects, some of which proved sufficiently powerful to submit for publication.

There is intuitive support for supposing a connection between the arts, on the one hand, and empathy/justice, on the other. If you reflected on my opening narrative, you may have noticed just such a connection. Moreover, it's common to view artists as social activists, claiming that artists/art are deeply implicated in key social movements throughout history. Many artistic works are aimed at making people aware of both social injustice and the need for social change. From Picasso's *Guernica* to Ai Weiwei's "Sunflower Seeds" to Banksy's street art, visual artists have famously made us aware of the tragedy of war, for example, and treating people like commodities, pointing as they also do toward peace and justice. Nonfiction narratives like *The Autobiography of Malcolm X* and *Black Like Me*, along with fictional narratives like *Uncle Tom's Cabin* and *The Color Purple*, powerfully communicate the savagery of slavery and racial segregation and generational poverty. I've already mentioned several songs that aim at moving the listener from racial bias to justice.

Does art really have the transformative power to cultivate empathy, again, empathy of the sort that moves people to justice?

Before proceeding, it behooves us to gain a more accurate understanding of empathy. Empathy comes in two shapes and sizes—affective and cognitive. Roughly speaking, *cognitive empathy* refers to the experience of comprehending and relating to another person's thoughts and perspectives. It differs from *affective empathy*, which refers to resonating with and sharing another's emotions. Like all human emotions, affective empathy has a cognitive aspect, but it is impossible and even undesirable for humans to have *affective* empathy for all other human beings. We are not able to sustain the energy required to actually share feelings with every suffering person to whom we owe mercy, respect and justice. Yet *cognitive* empathy, our understanding of what life is like for another being, can indeed be cultivated and consistently applied in order to create a more just world.

It is natural and often relatively easy to cultivate empathy for one's children, family, and tribe (i.e., similar and like-minded individuals). However, it is vastly more difficult—both evolutionarily and cognitively—to cultivate empathy for those *outside* of one's perceived tribe, including those who've been othered and dehumanized. We aimed at exploring some of the cognitive mechanisms that build bridges from in-group to out-group, from dehumanization to humanization.

Out-group divides take many forms—social, religious, political, economic, racial, and geographic—and they include forms of dehumanization grounded in stigma, shame and honor, scapegoating, etc. Symptoms of in-group/out-group divides include racism, religious persecution and exploitation, structural oppression, and social isolation through mocking, shaming, and denials of personhood, rights, and social participation. Such troubled divides actively perpetuate great harms around the world, inhibiting justice and preventing human flourishing at many levels. As such, we took in-group/out-group divides and dehumanization/humanization as sites of study. We recognized cognitive empathy as a bridge across such divides, and studies of its cultivation as critical to human well-being.

Finally, in-group/out-group divides inhibit *justice*—a concept which itself takes many forms. While the standard philosophical definition of justice may be something like "getting and giving what is deserved," social-psychological studies tend to operationalize the concept of "justice" by studying "cooperation," "prosocial behavior," "moral circles," or "fairness," all of which can be affected by cognitive empathy.[8] In other words, as a society, our collective pursuit of justice and

8. Karolina Urbanska, Shelley McKeown, and Laura Taylor, "From Injustice to Action: The Role of Empathy and Perceived Fairness to Address Inequality via Victim Compensation," *Journal of Experimental Social Psychology*, no. 82 (2019): 129–40; J. Decety and J. M. Cowell, "Empathy, Justice, and Moral Behavior," *AJOB Neuroscience* 6, no. 3 (2015): 3–14.

its related effects require that we develop a greater understanding of cognitive empathy and the ways in which it can be cultivated.

People are more likely to be just toward others for whom they have empathy, empathetic people appreciate the arts more than non-empathetic people, and empathetic people are more likely to benefit from the art's empathetic effects. Can, do the arts cultivate empathy, cognitive or affective, that finds expression in justice?

Our Pilot Studies

While evolutionary psychology suggests that music can increase one's sense of their collective, thus binding groups together, studies also suggest that music may expand one's in-group—one's sense of who is human and, therefore, deserving of care, respect, and justice. But we don't know how, cognitively and neuroscientifically, empathy creation happens, whether and how music uniquely or distinctively supports it, and whether and how these effects can be applied for the express purpose of humanizing populations in ways that prevent harm and encourage flourishing.

Our early pilots suggest (not unequivocally) that music can make us more empathetic; they also raise noteworthy questions such as: what kind of music generates this effect? How does music do this, for whom, and under what conditions? Are the effects short-term or long-term? And can these effects be generated via concrete, scalable strategies in order to meaningfully bridge deep and troubling divides?

Our international, interdisciplinary teams conducted original scholarly research in the USA, Israel, the UK, and Turkey—to understand the effects of the arts and, especially, music on empathy and justice across troubled divides. Such divides include social, religious, political, racial, economic, and geographic differences, as well as many forms of dehumanization grounded in stigma and shame. I will present the results of just three of our studies, two of which were quite robust and are headed for publication, and the third more suggestive at this state.

Sufi Music, Empathy, and Well-Being

Music has been used as a healing form from primitive times, with this having been witnessed all around the world. The primitive version of using the healing power of music pertained to it being a way to communicate with God. However, when Greek philosophers explored the special effect of music upon people via very basic experimental improvisations—for example, Plato played musical modes to make people sleep, laugh or cry when they gathered around him—it was found that producing or listening to music had an effect upon people's moods, even if those effects were not entirely clear. Rumeysa Nur Dogan (University of Ankara) conducted a pilot study on the effects of Sufi music on the cultivation of empathy. The modal music system known as "Sufi *makam* music" was one of the original theories of music therapy that was created in medieval times.[9] *Makam* refers to a predefined system that consists of scales that have dominant notes distinguished by *seyir*—its melodic progression. Over six hundred *makams* have been identified so far, although only a small number are currently used. Makam music theory lies at the heart of Turkish classical music; it can also be found in many cultures including Arabic (*maqam*), Persian (*dastgah*), Jewish and Israeli music (weekly *maqam*), Central Asian (in Uzbekistan and Tajikistan *shashmaqom*, in Western China *mukam*), and Indian (*raga*) music theories.

Although their effects differ from person to person, every kind of music may have a spiritual effect upon a person.[10] And although the words "spiritual" and "religious" may be used interchangeably from time to time, in the discipline of music the word "religious" indicates a narrower style, while the word "spiritual" finds its place in almost every musical genre. Religious music is defined as music pieces that are "composed for religious purposes or are focused on religious or sacred topics" (such as gospel, contemporary Christian, and Islamic rhymes [*ilahi*]).[11] Religious music and its therapeutic use within the mental health area have been newly incorporated into such investigations.[12] However, in contrast to religious music, no attempts have been made to identify a spiritual music genre. Some classical music pieces, which are commonly used within music therapies because of their ability to make the listener feel calm, serene and peaceful, have a spiritual effect.[13] However, no study related to spiritual music or its use in the mental health area has been undertaken to date.

The mechanisms of action of this type of music intervention are based on the belief that particular musical modes (*makams*), aided by the spiritual nature of

9. S. B. Benek et al., "An Example for the Application of Music Therapy in the Medical History: Divrigi Darüssifa," *Acta Medica Anatolia* 3, no. 2 (2015).

10. Willyane de Andrade Alvarenga et al., "The Effect of Music on the Spirituality of Patients: A Systematic Review," *Journal of Holistic Nursing* 36, no. 2 (2018): 192–204.

11. Matt Bradshaw et al., "Listening to Religious Music and Mental Health in Later Life," *Gerontologist* 55, no. 6 (2015): 961–71.

12. Jill B. Hamilton et al., "You Need a Song to Bring You Through: The Use of Religious Songs to Manage Stressful Life Events," *Gerontologist* 53, no. 1 (2013): 26–38; Jill B. Hamilton et al., "Younger African American Adults' Use of Religious Songs to Manage Stressful Life Events," *Journal of Religion and Health* 56, no. 1 (2017): 329–44; Hani Raoul Khouzam et al., "Use of a Religious Hymn in Remission of Symptoms of Social Phobia (Social Anxiety Disorder): A Case Study," *Psychological Reports* 96, no. 2 (2005): 411–21.

13. H. L. Bonny, "Music and Spirituality," *Music Therapy Perspectives* 19, no. 1 (2001): 59–62.

the Sufi instruments, impact specific diseases. Throughout the Seljukian Dynasty and Ottoman Empire Age, Turkish *makam* music played with Sufi instruments (combined with the sounds of water running in a fountain) was used to treat mentally ill patients. The earliest records of this music therapy in Turkish mental hospitals date back to the ninth century.

A number of randomized controlled trials (RCTs) of the effectiveness of Sufi music with *makams* has been published in recent decades. A systematic review and meta-analysis of the effects of Sufi music on mental well-being found evidence to suggest that it may reduce state-anxiety in patients undergoing an operation or treatment such as chemotherapy.[14] However, only a limited number of studies have examined the use of Sufi music in people with common mental health disorders. Moreover, the quality of the studies was low, and all of the studies have been conducted in Turkey. It is not clear whether Sufi *makam* music is beneficial for people from other cultures and those living outside of Turkey where they have not been exposed to Turkish culture. Moreover, none of the studies examined the effects of Sufi music on people with anxiety or depression. A recent feasibility study suggested that Sufi music therapy intervention was found to be feasible, acceptable and convenient to deliver, and the recruitment and retention rates in the intervention group were high. Furthermore, assessment of the clinical outcomes suggests that the intervention may reduce anxiety and improve mental and spiritual well-being. However, in this study, the results of listening to Sufi music were not compared with other musical genres and thus the clinical results in this trial were limited; even the authors conceded that the therapeutic benefits may be due solely to the act of listening to music in general rather than to Sufi music in particular.

Gurbuz-Dogan conducted a randomized study to evaluate whether Sufi *makam* music therapy is effective in improving empathy and spiritual well-being. Her team evaluated the efficacy of Sufi *makam* music in empathy, intergroup relations and spiritual well-being. The study sought to assess both the acceptability of Sufi *makam* music for well-being among contemporary students and to assess recruitment and retention rates of participants as well as their adherence to the intervention. Finally, and most importantly, the study sought to make a preliminary assessment of the effects of Sufi *makam* music intervention on empathy and spiritual well-being.

This study comprised a randomized, controlled, two-group design with assessments at the baseline, at the second week of the therapy, at the end of the

14. R. N. Gurbuz-Dogan et al., "The Effectiveness of Sufi Music for Mental Health Outcomes: A Systematic Review and Meta-Analysis of 21 Randomised Trials," *Complementary Therapies in Medicine* 57 (2021).

fourth and last session, and in a follow-up two weeks later. Participants were randomly assigned to the music therapy group ($n = 25$) and the wait list control group ($n = 25$). The study consisted of two different groups: (1) participants who listened to *makam* music weekly for four weeks, and (2) participants who attended regular activities at the university. The study was conducted in Ankara between January 2023 and February 2023.

For the music listening group, a quiet room was arranged by the university. All sessions took place in this room. Music listening was a group activity with participants listening to music pieces together. Participants received weekly emails/messages/calls as a reminder from the researcher throughout the four weeks. The music pieces, selected by the researchers, lasted about fifteen minutes. Applicants were encouraged to keep a log of notes for each listening activity. Control group participants were placed on a waiting list (and offered a chance to attend the musical activity after the intervention).

Outcomes were measured at multiple times: before randomization, at the end of the second session, at the end of the final session and two weeks after the last session. Outcome measures include:

1. The Empathy Quotient (EQ), originally a sixty-item self-report questionnaire aimed at measuring empathy[15] (with twenty items of filler and forty items for analysis). Each item is scored initially in a four-point agreement scale ranging from "strongly agree" to "strongly disagree." According to the sense of the item and the subject response, each item is then scored according to the magnitude of the empathic response, with 0 for a "non-empathic" response, and 1 for "slightly empathic" and 2 for a "strong empathic response." This version comprises twenty-eight items arranged in three different empathy dimensions: cognitive empathy (eleven items), emotional reactivity (eleven items), and social skill (six items).
2. The twelve-item Functional Assessment of Chronic Illness Therapy-Spiritual Well-Being Scale (FACIT-Sp 12) modified version for non-illness (also known as FACIT-Sp-Non-Illness) measures spiritual well-being of people under three sub-domains of spiritual well-being; peace, meaning, and faith. The scale was validated in both Turkey and the UK populations. The questionnaire uses a five-point Likert-type scale which represents scores 0 (not at all) to 4 (very much). Higher scores indicate higher level of spiritual well-being.

15. E. J. Lawrence et al., "Measuring Empathy: Reliability and Validity of the Empathy Quotient," *Psycholical Medicine* 34, no. 5 (2004): 911–19.

Data were collected at the eligibility, baseline, second week of the therapy, post-therapy (four weeks) and at two-week follow-up (six weeks). The follow-up (six-week) data were collected via telephone, post or email, according to participants' preferences.

A repeated-measures analysis of empathy scores across the four time points (T1 to T4) revealed distinct trends across the three groups: Sufi music, classical music, and control. The Sufi music group demonstrated a gradual decrease in empathy from T1 (M = 34.8, SD = 4.4) to T4 (M = 32.9, SD = 5.6) (where M = mean and SD = standard deviation). In contrast, the classical music group showed minor fluctuations, with empathy remaining relatively stable from T1 (M = 33.1, SD = 3.6) to T4 (M = 33.9, SD = 5.4). The control group exhibited a similar stable pattern, although with generally lower empathy scores, starting at T1 (M = 31.5, SD = 4.8) and fluctuating until T3 (M = 31.8, SD = 3.7), with no data available for T4. Overall, while the classical music group maintained relatively stable empathy levels, the Sufi music group showed a notable decline by T4.

The analysis of social distancing behavior scores revealed an upward trend in both the Sufi music and classical music groups. The Sufi music group saw a modest increase in social distance from T1 (M = 12.9, SD = 2.9) to T4 (M = 13.2, SD = 3.6), peaking at T3 (M = 13.9, SD = 3.3). Similarly, the classical music group exhibited a steady rise, beginning at T1 (M = 13.5, SD = 2.5) and increasing to T4 (M = 14.1, SD = 4.0). The control group showed relatively stable scores, increasing slightly from T1 (M = 12.7, SD = 2.2) to T3 (M = 13.4, SD = 3.0), with T4 data unavailable. The rise in social distance was more pronounced in the classical music group, indicating that the effect of classical music may lead to greater social distancing behavior compared to other groups.

The Sufi music group demonstrated a clear and steady improvement in mental well-being over time. Starting at T1 (M = 53.5, SD = 9.5), their well-being scores increased consistently, reaching the highest level at T4 (M = 59.2, SD = 9.4). In contrast, the classical music group experienced a decline, with well-being scores dropping from T1 (M = 53.0, SD = 11.0) to a low at T3 (M = 50.5, SD = 17.9), before recovering slightly at T4 (M = 52.5, SD = 15.9). The control group maintained relatively stable mental well-being scores, beginning at T1 (M = 52.4, SD = 8.1) and showing slight fluctuations up to T3 (M = 53.4, SD = 9.8), with no T4 data available. These results indicate that exposure to Sufi music was associated with consistent improvements in mental well-being, while classical music showed a more variable effect, with a notable dip at T3.

The findings across these three variables provide insights into the differential effects of Sufi and classical music interventions. The most significant outcome is the enhancement of mental well-being in the Sufi music group, which demonstrated a statistically significant improvement over time. This suggests that the meditative and spiritually rich nature of Sufi music may have a therapeutic effect on individuals, promoting a sense of well-being and mental balance. The classical music group, while maintaining stable empathy levels, experienced a decline in mental well-being and an increase in social distancing behavior, albeit less dramatic than in the Sufi group. These findings could suggest that, in this context, classical music does not offer the same mental health benefits as Sufi music and may even contribute to feelings of detachment or isolation and less empathy. The decline in well-being in the classical music group was notable but did not reach statistical significance. Finally, the control group, which did not receive any music intervention, showed minor increases in empathy and well-being and a slight rise in social distancing behavior. These changes were smaller in magnitude than those observed in the music groups, suggesting that the natural progression of time without intervention has less of an effect on these variables.

In conclusion, these findings highlight the potential for Sufi music to serve as an intervention to enhance mental well-being and empathy. Further research is needed to explore the mechanisms behind these effects, especially the impact of Sufi music on social distancing behavior. Classical music, while stabilizing empathy, may not be as effective in promoting mental health and may lead to some degree of social withdrawal.

Music, Religion, and Empathy

Onurcan Yilmaz (Kadir Has University, Istanbul), Gaye Soley (University of Barcelona), and Burak Dogruyol (Kadir Has University) explored whether exposure to two distinct pieces of music, which differ in qualities such as perceived holiness, would influence the moral behavior of religious individuals and atheists. This study sought to conceptually replicate the findings of Lang et al.[16] in a larger online sample. In their online experiment, one group of participants listened to Johann Sebastian Bach's "Sleepers Awake" (considered secular), another group listened to Bach's "Jesu, Joy of Man's Desiring" (considered religious), a third group was subjected to white noise (serving as an active control), and a final group was not exposed to any auditory stimulus (serving as a passive control).

To assess moral behavior, they employed the dictator game, a common tool used to measure generosity within behavioral research. In this game, a participant

16. Martin Lang et al., "Music as a Sacred Cue? Effects of Religious Music on Moral Behavior," *Frontiers in Psychology*, no. 7 (2016).

decides how much of a given sum of money to transfer to another participant, with the transferred amount serving as an indicator of generosity.

Their study had a sample size of 1717 with 47.1 percent female and a median age of 41.78; 843 participants identified as Christian and 874 participants identified as atheist.

Variables. There were four music conditions to which participants were assigned. Directly replicating Lang et al.'s methodology, they used the same music tracks in Lang's study for their manipulations. Participants listened to Johann Sebastian Bach's "Sleepers Awake" in the secular music condition. In the religious music condition, participants listened to Johann Sebastian Bach's "Jesu Joy of Man's Desiring." In the white noise condition, participants were exposed to white noise; in the control condition, no music was present. The music tracks played in the background while participants played the dictator game and answered the morality as cooperation questionnaire.

The dictator game is a one-shot economic game in which one player is active and the other is passive. In this study, the active player was given an endowment of fifty cents and asked to either share or keep some or all of this endowment. Both participants were assured that they were completely anonymous during and after the task and that no deception was used in the study. After the active player made their decision, the task ended. The dictator game allows the measure of participants' generosity in an incentivized manner.

Measures. The Morality-as-Cooperation Theory (Morality-as-Cooperation Questionnaire [MAC-Q])[17] proposes that morality evolved as a solution to cooperation problems faced by humans in their evolutionary past. The theory posits that there are seven fundamental elements to morality, and each is a solution to a different cooperation problem: The family element is related to favoring kin and blood-related individuals. Loyalty is associated with protecting the interests of one's in-group and not cooperating with out-groups. Reciprocity is related to returning favors and being trustworthy. Heroism is related to bravery and displays of hawkish behaviors in cooperative problems, while deference is related to dovish behaviors, respect for authority, and obedience. Fairness is associated with fair distribution of resources. Finally, property is related to respect toward ownership.

The TEQ (Toronto Empathy Scale)[18] is a single-factor scale used to measure participants' empathy levels. Finally, the study used the AOT (Actively Open-

17. Oliver Scott Curry et al., "Mapping Morality with a Compass: Testing the Theory of 'Morality-as-Cooperation' with a New Questionnaire," *Journal of Research in Personality* 78 (2019): 106–24.

18. R. Nathan Spreng et al., "The Toronto Empathy Questionnaire: Scale Development and Initial Validation of a Factor-Analytic Solution to Multiple Empathy Measures," *Journal of Personality Assessment* 91, no. 1 (2009): 62–71.

minded Thinking Scale) subscale of the Four-Component Thinking Styles Questionnaire[19] to measure actively open-minded thinking, which is how much an individual values reflecting on their beliefs and being open to change them when presented with counterevidence.

Procedure. Participants were randomly assigned to secular music, religious music, white noise, or control conditions. First, participants in conditions involving music were allowed to adjust the volume levels of their speakers or headphones while listening to a ten-second excerpt of their condition's auditory stimulus. After the training, participants proceeded to give answers to the dictator game and the MAC-Q, in exact order. The musical tracks in secular, religious, or white noise conditions played throughout these two tasks. Once they finished completing the MAC-Q, participants in the three music conditions were presented with the manipulation check question. Then, all participants completed the TEQ and the AOT scale. Finally, they answered the demographic questions and were directed to receive financial compensation.

Conclusion. Their findings indicated that, contra Lang et al., music exposure did not significantly affect moral behavior, despite their sample size being 2.5 times larger than that of Lang et al. While religious participants displayed significantly higher levels of generosity compared to atheists, musical exposure did not alter these patterns. But this was just one study with one type of music in one population. It is therefore important to recognize that the absence of evidence is not evidence of absence in such research. It is possible that music does have an effect, but detecting it might be challenging due to its small effect size, which could require larger sample sizes for detection. Additionally, there could be boundary conditions that moderate the impact, such as the volume of the music, listening online, or the duration of exposure to the music. Future studies should incorporate these boundary conditions as experimental variables, identify the limits of the effect, and attempt to replicate these phenomena using a broader variety of musical compositions.

Music and Meditation

Dr. Adam Green and Hemal Trivedi, PhD student, from Georgetown University's Laboratory for Relational Cognition conducted a pilot study investigating the relationship of music to empathy. This pilot study examined the effect of music-based[20] meditation on self-focused state of mind (i.e., ego dissolution). They

19. Christie Newton et al., "On the Disposition to Think Analytically: Four Distinct Intuitive-Analytic Thinking Styles," *Personality and Social Psychology Bulletin* 50, no. 6 (2023).

20. The Indian classical stringed instrument *tānpūrā*.

hypothesized that attention-directed meditation on music (*tānpūrā*) may experience selflessness, a decrease in the sense of self or ego. The presence of a self is associated with empathy that designates an in-group and out-group, a particular circle of concern. So, by decreasing the sense of self via music, participants may increase their circle of concern to include members in their out group. As a broader project, this study hypothesizes that meditation on music can increase empathy in religious individuals.

Participants included seven undergraduate students at Ibn Haldun University in Istanbul, Turkey. Ego dissolution was assessed using the Ego Dissolution Inventory (EDI),[21] before and after a mindfulness meditation session. Participants were led through a guided, twenty-minute mindfulness exercise while recorded *tānpūrā* music was played in the background. The meditation guided participants to draw their attention to three objects, in this order: the body, their breathing, and the music being played. Consistent with our hypotheses, a significant increase in ego dissolution was found. The results of this pilot study suggest that the ego may be influenced by both mindfulness and music-led meditation.[22]

Since this pilot supported the feasibility/achievability of the proposed paradigm in the proposed MRI scanner environment, we propose implementing a larger-scale study involving In-group/Out-group Empathy task performance and *tānpūrā* listening. We introduce the construct *interreligious empathy gap*[23] to measure the empathy bias religious individuals show toward their own in-group. Specifically, we will use the construct *cognitive empathy*, the ability to understand intentions, desires, and beliefs of another person.[24] A short mindfulness intervention was shown to improve cognitive empathy[25] and its related construct Theory of Mind (ToM), which refers to the ability to read the mental states of others. Furthermore, in Indian meditative practice, psychedelic therapy, and music ther-

21. Matthew M. Nour et al., "Ego-Dissolution and Psychedelics: Validation of the Ego-Dissolution Inventory (EDI)," *Frontiers of Human Neuroscience* 10 (2016).

22. It should be noted that confidence in the efficacy of the method requires replication in a larger sample.

23. S. Huang and S. Han, "Shared Beliefs Enhance Shared Feelings: Religious/Irreligious Identifications Modulate Empathic Neural Responses," *Social Neuroscience* 9, no. 6 (2014): 639–49.

24. Grit Hein and Tania Singer, "I Feel How You Feel but Not Always: The Empathic Brain and Its Modulation," *Current Opinion in Neurobiology* 18 (2008): 153–58; Don A. Vaughn et al., "Empathic Neural Responses Predict Group Allegiance," *Frontiers in Human Neuroscience* 12 (2018): 302; Leonhard Schilbach et al., "What's in a Smile? Neural Correlates of Facial Embodiment During Social Interaction," *Social Neuroscience* 3, no. 1 (2008): 37–50.

25. Anthony P. Winning and Simon Boag, "Does Brief Mindfulness Training Increase Empathy? The Role of Personality," *Personality and Individual Differences* 86 (2015): 492–98.

apy the sound of the *tānpūrā* is often the object and focus of attention or the accompaniment to meditation.

In this study, we hope to examine fifty Christian and fifty Muslim participants. Along with a series of questionnaires, participants will undergo the In-group/Out-group Empathy Task,[26] which asks for perceptions of pain in those related to one's in-group and out-group respectively. Three groups will be introduced: Meditation on Music (MOM), Meditation on Breath (MOB), and Non-Directed Music Listening (NDL). We hypothesize that after an eight-week intervention phase that involves Mindfulness Based Intervention (MBI) for ten–fifteen minutes a day, Music with Meditation (MOM) will be most effective in reducing the interreligious empathy gap. We hope that the design of this study will address the problem of interreligious conflict, which at its core involves challenges in empathy between in-groups and out-groups.

Conclusion

Our pilot projects delivered tantalizing and suggestive findings and not a few new questions about art's impacts on empathy and justice. In diverse studies not discussed, we were able to, for example, identify musical pieces by Jewish Israelis and Arab Palestinians expressing suffering, and test the effects of such pieces on expanding boundaries of concern (directed by Keren Sharvit of Haifa University, Israel); evaluate the impact of live music on empathy related to mental illness (directed by Tasha Golden, a musician and social scientist at the International Arts + Mind Lab at Johns Hopkins University). For the latter, Golden partnered with Sound Mind Live to analyze the impact of two concerts on attendees' empathy toward and perceptions of individuals with mental illness, as well as on their cognitive understanding of mental illness and related resources.

Again, from these pilot studies, associated research and in-depth discussion, we learned that people are more likely to be just toward those for whom they have empathy, that empathetic people appreciate music more than non-empathetic people, and that empathetic people are more likely to benefit from the empathetic effects of music. Findings from our pilot studies suggested (not unequivocally) that music can help generate empathy and potentially shift cognition and behaviors, and these early results illuminate critical opportunities to examine music's effects on empathy across genres, cultures, and time periods.

Our studies also raise such generative questions as: What kinds of music cultivate empathy? How does music do this, for whom, and under what conditions?

26. Vaughn et al., "Empathic Neural Responses," 302.

Are the effects short-term or long-term? And can these effects be generated via concrete, scalable strategies in order to meaningfully bridge deep and troubling divides? More broadly, how can music help overcome our cramped, tribal understandings of in-group/out-group and human/sub-human that prevent flourishing at multiple levels?

From the slavery and dispossession of Blacks in America to the Israel-Palestine conflict in the Middle East, fear keeps rearing its ugly head in ways that invite dehumanization, oppression, violence and even war. We know that empathetic people can resist the dehumanization and open moral circles to include out-groups. And we know that while the cultivation of empathy is possible (and even actual), we also know that it is not easy. Can a new generation and different cultural manifestations of Bob Dylans and Nina Simones provide songs that cultivate the empathy that opens doors and builds bridges across difficult social and political divides?

Contributors

Garrick V. Allen is Professor of Divinity and Biblical Criticism, University of Glasgow.

Marlene Sophie Altenmüller is Junior Professor for Science Reception, Leibniz Institute for Psychology.

Alejandro Bahena-Rivera is Research Assistant, School of Psychology and Neuroscience, University of Glasgow.

Bahador Bahrami is the Director of Crowd Cognition Group, Ludwig-Maximilians-Universität München.

Jonathan Berger is the Denning Family Provostial Professor in Music, and Director of the Center for Computer Research in Music and Acoustics, Stanford University.

Julio Bermudez is President of the Architecture, Culture, and Spirituality Forum.

Christopher R. Brewer is Principal Advisor for Templeton Religion Trust's Art Seeking Understanding grant-making strategy; and Honorary Research Fellow, School of Divinity, University of St Andrews.

Kutter Callaway is Associate Professor of Theology and Culture and Associate Professor of Psychology, Fuller Theological Seminary.

Eileen Cardillo is Associate Director of the Penn Center for Neuroaesthetics, University of Pennsylvania.

Anjan Chatterjee is Professor and Director of the Penn Center for Neuroaesthetics, University of Pennsylvania.

Alexander P. Christensen is Assistant Professor of Quantitative Methods, Vanderbilt University.

Kelly James Clark is Professor, School of Humanities and Social Sciences, Department of Philosophy, Ibn Haldun University.

Guy Dammann is a Senior Research Fellow, Department of Philosophy, Uppsala University.

Ophelia Deroy is Professor for Philosophy of Mind and Neuroscience, Ludwig-Maximilians-Universität München, and associate researcher at the University of London, School of Advanced Study.

Lexi Eikelboom is Senior Research Fellow in Religion and Theology, Australian Catholic University.

Jamal J. Elias is Annenberg Professor of the Humanities and Professor of Islamic History and Visual Culture, University of Pennsylvania.

Alejandro Erut is Senior Research Scientist, The University of Texas at Austin.

Julie J. Exline is Professor of Psychology, Case Western Reserve University.

Stacie Friend is Reader in Philosophy, University of Edinburgh.

Caleb Froehlich is Associate Lecturer in Theology and the Arts, University of St Andrews.

John Gibson is Professor of Philosophy, University of Louisville.

Mario Gollwitzer is Professor and Chair of Social Psychology, Ludwig-Maximilians-Universität München.

Carlos Miguel Gómez-Rincón is Associate Professor of Philosophy, School of Human Sciences, Universidad del Rosario, Bogotá.

Madeleine E. Gross is an Assistant Project Scientist at the University of California, Santa Barbara.

Faiz A. Hashmi is a doctoral researcher in psychology, the University of Texas at Austin.

Marina Iosifyan is Senior Research Fellow, School of Divinity, University of St Andrews.

Zorana Ivcevic is Senior Research Scientist, Yale Center for Emotional Intelligence, Yale University.

Alison Jack is Professor of Bible and Literature and Principal of New College, University of Edinburgh.

Robin M. Jensen is Patrick O'Brien Professor of Theology, University of Notre Dame.

Cristine H. Legare is Professor of Psychology, the University of Texas at Austin.

Elizabeth Mason is a recent MSc graduate in Psychology, Trinity College Dublin.

Valerie van Mulukom is Senior Lecturer in Psychology, Oxford Brookes University.

Yoshio Nakamura is Research Professor, Pain Research Center in the Department of Anesthesiology, Perioperative and Pain Medicine in the Spencer Fox Eccles School of Medicine, University of Utah.

Kate Nevin is a PhD Researcher in Neuroscience, Trinity College Dublin.

Fiona Newell is Professor of Experimental Psychology, Trinity College Dublin.

Carl Plantinga is Senior Research Fellow, Calvin University.

Kelsie G. Rodenbiker is Assistant Professor of New Testament at the University of Copenhagen.

Christoph Scheepers is Senior Lecturer, School of Psychology and Neuroscience, University of Glasgow.

Elisabeth Schellekens is Chair Professor of Aesthetics, Department of Philosophy, Uppsala University.

Jonathan W. Schooler is a Distinguished Professor of Psychological and Brain Sciences, University of California Santa Barbara.

David Shepherd is Professor in Hebrew Bible/Old Testament, Trinity College Dublin.

Zachary Taylor is Research Program Coordinator, the University of Texas at Austin.

Pablo P. L. Tinio is a Professor, Educational Foundations Department, Montclair State University.

Joshua A. Wilt is Senior Research Associate, Case Western Reserve University.

Brendan Wolfe is the Principal Editor of the St Andrews Encyclopaedia of Theology, University of St Andrews.

Judith Wolfe is Professor of Philosophical Theology, University of St Andrews.

Taylor Worley is Visiting Associate Professor of Art History, Wheaton College.

Index

www.ingramcontent.com/pod-product-compliance
Lightning Source LLC
LaVergne TN
LVHW050923080826
845145LV00001B/191